SILK FLAGS
AND
COLD STEEL

Silk Flags and Cold Steel
(The Civil War in North Carolina) Volume I: The Piedmont
by
William R. Trotter

DEDICATION
To Elizabeth, who gave me the courage to undertake these books
and then had to live with me while I wrote them.

Silk Flags
And
Cold Steel

The Civil War in North Carolina: The Piedmont

William R. Trotter

John F. Blair, Publisher
Winston-Salem, North Carolina

This book is printed on acid-free paper.

Library of Congress Cataloging-in-Publication Data

Trotter, William R.
Silk flags and cold steel : the piedmont / William R. Trotter.
    p.   cm. — (The Civil War in North Carolina ; v. 1)
Includes bibliographical references and index.
ISBN 0-89587-086-X (pbk.)
1. North Carolina—History—Civil War, 1861–1865—Campaigns.
2. United States—History—Civil War, 1861–1865—Campaigns.
I. Title. II. Series: Trotter, William R. Civil War in North Carolina ; v. 1.
E470.6.T76 1991
973.7'456—dc20
90-28706

TABLE OF CONTENTS

INTRODUCTION

"I have always found more dead North Carolinians on the Virginia battlefields than from any other state..."

— General James Longstreet

North Carolina's role in the Civil War was more strategic than tactical — the big, epic battles were fought elsewhere. But battles there were, nearly a hundred of them, if you count the skirmishes, and on their outcome depended the strategic health of the Southern cause. As long as the railways of North Carolina were operating freely, and the state's farms were producing to capacity, Robert E. Lee's Army of Northern Virginia could move, eat, fight, and replenish itself — if not on a luxurious scale, then at least on a subsistence level, enough to keep it in the field and fighting. As long as the coast of North Carolina continued to be reachable by the blockade runners, some trickle of vital imported supplies could get through.

Although the battles waged in North Carolina were not fought with huge numbers of men, and though they perhaps lacked the poetic drama of Gettysburg or Shiloh, they were just as harrowing in their intensity for the men who participated, and they formed vital pieces of the whole strategic pattern.

If the Confederates' situation in North Carolina was under control, the entire Confederate cause benefitted — even in the faraway theaters of war. When the situation in North Carolina began to fall apart, politically as well as militarily, the rebel cause suffered. In the end, when the conquest of Fort Fisher brought the coastline of the state completely under Federal control, the Confederacy staggered under a mortal blow.

North Carolina's relations with the Confederate government of Jefferson Davis were complex, touchy, and often antagonistic, for the state had been reluctant to secede and there was strong Union sentiment in many regions. President Davis never particularly trusted North Carolina, and this blinded him to the state's vital strategic value. It can be said that Richmond's neglect of North Carolina's coastal defenses amounted to criminal negligence.

Paradoxically, no other state contributed more to the Confederate cause in terms of manpower and resources. If you count the Home Guard units — many of which did see some action — North Carolina's flesh-and-blood contribution to the war amounted to 125,000 men, considerably more than the entire voting population of the state. Depending on various numbers, that works out to either one-sixth or one-seventh of the entire Confederate Army. In fact, there were periods during the last two years of the war when 50 percent of Lee's army was comprised of North Carolina regiments.

Moreover, only about 20,000 of those men were conscripts. The rest were volunteers — 72 regiments' worth.

The most revealing statistics, however, concern the Confederate dead. North Carolinians accounted for one-fifth of the Southern losses in the Seven Days' Battle, one-third of the losses at Fredericksburg, and one-fourth of the losses at Gettysburg. (One regiment at Gettysburg, the 26th North Carolina, suffered 86 percent casualties.) In all, one-fourth of the total Confederate battlefield deaths were North Carolinian — close to 20,000 men. Another 23,000 North Carolinians died from diseases contracted under field conditions. And although it is true that 23,000 more deserted during the course of hostilities, one-third eventually returned to their units once they had finished their business at home. (That desertion rate may seem high, but it's almost exactly the same as for all the other states in the Confederacy, as well as for many Union states.)

But a history of North Carolina *in* the Civil War is a far different thing than a history of the Civil War *in* North Carolina, and the purpose of this trilogy is to examine the events that took place within North Carolina's borders. Civil War buffs, and some casual readers as well, may already be familiar with the amphibious campaigns that were mounted on the Outer Banks and along the great riverine estuaries of Pamlico and Albemarle Sounds; but generally, the Civil War era in North Carolina has received far less attention than the events of the Revolutionary War. And while it is true that there was no single Civil War campaign in North Carolina that matches, for epic drama, the 1781 contest between Lord Cornwallis and Nathanael Greene, it is manifestly untrue that "nothing much happened" in the state during the years 1861-65. A great many things happened, in both the political and military spheres, and they were nothing if not dramatic. Even in those localities which saw little or no fighting, there were profound disturbances in the old order of things — changes which led to new attitudes, opened new possibilities, and which helped, ultimately, to create a "New South" in which the Old North State would never again assume the Rip Van Winkle role she had filled so comfortably since the dawn of independence.

In organizing this trilogy according to geographical regions, I inevitably encountered some areas of overlap and ambiguity. When that happened, I followed the guidance of common sense rather than strictly adhering to the rules. For instance, although Stoneman's Raid spilled over into large areas of the Piedmont, it began, ended, and was most effective in the mountain region. Therefore, the entire story of the raid will be found in Volume II (*The Mountains*), and not arbitrarily split along geographical lines between that book and this one. Similarly, I defy anyone to draw an exact line on the map and claim that the coastal plain begins on one side and the Piedmont on the other. For events taking place in the eastern portion of the state, I have used the course of the Wilmington and Weldon Railroad as a handy line of demarcation. In other words, what happened east of Goldsboro, the central stop on that line, will be found in Volume III, *The Coast*, and what happened in Goldsboro and points west will be recounted in *The Piedmont*.

I wish to extend my thanks to Robert Lock, for first suggesting and then actually commissioning this work. The daunting task of research was made considerably easier by the kind help of Steve Cattlet, archivist of the Greensboro Historical Museum, and by Doug Kerr and the rest of the gracious, helpful reference staff of the Greensboro Public Library, whose Carolina Collection is a treasury of source material, some of it exceedingly rare.

SILK FLAGS AND COLD STEEL

*Too clearly, even then, [North Carolina] saw the end from the begin-
ning; but what was left for her, when the clouds lowered and the
storm at last broke, but to stand where the God of nature had placed
her, and where affection and interest both inclined her — in the
South and with the South....*

— Cornelia Phillips Spencer

It was a scene that could have been an out-take from *Gone With the
Wind*. The time: ten o'clock in the morning, May 5, 1860. The place:
a green field framed by a grove of oak trees. It was a clear, spring
morning in the central North Carolina region known as the Piedmont, warm and scented with flowers. In the background stood the
stolid prim-faced buildings of the Edgeworth Female Seminary —
rectitude sculptured in red brick — and in the foreground, frocked
and top-hatted, stood the citizens of Greensboro, North Carolina,
their ears cocked toward Market Street to catch the first tap of drums
on the breeze. Off to one side of the field, in formation, stood the
band from Salisbury, renowned as the finest in the Piedmont.
Golden coronas of light blazed from the bells of their cornets.

For the ladies of Edgeworth Female Seminary, the day was doubly
exciting. It was a spring holiday for them, highlighted by the corona-
tion of the Queen of the May. There would be a gala parade, with
costumes, bowls of punch on the lawn, music and chatter, quadrilles
to be danced. What's more, every reputable bachelor in Guilford

County would be on hand.

The day would open with a special ritual: a grandly ceremonial presentation, by the May Queen, of a new battle flag to the Guilford Grays, the county's first and fanciest company of soldiers.

The May Queen's name was Mary Harper Morehead (Mamie to her friends and erstwhile beaus) and this was a day she had been looking forward to all spring. Her uncle, former Governor Morehead, was one of the founders of Edgeworth Female Seminary. Like most of the Morehead girls, Mary Harper was more endowed with grace and bearing than with good looks. But on this day, in her elegant yellow gown, with her chestnut hair carefully coiled in ringlets and her cheeks aglow beneath her May Queen's crown, there was a radiance about her, a luster in her eyes that would draw many young men to compete for a place on her dance card.

Mary Harper stood now in the morning light, trying to curb her impatience by studying the ribbons and pom-poms and gaily colored lanterns that festooned the trees around the "royal grove." As soon as the Guilford Grays arrived and took their position at the end of the procession, the cortege would advance across the lawn for the opening ceremonies: the crowning of the Queen and her presentation of the flag.

It was a lovely flag, and Mary Harper had spent a long, rapturous interlude studying it earlier that morning, running her groomed, articulate fingers over the sensuous, heavy, blue silk. The design had been executed in Philadelphia (it would have been preferable to do it locally, rather than in the North, but the machinery and workmanship were just not to be found in this part of the South), and no expense had been spared. Measuring five by six feet, it was a brave and commanding ensign. On one side was the coat of arms of North Carolina, encircled by a wreath of oak leaves and acorns. Atop the wreath was a spread-winged eagle clutching a scroll embroidered with the motto "E Pluribus Unum." Below the wreath was another symmetrical scroll bearing the words "Greensboro, North Carolina." The same motifs were repeated on the flag's reverse side, except that the scroll above the wreath said "Guilford Grays" and the scroll below said "Organized March 5th, 1860." In the center of the wreath were the words "Presented by the Ladies of Edgeworth Female Seminary, May 5th, 1860."

While Mary Harper Morehead waited, palpitant amid her costumed attendants, the Guilford Grays themselves were marching down Market Street toward the Seminary Grounds, cheered by citizens on the curb and tagged by yelping urchins. Founded in January, in the Guilford County Courthouse in Greensboro, the Grays were typical of the many hundreds of local militia companies that were springing up spontaneously, all over the South. While most of the young men who joined the Grays were, at this point, more sympathetic to the Union than to the concept of secession, they were all motivated by a feeling of unease about the future and a conviction that, whatever happened in terms of national politics, the South would be better off if her states at least presented a picture of military preparedness.

An all-volunteer unit, the Grays also elected their officers, as was the common practice in those days. The officers were drawn from some of the most prominent families in Guilford County. Handsome young John Sloan was elected captain; a Morehead boy, James, was his second lieutenant; and Henry Gorrell, son of a widely known attorney, was the ensign. The officers received their commissions from Governor John Ellis on March 15, 1860 — the 79th anniversary of the historic Revolutionary War Battle of Guilford Courthouse.

Drill was conducted every Friday night in the vacant second story of an old cotton factory. In early April, the company received its arms: 50 stand of unrifled flintlock muskets from the Fayetteville Arsenal (not until war actually broke out would the Grays receive modern percussion-cap rifles). A "stand of arms," in those days, was standard nomenclature for a single musket with accessories: cartridge pouch, bayonet, and belt.

The Guilford Grays drilled with their muskets according to the tactical doctrines set forth by General Winfield Scott back around the time of the Mexican War. By the time of the May Day parade, their marching was still more notable for its zest than for its precision, but that mattered little. Most of what they would learn about the realities of modern warfare would be derived from brutally direct on-the-job training.

Still, the Guilford Grays made a brave sight on that sun-washed morning in May, stepping out manfully, chests swelling in their splendid uniforms. They were outfitted in single-breasted frock coats with two rows of brass buttons, matching gray pants with black stripes along the outward seams, waist belts of shiny black leather, cross belts of white webbing, with the entire ensemble topped by a jaunty gray cap with pom-pom.

The sun flashed on their bayonets and the store-bought polish of the officers' new swords as they swung down Market Street and approached the grounds of the Seminary. At the head of the column, a kettle drummer, a bass drummer, and a bandy-legged fifer named "Old Jake" Mebane shrilled and whomped and thundered bravely.

Swinging smartly onto the grounds to the cheers of the crowd and sighs of the ladies, the Grays took their position at the end of the May Queen's procession, and the ceremonies began. The Salisbury band crashed into a triumphal march, and 14 gaily dressed Maids of Honor led the parade. Following them came ten flower maidens who scattered petals from overflowing baskets, laying down a fragrant carpet for those who walked behind. Next came two pages, bearing the Queen's crown and scepter. Mary Harper herself followed in the center of the procession, flanked by Miss Mary Arendell costumed as "Lady Hope" and Miss Hennie Erwin costumed as "The Archbishop." Behind the Queen came more maids of honor and pages, and behind them — a dazzle of steel and brass — the Guilford Grays.

Inside the sacred grove, the Archbishop crowned the Queen. A standard bearer came near and handed Mary Harper the banner. She advanced to the head of the Grays' formation and addressed them in the high-flown Victorian rodomontade that seemed to come so naturally to educated people during this period:

> In the name of my subjects, the fair donors of Edgeworth, I present this banner to the Guilford Grays.
>
> Feign would we have it "a banner of peace," and have inscribed on its graceful folds "peace on earth, good will to man," for our womanly natures shrink from the horrors of war and bloodshed.
>
> But we have placed upon it the "oak," fit emblem of the firm, heroic spirits over which it is to float. Strength, energy, and decision mark the character of the sons of Guilford, whose noble sires have taught their sons to know but one fear — the fear of doing wrong.

Miss Morehead's concluding remarks — which were censored out of John Sloan's postwar account of the event — revealed something of the political climate in this part of North Carolina, only one year before the war: "Proudly in days past have the banners of our country waved o'er yon Battlefield, where our fathers fought for freedom from a tyrant's power. This their motto: 'Union in Strength,' and we their daughters would have this, our banner, unfurled only in some noble cause, and quiveringly through our soft Southern breezes echo forth the same glorious theme: Union! Union!"

Ensign Gorrell accepted the flag on behalf of the company, and responded to her word-bouquet with a few verbal flourishes of his own:

> Most noble Queen, on the part of the Guilford Grays, I accept this beautiful banner, for which I tender the thanks of those whom I represent.
>
> Your majesty calls to remembrance the days of "Auld Lang Syne," when the banners of our country proudly and triumphantly waved over our own battlefield, and when our fathers, on the soil of Old Guilford, "struck for their altars and their fires." Here, indeed, was fought the great battle of the South; here was decided the great struggle of the Revolution; here was achieved the great victory of American over British generalship; here was evidence the great military talent and skill of Nathanael Greene, the blacksmith boy, whose immortal name our town bears.
>
> If any earthly pride be justifiable, are not the sons of Guilford entitled to entertain it? If any spot on earth be appropriate for the presentation of a "banner of peace," where will you find it, if it be not here, five miles from the battlefield...here, at Guilford Court House, in the boro of Nathanael Greene; here, in the classic grounds of old Edgeworth, surrounded by beauty and intelligence, in the presence of our wives, our sisters, and our sweethearts....

Flinging wide his arm, Gorrell declaimed a verse in honor of the ladies: "No braver dames had Sparta/No nobler matrons Rome/Then let us laud and honor them/E'en in their own green homes."

And there can be no doubt that every man in the company felt a thrill of emotion at Gorrell's concluding words:

> ...and while we pay to their memories the grateful tribute of a sigh, we would again express our thanks to their daughters for this beautiful banner, and as a token of our gratitude, we, the Guilford Grays, do here beneath its graceful folds pledge our lives, our fortunes, and our sacred honor, and swear for them to live, them to love, and, if need be, for them to die.

That last pledge would certainly be kept. Not quite a year later, on

April 18, 1861, the Guilford Grays said farewell to their mothers, sisters, and sweethearts, marched to the Greensboro railroad depot beneath that same blue silken banner, and went to war. After a dreary and uneventful period of garrison duty at Fort Macon on the Outer Banks, the Grays received their baptism of fire at the Battle of New Bern and slogged through the rest of the war in the thick of things, seeing action at Fredericksburg, Spottsylvania, The Wilderness, Cold Harbor, Petersburg, and a host of smaller engagements. Early in the war, Ensign Gorrell returned to Greensboro and raised his own company of men; he died, on June 21, 1862, leading a charge against a Federal stronghold at Chickahominy. Of the other 180 men on the original muster of the Guilford Grays, one dozen were still in the ranks at the time of Lee's surrender. The rest were dead, or maimed for life.

The blue silk flag, caressed on that soft clear morning by both the sun and the May Queen's gentle hands, hangs today in the Confederate Museum in Richmond, Virginia. On its tattered surface can be read the story of what happened between that glorious spring morning in 1860 and the ashen day in May 1865 when General Joseph E. Johnston surrendered the last Confederate army east of the Mississippi — at a railroad siding only one mile distant from the oak-shaded lawns of Edgeworth Female Seminary.

All that is left of the cause they went to war for — so innocent, so ardent, with such full and tender hearts — are some fading flags and the last stubborn embers of pride.

North Carolina On The Eve Of War

The Confederacy, by definition, was not a nation. To the detriment of its wartime effectiveness, it was not even a monolithic political bloc. Instead, it was subdivided between the hard-core cotton-producing states of the Deep South and the more diversified tier of states of the Upper South. The former bloc seized upon the idea of secession early and with an emotional commitment that was simply not duplicated, except in scattered areas, in the latter group of states. Most of the inhabitants of the Upper South sought respect for Southern rights and advantage for Southern economic interests within the accepted framework of the Union. They were wary of rabid secessionists and abolitionists alike.

This attitude was common in the Upper South among those who did not own slaves as well as among those who did. Those who didn't hold slaves were wary of the abolitionist movement because it would not only set loose all the Negroes, but also would establish them on an equal legal footing with the lower class of whites — and virtually all of these whites viewed with dire alarm the prospect of having to compete with blacks for scarce economic resources.

As the events of the 1860s began to unfold, North Carolina was in no hurry to secede from the Union. All things considered, the Federal system had been pretty good to the state. Agricultural conditions in North Carolina did not favor the creation of vast cotton plantations — in most places where it was planted, the soil yielded a mediocre grade of cotton, and that grudgingly — so the state was spared the labor-intensive economics of the plantations and their consequent dependence on slavery. The dirt farmers of the Piedmont and the mountainous western areas of North Carolina had never owned slaves, and most didn't particularly want to own them, either. They certainly weren't anxious to spill their blood to preserve such a dubious institution. So long as the main issue was one of abolitionist versus plantation aristocrats, slavery was not an issue likely to draw North Carolina into a war.

According to the census of 1860, the state's population totaled 992,622 people, making it the twelfth most populous state in the nation. Included in that figure were 331,000 slaves, 30,500 free Negroes, and about 11,000 American Indians. Only one-quarter of the population was living in urban areas.

Despite the construction of 60 new miles of railroad and another 500 miles of plank road during the late 1850s, North Carolina in 1860 remained essentially a backward, undeveloped, agricultural state. Her vast coastline was treacherous, and of her many ports, only Wilmington did any significant business with the outside world. The other ports were largely intracoastal centers of commerce. Agricultural development was retarded by poor transportation and obsolete technology. Nevertheless, even if the state's red-clay soil was not much good for cotton, it was just fine for corn, oats, barley, tobacco, sweet potatoes, rye, and rice, so the state ranked near the top in the Confederacy in terms of agricultural output.

North Carolinians had a deep, traditional aversion to taxes, and the statewide tax base — only about $1 million for all of 1860 — was too shallow to permit much in the way of dramatic improvements. The various sections of the state were still, in 1860, more isolated from one another than they were from neighboring states. Conservatism and sectionalism go hand in hand, and those two adjectives clearly apply to antebellum North Carolina. Individualism, too, was one of the more endearing by-products of the state's provincial, socially stratified way of life, and with it came a certain impatience with enshrined authority — a trait that later would be reflected in Governor Zebulon Vance's squabbles with the Confederate government in Richmond and in the citizens' unending complaints to the governor.

The average small farmer and his family owned no slaves, lived in a crude log house of one or two rooms, wore the simplest kind of clothing, and survived on a limited, monotonous, but basically healthy diet. Domestic labor was apportioned as it had been a century before: the men farmed and the women did all the household chores. Toil was constant and life followed a predictable yearly cycle, with the exception of special events such as church picnics or rousing public hangings. Social life revolved around militia musters and court sessions, both of which furnished a good excuse to leave the plow for a day or to catch the local horse races.

Here and there were pockets of real hillbilly squalor and degeneracy — the type of "poor white trash" that even poor whites disdain to associate with — but you had to travel some bad back roads to find them. The vast majority of lower-class whites in North Carolina were industrious, honest, God-fearing, stoutly independent people. They would need all the strength they possessed, for upon them would fall all of the war's most terrible burdens, both at the fighting fronts and at home.

When North Carolina signed the freshly inked Constitution as one of the original 13 states in the Union, it was a marriage vow the state took seriously. In the two generations since the Revolution, links had been forged in commerce, culture, and politics between the state and the Union. The connections were not tenuous.

Yet neither was the connective tissue that bound the state to the rest of the South. In the last years before the war, there was growing resentment, not uncolored by envy, of the industrial might and commercial clout of the Northeast. There was also a pervasive attitude that while slavery was not an especially laudable institution, it was a necessary social mechanism for "keeping order" (controlling the Negroes).

At the start of 1860, the state's electorate was divided into four more or less distinct groupings. On the extreme left were the pro-Union zealots, and on the far right were the passionate pro-slavery secessionists. In the middle could be found those who sought, with diminishing success, to remain strictly neutral, along with a much larger faction that was pro-Southern. That is, they were vaguely pro-slavery (or anti-abolitionist; the distinction is subtle, but for many it existed) and strongly pro-North Carolina. This middle-of-the-road mass of people was against secession until Abraham Lincoln's election. A lot of them changed their minds quickly afterward.

In the context of the times, the fact that most North Carolinians did not own slaves turned out to be less important than it might appear. There were more ties between slaveholders and non-slaveholders than there were differences. Aside from sharing the same landscape, they were bound together by a backward economic system in which the prosperity of one class bore directly on the prosperity of the other. Both classes held to, or were at least constantly exposed to, the same ideologies, the same folklore, the same shared assumptions about "how things ought to be" in the world around them. Finally, there was a lot of blood kinship between slaveholders and non-slaveholders. Rich cousin and poor cousin alike, all shared a common identity as North Carolinians — although as the war dragged on and the system grew strained and fragmented, that particular bond tended to break down before the demonstrably true popular notion that it was "a rich man's war and a poor man's fight."

It is not wise, however, to categorize antebellum North Carolinians too rigidly. The situation in 1860 was fluid and extraordinarily complex, and many conflicting impulses tugged at the minds and hearts of the electorate. Documentation from the period is useful only for pinpointing specific examples and mapping out trends. Unionists, neutrals, and secessionists all coexisted, intermingled, and intermarried. Pockets of ideological concentration can be identified here and there — such as the pro-Union "Quaker Belt" centered in Guilford, Forsyth, and Randolph Counties — but on the whole, the picture that emerges from the historical records is more mottled than clear-cut. The lines between political positions tended to become very blurry on a personal level. A man who might, in theory, advocate remaining in the Union might also, at the same time and for strictly personal reasons, be passionately pro-slavery. Things were not simple, and the issues were not clearly defined. It required the galvanizing force of outside events to make them seem so.

Having a general sympathy for the concept of the Federal Union was one thing, but knowing where to draw the line in support of states' rights was another. It was common in 1860 for editors and politicians in North Carolina to declaim that secession should be resorted to only "as a last resort," but exactly what conditions should trigger a last resort? How much pressure from the North should the average citizen tolerate before drawing the line?

Things began to change quickly in November 1860 when Lincoln was elected to the Presidency. North Carolinians felt and voiced dismay. The mere fact of Lincoln's victory was enough to catalyze secession among the states of the Deep South. Yet even after the election, secessionist rhetoric in North Carolina remained oddly muted, cautious, and speculative. Newspaper editorials from the era give some idea of the state's prevailing mood: If Mr. Lincoln contented himself with moral and legal moves against secession as a political fluke and slavery as an undesirable system, North Carolina, thank you very much, would prefer to sit out the whole business of seceding from the United States. But, the editors continued, if the North mobilized its troops, if Mr. Lincoln brandished the threat of armed force...at that point, North Carolina would have to take its stand.

Still, most North Carolinians prayed it would not come to that. They weren't spoiling for war. There was much talk in Raleigh of calling a special statewide convention to debate the issue of secession, but the idea didn't really get off the ground until 1861.

One advocate of secession, a Mr. Rayner of Raleigh, wrote to his friend Thomas Ruffin on Christmas Day 1860, to describe the mood in Hertford County, up in the northeast corner of the state. Rayner had gone home "to attend to the putting up of my port," and he was "mortified to find as far as I could ascertain that the feeling in that section was in great measure in favor of the Union at any and all hazards...[the population] would not lift a finger to protect rich mens' Negroes. You may depend upon it, my dear Judge, that this feeling prevails to an extent you do not imagine."[1] Rayner concluded his letter by stating that, although he had hoped to stand for election to the secession convention, he now doubted he could win in his home district unless he declared himself a Union man, and this he would not do.

When North Carolina sent a delegation to the Confederate States organizing conference in Montgomery, Alabama, the representatives were in such an anomalous position that they were officially designated "observers" rather than participants. As such, they were excluded from all of the nonpublic functions of the conference where most of the real wheeling and dealing was actually done. One prominent newspaper began referring to the North Carolina group as "political hermaphrodites" because they were "sorta so and sorta not so."

Nevertheless, the state was courted while its representatives were in Montgomery. In a resolution drafted on February 8, 1861, North Carolina was cited as being bound to the Confederate states by "common history, common sympathy, a common honor, and a common danger."

Back home, however, a typical expression of the majority opinion was embodied in a statement issued after a citizens' courthouse meeting in Alexander County on January 4: "...although frantic and bad man [sic] in the Northern States have adopted obnocious [sic] laws...calculated to rouse the indignation of the South," redress should first be sought within the Union, not out of it. The gist of the Alexander County manifesto was that North Carolina should not allow itself to be stampeded into a rash course of action, but should stand true to its best convictions and allow President Lincoln a chance to work out a solution. North Carolina, after all, had invested 80 years in the Union and had even contributed significantly to its founding. Such an investment was not to be shrugged off in a fit of petulance or anger.

In some counties, pro-Union sentiment was so entrenched that secessionist politicians, in order to stand a chance of being elected to the convention, had to label themselves as belonging to a "States Rights Union Ticket" — a semantic sleight-of-hand that must have thoroughly confused many a man in the street.

Politics was the grand passion in North Carolina, a passion that cut across geographical and economic lines and was shared with equal zest by the rich coastal planter and the red-clay farmer. During the quarter-century preceding the outbreak of war, two political parties dominated the regional scene: the Democrats and the Whigs. Both parties were fairly evenly matched most of the time, and both were blessed with vigorous, able leaders, factors which made North Carolina a "close" state. Both Democrats and Whigs were active in their respective national party organizations, and North Carolinians held a number of high administrative and cabinet posts during the presidencies of Harrison, Fillmore, and Pierce.

Matching local affiliations to national issues, one finds that the

North Carolina Whigs were in favor of protective tariffs, of the distribution to the states of profits obtained from the sale of public lands, and, in general, of a strong central Federal government. Toward the Constitution, the Whigs maintained a broadly constructionist attitude. Democrats favored a stricter interpretation of the Constitution. They identified passionately with the cause of states' rights and looked with suspicion on any high-profile Federal interference in state affairs.

Although each party slanted its rhetoric somewhat differently on the slavery issue, both were in basic agreement. They were in favor of maintaining the system, and orators from both parties were often heard lambasting the abolitionists. Both parties also agreed on the slavery issue as it pertained to newly opened territories. They believed that the frontier should be open to settlement by any citizen from any state in the Union, along with whatever property he elected to take with him into the new territory — including slaves, if he owned them.

Gradually, however, the Democrats assumed the mantle of the protectors of slavery. North Carolina Democrats drew much of their strength and most of their leadership from the plantation districts in the eastern part of the state. As time went by, the Democrats' anti-abolitionist rhetoric grew more strident, and much of their ire was directed toward Unionists who wanted to separate the ownership of slaves from other property-rights issues.

The Whigs dodged the slavery issue whenever possible for the simple reason that they could not reach a consensus on what their platform ought to be. The so-called Federal Whigs — in whose ranks could be found such important figures as Governors John Morehead and William Graham — believed that no state had a right to drop out of the Union. The more ideologically severe party members, who called themselves States Rights Whigs, became more and more aligned with the Democrats over issues such as secession and the extension of slavery into newly opened lands.

There were men from every social and economic caste represented in the ranks of the Whigs, but generally it was not a party dominated by the so-called "slavocracy." In counties where the slave population was small, the Whigs were usually the dominant political party. It was the Whigs who counterbalanced the emotional pull toward secession, at least until Lincoln's call to arms pulled the rug out from under them.

Fifteen years earlier, the Whigs had opposed the Mexican War, regarding it as an "unjust war against a weak neighbor" fomented for the benefit of Democratic policies. The Democrats supported the war against Mexico and were gleeful over the annexation of Texas. This forthright stand cost the Whigs a lot of support. The Democrats painted the Whigs as "unpatriotic." The tide of history seemed to be turning against the Whigs, and sometime after 1850 they lost their edge. Their leadership declined in eloquence and effectiveness, and the Democrats gradually exercised more and more control over North Carolina's political machinery.

The Great Compromise of 1850 caused remarkably little stir in the state. Most of North Carolina's Congressmen supported it, and most citizens felt relieved that the nation was, for the moment, able to settle back down to business as usual. In truth, few of the state's voters really cared all that much what happened in California, Oregon, or New Mexico — places that seemed, to most North Carolinians, about as remote as Mars.

In 1854, however, the Kansas-Nebraska Act did cause a tense quickening of events. The national Whig party structure collapsed, the anti-slavery Republican Party suddenly achieved national prominence, and sectional debates in Congress became much more acrimonious than had hitherto been the case. The gloves were coming off. During the Presidential election of 1856, North Carolina's powerful Radical Democrats came out in favor of secession in the event of a Republican victory by John C. Fremont, an avowed abolitionist. But when the Democratic candidate, James Buchanan, won, the crisis atmosphere rapidly eased. For the moment.

The 1859 gubernatorial campaign in North Carolina was a cliffhanger made even more dramatic by the shocking news, on the eve of the election, that John Brown had sparked a slave revolt in Virginia and had seized the arsenal at Harper's Ferry. During the gubernatorial campaign, the state's Whigs had made a furious effort at reorganization, and their candidate, John Pool from Pasquotank County, ran a very close race with Democrat John Ellis, a secessionist from Rowan County. Pool lost by only 6,000 votes.

Lincoln was not on the ballot in North Carolina, in the presidential election of 1860. John C. Breckinridge carried the state, but only because he ran as a moderate (but pro-Southern) candidate, and then only by 4,000 votes. In October, Governor Ellis had probably spoken for the majority of North Carolinians when he declared that the mere election of Lincoln was not "sufficient ground for dissolving the Union of States." A mere two weeks after Lincoln's election, however, with secession imminent in the Deep South, Ellis moved to a more belligerent position. He stated that the time had come for North Carolina to hold high-level talks with the governments of the Deep South states, "states identified with us in interest and in the wrongs we have suffered."

Until Lincoln's election, the emotional climate in North Carolina had remained fairly stable. Now, blood grew hot and feelings ran high. Those who spoke for reason, for freedom of expression, and for calm, found themselves increasingly drowned out by the shriller voices of hatred, sectionalism, and secession. Those who spoke out against the growing irrationality were now likely to find their patriotism, if not their moral character, under challenge.

By the end of 1860, secessionist passions were swelling all across North Carolina. When the news arrived, on December 20, of South Carolina's break with the Union, the people of Wilmington — long a hotbed of radical fervor — fired a 100-gun salute and held torchlight parades.

During the winter of 1860-61, seven Southern states left the Union. In February 1861, they formed the Confederate States of America.

To be sure, there were plenty of voices in North Carolina openly decrying South Carolina's action as reckless and provocative. But even citizens who condemned their hotheaded neighbors to the south were strongly opposed to any attempt by the Federal government to coerce South Carolina back into the Union through armed force. That possibility made "Unionists" into "Southerners" as quick as a finger-snap. In the Piedmont, and in the mountains, Unionist sentiment was still strong, but something new had crept into the rhetoric. At many pro-Union rallies, the message was clear: If compromise can be made to work, let us remain in the Union. If they send men against us with guns, then we must take a stand with our neighbors.

Virginia, too, was reluctant to leave the Union without first giving compromise a chance to heal the rift. It was largely at Virginia's urging, therefore, that the Washington Peace Conference was held in February 1861. North Carolina sent a distinguished delegation to that affair, including two former Governors (Morehead and David Reid), a former chief justice (Thomas Ruffin), and George Davis, who would later serve briefly as attorney general of the Confederacy. Dealing from its new position of strength, however, the Republican Party refused to make the sort of compromises needed to head off open conflict and the conference was a failure.

One North Carolina Congressman who was in Washington at this time, representing the Fifth District, was John A. Gilmer. Gilmer was a Unionist. His oratory on the subject was so eloquent that his speeches sometimes moved men on both sides of the aisle to tears. Lincoln thought highly enough of Gilmer to offer him a cabinet post. Lincoln badly wanted someone from the South in a high-profile position in his administration, and he was even willing to offer Gilmer the job of secretary of war. Gilmer declined. On January 26, Gilmer made the most stirring pro-Union address of his career. After he was finished, he was mobbed by enthusiastic colleagues from all parts of the nation.

Ten weeks later, that same John Gilmer rose in the courthouse in Greensboro and staunchly admonished the assembled Guilford Grays to defend the Old North State against any invader, no matter from whence he came. That Gilmer, so loyal a Union man that Abraham Lincoln wanted him as secretary of war, could revise his politics so drastically, in so short a time, is a good measure of the impact generated by the looming prospect of a Northern attack.

Now it had become clear to most North Carolinians where the line would be drawn. It would be drawn at the threat of armed invasion. When Lincoln issued his call for troops, all other issues and considerations faded. Secession and resistance, which until that moment had been "political" issues — cloudy, messy, fraught with ambiguity — suddenly became urgent, hard edged, crystalline. As the momentous new year of 1861 dawned over the land, it was clear to most North Carolinians that the line had, indeed, been drawn.

"YOU CAN GET NO TROOPS FROM NORTH CAROLINA!"

Early in 1861, a clear division could be seen in the ranks of the North Carolina General Assembly. On one hand were the radicals who favored dramatic and immediate action: secession and mobilization. On the other hand, there were the conservatives — still identified, though rather uncomfortably now, as Unionists — who regarded secession as perilous at worst, premature at best. Both factions, however, lined up behind Governor Ellis's contention that the state militia needed dusting off and the state's defenses upgrading. On January 8, therefore, the legislature voted to appropriate $300,000 for the purchase of military goods and the establishment of training facilities.

January was a busy month for the General Assembly.[1] Much of the lawmakers' activity centered around the idea of holding a special state convention to resolve, once and for all, the question of secession. The convention was intended to be a supra-normal legislative body, an extraordinary entity convened to resolve extraordinary issues. Numerous proposals for such a conclave had been introduced in the closing weeks of 1860, and on the first day of the new year the process got under way.

On January 1, Governor Ellis was authorized by the General Assembly to issue an official proclamation to all county sheriffs in the state, ordering them to open the polls on February 28 for a statewide referendum on the convention. If the proposal carried, the voters would then elect 120 delegates, each county allowed the same number of delegates as it had Assemblymen. The convention's legal powers would be equal to those of the General Assembly.

Results of the February 28 voting showed that North Carolina was not quite ready to jump into the uncharted waters of secession. If there was a consensus to be read in the numbers, it probably was this: That the very existence of such a convention, with its waves of impassioned oratory and its potential for grabbing headlines, might itself be enough to launch the state impulsively toward the road of rebellion. So the idea was rejected, at least for the moment, although the margin was paper-thin: 47,323 votes to 46,672.

Meanwhile, the failure in February of the so-called Peace Conference in Washington further undermined the Unionists' case. On March 4, Abraham Lincoln was inaugurated President, and one of his first acts was to authorize the shipment of supplies to the garrison of Fort Sumter, which was isolated on an island in Charleston harbor. When news of this reached the Confederate firebrands in South Carolina, they commenced a bombardment of the stone fort. After two days of incessant pounding, Fort Sumter surrendered on April 13, 1861.

When North Carolina Congressman John Gilmer heard the news of the firing on Sumter, he wrote to Lincoln's new secretary of state, William Seward, in Washington: "If what I hear is true that we are to have fighting at Ft. Sumter...I seriously apprehend that it will instantly drive the whole South into secession, and that before the end of another sixty days...there will be a contest that makes me shudder to contemplate. Truly, indeed, may it be said that madness rules the hour..."[2]

Another reaction to the news from Fort Sumter was expressed in the following editorial from the *Greensboro Patriot*, dated April 18: "It is with deep regret and most painful anticipation of the future, that we announce to our readers that war has commenced; that the first gun has been fired, and that Fort Sumter, instead of being evacuated, as should have been done, has been violently seized upon, and that the flag of the Confederate States now floats upon its walls...Events of the most startling character so crowd upon one another, that the mind becomes bewildered and confused, no time being afforded for reflection. But yesterday, all was quiet, peace, and happiness; today, terror, excitement, and confusion rules the hour."

The editor concluded with some fairly ineffectual remarks that cautioned against unleashing too much emotion. He called upon his readers to have faith in the Union, and he closed by voicing skepticism that matters would ever become so dire that one state could actually attack another.

By the time the ink was dry on the page, however, Virginia had followed the Deep South and withdrawn from the Union. This was done in secret on April 17 and not made public until April 24.

By the end of January, four states had followed South Carolina out of the Union (Florida, Mississippi, Georgia, and Alabama), and Virginia's defection probably would have been the last straw that tipped North Carolina into the Confederate camp. But even Virginia's secession did not have as dramatic an impact as Lincoln's call to arms.

On April 15, two days after Fort Sumter surrendered, Lincoln issued a mobilization order for the purpose of quelling what he described as a "Southern insurrection." Governor Ellis duly received a telegram from the secretary of war, ordering him to furnish two regiments of state militia for active duty against the rebels. Ellis's reply is worth quoting in full, for it vividly captures the essential reasons why North Carolina joined the war on the Confederate side. It is noteworthy that it contains not a single word about slavery:

> Your dispatch is received, and if genuine, which its extraordinary character leads me to doubt, I have to say in reply that I regard the levy of troops made by the administration for the purpose of subjugating the states of the South, as in violation of the Constitution, and as a gross usurpation of power. I can be no party to this wicked violation of the laws of the country, and to this war upon the liberties of a free people. You can get no troops from North Carolina.

Zebulon Vance, at that time serving his first full term in Congress, was stunned by the news of Lincoln's proclamation. Vance was politicking in the North Carolina mountains when the news broke. He was, in fact, politicking on behalf of the Union and was engaged in a spirited debate with a confirmed secessionist. "For myself...I was canvassing for the Union with all my strength. I was addressing a large and excited crowd, and literally had my arm extended upward, pleading for peace and for the Union of our fathers, when the telegraphic news was announced of the firing on Fort Sumter and the President's call for 75,000 volunteers. When my hand came down from that impassioned gesticulation, it fell slowly and sadly by the side of a Secessionist. I immediately with altered voice and manner, called upon the assembled multitude to volunteer, not to fight against, but for, South Carolina. I said: 'If war is to come, I prefer to be with my own people.'"

Events now moved swiftly. After Governor Ellis received word that the three most important posts on the North Carolina coast (Forts Caswell, Macon, and Johnston) had been seized from Federal control, he moved against the most important Federal positions in the Piedmont. On April 20, a company of the Charlotte Grays seized the branch mint in Charlotte. The U.S. Arsenal at Fayetteville was taken two days later, yielding 37,000 stands of arms, several cannon, a large quantity of powder, and a respectable stock of miscellaneous military stores — great booty indeed for a state that possessed virtually no industrial war-making capacity.

Sometime during the ten-day period between the fall of Fort Sumter and the takeover of the Fayetteville arsenal, Unionist sympathies died in the minds and hearts of most North Carolinians. There are hundreds of letters, diaries, and memoirs which echo virtually identical emotions: a sense of profound and tragic sorrow that the break had come and a sense of agonized regret at the seemingly inexorable march of events, coupled with a rock-solid determination to take up the sword and fight for the right to be left alone. The last emotions are sometimes expressed in terms of apocalyptic blood-thirst, but more often the tone is one of deeper, more dignified resolve. North Carolina didn't want disunion, but it seemed inevitable now, and her population, for the most part, was resolved to stay the course.

Governor Ellis immediately moved to put the state on a proper war footing. A special session of the General Assembly was proclaimed for May 1, and an inspector generalship was created to coordinate the state's military preparations. New companies of militia were sprouting like spring onions all over the state, and by the end of

April, 5,000 eager young men were bivouacked at Camp Ellis, near Raleigh. Fresh troops, including the Guilford Grays, were rushed to the newly captured coastal forts. A law was passed authorizing $5 million worth of defense bonds. Another was passed making it illegal to administer an oath upon the U.S. Constitution. The Governor was still anxious to handle the secession matter "by the book," so the issue of the statewide convention resurfaced. As soon as the special session of the General Assembly opened on May 1, the calling of such a convention was authorized. Delegates would be elected on May 13, and the actual convention would open deliberations on May 20 in the North Carolina House of Commons.

The convention that took North Carolina out of the Union was a creation of the secessionists, and they were willing to sell the idea to the public by assuring fence-sitters that the convention would help preserve the Union. It didn't, of course, for it promptly took the state out of the Union, as its advocates had known all along. (For that matter, none of the first five states which seceded had dared to put the issue up for a public plebiscite.) Predictably, most of the delegates elected to the convention were secessionists, who, for the first time, found themselves in a dominant position among the state's various political factions. Their timing was exquisite: two weeks after Virginia had left the Union and three days after the proclamation of the Federal naval blockade. The secessionist cause had evolved from an option, to a matter of theoretical debate, to finally an emotional and psychological juggernaut.

When the secession convention met on May 20, the mood in Raleigh was ardent and bipartisan. An ordinance of secession was rapidly and enthusiastically passed, and the news of its passing triggered cheers, singing, and volleys of musketry in the streets outside the capitol building. As soon as some degree of order was restored, the convention swiftly ratified the Provisional Constitution of the Confederate States of America and adopted a new state flag: a white star centered in a red field, surmounted by a semicircular inscription ("May 20, 1775" — the date of the elusive Mecklenburg Declaration of Independence) and a symmetrical inscription below bearing the legend "May 20, 1861." (Actually, the present-day flag of North Carolina differs little from this design, except that the red field is now blue and the inscription "April 12, 1776" supplants the date of secession.)

Formal documents of secession were signed amid much pomp on the following day in the hall of the House of Representatives. It was oppressively hot and muggy, and the hall was jammed with spectators who had come to witness the historic event. As each of the 120 delegates signed his name, the hall reverberated with cheers. Outside, a band stood by, ready to cut loose with the song "Old North State," and a battery of cannon was preparing a 100-gun salute.

A white handkerchief was waved from one of the capitol's windows to signal to the crowd outside that the momentous deed was done. Cannon thundered, bells rang in the steeples of every church in Raleigh, and the crowd went wild. Strangers embraced and pounded one another on the back, people began to sing, and then started to dance in the streets. As one eyewitness charmingly put it, "All sorts of extravagances were indulged in."

On the fringes of this delirious mob, their heads bowed, their eyes clouded by tears, and their minds haunted by a dark and troubling presence, the Unionists saw something dreadful beyond the flag-waving, the hoopla, and the naive bloodthirstiness. Where the secessionists saw a wild and romantic beginning, a crusade, and an adventure beyond compare, the more reflective citizens in the crowd saw instead the end of something: the end of the genteel, decent, slow, yet gradually progressive way of life that had characterized North Carolina's culture since the end of the Revolution. But most of the Unionists, too, would take up the gun and fight.

GIRDING FOR A LONG WAR

North Carolina was the last Southern state to leave the Union, but once the commitment to war was made, her people joined the cause with determination and zeal. As was too often the case with the Confederate states, however, zeal was the only war commodity in adequate supply.

Consider the relative strength of the two opponents. The South had a total population of 9 million, the North almost 23 million. Discounting the 3.5 million slaves, the manpower odds against the South were 5 to 2. The North had 6 times as many factory workers and a powerful industrial base capable of rapid expansion. It also had a functioning government in place, not a provisional government starting from scratch like the one in Montgomery (soon moved to Richmond). The South's only significant economic resources were surplus agricultural goods which could be traded in Europe for finished goods — an exchange which became increasingly difficult as the Union blockade tightened.

In the beginning, the South's interior lines of communication, the sheer valor of her troops, and the remarkably consistent excellence of her commanders all helped offset these profound disadvantages. But not for long. The North's basic strategy was dictated by geography: split the Confederacy by gaining control of the Mississippi River, cut off the flow of European supplies by means of blockade, and defeat the Confederate armies in the field before Richmond. The South's basic strategy was to defend itself, to go on the offensive when an opportunity seemed to arise, and to seek outside help. Robert E. Lee himself thought that the South's best chance lay in the possibility of foreign intervention.

But Queen Victoria had no intention of being drawn into this internecine war. The wheat England imported from the North was more important to her balance of trade than was the cotton she bought from the Confederacy. The British did turn a blind eye when the South sought to purchase commerce raiders and blockade runners from English shipyards, and the British Enfield rifle was found in large numbers in the Confederate Army, but beyond that, the South got disappointingly small play from her "British card."

Proportionally, North Carolina's industrial base was even more minuscule than that of the South as a whole. Out of the state's population of one million, only .01 percent was engaged in manufacturing. There were more cobblers than iron workers. The few factories that could be converted to arms manufacturing were small, usually one-room, affairs that depended on hand labor to forge, assemble, and fine-finish their weapons. A weekly production quota of 50 rifles was good for such an establishment. In fact, during the first spring of the war the state was virtually defenseless. A "preparedness program" had been voted into place by the General Assembly, but it came only a few weeks before hostilities opened and had no practical effect on the state's military posture in early 1861.

Still, there was no dearth of manhood from which to forge an army. The state's young men flocked to its towns and cities in impressive numbers. Training camps sprang up in Raleigh, Warrenton, Halifax, Smithville, High Point, Asheville, and Carolina Beach.

They had gallant and colorful names, these motley companies of local boys: the Guilford Grays, the Cape Fear Minutemen, the Scotland Neck Mounted Riflemen, the Rough and Readies. Some of them sound, today, like the monikers of bellicose high school football teams: The Lexington Wildcats; the Rockingham Invincibles. They invariably went to war with the cheers of ladies and the shouts of fellow volunteers in their ears. Young girls stepped up to the roadside and hurled bunches of flowers; tied to the stems were messages admonishing the recipient to "defend the soil they grew on."

They went to war, in that first ebullient wave of volunteering, as though they were off to a grand Victorian picnic. One observer described the arrival of the Warren County Guards in these terms: "When this company arrived in Raleigh and came into the camp

28

(which was commanded by D.H. Hill...), it came with a train of wagons which would have sufficed, a few years later, to transport the baggage of Stonewall Jackson's [entire] corps, and the quality of the baggage was remarkable. There were banjoes, guitars, violins, huge camp chests, bedsteads, and other material startling in amount and unique as to quality, while the soldiers, a number of them large landed proprietors, were uniformed in a style of magnificence, as to gold lace, plumes, and epaulets, that would have required the genius of Sir Walter Scott to describe with proper effect...."[1]

Up to this time, the state's militia units were not really serious military organizations and were refered to as "holiday soldiers." They had dressed up for the Fourth of July in fanciful Napoleonic outfits decorated with gold trim, swishing epaulets, and clanking swords. The heavily plumed caps of the fancier outfits gave them the appearance of marching ostriches. They drilled once a month or once a week, held target practice a few times each year (rarely hitting anything), and their classroom study of tactics was perfunctory in the extreme. Until they learned how to fight, about all they could do was die bravely. They were to do a lot of that.

There were two kinds of enlistment arrangements at the start of the war. Under the old, prewar state laws, volunteers enlisted for a period of 12 months. Under the new emergency laws drafted at the secession convention in May, men enlisted after that time were in uniform for a period of three years or for the duration of the war, whichever came first. These new formations were called State Troops, and the herculean job of organizing them into trained regiments was the responsibility of the very able Major James G. Martin, a combat veteran who had left one arm on the battlefields of Mexico.

Martin proved an excellent administrator. By the middle of 1861, he was promoted to Adjutant General for the whole state, answerable only to the governor himself. During the first 12 months of conflict, Martin organized, trained, equipped, and sent forth no fewer than 41 regiments of North Carolina troops.

The First North Carolina Regiment departed from Raleigh for Richmond in May 1861. Its commander was D.H. Hill, whom Governor Ellis had promoted from a post at a military academy in Charlotte. It seemed as though the entire capital turned out to see the boys off to war. The regiment marched down Fayetteville Street, bands playing, women waving handkerchiefs, enjoying the whole wonderful, naive, romantic send-off that was such a common outlet for popular emotions at the time. The memory of those colorful farewells sent thousands of North Carolina boys into combat with heads erect and steps firm. But the first time a round of lead slammed into human flesh, the echo of the cheering faded quickly, and in the aftermath of the first battle — wherever it occurred for each fresh unit — it was drowned out, finally and for good, by the screams of the mutilated.

For the moment, though, it was all a grand adventure. The first North Carolina troops to arrive in Richmond found the new Confederate capital a dazzling place. Its paved streets, its gracious and substantial architecture, and its sheer size and sophistication excited them and filled them with wonder. And the Virginians welcomed them not as the gawking rural bumpkins many of them were, but as noble crusaders. What young soldier's head would not be turned by the sort of review that appeared in the *Petersburg Express* on May 20, 1861: "North Carolina marshals her bravest and her best for the coming contest and sends to Virginia men who will uphold and transmit without blemish to posterity the honorable and enviable glory and fame of their patriotic sires. Drilled to perfection and armed to the full — with brave hearts to lead and brave hearts to follow — they will do their duty and that nobly."

For the second wave of raw recruits who followed those first regiments, disillusionment began not on the battlefield but in training camp. One of the best-appointed camps in North Carolina was the big compound near Raleigh named after the governor. The "barracks" at Camp Ellis consisted of crude log huts. The beds were wooden planks laid down along one side of the huts. Not only were there no mattresses, there was no straw. The recruit threw his blanket down on the raw pine lumber and got whatever rest he could. Food was utilitarian at best, and cooking utensils were scarce. One recruit wrote of having to use the same tin pan for washing, baking bread, making tea, cleaning dishes, and bathing his feet after a hard day's drilling on red clay parade grounds. Dirt, he complained, got into the food constantly, and when it rained "it pours through the roof wetting the bedding and everything else."[2] Conditions in the cruder rural camps were even more primitive.

Building a War Industry

In May 1861, Governor Ellis unexpectedly died and was succeeded by Henry T. Clark, speaker of the senate. Clark's first duty as governor was to inform the General Assembly that the $5 million they had raised for the war effort was already spent and that they needed $6.5 million more. The war was scarcely a month old, the regiments were still largely untrained, no major battles had been fought, and already the state's financial resources were stretched uncomfortably thin. In late June, some of the burden was shifted, indirectly at least, when command of and responsibility for maintaining forces in the field was taken over by the Confederate government in Richmond.

Improvisation was one way to compensate for the state's backward industrial condition, and those in charge of such matters learned to do so with considerable ingenuity. Many of the weapons confiscated at the Fayetteville Arsenal, for instance, were obsolete flintlock smooth-bore muskets that had been in storage since the end of the Revolution. One fired some of these weapons at one's own peril, not the enemy's. Crews were set to work converting these antiques into modern firearms by rifling their barrels and replacing their flint and steel mechanisms with modern percussion caps.

In the autumn of 1861, it finally became possible for the state to produce modern weapons. Early in the war, when Union troops had abandoned and set fire to the arsenal at Harper's Ferry, some Virginia soldiers had managed to rescue the gun-making machinery. It was shipped to Fayetteville, a much more secure location than Harper's Ferry, but it languished there for months until workmen could be found to repair it and forge some of the missing parts. Once the repaired machinery was cranked up, the Fayetteville shops could turn out about a thousand finished rifles per month, although wartime shortages often made this quota elusive.

A report on a proposed new arsenal, submitted to Governor Ellis in January 1861, illustrates the economics of gun-making in those days. An armory capable of making 5,000 rifles a year would cost $48,000 to set up. For an additional $10,000 in start-up costs, the same plant's output could be increased to 15,000 weapons per year.

However, these estimates didn't include the gun-smithing machinery. That would cost a whopping $176,000. The master armorer's salary would be $3,000 per year, handsome wages in those days, and his foremen would receive $1,000 annually. After production began, it would cost about $14 to manufacture one rifle. A cannon foundry, requiring somewhat less sophisticated machinery, would cost in the neighborhood of $100,000. For any state in the Union, these figures were a major expense. For North Carolina in 1861, they were simply beyond reach. Throughout the entire war, no arsenal of this scope was ever constructed from scratch in North Carolina.

Instead, small manufacturing operations were opened wherever a suitable building and population of skilled workmen could be found. Pistols were made at New Bern, paper cartridges at Raleigh and Lincolnton, cannon shells at Wilmington, Charlotte, and Salisbury, bayonets and sabers at Kenansville, and rifles at Asheville and Fayetteville. To meet the gunpowder shortage, manufacturing plants were opened in Charlotte and Raleigh.

A thriving cottage industry in small-arms manufacture sprang up in Guilford County. There were half a dozen factories scattered through Greensboro, High Point, Jamestown, and Cedar Hill, making this region the fifth-largest center of gun production in the Confederacy. One interesting weapon manufactured in Greensboro, the .52-caliber Tarpley Carbine, patented in 1863 by gunsmith Jere H. Tarpley, had the distinction of being the only breech-loading firearm designed and manufactured solely in the Confederacy. It was also the only Confederate-made weapon ever offered for sale to the general public, as revealed in an advertisement from the April 14, 1863 issue of the *Greensboro Patriot*. An uncommonly ugly weapon, the Tarpley was plagued by recurring problems of gas leakage at the breech and by the lack of a forestock under its barrel, which made it too hot to hold after a few rounds were fired. By the end of the war, only a few hundred had been manufactured.

By mid-1862, North Carolina's regiments would be about as well armed as any in the Confederate Army, but the rifle deficit was still critical during the winter of 1861. General Martin's office reported that up to 10,000 additional men could have been fielded if there had been arms for them to carry.

Even more critical, in view of the need to defend the state's long coastline, was the shortage of artillery. Aside from the modest quantity of artillery seized at Fayetteville and at the coastal forts, North Carolina began the war with four smooth-bore Napoleonic field guns, appropriated by the state from military academies in Hillsborough and Charlotte. Patriotic collections of church bells and scrap iron made the donors feel useful, but did not, in practical terms, amount to more than a drop in the bucket. This shortage of artillery was never entirely solved and was a major factor in the Confederates' inability to defend a number of important coastal positions.

Inventive minds came up with practical designs for belts and cartridge boxes that could be made from multiple layers of cotton cloth rather than from scarce and expensive leather hides. As the winter of 1861-62 drew near, and a scarcity of warm clothing began to affect the troops in the field, General Martin mobilized the state's textile industry. First he established a clothing factory near Raleigh, then he commandeered the output of every textile plant in the state (9 cotton and 39 woolen mills) and had the cloth shipped to the capital. There, in one tight, centralized operation, the cloth was turned into uniforms and shipped to the troops. Generous donations of quilts, blankets, carpets, shirts, and socks poured in from all over the state and helped make up the shortfall during that first winter. If North Carolina's soldiers were not the smartest-looking in the land, most of them were at least adequately protected from the elements.

There was one major Confederate facility opened in the Piedmont which seems, at first glance, laughably incongruous: the Charlotte Navy Yard, located about 200 miles from the nearest body of navigable water. The creation of a navy yard so far inland came about when Norfolk's main navy yard at Portsmouth, Virginia was threatened by Federal advances. Confederate naval authorities in Richmond looked around for a suitable place to relocate Portsmouth's machinery and technicians. Charlotte was chosen because it was about as safe from Yankee attack as any place in the South, and because it had good rail connections not only with Richmond but also with the North Carolina coastal cities of New Bern, Wilmington, and Beaufort. Naval repairs and new construction could be undertaken in Charlotte in relative safety, and the finished vessels and other materiel could be dispatched to their places of deployment in a reasonably efficient manner.

The first men to staff the new navy yard were former crew members of the famous Confederate ironclad C.S.S. *Virginia*, formerly U.S.S. *Merrimac*. After its epic battle with the *Monitor* off Hampton Roads, the *Virginia* had been burned and scuttled to keep it from falling into Union hands. The *Virginia*'s chief engineer, Ashton Ramsey, became head of the Charlotte Navy Yard. A number of big frame buildings were erected on the Trade Street lot purchased for the yard, including a laboratory, a torpedo shop, a large-scale forge, and a gun carriage shop. The largest steam trip-hammer in the South was constructed there and was used to forge the propeller shafts for all the ironclads built in the Confederacy, including the *Virginia II* and the legendary *Albemarle*. Naval and coastal defense mountings, solid shot, explosive shells, and torpedoes were also made at Charlotte.

So the idea of establishing a navy yard at Charlotte turned out to be not whimsical but eminently practical, for the facility functioned quite well for most of the war, hampered only by the same shortages of raw materials that choked so many other Confederate improvisations.

Nothing better illustrates the seat-of-the-pants quality of North Carolina's industrial mobilization than the saga of the state's first powder factory. Early in the war, Governor Ellis put the word out that powder-makers were urgently needed and that anyone who was conversant with that arcane and dangerous craft should report at once to him in Raleigh. Two men showed up who were equipped with both zeal and ideas. Their names were James Waterhouse and Michael Bowes, both Englishmen by birth, and both former citizens of Canada who had emigrated to North Carolina during the 1850s. Ellis liked their confidence and energy. The only problem was that neither man knew the slightest thing about making gunpowder. Until now, they had been employed at the Raleigh gas works.

Undaunted, and armed with official blessings and funding, Waterhouse and Bowes immediately undertook to educate themselves. They found enough references to existing powder plants to come up with an inventory of machinery and facilities, and they learned the powder-makers' art simply by reading a lot of chemistry books.

From Richmond, they acquired a powerful tobacco press, which seemed ideally suited for pressing the raw powder into sheets. They found a suitable location on the outskirts of Raleigh on the banks of Crabtree Creek, and erected eight water wheels to supply power to eight different buildings. Obtaining the sulphur, nitre, and saltpeter proved difficult at first. Until regular supplies could be manufactured or imported from other states, quantities of these chemicals were hacked out of abandoned mine shafts, scraped out of old smokehouses, and retrieved from caves and moldy cellars. Vast supplies of willow wood were obtained from trees that grew in the Raleigh area, and this was converted to charcoal on the spot. A cooper set up shop on the edge of the site and began crafting wooden kegs for storing and shipping the finish products.

In an amazingly short time, the two entrepreneurs had mastered their craft and were turning out high-grade gunpowder, starting with a paltry 300 pounds per day and quickly working up to an average of 1,600 pounds per day. The factory's total output went to North Carolina, and the state in turn sold vast quantities to the Confederacy. Robert E. Lee's artillery devoured tons of it during the great campaigns in northern Virginia, and it is known that Waterhouse and Bowes's powder was used in the duel between the *Monitor* and the *Virginia*.

Powder-making was dangerous work. Every building on the site was ringed by deep underground bunkers where the workmen could take cover in the event of a fire or accidental detonation of the product. The bunkers were used often; a total of 15 men died in pyrotechnic mishaps during the three and a half years the plant was in operation. When General Sherman's Union army drew near in April 1865, the last kegs of powder were shipped by rail to storage bunkers near Greensboro and the plant was set afire. Waterhouse died not long after the war, but Bowes lived into his eighties, a prosperous Raleigh businessman.

Although the Confederacy overlooked few resources in its struggle to win the war, no formal attempt was ever made to organize the state's women for the war effort. There were no women's auxiliary corps, no WACS, no Rosie-the-Riveter factory jobs for the ladies. But the hardships, sacrifices, and contributions made by the women of North Carolina, entirely on their own, were immense. To begin with, most women functioned in a domestic setting that was rural and, on the average, dependent on a subsistence economy with marginal surpluses, even in times of good harvest. The number of women who had slaves to help them was statistically insignificant. Most married women had children and/or elderly dependents. Their husbands, absent in the service of their country, did not receive enough pay to send much home, and what they could send bought less and less as inflation diluted the economy. The demands on the womenfolk were great at the start of the war, crippling by the end of it. They plowed, planted, harvested, cooked, washed, nursed, and raised the kids; they carried on. The war brought hardships that bent them down, and after years of unrelenting toil and deprivation, broke not a few of them. But the vestiges of coherent society left for the men to come back to in 1865 had largely survived thanks to the resourcefulness and endurance of the women.

Early Action

The Union's opening act in the war was President Lincoln's declaration of a naval blockade of the Confederacy in April 1861. At this time, however, the U.S. Navy was still a fledgling force spread dangerously thin, and most of its vessels could not be spared for routine patrol duties. During the first year of the war, the blockade existed for the most part only on paper, and North Carolina had little trouble supplementing its strained resources with cargoes from overseas.[3]

Early in June 1861 came electrifying news: The first battle of the war had been fought and had resulted in a Confederate victory! Not a big victory, to be sure, but a respectable one. A numerically superior Union force under General Butler had been whipped by a feisty Confederate force under Colonel John Magruder at Big Bethel, Virginia, not far from Yorktown. The First North Carolina Regiment boasted a prominent role in the victory, conducting itself boldly under its able commander, D.H. Hill. A soldier in the ranks of the First North Carolina, Henry L. Wyatt, from Edgecomb County, was the first Confederate soldier killed in the engagement — and, so far as anybody knows, in the entire war.

Shortly afterward, on June 21, came news of a much more significant victory: the Battle of First Manassas (Bull Run). Three North Carolina units participated in this Virginia battle. In Raleigh, in Charlotte, in Greensboro and Salisbury, citizens thronged the streets to grab the freshly printed news sheets describing the Yankees' rout and the glorious sweep of the rebel forces across the field. Here, surely, was proof that the inherent martial prowess and natural gallantry of Southern manhood could more than cancel out the North's numerical and industrial advantages.

Of more tangible significance to North Carolina was the fact that the Battle of Manassas eliminated Virginia as a major campaign theater for the remainder of 1861. Federal strategists were encouraged to look elsewhere, for places where they might obtain significant results on the cheap. Their attention was inevitably caught and held by the strategically vital and seemingly vulnerable coastline of North Carolina.

The state's coastal defenses were scandalously neglected by Richmond and incompetently defended by most of the Southern commanders in the area. One after another, important points fell: Fort Hatteras in August 1861, Roanoke Island in February 1862, New Bern and Washington in March, Fort Macon in April, and Plymouth in December 1862.

After 1862, things settled down to a stalemate along the coast. The state managed to muster enough forces to keep the Federals pinned in their coastal enclaves, but never had enough to actually drive them out. When Lee finally got around to making a serious effort to "clear the state" in April 1864, it was too late to make much difference, and General Robert Hoke's brilliant campaign was cut short by renewed interference from Richmond before it could reap its full potential for victory.

Significant military action was absent from the Piedmont until the last spring of the war, when Sherman thundered over the border from South Carolina and the Army of Tennessee, hastily assembled from camps all over the South, mustered for one last trial of arms at a piney-woods village known as Bentonville. But there was political action aplenty in Raleigh as the state mobilized for total war under a proud and charismatic leader named Zebulon Baird Vance.

SLAVES AND FREE NEGROES

To use modern terminology, North Carolina was never a hard-core slavery state. The reasons why were social and economic in nature. For one thing, the plantation system, with its huge feudal estates, never took root in North Carolina as it did in the more lush climes of the Deep South. Except for limited areas along the coast, the state's soil simply did not support that kind of farming, nor the kind of crops that are economically feasible under that kind of system.

The "plantation class" in antebellum North Carolina amounted to only 6 percent of the population. According to the last prewar census, slightly more than 4,000 planters in the entire state owned 20 or more slaves. In all of North Carolina, in fact, there were only 311 farms with more than a thousand acres of land. Of all the state's landowners, only about one-quarter owned any slaves at all, and the number of slaves owned by any one family was likely to be small. Of the 11 states which seceded in 1861, North Carolina ranked eighth in its ratio of slaves to whites.

There was never a genuine slave uprising anywhere in the state, and there were relatively few acts of individual violence. The yoke of servitude was simply not as harsh in North Carolina as it was in most Southern states and, although economics certainly was the primary reason for this, there was in many areas of the state an attitude of genuine enlightenment.

Thanks in large part to the anti-slavery attitudes of the Quakers, the Wesleyan Methodists, and other well-organized sects in the Piedmont region, North Carolina made real progress during the first third of the 19th century in liberalizing its slave codes. Free Negroes were permitted to vote in some state elections, and programs were implemented to spread literacy among the Negro population.

In the mid-1830s, however, the widespread fear of slave uprisings, together with a growing defensiveness on the part of landowning Southerners about the "peculiar institution" to which their region subscribed, created a changed intellectual and emotional climate. Most of the humanizing legislation enacted during the first three decades of the century was undone by a major constitutional revision in 1835. Manumission (the freeing of slaves by their owners, often as a deathbed gesture to repay decades of docile loyalty) was made much more difficult, and the vote was taken away from free Negro men.

The tempo of restrictive legislation picked up as the war approached. By 1860, these laws, taken as a body, formed a rigid and effective system of controls designed to restrict the Negroes' freedom of movement, to force them into positions of economic subservience to lower-class whites (by making it difficult and/or dangerous for them to compete for the same jobs), and to prevent them from organizing insurrections.

The slave population of North Carolina had a deserved reputation for docility. Abolitionist activity did generate plenty of passengers for the Underground Railway, but it never stirred up a single recorded incident of violent rebellion. Nevertheless, North Carolina caught the contagion of fear — Nat Turner's Syndrome, as it were — which spread across the South during the last three or four years before the war. The paranoia over "outside agitators" was not unlike that which surfaced a century later during the early civil rights movement. Even Governor Ellis — normally a level-headed man — was ranting in 1860 about "organized societies [that] have sent emissaries among us to incite insurrection and bloodshed...." He laid the blame for those societies at the feet of the Northern political establishment.

Newspapers and incendiary pamphlets warned citizens to be ever vigilant, to vigorously quash any revolutionary tendencies found in the local black population, slave or free. Lurid stories made the rounds about white families poisoned en masse by hitherto trusted black servants. Yet even the secessionist papers printed these tales as rumor, not fact, and no documented case of such an atrocity is recorded in the standard reference sources for the period.

With the approach of almost certain war, the white population
became even more jittery. The entire coastline of North Carolina lay
open and practically defenseless against Federal incursions — it
seemed only a matter of time until Union forces gained beachheads.
And it so happened that the vast majority of North Carolina's slaves
were concentrated in the northeastern counties, where they would be
within easy reach of the enemy, and where they could be enlisted in
his war effort. The thought of vengeance-inflamed gangs of rebellious slaves, armed with Yankee rifles and running amok, must have
kept a lot of people awake at night.

The legal machinery erected to eliminate this potential nightmare
was called Negro Control, a label as honest as it was repugnant. As
the war drew closer, and especially after hostilities began, those
controls grew more rigorous, more stifling, until every inch of social
progress the state had gained from 1800 to 1835 was wiped out and
replaced by draconian and openly repressive laws.

Policies were formulated to grind the Negroes down, keep them in
their place, and control them by means of legalized vigilantism,
while at the same time maximizing the contributions of Negro labor
in the war effort. It occurred to some thoughtful people that there
was a serious contradiction between these two policies — men do
not work hard or willingly to defend their oppressors — but the
lonely voices of reason were drowned in the tides of passion and
fear.

The specter of insurrection was addressed in February 1861 when
a measure was introduced in the General Assembly to make it a
felony for anyone to publish or bring into the state written material
which would "cause slaves to become discontent with the bondage in
which they are held" or "free Negroes to be dissatisfied with their
social status." Interestingly, the wording implies the assumption that
outside provocation was required to render slaves "discontent with
the bondage in which they are held."

A more stringent law was enacted on May 11, 1863, condemning to
death anyone caught "advising or conspiring" with Negroes for the
purpose of fomenting insurrection. The death sentence would be
meted out regardless of whether an act of rebellion actually took
place as a result of the advising and conspiring.

Starting in 1862, the presence of Federal enclaves on the coast exacerbated fears of slave uprisings to a fever pitch throughout the state. One Piedmont newspaper — the *Charlotte Western Democrat* — spoke openly about the imminent return of "Judge Lynch."

It had long been a practice in antebellum North Carolina for slave owners to permit individual slaves to hire themselves out for work on other farms, in other counties or in other parts of the state. But wartime conditions virtually demanded a change in this policy. The whole system, it was felt, might disintegrate without tight supervision and control of every black in the state. Bills were introduced to outlaw the practice, but the General Assembly never passed them — perhaps because many of the legislators were slave owners, and slave owners usually made a profit from these subcontracting arrangements.

Several communities, however, did enact local laws to regulate slaves' movements. An ordinance passed in Hillsborough in April 1861, made it illegal for slaves to be inside the city limits between sunset and sunrise and all day Sunday, on pain of imprisonment. One law passed in Charlotte at about the same time was even more strict, stating that "no slave shall go at large as a free person exercising his or her discretion in the employment of their time." Any slave owner convicted of allowing his blacks to roam free, or of hiring them out without written permission, was subject not only to a stiff fine, but also could have the slave confiscated by the city, which auctioned off the slave's services to the highest bidder for the remainder of the year.

Other more minor but equally repressive new laws forbade a slave to "keep house...as a free person," or to trade in "spirituous liquors." Slave trading was also tightly regulated by means of rigid new licensing laws.

Paradoxically, the lot of the free Negro was, in many cases, even worse than that of the slave. North Carolina's 30,000 free Negroes lived in a curious kind of social and moral limbo. The dominant white society recognized two classes of human beings: those who were free and those who were slaves, and slavery was regarded as the natural condition of the black person. Free Negroes had no niche to fill. With very few exceptions, they lived isolated, impoverished lives, regarded with suspicion by those around them and viewed by the state's lawmakers as a destabilizing influence on the whole system.

State policy toward the free Negroes during the Civil War period was neither enlightened nor farsighted. Properly motivated, and given a stake in their society, free Negroes might have contributed something to the war effort; but, of course, to give them a stake in society would be to undermine the very foundations of that society. Once again, the cause of the South was torpedoed by the social dynamics that made the South so different in the first place.

A sizable body of laws was enacted to regulate free Negroes, and the net result left these unfortunate people, for all practical purposes, no freer than their brothers and sisters in actual bondage. They were watched, their activities monitored closely, day in and day out. Close contact between them and the slave population was forbidden and punishable. And, perhaps worst of all, the economic possibilities open to them were so narrowed, and so circumscribed, as to drive many of them either out of the state or actually back into slavery.

The first major piece of wartime legislation regarding free Negroes was a law that sought to keep this population from expanding. After December 8, 1860, it became illegal for any North Carolinian to emancipate a slave in his last will and testament — the most common path to freedom for Negroes.

Laws were also introduced to permit "voluntary enslavement" — that is, to allow desperate free Negroes to chose a master and indenture themselves to him. Perhaps some residual sense of common decency prevailed, however, when the North Carolina Supreme Court finally ruled that "the [state] Constitution recognizes free persons of color as citizens of the state and…the law must protect them in the enjoyment of life, liberty, and property, except where they have forfeited the same for crime." A constitutional amendment would have to be passed, the court declared, to make it legal for free Negroes to return to slave status. Thwarted by the court's decision, one senator (John Murell of Onslow County) tried to introduce a bill providing that all free Negroes who had not "voluntarily" sold their services for a period of 99 years, as of January 1, 1864, should be forcibly ejected from the state. This measure, fortunately, went much farther than most lawmakers were willing to go, and it was tabled for good after some lively debate.

Law or no law, a large number of free Negroes sank back into slave status during the war. For one thing, free Negroes who ran afoul of the law and were unable to pay any imposed fines were hired out — slaves in all but name — to anyone who assumed those fines. During the period in which they worked off their fines, these people were as tightly regulated as most slaves.

One situation that was regarded as highly volatile was the owner-ship of slaves by free Negroes — not a common phenomenon, to be sure, but one which struck most whites as doubly unnatural and sinister. The number of slave-owning free Negroes in North Caro-lina was minuscule (a grand total of eight, according to one estimate based on census figures for 1860), but the amount of legislative ink spilled over the subject was enormous. A law was swiftly passed in February 1861 making it illegal for a "free person of color" to own slaves.

A mere ten days after that came a law forbidding any free Negro to bear arms — including a shotgun — even if the weapons were for hunting or self-defense. Ninety days later, another piece of legisla-tion provided a mandatory death penalty for any free Negro con-victed of plotting with a slave for the purpose of insurrection.

A statewide system of licensing free Negroes — compelling them to carry their papers at all times — was debated but not passed, perhaps because the state had all the bureaucratic headaches it could handle by the end of 1861.

The failure of such legislation on a statewide level, however, did not prevent some counties and towns from enacting similar ordinances locally. The city fathers of Hillsborough proved excep-tionally severe. The only time a free Negro was allowed to walk abroad in that town without his local permit was on Sunday morn-ing, going to or from church. A similarly repressive law passed in Charlotte mandated "registration papers" for all free Negroes in the city. Anyone caught without his or her papers was subject to fines, imprisonment, flogging, or indentured labor for a period of up to six months.

The result of all these restrictive measures, quite predictably, was a great increase in both runaway slaves and refugee free Negroes — particularly after many of the coastal counties fell under Federal control in 1862. Intended to nail the state's black population in one place for the duration of the war, these laws may actually have increased manyfold the amount of unsupervised movement.

Taken as a whole, North Carolina's wartime Negro policies were designed to reinforce the existing system by means of tighter controls over every aspect of blacks' lives. Although the state was never as heavy-handed as some of its Confederate allies in the Deep South, it did come down hard; hard enough to force hundreds of free men to fall back to the status of slaves.

Although North Carolina's slave population was neither large nor generally ill-treated, it would give a false impression of historical reality to gloss over the harshness of the slaves' lot, or to presume that the "freedom" enjoyed by "free Negroes" was anything like the freedom available to the poorest white man in the state. In Salisbury, for instance, in 1861, a free Negro who took a swipe at a bullying magistrate with a stick was arrested and given his choice of 500 lashes or a hanging — the poor man understandably chose the noose. Perhaps the difference between North Carolina's attitude and that of the Deep South states is illustrated by the fact that, at the last minute, some of the onlookers took pity on the man and cut him down just seconds before he would have died. In Georgia or Alabama, they would undoubtedly have left him dangling.

THE UNDERGROUND RAILWAY

At the start of the war, there was still considerable ambiguity in North Carolina about the issue of slavery. Thirty years earlier, there was less. Until the mid-1830s, in fact, the state was gradually turning its back on the "peculiar institution." It was strongly rumored that an informal poll of the General Assembly on the resolution "Shall slavery be abolished?" had fallen short of passage by a mere seven votes.

This attitude, not exactly pro-abolitionist, but decidedly uncomfortable about slavery as an institution, germinated from the upper Piedmont section of the state. The Piedmont's center of gravity was in Guilford County, where three of the four original chapters of the Manumission Society were formed in 1816. In ten years, the Society had grown to 28 chapters with more than 16,000 members.

At the vanguard of this movement were the Quakers. The Society of Friends (as they were more formally known) had done away with slavery as far back as 1774, and they had worked vigorously, through lectures and pamphleteering, to spread their enlightened attitude throughout the state. One of the Manumission Society's chief allies was the editor of the *Greensboro Patriot*, William Swain (the writer O. Henry's grandfather), who wrote eloquently about the evils of the system. Given this environment, it is perhaps not surprising that in all of Guilford County in 1860 there were less than 200 slaves.

It was this attitude that led to the founding of the legendary Underground Railway — a shadow-system that functioned, with remarkable success and in near total secrecy, for more than a quarter-century. The concept of the "railway" is generally attributed to two ardent Quaker abolitionists, Levi and Vestal Coffin.

It worked like this: If a slave decided to seek his freedom via the railway, he would ask around until he learned the name and address of the nearest "railway agent." The slave would then slip away from his quarters one night and submit to an extensive interview by this agent. Not every slave who wanted to make the trek was accepted. The organizers had to consider the safety of the system as a whole, and slaves who were in poor health, who were half-hearted in their commitment, or who were of below-average intelligence were turned down for the sake of hundreds of other candidates better equipped to withstand the rigors of the journey.

The railway agent would therefore examine the candidate from several angles: Was he sincere? Strong? Motivated? Smart? If the examining agent felt the candidate could make the trip, he would be welcomed into the system and given instructions on how to find the next agent "up the line." This stringent screening process seems to have worked very well, for in the 30 years the railway functioned, there was no known instance of a chosen candidate ever divulging any of the network's secrets.

In the beginning, two main routes were established: from North Carolina through Virginia into Pennsylvania, and from North Carolina via the Virginia Turnpike to the junction of the Ohio and Kanawha Rivers. By 1835, the railway had grown to include regular "depots" in Ohio, Indiana, and Illinois. These "safe houses" were set up every 20 or 30 miles in the attics, outbuildings, and cellars of dedicated abolitionists.

Starting in or near Greensboro, and continuing all the way to the Virginia Turnpike, the route was marked by secret signs likely to be ignored or overlooked by those not privy to the railway's workings. If there was a fork in the road, for instance, a nail driven into a tree on either the right or left side of the trunk would tell the escapee which branch he should take. The fleeing slave would simply walk up to the tree, encircle it with his arms, and run his hands down the length of the trunk until he encountered the nailhead.

If there were no trees, then rock markers or nails driven into fence posts served the same purpose. For escapees from the eastern counties making their way toward Greensboro along the inland waterway system, there were nautical markers denoting hidden channels and navigable streams. In fact, though, little is known about just what sort of secret signs were used along the nautical routes; most of the men who knew those secrets took them to the grave.

River crossings were often undertaken on rafts made from fence rails. Once the refugee was safely across, he untied the cords holding the raft together, and the little craft literally fell to pieces, turning into just so much innocuous driftwood.

The courage and resourcefulness of those who established the Underground Railway and kept it functioning without a major lapse for 30 years were remarkable. Today, the story of the Underground Railway has become one of the great folk epics of antebellum America. Several spots have been singled out in Guilford County as the epicenter of the system. Some say the original starting point was in the New Garden community, near what is today Guilford College; others maintain that the site was actually inside the Greensboro city limits, near present-day Cedar Street; still others have traced it to the southwestern corner of the county, where Guilford borders Randolph and Davidson Counties. It is possible, of course, that all these educated guesses are correct. As the railway developed beyond its tentative beginnings, there must have been more than just one or two embarkation points.

It is also interesting to note that, after the war, one of the Coffin men and several other Underground Railway "conductors" found additional employment for their skills — as the masters of wagon trains heading west.

NEGRO LABOR AS A STRATEGIC RESOURCE

There were approximately 4,200,000 black people living in the South at the war's beginning. By the time the Confederacy's white male population had been thinned out, first by the initial wave of volunteer enthusiasm, and later by successive waves of conscription, the secessionist states were faced with a chronic shortage of labor, particularly in areas of employment from which blacks had traditionally been excluded.

Here, again, the system of slavery worked against itself. In order for the South to remain true to its antebellum identity, slavery had to be perpetuated, even strengthened. And yet for the South to make efficient use of the immense reservoir of manpower represented by its Negro population, the whole system would have to be dismantled and the Negroes given some stake in a Southern victory. This was a paralyzing contradiction; all the incentives for black people lay on the enemy's side. To form combat units of armed Negroes was unthinkable because the only prize they would fight for — freedom — was an incentive the South could not offer without inviting economic collapse.

There was only one possibility for getting the most out of the Negroes, and that was to expand the limits of employment, to permit the training of Negroes as train engineers, factory workers, craftsmen, and clerks. The system had to yield and grow flexible in this regard, or North Carolina's economy would have collapsed by the end of 1863 or the start of 1864.

In late 1862, the General Assembly authorized the governor to impress slaves for work on defensive construction projects. There was even a complicated sliding-scale arrangement in the bill so that slave owners in a given county would be liable to provide an equal percentage of their "property" regardless of whether they owned 3 slaves or 30. The statute promised that slaves requisitioned for these projects would be returned "forthwith" to their owners as soon as the fortifications were completed, but they seldom were. In return, owners were compensated on a per-month basis for their contribution. An ordinary field hand was valued at $15 per month, and a skilled workman or mechanic at twice that amount. Should a slave die, become maimed, or flee to the enemy while so employed, the state government would compensate the owner fully for the loss.

Because many defensive works were naturally being constructed in fairly close proximity to the enemy, slave owners feared that their "property" would simply vanish on the first dark night. As a result, some nervous slave owners moved their slaves into the Piedmont region. This made it harder for the slaves to run away, but also made it harder for the state to find enough laborers to build the defenses it needed.

Another problem was the reluctance of slave owners to loan out their fittest hands when there were large numbers of free Negroes in the same neighborhood. So great was the outcry among the landed gentry that a law was passed in 1862 making it mandatory that labor requisitions be drawn first from the population of free Negroes, with the slave population being held in reserve.

Amazing as it may seem, there were isolated bursts of genuine Confederate patriotism among some of the free Negroes (and even on the part of a few slaves), although it seems to have lasted for only the first few weeks of the war, before the legislative screws were put to the freemen as a class. In May 1861, for instance, the *Winston-Salem Press* carried a story about "fifteen free men of color [who] left Salisbury Monday morning for the mouth of the Cape Fear, volunteers for the service of the state. They were in fine spirits and each wore a placard in his hat bearing the inscription: 'We will die by the South!'" There was also this account in the *Greensboro Patriot*, dated May 7, 1861, describing "a Negro hackman who came to his master and insisted with tears in his eyes that he accept his savings of one hundred dollars to help equip volunteers."

Whatever laws and priorities were promulgated by Raleigh, actual conditions in the field varied from place to place and from situation to situation. If a military commander needed earthworks thrown up in a hurry, and there was a supply of slave labor handy, he probably wouldn't bother to write to Raleigh for permission. Most likely, he would simply commandeer the men he needed and sign a chit to the owner which might, or might not, be honored at some later date by the state treasurer.

Rations, housing, and medical care for labor detachments tended to be much poorer than what was enjoyed by the regular rank and file — which is to say that conditions could be appalling. Word got around via the slaves' informal network, and after a while nobody harbored any illusions about what life would be like near the battlefield. Artillery fire was color-blind, the work was brutal, the food inadequate, and the medical care usually nonexistent. Unless a slave was motivated by an intense desire to escape to Federal lines, he was no more eager to participate in front-line labor service than his master was to lose him for it.

Throughout the conflict, vast numbers of black men, slave or free, were coerced, cajoled, or simply impressed into the building of defensive works — but the entire process was cumbersome and grossly inefficient in terms of the results versus the effort expended.

Back on the home front, the story was somewhat different. Farm labor, factory tasks, and especially railroad jobs offered better conditions for the laborer and much more potential profit for the owner. The result was an inflated slave-labor market in which demand was always greater than supply. In 1863 alone, the Piedmont and Chatham Railroads advertised for a total of 800 laborers, trying to fill positions not only in construction but also in maintenance and clerical work. As the strain on the state's railroad system increased, Negroes were even trained as locomotive engineers. For a small number of blacks, the war actually provided a chance to acquire job skills that would prove very valuable during the Reconstruction period.

Newspaper advertisements placed by the railroad companies sought to entice owners to hire out their slaves by making promises such as this one, from the *Fayetteville Observer* (February 16, 1863): "The line runs through healthy country, on a high ridge, and all hands employed on the road will be well fed and cared for." The effectiveness of these ads may be deduced from the fact that some of them ran, issue after issue, for five or six months. Other notices were run by farmers, construction contractors, and municipal utilities, and there were always steady jobs to be had at the salt works along the coast.

By the middle of 1863, the cost of hiring slaves had gone through the roof. A man who could have been hired in 1861 for $100 now commanded $300 (or, to be precise, his owner did). By 1865, an average field hand couldn't be hired for less than $500, and a strong man in his prime might fetch as much as $1,200. Mechanics (a term which encompassed a much broader range of skills in 1865 than it does today) were going for $1,000 to $2,400. And a healthy female "without encumbrances" (slaveownerese for "no children") was worth anywhere from $300 to $1,000.

If it was expensive to hire a slave, it was ruinously so to actually buy one. Few slaves went on the market, and those who did, even if past their prime, commanded prices in excess of $5,000.

Simple demand alone does not explain these wildly inflationary figures. The state government was forced to pay high rates to hire slave labor, so private contractors were forced to match or exceed those rates in order to compete. The official rate in late 1864, as fixed by the Board of Commissioners of Appraisement, was $45 a month plus room and board, or $540 per year.

It did not escape notice, especially by those who had become disillusioned with the Confederate cause, that the soldiers in the field who were bleeding and dying to protect the Southern way of life were paid — if they were paid at all — at the rate of $132 a year.

A WORD ABOUT THE RAILROADS

The only strategic advantage the South possessed over the North was in the category of interior lines of communication. As limited and half-formed as the Southern railway system was by 1861, it was still extensive enough, and efficient enough, to permit the Confederates to concentrate their forces rapidly and gain localized parity — or even, in some battles, superiority.

As the war progressed, and the Confederacy's coastal and riverine lines of communication fell under Federal control, the railroads assumed even more importance. They alone allowed the South to concentrate its dwindling manpower to meet new threats in different areas, and they alone provided an unbroken and reasonably reliable conduit for the supplies that squeezed through holes in the Union naval blockade. Time and time again, the use of her internal rail network — bumbling, chaotic, and as politically corrupted as that use sometimes was — allowed the South to check Federal advances first in one theater, then in another. Both the first great battle of the war (the victory at Manassas) and the last (the gallant, foredoomed stand at Bentonville) were fought with concentrations of troops that could not have reached the field without rail transportation.

By January 1861, there were 8,783 miles of track in the Southern states — compared to a national total of about 31,000 miles. Unfortunately, the South's resources of rolling stock, iron, and support facilities made up only about one-quarter of the national inventory, and the South had virtually no way of replacing war-worn equipment and track.

In the decade from 1850 to 1860, a progressive policy of state support enabled North Carolina's railroads to grow at a healthy rate: track increased from 283 miles in 1850 to 922 miles on the eve of hostilities. The system was not well-suited for military purposes, however. For one thing, the track gauge (width between the rails) had not been nationally standardized by 1860; locomotives and rolling stock designed to run on some tracks wouldn't fit on others. In North Carolina, the gauge was a paltry but troublesome inch and a half narrower than the gauge used from Danville north and from Charlotte south. Another problem was that North Carolina's rail system had been built to function in east-west directions, to move goods and people from the interior of the state to the ports on the coast and vice versa. The war effort required most rail traffic to move in north-south directions.

The most important of the North Carolina railways was the Wilmington and Weldon Line, which connected Wilmington (North Carolina's most vital port, especially after the Union captured the state's other ports) with Virginia. By means of connections at Goldsboro, the Wilmington and Weldon Line also linked Wilmington with the western Piedmont and the Deep South states. Not without reason was this railroad often referred to as the "lifeline of the Confederacy." From the opening weeks of the war, a large percentage of the supplies needed to keep the Army of Northern Virginia in the field — from British-made Enfield muskets imported through the blockade to home-grown corn and uniform cloth — came up this line. As supply routes from the Gulf of Mexico and the West were severed, one by one, the importance of this lifeline grew accordingly. By the middle of 1864, about 60 percent of the food consumed by Lee's army moved along this one railroad, as did a comparable percentage of military equipment. The importance of the line decreased after the Federals captured its terminus at Petersburg, Virginia, in August 1864, but blockade-runner supplies continued to get through along the North Carolina tracks right up until the capture of Fort Fisher at Wilmington.

The other major north-south line in the state was the North Carolina, Richmond, and Danville Line (sometimes called the Piedmont Line), which connected to South Carolina via Charlotte, to the Western North Carolina spur line via Salisbury, and to the eastern part of the state via the Atlantic and North Carolina Line, whose western terminus was in Greensboro. The NCR&D tracks continued north beyond Greensboro almost up to the Virginia Line, but at the start of the war there was a 40-mile gap between the end of the tracks and the Danville connection. Goods that were shipped on this line, therefore, had to be unloaded onto wagons for that stretch of the trip.

A typical east-west prewar run on the North Carolina Railroad went like this: A train would depart Goldsboro at 6:30 a.m., arrive at Raleigh about 9:30, then proceed about 44 miles to Hillsborough and pull into the station there at about noon. Greensboro would be reached by about 3:30 p.m., Salisbury sometime around sunset, and Charlotte at about 9:15 — if everything went without a hitch. The total run of 225 miles took about 15 hours, for an average speed of about 15 miles per hour (including stops).

Passenger fares were rather steep. A ride from Weldon to Richmond cost $4, for example, including a horse-drawn cab ride between stations in Petersburg. Aside from passengers, the most common prewar cargos were lumber, salt, pork, copper, gold (1,500 tons in 1860, statewide), flour, beeswax, and liquor.

During the first year of the war, control of the Confederate states' railroads remained firmly in the hands of various — and sometimes competing — state and private authorities. In a belated effort to establish some sort of centralized order, President Davis appointed William M. Wadley to clean up the mess.

During an inspection tour of North Carolina's rail system, Wadley found a state of barely tolerable confusion. At every station, he beheld pestilential swarms of Confederate government agents badgering railway employees to expedite their particular shipment of goods ahead of everyone else's — a situation that invited wholesale graft. Train and station crews were found to be in a constant state of irritation over outside interference with their jobs and in a state of smoldering anger over the Confederate government's chronic inability to improve, or even maintain, rolling stock and roadbeds. Iron that was urgently needed to maintain the rails was diverted instead to be fashioned into armor plate for Confederate ironclads. As the rails wore out, an effort was made to preserve them by running trains at slower speeds...much slower: "A traveler on the Wilmington, Charlotte and Rutherford Railroad during the war facetiously reported that the speed of the train was so slow and stops so frequent that the train was repeatedly passed by an old Negro laden with farm implements. To each and every invitation from the passengers to get on the train as it overtook him, the Negro politely replied: 'Much obliged, boss, but I hain't got time.' "[1]

Wadley was amazed to learn that at least 25 percent of the state's rolling stock had deteriorated to the point where it was neither reliable nor safe to operate. By the end of 1863, only six out of the 26 "operational" locomotives running in North Carolina were classified as being in "good order." On their best days, when everything worked without a major breakdown, each of the main north-south lines could handle about 200 tons of freight.

Wear and tear on the depots was also taking a toll. The main depot in Raleigh, for instance, was described by one local newspaper as "a hog wallow"; depots in lesser destinations were correspondingly worse.

Despite these troubles, North Carolina was the site of the only major railroad construction project successfully completed by the Confederate government — the linkup of the Greensboro-Danville connection.

The necessity of completing this link had of course been understood early in the war, but finding the resources and the money to do the job was not easy. There was not enough iron for the rails, not enough men for the work, and too much political footballing of the necessary financial schemes. Work progressed in spasms of activity separated by long intervals of inertia. The two ends of the line crept closer to each other with agonizing slowness, and the first trains didn't begin to venture timidly over the rickety rails until May 22, 1864.

One reason it took two years to build a 40-mile line that shouldn't have taken more than eight months to construct, even under wartime conditions, was the opposition of Governor Zebulon Vance. Richmond wanted the link so the Confederacy would have a reserve line in case the enemy overran the Wilmington and Weldon Railroad in the eastern part of North Carolina. Governor Vance, whose strategic thinking was often remarkably subtle — indeed, on occasion, too subtle — viewed the Greensboro-Danville project with a jaundiced eye.

Already, by mid-1862, Richmond had shown an astonishing reluctance to defend the strategically valuable, and vulnerable, eastern third of North Carolina — through which, of course, ran the Wilmington and Weldon Line. Vance figured that if the new Greensboro-Danville line were completed, Richmond would have even less incentive to protect the vital breadbasket region of North Carolina. Vance wanted Richmond's help in regaining the lost eastern counties; he didn't want to retreat even farther from them.

Still, the Greensboro-Danville Line was so obviously a vital strategic asset that it would have been politically unwise — if not slightly treasonable — to oppose it openly. So Vance took an indirect approach. He gave his official blessing to the project, then quietly turned his back on it. He didn't interfere with the construction in any direct way; he simply didn't help it. And the lack of active interest by the governor was almost fatal. No better illustration exists of how pervasively Vance influenced wartime activities within the state. If he got behind a project, things moved, things happened, and results were obtained. If he didn't sponsor a project, things languished, wallowed, and drifted on the bureaucratic tides.

Governor Vance did raise some open objections which were based more on practical concerns than on subtleties of strategy. While the existing, still-functioning, railroads were desperately in need of repair, did it make sense to lay down 40 miles' worth of priceless rail-grade iron to create a redundant line?

But even Vance had to withdraw his objections in the end, for once the rail lines south of Petersburg had been severed, the Greensboro-Danville supply line made it possible for Robert E. Lee's army to stay in the field and continue to offer resistance. In the words of one authority, "It is hardly too much to say that the Piedmont Railroad (as it was called locally) added months to the length of the Civil War."[2]

It was a frail asset indeed. Just a basic line of track, without adequate wood supplies, water stations, sidings, or depots — a raw iron scrawl across the pinewoods and fields of the northern Piedmont. When General Robert Hoke, in December 1864, tried to move his division from Richmond to Wilmington, it took three days for one of his brigades to cover the 40 miles between Danville and Greensboro by train. In disgust, Hoke finally abandoned the rail line altogether and ordered his men to march on foot instead of risking even more delays.

The new line was hampered by administrative incompetence,

political vacillation by Raleigh, and bureaucratic inertia from Richmond as much as by the chronic shortage of iron and labor. For a nation "in extremis," the Confederate government clung with amazing stubbornness to the torpid processes of business as usual. In January 1865, one report cited "immense quantities" of corn and salt which had been found abandoned alongside the tracks, rotting away in the winter rains. Lee's army had no soap, yet there were 800 barrels of the stuff sitting in a depot in Charlotte. Perhaps the railway's most critical failure occurred during the attempt to concentrate forces for the showdown at Bentonville in March 1865. From Danville all the way down to South Carolina, the system simply collapsed, and General Joseph E. Johnston — who had only a forlorn hope at best of stopping General Sherman's invading army — was compelled to enter battle with only part of the forces theoretically available to him.

ZEBULON VANCE — AN OVERVIEW

I am aware that my character is somewhat two-fold — that from cultivating the practical part of life, and especially the rough and unpolished ways which I so early affected as stepping stones to popularity among a rude mountain people, I stand in great danger of being mistaken for a man of no sentiment and heavy nerves. But those who suppose me so will seriously mistake me. I am quite the contrary.

— Zebulon Vance, in a letter to Mrs. Cornelia Spencer, dated February 27, 1869.

One reason why the Civil War — more documented and minutely dissected than any other event in American history — continues to grip the imaginations of succeeding generations is surely the Shakespearean stature of its major characters. The principal figures have been examined under the most intimately revealing microscopes; we know almost everything about Abraham Lincoln and Robert E. Lee, for example, that is of legitimate or even marginal historical interest, including the details of their daily toilette. And yet, unlike many modern personages, the men of the Civil War era seem little diminished when subjected to the glare of such scrutiny.

It is possible that, in certain periods of certain cultures, the times do summon forth the man. The mid-Victorian period was a time when one could write words such as "Honor" with capital letters and not draw a smirk from the reader. There was as much hypocrisy as there is now, of course, but it was a time when politicians had to sell themselves "on the stump" in grueling, face-to-face encounters with voters, not as images prefabricated in conference rooms and then disseminated via the slick machinery of modern media to an increasingly passive and voiceless electorate. Rough and approximate as the process was, it gave the voters a chance to measure their candidates in the flesh, to pepper them with unscreened questions, to gauge their ability to think on their feet, to witness their quickness with verbal parries, and to evaluate the depth and genuineness of their humor.

The 19th-century political system may not have cast up a higher percentage of honest men than our own high-tech apparatus, but it did give the electorate a fair chance to determine whether or not a man was a scoundrel or a nitwit — qualities which can often be masked today by media glitz and a photogenic smile.

Fortunately for North Carolina, the times definitely did summon forth the man. The Civil War period provided a matrix of circumstances in which an ambitious natural-born politician from the mountains could come to embody the hopes, fears, and sometimes conflicting aspirations of an entire state, and thereby attain true greatness as a leader.

Even if the war had never happened, though, this man's career might have been essentially the same, for he was a consummate politician, born to the arena, and his combination of ambition and ability would surely have carried him far no matter what transpired after 1860. As it was, he became a county solicitor at 21, a Congressman at 28, the governor at 32 (for a total of three terms), and four times was elected U.S. Senator. No doubt about it: Zebulon Baird Vance was an important regional politician.

Of course, American history is littered with the careers of regional politicians whose historical importance ended with their last term in office. By contrast, Vance's wartime leadership of North Carolina continues to fascinate historians to this day, for he was unique, and in that uniqueness he embodies the spirit that made the Confederacy such a rich historical experiment — as well as such a hopeless practical failure.

Fate placed Zeb Vance in a difficult and ambiguous position. He interposed himself between his state and the central government in

Richmond and sought, through often contentious argument, to define the proper spheres of authority and responsibility ascribed to each political entity. Vance used to say that his main activities, as governor, were "fighting the Federals and fussing with the Confederacy."[1] Other state governors "fussed with the Confederacy" over one thing or another, but no other state leader had the audacity, the clout, or the rhetorical energy to engage Jefferson Davis and his cabinet in a three-year-long civics debate.

Time and time again, in his postwar writings, speeches, essays, and letters, Zeb Vance claimed that his proudest achievement as governor was to ensure that "the laws were heard amidst the cannons' roar." The vast collected correspondence that flowed between Raleigh and Richmond is for the most part gentlemanly and dignified, except on occasions when Vance got on his soapbox and began first to lecture, then to harangue, President Davis or members of his cabinet. Davis must have grown exceedingly vexed at having to spend so much of his time debating the fine points of civil rights with an inflated backwoods politician from a politically suspect state.

Vance could be stubborn, even obnoxious, and on some few occasions, outrageous — as when he threatened to call out the militia and "wage actual war" on some ill-behaved Confederate cavalrymen who were stealing provisions in the mountain counties. But he was the voice of North Carolina, and the fears, angers, and suspicions he voiced to Richmond were an accurate reflection of what was in the minds and hearts of North Carolina's people. An astute politician himself, Jefferson Davis understood this and respected it — unless, in Davis's opinion, it got in the way of running the war. As for the people of North Carolina, they too understood Vance's perspective, and they loved him for it.

Because of the way it defined itself, the Confederacy was stretched on a rack of paradox. It was fighting the first "total war" in American history, a conflict in which the political, social, and economic dimensions were as important as the military actions, and it was fighting against an enemy which had mobilized vast industrial resources and enormous numbers of men. To fight such a war, a government must be able to coordinate all the resources it can command. Planning, on both the strategic and economic levels, must be centralized and efficient. Historically speaking, nationalism is usually the binding force that permits such centralized authority to function. But that particular glue was absent in the Confederacy. To prosecute the war more efficiently and with greater vigor, Richmond required strength of will and coercive power; and to a certain extent, that required setting aside civil and local authority and rights in the name of the larger common cause.

Unfortunately, this tended to clash with the main pillar of Confederate ideology — the concept of untrammeled states' rights. When wartime necessity conflicted with sectional autonomy, the friction was particularly intense and disruptive. In North Carolina, especially, with its long tradition of Unionism and its recent history of reluctance to secede, states' rights were taken very seriously. By late 1862, when Richmond's tendency to consolidate centralized power had become a clear and pervasive policy, there were many people in North Carolina who feared Confederate oppression as much, if not more, than Yankee invasion. It was a fear that cut across economic and party lines, and it was widespread enough to get Zeb Vance elected twice as governor during the war.

The central theme of all these political conflicts was as old as political philosophy itself: the tension between individual liberties and those whose highest priority is to preserve them, versus the needs of a strong central government, which occasionally has to curb some of those liberties in order to meet its own highest priorities. Today's readers, perusing an account of these disputes, may tend to wonder why Zeb Vance and the many North Carolinians who supported him were so "hypersensitive" about certain issues. After all, compared to the powers wielded by Washington today — even in peacetime — the policies of the Davis administration would seem from a modern perspective to be the minimum measures needed to continue the kind of war the Confederacy was waging. Today, we're accustomed to such concepts as the military draft, heavy income taxes that support a vast defense establishment, and snooping by Federal agencies into the private affairs of citizens. But from the point of view of citizens in the mid-19th century, we are alarmingly insensitive to the state's power to poke into our private affairs, whether they be financial, ideological, or even moral. Viewed against a modern context, therefore, Vance and his fellow libertarians seem to be obsessed, constantly making thunderous orations against some fairly mild centralist measures: a military draft, a tax-in-kind to finance the war and feed the troops, and legal actions to coerce and punish people whose activities, as perceived by the central government, were detrimental to the war effort.

What, in short, was all the fuss about? Was it sheer paranoia that prompted Vance and his contemporaries to constantly strike such seemingly extreme political postures? If so, it was a widespread paranoia indeed. The same fears expressed so passionately by Zeb Vance were also expressed, in thousands of diaries and letters, by the ordinary citizens of every state in the Confederacy — by men and women in all walks of life who lacked a shred of political ambition as possible motivation. To modern readers, the recurrence of these themes and the shrillness of emotion seems almost to argue for a strange kind of dementia, so often did they rant and rage against "tyranny and despotism" in Richmond. Yet, their complaints were directed not against the brutal excesses of a cruel dictator, but rather against policies which today seem relatively mild.

The whole business becomes much clearer, and the issues more informed by genuine passion, when we make an effort to view them as they were seen by North Carolinians in the mid-19th century, rather than from the vantage point of people who have lived through the crises of the mid-20th. If we make that effort, it becomes clear why, in 1864, reasonable men could label as "vile despotism" measures which would seem by 1964 standards to be fairly benign.

If you lived in North Carolina in 1860, about the only time you came in contact with the Federal government was when you conducted business with the local postmaster (or, if you lived on the coast, with the local customs agent). The only other common occasion of contact was if you voluntarily enlisted in one of the armed services, which were, before the war, relatively small, tight, professional bodies. Of course, the policies and actions of the Federal government did influence your life, but they rarely interfered with it.

In modern America — after two world wars, not to mention Korea, Vietnam, and the various other crises that have wracked the United States since the 1950s — we have become accustomed to a degree of governmental interference with our freedoms in the name of national security that is more sustained and pervasive than anything contemplated by the Davis administration. Yet, under normal circumstances, we are scarcely aware of it. But back in 1860, the citizens of North Carolina had been nurtured on the ideals and fears expressed in the Revolution. To them, the Revolution was not a remote and dusty event, but something quite close and vibrant. Many people in the prime of middle age had grown up knowing relatives who had experienced the passions of that era firsthand and who communicated those passions to their descendants. To a great degree, the issues of 1776 still retained their original force and luster in 1860.

Now, here was the Confederate government committing some of the same sins against personal liberty that had pushed the original colonists into rebellion against George IIIrd: burdensome taxation, confiscation (or "impressment") of private property, suspension of the writ of habeas corpus, the seemingly arbitrary arrest of civilians by armed men in uniform. To people raised in the traditions of the great Revolutionary ideals, these things evoked a genuine sense of looming horror, a dread great enough to justify their use of such terms as "tyranny" and "despotism." The North Carolinians of 1860 were, in short, exceedingly touchy about certain kinds of political activity that we tolerate with complacency today.

To those people, the very essence of liberty was found in one's freedom from arbitrary central authority. This was an ideal that had been handed down to them straight from the Revolution. A "free man" was, by definition, a man protected by the law from arbitrary arrest, burdensome taxation, censorship, and interference with his private property. By extension, a white man who was stripped of these things was regarded as condemned to a state of bondage no different from that endured by a slave.

Such an ideal of liberty contains tremendous strength. Yet liberty was perceived as a fragile and vulnerable condition, a blessing from God and the Forefathers that had to be guarded vigilantly and passionately, or else it would be eroded, if not snatched away altogether. As one prominent conservative wrote in a letter to Zeb Vance in the spring of 1863: "We must retain our self possession, and our liberties too, in the progress of this war, or we will look in vain for them at its close."[2]

When the war started in 1861, President Lincoln suspended the writ of habeas corpus, a right so highly valued by the nation's founders that they had written it into Article I of the Constitution ("The privilege of the writ of habeas corpus shall not be suspended, unless when in cases of rebellion or invasion the public safety may require it"). Despite the "rebellion" clause, the U.S. Supreme Court held that Lincoln had exceeded his powers, so Congress voted to suspend the writ for the duration of the war. When Northerners accepted this, many Southerners, and most North Carolinians, viewed them as being but one step removed from slavery itself. Although more than a century's worth of biographies, stories, legends, novels, poems, songs, lectures, and movies have generally portrayed Abraham Lincoln as a mythological saint in a stovepipe hat, it's possible to understand why the North Carolinians of 1861 could perceive him as a "tyrant," and why they passionately believed that "all that is left on this continent of Constitutional Liberty must be looked for in the Confederate States."[3] And in turn, it becomes possible to understand why they bridled so angrily when Jefferson Davis — moved as Lincoln was by the exigencies of national crisis — began to take similar actions in the South.

Believing that any encroachments on liberty would begin with and be enforced by the armed forces of the central government, North Carolinians believed that civil power must always be held superior to military power. To that end, a strong state government had to be maintained as a shield, a buffer between them and the central authority. To fulfill this difficult and complicated job, they could not have chosen a better leader than Zebulon Vance.

The young governor came to embody the hopes of his electorate, and he became their bulwark against both the battlefield enemy and the dangers perceived in the policies of Richmond. Vance's understanding of the people's mood was partly intellectual — when they asked him questions out on the stump, he listened — and partly intuitive; he knew their concerns and their fears because he had not lost touch with them.

They were struck by the energy with which he sought to improve North Carolina's military situation, and by the boldness with which he implemented his swashbuckling program of blockade-running. They put their concerted efforts behind his programs to mobilize the state's resources for the good of her men in the field, and were proud that North Carolina's regiments had medicine and shoes and decent overcoats, while the regiments of other states were not so fortunate.

They cheered Governor Vance when he denounced profiteers and speculators, and also when he sent relief supplies to areas of the state beset by hunger and poverty. They wrote him hundreds of letters and petitions, begging his help or thanking him for an act of intervention already performed. Every person who wrote him received a gracious answer, if not satisfaction.

And they loved him for his warmth, his humanity, his vitality. "Laughter," he used to say, "does for the body what sleep does for the soul," and they adored him for his robust, Will Rogers-like sense of humor.

He looked his part, too. Strong brows, a spacious forehead, a determined mouth, a modest and dapper moustache, and clear blue eyes that flashed when he spoke. At the time he took office, he wore his hair long and brushed straight back, without a part, tucked fastidiously behind the arch of his rather prominent ears. He didn't look like a nonentity: His visage had character and force, without arrogance, yet also without false modesty. His gestures, as a great politician's should be, were forceful and eloquent, yet never studied-looking.

From his earliest political appearances, Vance acquired a reputation for great oratory — not high-flown, but always pitched exactly to the level of his audience without ringing a false or condescending note. He had a vast repertory of jokes, anecdotes, Biblical phrases, dialects, and mimicry, and he knew exactly when to switch from one to the other. Florid rodomontade was not his specialty; his speeches were notable for their pungency rather than their polished elegance. He rarely raised his voice — and rarely had to, to make himself heard — but rather coaxed and caressed and befriended his audience with tones as smooth as aged bourbon. He believed that political oratory was an art, and he was the leading virtuoso of his day.

At a big pro-Union rally in Salisbury in the autumn of 1860, Vance shared the speakers' platform with some of the most famous and venerable of North Carolina's politicians. Not a man spoke that day who was not a superb and experienced orator. But Vance, barely 30 years old, stole the show. By popular demand, he was thrust onto the stage several times, both afternoon and evening, and forced to speak.

After the rally, one old-time political pro, who had spoken after
Vance had finished (with no voice left), found himself being con-
gratulated on his own speech by a friend who had arrived at the rally
somewhat late.

"Yes, yes," growled the veteran orator, "but you should have
heard young Vance. He is the greatest stump speaker that ever was."
The old politician paused for an instant, then repeated himself with
fierce emphasis: "The greatest that ever was!"

VANCE TAKES THE HELM — THE ELECTION OF 1862

Zebulon Baird Vance was descended from distinguished forebears on both sides of the Mason-Dixon Line who had played important roles in the early history of America and North Carolina. His grandfather, David Vance, had come to North Carolina sometime between 1744 and 1752 as part of a wave of Scotch-Irish immigrants. He settled in what is now Burke County and married a Rowan County woman named Priscilla Bank in 1755. David Vance served with honors in the Continental Army, seeing action at Brandywine, Germantown, and Kings Mountain. He also endured the winter at Valley Forge with Washington's army. When the Revolution was over, Captain Vance returned to his family and resettled on Reems Creek, about 12 miles north of Asheville. There he constructed the log cabin home — still standing and nicely preserved — where Zebulon Vance would be born 35 years later.

Captain Vance, like his grandson, believed in public service. He sat in the North Carolina General Assembly and was a member of the commission that finally settled the boundary line between North Carolina and Tennessee. He served four terms in the state legislature. When Buncombe County was formed out of parts of Rutherford and Burke, he was appointed clerk of court for the new district, a position he filled honorably until his death in 1813.

The name Zebulon came into the family when the captain's son, David Vance Jr., married Mira Margaret Baird, the daughter of Zebulon Baird. The Bairds were a very prominent Buncombe County clan, descended from some of the region's earliest settlers.

Zebulon Baird and his brother had opened one of the first mercantile businesses in the Asheville region and had done well. They also speculated in real estate, buying up large tracts of land near the French Broad River — land on which a good portion of the city of Asheville would later be built. Zebulon Baird, too, was active in state politics, representing Buncombe County four times in the lower house and serving two terms in the state senate.

The future governor of North Carolina was named for his grandfather, Zebulon Baird, and was the second child of the union between Mira Baird and David Vance Jr. For those who believe in the predispositions of heredity, a future career in politics might seem to have been inevitable.

Zebulon Baird Vance entered the University of North Carolina at Chapel Hill when he was 21. Until then he had enjoyed only a meager formal education, but he was exceptionally well-read. His deep acquaintance with Shakespeare and the King James Bible was reflected in the rhythmic vigor of his writing and speaking style almost from the beginning. He was well-liked at UNC; even if some of the "I-knew-he-would-be-a-great-man-one-day" stories that later circulated about him were the product of hindsight, his record at the university indicates a gregarious and companionable personality. His repartee was stimulating and his fondness for a well-turned joke became legend.

He took the state law examination and was admitted to the bar in 1852. The qualities which had made him popular at UNC — his charm, his good nature, his quickness, and his facility with words — made him a successful lawyer almost from the day he hung out his shingle in Asheville.

Vance married in 1853 and one year later ran for the lower house of the General Assembly on the Whig ticket. He served for three years with middling distinction, was defeated in a state senatorial campaign in 1856, and returned for a time to private law practice.

His second call to political service came in 1858, when the Congressman from North Carolina's Eighth District, Thomas L. Clingman, resigned in order to become a U.S. Senator. Vance promptly began campaigning to fill the remainder of Clingman's unexpired term. Although his opponent was older and more experienced, Vance won the election by a respectable majority and took his seat in

Congress on December 7, 1858.

His first year in Congress seems to have been fairly routine. He kept his eyes and ears open, learned how the system functioned, and diligently applied himself to committee work. He stood for reelection after filling out Clingman's term and won handily.

His second term in Congress was anything but routine. When he took his seat for the opening of the 36th Congress, the nation was still reeling from the shock of the aborted slave revolt masterminded by John Brown at Harper's Ferry in October 1859. Events began plunging recklessly ahead, acquiring a momentum of their own. By the time Lincoln was inaugurated on March 4, 1861, seven Southern states had seceded. North Carolina, however, was not yet one of them, and there was considerable doubt that she would be. Vance believed in the Union and felt that the men leading the South into rebellion were unrealistic hotheads. Indeed, he spoke passionately in favor of the Union right up until news arrived of Lincoln's call for troops to put down the rebellion. (See Chapter 3.)

A few weeks after his momentous commitment to the Southern cause, Vance marched at the head of a volunteer company (the Rough and Ready Guards) to Raleigh, where his unit was absorbed into the 14th North Carolina Regiment. Several months later, Vance was promoted to his own command, the 26th North Carolina. After taking part in the ill-fated attempt to recapture Roanoke Island, the regiment saw action in the battles of New Bern and Kinston before being ordered up to the main front near Richmond.

Meanwhile, back home, Governor John Ellis died in office and was succeeded by Henry T. Clark, speaker of the state senate. When new elections were scheduled for August 1862, Zebulon Vance's name figured prominently from the start. Vance played a cool hand, remaining at the front with his regiment and permitting the election campaign to be fought, for the main part, by the state's numerous pro-Vance editorial writers. He made his position clear in a letter which appeared in the *Fayetteville Observer* shortly after he was first offered the nomination:

> I took the field at an early day, with the determination to remain there until our independence was achieved. My convictions in this regard remain unchanged...A true man should, however, be willing to serve where the public voice may assign him. If, therefore,

> my fellow citizens believe that I could serve the great cause better
> as governor than I am now doing, and should see it proper to con-
> fer this great responsibility upon me without solicitation on my part,
> I should not feel at liberty to decline it....

He was, of course, being a bit disingenuous here, but he was also right: The South had plenty of fair-to-middling colonels, but a chronic shortage of great political leaders.

As if to confirm his commitment to uniform, Vance's regiment took part in the Battle of Malvern Hill on July 1, 1862. Some of Vance's men tried to persuade him to sit out the engagement. Instead, he ably led them through some of the battle's hottest fighting. (Lee's Army of Northern Virginia on this occasion was 20 percent North Carolinian; 20 percent of his 6,600 casualties at Malvern Hill were North Carolinian as well.)

Vance's absence from the state during the gubernatorial campaign of 1862 was only one example of the unusual circumstances that marked electoral politics during the war. Normal party politics were more or less held in abeyance during the war, on both sides. The mere fact of secession, after all, had effectively done away with national political parties, and, with them, much of the normal state-level political machinery. The main issue of debate before Fort Sumter had been secession, and once that was accomplished, a kind of universal "platform" was established throughout the Confederacy. This was reinforced by a provision in the Confederate Constitution which limited the President to a single six-year term (an innovation which continues to have plenty of advocates to this day). Jefferson Davis (and his successors, had there been any) were therefore placed above party politics. The practical result of these changes was that candidates for state and local elections tended to run as individuals rather than as spokesmen for a party. The usual host of purely partisan squabbles receded into the background, becoming a muted and irrelevant babble.

One exception was North Carolina, where partisan politics continued to display rough, discordant vigor throughout the conflict, thanks in large part to the drum-beating efforts of the state's outspoken and contentious newspapers. Chief among these was the *Raleigh Standard*, edited by William Holden, whose editorials kept drawing party lines even when most people didn't care to have them drawn. Long-time Whigs and staunch old Unionists, crowding under Holden's editorial umbrella, unfurled the banner of something called the Conservative Party. Meanwhile, the original fire-breathing secessionists who had pushed North Carolina into the war in the first place rallied under the name of the Confederate Party.

The Conservatives decided they needed a gubernatorial candidate who was not only available, but who also met a rather particular set of political criteria. Zebulon Vance fit the bill nicely. He was a natural-born politician with no taint of the tub-thumping seces-sionist; yet, when war had come, he had unhesitatingly turned in his credentials as a U.S. Congressman and marched bravely toward the sound of the guns. Last but by no means least, Vance had actually been off fighting the Yankees while the state's old political structure was breaking up and reforming along the fault lines created by war-time pressures.

The gubernatorial election of 1862 would therefore be a crucial watershed for state politics, and most informed citizens were well aware of it; Governor Clark had been recognized as a caretaker from the day he took office after Ellis's death. So August 6 was decreed as the election day for selecting a new governor. (North Carolina troops serving in Virginia were permitted to mark their absentee ballots during the last week in July.)

Vance was certainly widely known and well-thought of, but at first the odds-on favorite was former governor William A. Graham. But Graham, at 58, made it known that he was not a candidate. A greater measure of attention was then directed toward Vance, whose name began to appear in the state's leading newspapers with growing frequency and accompanied by more fulsome praise. In addition to Holden's *Raleigh Standard*, probably the liveliest and most influential paper in the state, Vance also picked up the endorsement of Edward Hale's *Fayetteville Observer*, a journal of smaller circulation but nearly equal prestige.

Friends and advisers wrote to Vance in the field (his regiment was now guarding the rear of Lee's position at Petersburg, licking its wounds from Malvern Hill), anticipating a reluctance to serve that Vance himself may not have actually shared. They argued that he would be more valuable to the cause in the State House in Raleigh than he would be leading bayonet charges in Virginia.

Vance's only opposition came from a candidate picked — almost at random, it seems — by Holden's chief competitor, the *Raleigh Register*. The candidate was William Johnston, a little-known railroad executive who lived in Charlotte but whose main business interests, as Vance's supporters were quick to learn and point out, actually lay in South Carolina. At the beginning of the race, there were probably more newspapers supporting Johnston than Vance, but they were not the most influential papers and their editors made the gross tactical mistake of trying to portray Vance's military record in an unflattering light.

In particular, Vance's conduct on the battlefield at New Bern was singled out, and that proved to be a serious blunder. New Bern had not been an especially good day for Confederate arms — the Federals had crashed through Confederate lines with embarrassing ease and had put several regiments to rout at little cost. However, there were plenty of eyewitnesses who could vouch for the fact that Vance's conduct had not only been valiant, but also that his leadership had been markedly more effective than that of nearly every other Confederate commander on the scene. Accurate accounts of the battle, written by men who had been there, soon appeared in print and thoroughly discredited the hatchet jobs of the opposition.

Johnston did campaign fairly actively, but by all accounts he was a dull orator and a man utterly bereft of personal charisma — the very qualities Vance had in abundance. Actually, though, the electorate saw little of Vance's qualities in the campaign, because he still chose not to take the stump. He remained with his regiment in Virginia, performed his duties, and made not a single speech. Instead, he conducted his campaign by issuing statements to the newspapers, and these were duly reprinted all over the state.

Editor Holden has sometimes been credited as the kingmaker of this election, but that title perhaps assigns more influence than he probably had. Holden was a zealous Vance partisan, to be sure — and that very zeal would in time make him one of Vance's biggest headaches — but he was, when all was said and done, just a newspaper editor and not a political power-broker. Forty-four years old, and solidly in control of the most influential Democratic organ in the state, the outspoken, intelligent, but frequently sharp-tongued Holden was too prone to extremes of enthusiasm ever to capture a large measure of popular support. For all his undoubted brilliance, there was a reckless edge to him that some people interpreted as shiftiness, and others as simple fanaticism.

One interesting and subtle factor working in Vance's favor was the simmering resentment many North Carolinians were starting to feel toward Virginia. The *Richmond Enquirer*, not long before the election, began running a series of snide, critical articles belittling North Carolina's war effort. This was in spite of the fact that the North Carolina regiments, Vance's among them, had already saved Richmond's bacon a time or two. The newspapers in North Carolina, stung by the haughtiness and ingratitude of their neighbors, retaliated in kind.

Wide circulation was therefore given to the story of Zeb Vance's stinging retort to a Virginian's insult following the defeat at New Bern. As Vance was leading his company past some Virginia troops lying by the roadside, one of the Virginians called out derisively, "Oh, you tar heels!" Vance, never at a loss for a quick comeback, snarled, "Yes, and if you fellows had had some tar on your heels you would have stuck yesterday in that fight, instead of running." Given the anti-Virginia sentiments at the time of the election, the resurrection of that little yarn was probably enough to win Vance thousands of votes.

The soldiers who voted were overwhelmingly for Vance: 11,683 to Johnston's 3,691. The civilian vote was similarly lopsided: 54,423 to 20,448. Of the 80 counties that made up North Carolina at that time, only 12 went for Johnston.

Vance's departure from his beloved 26th North Carolina Regiment was an emotional occasion. He made arrangements for the regimental band, the renowned Johnny Rebs from Salem, to perform at his inaugural. Then he left for Raleigh. His first speech, on August 16, 1862, to a Saturday night crowd in front of the Yarborough Hotel, was designed to unify the populace. He called upon them to set aside all political partisanship and get on with the great struggle at hand: "Now the first, great, absorbing purpose should be to beat back our invaders and establish the independence of this glorious Confederation of States...I want all the people of this State to aid me with all their Energies, all their means, and all their confidence...until the Confederate States shall stand proudly among the nations, free and independent."

Before assuming his duties as governor, Vance made a brief visit home to the mountains. The mountain folk admired Vance — he was one of them, to be sure, and his roots went deep — but they were by far the most skeptical North Carolinians where the Confederate cause was concerned. Speaking from the courthouse steps in Asheville, Vance gave it to his audience in plain language. He had heard, he said, that many of them were complaining about the war, when in reality they knew nothing of its horrors. "You should go to our sister state of Virginia! See her bloody fields, blackened homesteads, and fleeing families, to learn what war is."

He had heard, he continued, that many of them had voted for him out of their belief that he would not enforce the hated conscription law. On the contrary, he told them, that law was necessary and proper. "If there is any [man] in North Carolina who ought to be in the army, and who is not there, I will make the state too hot to hold him!"

The inauguration in Raleigh managed to achieve almost a prewar level of gaiety. The Johnny Reb Band paraded and played concerts, featuring the brand-new "Governor Vance's Inauguration March." The crowds were big and enthusiastic, the mood was positive. Vance made a short, punchy speech, calling again for unity and resolve, and successfully positioned himself beyond all the recent partisan bickering. Newspapers from both sides gave the speech good reviews. Every sign indicated that Zebulon Vance had as strong a public mandate as any candidate could hope for. He would need it.

Vance also received some good advice from an old mentor, former governor David L. Swain, who had taught him at the University of North Carolina at Chapel Hill. "Discard party and the selfish tools of party," Swain advised his star pupil, reminding him that his election had truly been "by the people" rather than by the politicians. "Beware of hasty committals to applicants for office...will not one able and trusty friend suffice?"

Swain proffered the names of two men who, in his opinion, would make excellent private secretaries for the new governor, men of "learning, talent, and integrity." Vance selected Richard H. Battle, whom he had known at Chapel Hill, and appointed him to be his confidential secretary. Battle would indeed prove to have talent and integrity, and the governor would indeed need men of that stripe around him during the hard and increasingly bitter days to come.

Mobilizing For Total War — Vance As Economic Commissar

When Zebulon Vance took the oath of office in late 1862, he was 32 years old and in the prime of life. He was a big man — 230 pounds — but carried most of his weight in the upper part of his body, in massive shoulders and a barrel chest, not in his middle. He had a powerful-looking head centered on a muscular neck, a virtuoso's speaking voice, clear, vital eyes, and he possessed in full measure that indefinable spark of personality that commands respect and attention: "charisma," as it's called today, or "magnetism" to the Victorians of his own time.

He inherited an office whose responsibilities were made even more daunting by the fact that neither of his predecessors had served a complete term. Neither Ellis nor Clark had the chance — nor, in Clark's case, had the ability — to fully organize the state and its intractably independent population for the kind of struggle North Carolina was now engaged in.

In addition to Richard Battle, Vance's staff consisted of three other men: an executive clerk named McPheeters and two aides named George Little and David Barnes. The workload these men carried throughout the war was enormous, for Vance's office, and indeed Vance himself, was accessible to a degree that would be regarded as both foolhardy and impossible today. He was available, most of the time, to any North Carolinian who sought an audience. Many of the problems laid before him were, in the great scheme of things, rather trivial, but they were important to the supplicants, and Vance knew that these interviews and exchanges of letters served the useful purpose of keeping him directly in touch with the people.

In contrast to the modern way of doing things, the governor enjoyed a great deal of executive power. Many things could be accomplished with a simple decree and his signature. Petitions for redress of grievances, for commissions to officer rank in the armed forces, for jobs, or for some form of assistance were addressed directly to the governor and usually answered by him. The General Assembly was still the official lawmaking body, of course, but the Assembly was not in session in Raleigh all day, every day, as the governor was. Also, there was a longstanding tradition among the people which held the governor as a symbol of justice. Vance understood this and accepted the role of Solomon as part of his job. He wore those robes rather well, although not all of the decisions he had to make were pleasant. As the war continued to grind on, month after sullen month, more and more of those decisions came down to a choice between equally unpalatable options.

The majority of the governor's time, both during "business hours" and at home in the pretentiously named Governor's Palace at the southern end of Fayetteville Street, was devoted to unending correspondence. Richard Battle helped him immeasurably with the copying and editing, but virtually all of the composition was Vance's, and he spent hours at it every day. A great many of the hundreds of surviving Vance letters are in the governor's own hand. He developed special pen-pal relationships with several correspondents, including Robert E. Lee, with whom he felt free to indulge from time to time in a bit of droll humor.

Vance did not let the burden of his duties completely isolate him from his family, however. He remained devoted to his four sons and to his slight, vivacious, red-haired wife, Hattie. Somehow, he also found time to pursue personal reading. He found special solace in Motley's *The Rise of the Dutch Republic*, which chronicled the struggle of the Dutch people against Philip II. Vance saw in that story a direct analogy to the birth-pangs of the Confederacy. His reading list was also heavily weighted with military history, for he did not see how it was possible to govern a state in wartime without the deepest possible knowledge of the military problems and exigencies to be encountered. As Vance himself would have been the first to admit, his soldiering to this point was strictly that of a gentleman amateur. The campaigns of Alexander, Napoleon, Caesar, and Hannibal all underwent his scrutiny. He grasped the gist of their strategies quickly and he tried to apply them to his own military problems, often to find that those problems were much more elusive and stubborn than they appeared in the history books.

In toting up the assets and liabilities of North Carolina, Vance found that he now governed a state vast in size, diverse in population and attitude, and, though woefully lacking in manufacturing capacity, not without certain resources which could be developed. Although North Carolina was still an agricultural state, it had a fairly dynamic economy and much less severe class distinctions than those found in the Deep South cotton states. True, there was an important and powerful plantation caste, but it was small and located mostly along the coast and the sandhills region that marked the boundary between coast and piedmont. The vast majority of acreage under cultivation in North Carolina belonged to thousands and thousands of small farmers.

In only three counties — Edgecomb, Halifax, and Warren, all near the Virginia border — did the black population outnumber the white. Wake County, site of the state capital, also had a sizeable slave population. But the further west one traveled, the fewer slaves one was likely to encounter. In the mountain counties, the slave population numbered only in the hundreds. North Carolina was the third most populous state in the Confederacy, if you counted only the free inhabitants.

Among the 11 seceding states, North Carolina ranked fourth in agricultural production and third in manufacturing — although the latter rating sounds more impressive than the reality, given the South's near-total dependence on imported manufactured goods, from sewing needles to locomotives.

The sheer diversity of North Carolina must have given Vance pause. The interests and preoccupations of the mountaineers were as different from the concerns of the coastal planters as the topography of Mount Mitchell was from the swamplands around Albemarle

Sound. Yet Vance's task was to forge from such diverse material a unified response to the crisis at hand, to lead his people to pursue the war with one mind and heart. It was, of course, an impossible assignment — but it is a measure of Vance's commanding personality and sheer industry that North Carolina stayed in the war and contributed as much as she did to the cause.

Given the factors working against him, Vance accomplished a lot. He mobilized the state's fledgling industrial base and squeezed out a surprisingly high level of production. He did even better with agriculture, actually achieving in some counties a new level of vigor and efficiency during the war. And most of all, he kept North Carolina's regiments in the field, at or close to full strength, clothed and armed by the state. On the whole, they were better clad, shod, and equipped than most of the regiments maintained by the Richmond administration.

Some historians have judged Vance's policies too locally directed; some have even accused him of hoarding supplies and arms in the state which should have been passed up to the front in Virginia. It is true that North Carolina's warehouses were more fully stocked in April 1865 than any other state's, often with an excess of certain types of supplies. But some of that surplus can be explained by the fact that the ailing Confederate supply system, especially the railroads, simply could no longer get the stuff up to the battlefront when it was needed. Vance did begin to hoard supplies in the late winter of 1864, but only because both common sense and military logic told him that several enemy armies were converging on North Carolina and the state was likely to become the last major theater of war.

Generally, Vance shared his supplies generously with the Confederacy. To cite one example, he shipped 5,000 uniforms to Longstreet's needy corps, in spite of the fact that not a single North Carolina unit fell under Longstreet's command at that time. And it should not be forgotten that during the last year of the war as much as 60 percent of Lee's food and medicine came from North Carolina, even when many North Carolina counties were on the brink of starvation.

By the time Vance had restructured the state's economy in such important areas as wool, cotton, leather goods, and some kinds of ironwork, North Carolina was able not only to fill its own requirements, but also to actually sell substantial amounts of surplus goods to other Confederate states.

In particular, Vance encouraged the state's infant textile industry, building successfully on Governor Ellis's early policies. At the start of the war, the state had clothed its own soldiers and was reimbursed by Richmond at the rate of $50 per year per soldier. Raleigh had signed contracts with the state's factories, creating, in effect, a state-run monopoly. This system was ended in October 1862 when Richmond assumed responsibility for clothing all Confederate units. The idea was to force a more equitable distribution of the South's total resources.

The Confederate Quartermaster Department waited in vain for Vance to relinquish control over North Carolina's seven woolen mills and 39 cotton mills. Vance instead negotiated a renewed agreement with Richmond that permitted his administration to continue clothing North Carolina troops while receiving full reimbursement from the Confederate treasury.

Vance spent a good deal of time and energy in the winter of 1862-63 negotiating new contracts with the state's textile plants. The cotton mills were agreeable, but the woolen manufacturers held out for higher profits. Vance addressed the state legislature on the problem (November 17, 1862): "The woolen factories seem more incorrigible. Some of them when asked to furnish their goods at 75 percent profit, decline entirely, and others agree to do so by fixing enormous profits on the cost of raw materials and then adding the 75 percent on the finished article, making their profits even greater than before. I recommend them to your tender mercies, gentlemen...."

But too many legislators owed favors to the textile magnates, or were themselves investors, so no draconian measures were ever enacted against the woolen mills. When a shortage of winter clothing loomed at the front, Vance appealed directly to the populace. Thousands of blankets, rugs, and overcoats were donated to the cause from all parts of the state.

To overcome the shortfall in textile production, Vance adopted a twofold strategy. First, he put North Carolina into the blockade-running business in order to obtain from Europe the goods that could not be manufactured at home. Second, he initiated a general nurturing of the state's textile industry. Vance established new plants, encouraged cottage-industry output by women and children, permitted his purchasing agents to offer attractive prices for suitable goods, and strove mightily — and mainly through the force of public proclamation and patriotic appeal — to keep the profit-hungry mills from gorging themselves beyond reason. In time, places which had never before been active in textile production were actually doing good business. Fayetteville, for example, became one of the South's leading centers of cotton-goods production. By the end of 1864, when the loss of skilled labor began to seriously hamper manufacturing, North Carolina had ceased importing most cotton fabrics from other Confederate states and had even begun limited exports.

To do all this, however, Vance had to fight a major paper-battle with the Confederate bureaucracy. His main enemy was Abraham C. Meyers, a South Carolinian whom Jefferson Davis had appointed head of the Quartermaster Department. Their first clash concerned leather goods. With so many Confederate soldiers going barefoot, Vance argued, why not explore the possibility of making harnesses out of heavy-gauge cotton cloth and diverting all the tanneries' output to the manufacture of shoes?

The military priorities seem obvious, and Vance's suggestion seems practical, but, of course, practicality was never Richmond's strong suit. It was impossible to streamline the leather requirements, Meyers told Davis and Davis wrote to Vance, because shoes fell under the Quartermaster Department and harnesses fell under the Ordnance Bureau, and never the policies of the twain would meet. This ludicrous and wasteful distinction was something that Davis, had he been more decisively inclined, could have corrected with one stroke of his pen.

Though Vance's efforts were often frustrated by these maddening bureaucratic policies, his centralized economic planning brought about dramatic improvements. By mid-1862, North Carolina's regiments had worn out their first set of clothes and were just as shabby and disreputable-looking as the rest of the Confederate army. One year later, thanks to Vance's stimulation of the textile industry and his aggressive blockade running, North Carolina fielded the best-dressed units in the Confederacy.

Wartime profiteering and speculation were, of course, rampant, and Vance couldn't spare the manpower to prevent such excesses by means of on-the-spot inspections. He did make things as uncomfortable as possible for the speculators, though, by issuing public bulletins that exposed some of their scams and painted them in traitorous colors. Vance's most important press ally, William Holden of the *Raleigh Standard*, helped by regularly publishing a "Roll of Honor" in which civilians were singled out by name for acts of generosity and restraint on the home front. The degree of prestige associated with having one's name in this column cannot be accurately determined a century later, but it's unlikely that Holden would have continued the feature if the response was not favorable. Also, the Roll of Honor demonstrates Vance's success in making people aware that there even *was* such a thing as a home front, and that its stability was absolutely essential to victory.

Vance was deeply touched by letters such as this one, from a Methodist minister in McDowell County, on the eastern slopes of the Blue Ridge Mountains: "Here in Marion, beef is being sold to poor wives of soldiers who get $11 per month in the field, at the enormous price of 11 and 12 cents a pound! Leather at $4 per pound! Bacon at 40 and 50 cents per pound…If this thing is not put down, our Country is ruined forever. Many children of the soldiers in the Camps are nearly barefoot and naked, without the possibility of getting clothes or shoes…if your position as Governor of North Carolina gives you the power to do so, in the name of God, of suffering humanity, of the cries of widows and orphans, *do* something to put down the speculation and extortion in this part of the state…."

In a proclamation designed to counter such exploitation, Vance admonished the citizens to shun the speculators: "For they are the vilest and most cowardly of your country's enemies."

One of Vance's most drastic "total war" measures was a law forbidding the planting of any new cotton and tobacco crops for the duration of the conflict. Food was needed; cotton was piling up and no recipe ever invented could make it palatable. This law hit the plantation class where they were most sensitive and caused deep resentment, but it was an effective method of boosting agricultural production. The crops thus produced would mean more to the survival of Lee's army than any amount of cotton.

Vance also addressed himself, in November 1862, to the matter of wartime prohibition, pushing through the legislature a law prohibiting the distillation of liquor anywhere in the state. This law almost certainly enjoyed keener observance in the Piedmont and coastal counties than in the mountains. As a mountain man himself, Vance understood the hardship he was imposing, but he felt it was a proper policy, one that would save tons of grain every year. He did relent a year or so later under pressure from Richmond, permitting the establishment of a government-run distillery near Salisbury for the purpose of producing medicinal whiskey — the poor man's chloroform. But for a while, at the start of his administration, North Carolina was legally dry.

Hundreds of private citizens petitioned the governor for exemptions from the distillery law, often citing dire personal and family needs. Some of the letters make droll reading — one mountaineer claimed that it was a bad season for snakes in his neck of the woods and he really needed to keep a small supply on hand in case of bites. Another gentleman appealed to Vance on a man-to-man basis: If he could distill but ten gallons, he would send the governor a quart. Vance replied with tongue in cheek that he could not think of violating his oath of office for less than a gallon.

Saltpeter, essential to the making of gunpowder, was now a highly marketable commodity. Vance opened some long-idle mines and had them worked intensively. He sponsored collection drives for scrap metal, especially church bells, to melt down for cannon, and lead window weights to melt down for musket balls. Once the prohibition law went into effect, he even had the copper tubing from the state's distillery plants melted down and turned into percussion caps.

At the same time, Vance exempted more men from conscription than any other Confederate governor. His liberality in this matter irked Richmond, but Vance was determined to preserve the state's economy, figuring that a sound economic base in North Carolina was worth more to the cause than a few hundred more pieces of cannon fodder. In view of North Carolina's already enormous contribution of manpower to the Confederate army, Richmond generally let him get away with it.

Vance encouraged dozens of small gunsmithing and manufacturing plants in all parts of the state, opened iron mines in Avery County, and established iron-mongering plants in Lincoln, Gaston, and Cleveland counties. When added together, these facilities comprised the second-largest complex of iron works in the Confederacy.

If some historians maintain that Vance's policies were too local-ized, too state-oriented, and too downright selfish with regard to the Confederate cause as a whole, there are other historians who con-tend that without Vance's programs and the stability they brought to North Carolina — which was, after all, the breadbasket and back-stop of the Army of Northern Virginia — the Confederate cause would have collapsed much sooner than it did.

Moreover, this vast and voluntary effort took place while Vance, more than any other Confederate governor, was steadfastly uphold-ing every peacetime standard of individual liberty, maintaining civilian control over the military, and protecting civil rights from the usurpations common in so many other places. Rather than coerce his people, Vance took them into his confidence. They remained in the war a lot longer than they would have without him.

Vance understood, better than most Confederate leaders, the essential economic dimensions of the conflict. While he had the keenest appreciation for personal bravery, he knew that gallantry alone would not prevail against the North's enormous advantages of manpower and industrial might. Only by mobilizing all existing resources, and by developing new ones as expeditiously as possible, could the South hope to offset those advantages, no matter no vali-antly her men fought and died.

If North Carolina did not, then, produce a battlefield general comparable in fame to Lee, Jackson, or Forrest, it did at least produce a civilian wartime leader of similar stripe.

Vance himself came out of the conflict filled with new admiration for the people of his state. In one postwar essay he argued for a new kind of war history, one which would detail the "feelings, hopes, patriotism and...despair" of the common people. "The broad, catholic, cosmopolitan history of this most remarkable struggle has yet to be written," he said, "wherein the story of the people shall be told; wherein, when it is said how a great general won a victory, it will also be mentioned what troops and where from fought it for him; how the artisan in his shop, the plowman in the field, the little girls in their factories, the mothers at the old hand looms, the herds-men on the mountain side, the miner in the earth's bowels, the drivers and brakesmen on the railroad engines, how *all these* felt, and strove, and suffered equally with the soldier, and yet without his stimulus of personal glory."

Vance As Confederate Warlord

One of the most effective military programs undertaken by Governor Vance was the total overhaul of North Carolina's Medical Department. To run that operation, Vance chose one of the most colorful individuals to be found anywhere on the home front, Doctor Edward Warren.

Warren was born in Tyrell County, on the southern shores of Albemarle Sound, raised in New Bern, and educated at the Jefferson Medical College of Philadelphia. He was forced by the outbreak of war to abandon an important chair at the University of Maryland. Although he scarcely knew Vance at the time the governor appointed him surgeon general of North Carolina, he soon became a devoted friend and remained so for the duration of his long and eventful career — which, after the war, included a stint as the Khedive of Egypt's personal physician.

The two men were bonded, and the governor's interest in the Medical Department stimulated, by events that took place soon after Vance's inauguration. Only nine days after the new governor took office, the single bloodiest day in American military history unfolded in Sharpsburg, Maryland, along the banks of Antietam Creek. Many North Carolina troops fought in the battle, including Vance's old company, the Rough and Readies (now part of the 14th North Carolina Regiment). The two opposing armies — not as adept at the quick preparation of field entrenchments as they would soon become — clashed more or less in the open, and they slaughtered each other with a ghastly proficiency that would never be surpassed in all the remaining years of the war.

As soon as reports came back of the scope of the bloodletting, and of the disproportionate suffering of North Carolina troops (who had arguably saved Lee's army at one and possibly two critical moments in the battle), Vance summoned Surgeon General Warren, collected a large quantity of medical supplies, and went to Virginia to meet his troops when they returned.

Vance was staggered by what he saw in the hospitals. Himself a veteran of Malvern Hill — no slouch of a battle, either, when it came to butchery — he was not surprised by the gruesomeness and agony he beheld on every hand, but he was distressed by the raggedness of the North Carolina troops, by their destitute appearance, and by the way the sheer numbers of casualties overwhelmed existing resources and multiplied the suffering of the wounded. Governor Vance resolved then and there to do everything in his power to find better ways for the state to take care of her sons in the field.

While Vance did what he could in the Richmond hospitals, Doctor Warren and his team of assistants went ahead to the forward casualty collection point at Staunton, Virginia, where a thousand wounded men were arriving by train every day. The place was a reeking, screaming abattoir. Warren and his aides worked themselves to exhaustion but could scarcely make a dent in the ocean of suffering that rose all around them.

Warren penned an emotional report to Vance, written with the blood still fresh under his fingernails, telling him of "the poor creatures in the hospitals...dirty, naked, without shoes, hats or socks, wounded in every possible manner, they present a picture of wretchedness and misery which no tongue or pen can describe...the condition of these poor unfortunates is enough to wring tears from hearts of stone, and to stamp the authorities of the Confederacy with a brand of unutterable disgrace, Thank God I have been able to do something at least for the poor fellows from North Carolina."

Warren worked until he dropped, visiting every wounded North Carolina boy he could find. When he could do nothing for their injuries, he at least spoke kindly to them, promised them that their suffering was being reported to the governor, and that he would do all he could back in Raleigh to see that conditions improved in the future. Before leaving the scene, Warren bought clothes for some of the most destitute men with his own money.

Vance prevailed upon the state legislature to appropriate $100,000 (later boosted to $300,000) for the maintenance of the surgeon general's office. Using this fund, Warren set up hospitals at logical and convenient places throughout the state. He also created a Soldiers' Home in Richmond, where North Carolina men in transit to or from Lee's army could find food, clothing, shelter, someone to write letters for them, and perhaps a kind word. It was, in effect, a prototype USO facility. Thousands of men availed themselves of these services, and the Soldier's Home became a model for subsequent homes established by other state governments.

Warren also used Medical Department funds to obtain large shipments of medicine and surgical supplies from Europe, the best money could buy, and oversaw their distribution to North Carolina units. He also found time to organize the collection and distribution of clothing and bedding donated by civilians. Regular monthly shipments of blankets and underwear were sent to the front, where they were mightily appreciated by North Carolina troops and mightily envied by others.

A surgeons' corps was organized, and several excellent physicians were kept as a kind of medical "strategic reserve," dispatched first to one battlefield and then to another, wherever the need was greatest.

One of Doctor Warren's severest tests came early in his tenure when smallpox broke out in the Piedmont region of the state. Warren quickly obtained a large quantity of good serum, appointed vaccinators for each county, oversaw the inoculation of 70,000 people, and stamped out the plague before it could really take hold.

Warren's devotion to Zebulon Vance grew with each passing month. In a vivid collection of memoirs, written in the twilight years of his career when he was a lionized fixture in Parisian high society, Warren described the governor in glowing terms: "In my judgement no nobler man than Zebulon Baird Vance was ever created — with an inherent kindness of heart which tempers and softens his entire nature; a respect for justice and right which asserts itself under all possible circumstances; a sense of the ridiculous from which wells out a stream of humor at once copious, sparkling, and exhaustless...I have analyzed his heart from core to covering, and I know that in its every cell and fiber it is of purest gold, without the trace of alloy or a trace of counterfeit."

Military Troubles Along The Coast

After Governor Vance settled into office and recovered from the emotional strain of his post-Antietam tour of the hospital wards, he faced a whole new set of military problems that were far more intractable, and perilous, than the shortcomings of the Medical Department. To a large extent, he had mended the medical service's ailments; the strategic situation he inherited was not so amenable to action.

Even though General Ambrose Burnside had withdrawn his Union corps from coastal North Carolina in July 1862 to join General George McClellan's ill-fated drive on Richmond, there were still some 25,000 Union troops poised just over the state line in Suffolk, Virginia; 12,000 Union troops in garrison at New Bern; and smaller Federal enclaves at Washington, Plymouth, and Elizabeth City. The only North Carolina port remaining in Confederate hands was Wilmington.

After losing New Bern in March 1862, Confederate forces in the eastern part of the state had fallen back to Kinston, seeking to protect the vital Wilmington and Weldon Railroad. The Confederate commander on the coast, Major General Samuel G. French, had enough troops to achieve a strategic stalemate, but never enough to either eject the Federal garrisons or to protect the fertile eastern counties from raids and foraging parties. The inhabitants of the eastern counties felt vulnerable, and they were. They also felt, after the string of missed opportunities and humiliating reverses that had hobbled the fighting along the coast in the war's first year, that they were being left unprotected by the Confederate government.

Governor Vance could not understand — even as many modern historians have difficulty understanding — why the Confederacy did not simply wait for a lull in the Virginia fighting, move a few divisions of crack troops down to North Carolina by rail, and then smite the isolated Federal garrisons hard enough to eject them for good. The coast could then be defended, rather economically, by a combination of shallow-draft gunboats and strong fortifications — designed to correct the weaknesses already revealed by the fall of the

Outer Banks defenses. With the North Carolina coast secure, the Union blockade's death grip would be loosened, more supplies would flow in from overseas, and the entire Confederate strategic posture would improve.

But as matters stood when Vance took office — as delegation after delegation from the vulnerable eastern counties told him in person and by petition — the residents of this fertile and productive region were utterly dependent on the inertia and lethargy of the Confederate government. They felt the Confederacy had left them abandoned, ignored, and doomed to their fate. Loyalty to Richmond, never exactly passionate in the coastal counties to begin with, began to waver badly.

Governor Vance wrote increasingly angry and remonstrative letters to Richmond, begging for either reinforcements or for permission to raise a state army that could be deployed without fear of sudden diversion to meet some crisis in Virginia. President Davis addressed Vance's concerns in a letter written in mid-October, 1862: "I have not been unmindful of the condition of the Eastern portion of your state," he began, before continuing in a more condescending vein, "and can make allowance for the anxiety of those who reside there...." He promised that a force of cavalry would be raised — from what quarter, he did not say — to protect the interior of North Carolina from Federal raids. He went on to stroke Vance's feelings by acknowledging North Carolina's great contribution to the Confederate cause and closed by assuring him of Richmond's continued concern for the welfare of the Old North State.

A case can be made for Vance as the boy who cried wolf, sending Richmond dire warnings every time he got word of a Federal cavalry patrol foraging beyond the picket lines at New Bern. It is certainly true that Vance raised the alarm on some occasions when the overall strategic situation clearly didn't permit Davis to detach significant numbers of troops from the Virginia front. Also, Davis had to deal with many desperate pleas from all over the South, and North Carolina's pro-Union history and growing problems of desertion and dissent did not inspire confidence in Richmond. Still, it remains a mystery why the Confederacy was so blind to the strategic opportunities offered by the situation on the North Carolina coast.

When General Lee finally did release some good troops to North

Carolina under an aggressive commander (General Robert Hoke, in 1864), the Confederates tore up the bothersome pea-patch with a brilliant offensive against Washington and an effective threat against New Bern — before his troops were, with sad predictability, ordered back to Virginia. If similar action had been taken earlier in the war, certainly the Confederacy could have gained local superiority over the coastal garrisons. The advantages, both psychological and tangible, of clearing the Yankees from the North Carolina coast were surely greater than anything that was gained from invading Pennsylvania.

Perhaps the answer lies in the vague but pervasive antipathy Jefferson Davis seems to have felt toward Governor Vance, almost from their first contact. The reasons for this remain elusive, as do so many of Davis's motivations. Possibly it was the instinctive distaste of the aristocrat for the mountaineer. Perhaps it was a lingering suspicion on Davis's part that Vance was secretly halfhearted about the Confederate cause — even though Vance's actions, from the first day he took office, should have put to rest that idea. Perhaps it was even that old, sly, persistent animosity between the Virginian and the Tar Heel. Whatever the case, relations between the two men, though nearly always gentlemanly on paper, were never really warm. And they were destined to grow increasingly antagonistic as the war dragged on and North Carolina's internal problems grew more serious.

A Rival Governor

If the Confederacy was dim when it came to the strategic possibilities of the Carolina coast, the Union was not. Not long after New Bern fell into Union hands, President Lincoln conceived of a political ploy to begin a partial "reconstruction" in the occupied parts of North Carolina. He chose a political puppet named Edward Stanly and attempted to install him as a loyalist governor.

Stanly had served in Congress and had held the post of state attorney general before choosing to migrate to California, where he became one of the leading Republican politicians in that new territory. A capable man of no small intelligence, Stanly was also a frustrated man. He had lost, first, his North Carolina Congressional seat, and then a hotly contested gubernatorial bid in California in 1857. Stanly seems to have convinced himself that Lincoln's perception of North Carolina as a state which remained Unionist at heart was true. After Lincoln appointed him governor, Stanly took his oath of office in New Bern — backed up by a Yankee fleet and a fancy proclamation from Washington. Technically speaking, North Carolina then had two governors.

In October 1862, Governor Stanly had the temerity to write Governor Vance, requesting an interview. In his letter, Stanly said he had been motivated to take the Federal post only out of "strong affection...for the people of my native state," and suggested that the war was little more than a quarrel between family members. His new position, he averred, would allow him to "confer blessings" on the people of the state, especially if those in high office would lend him their support. It was an astonishingly naive letter; not only did Stanly leave undescribed the nature of the "blessings" he might confer, or the strings he might attach to them, he also rather pointedly omitted to address Vance as "governor" anywhere in the document. Instead, he headed his letter merely "Your Excellency."

Vance had many important things on his mind at this time. He must have perceived Stanly's letter as nothing more than the presumptuous squeaks of a Quisling. His reply bristled with indignation: "Your proposition is based on the supposition that there is a baseness in North Carolina sufficient to induce her people to abandon their confederates and leave them to suffer alone all the horrors of this unnatural war, for the sake of securing terms for themselves, a mistake which I could scarcely have supposed anyone so well acquainted with the character of her people as yourself could have committed."

Stanly took umbrage and wrote a petulant reply accusing Vance of "unbecoming remarks." Vance, who generally preferred sharp irony to outright anger in his correspondence, replied with a blast of molten rhetoric: Stanly should know that his name was daily cursed throughout the state. "How could you expect it to be otherwise?" Vance asked, "coming to the people who have often honored you, in the wake of destroying armies; assuming to be governor of a State by the Suffrages of abolition bayonets red with the blood of your kindred and friends...."

It was possible, Vance conceded, that Stanly might one day sit in the Governor's Palace, but "you can only do so over the dead bodies of the men who once respected you, through the smoking ashes of the homes which once greeted you with hospitable welcome, and through fields desolated, which once gladdened your eye...with the glorious harvest of peace."

As things happened, Stanly's term in office proved to be brief. Undoubtedly he was stung to the quick by Vance's outrage. He must have seen, rather soon, that his writ as governor didn't extend beyond the farthest line of Federal rifles. His very presence on North Carolina soil was an irritant, not a balm. And when the Emancipation Proclamation was issued on New Year's Day, 1863, it undercut whatever hope Stanly may still have harbored about gaining any real popularity.

In his heart, Stanly had never really been an abolitionist. He felt that the Proclamation changed the whole purpose of the war — for him, at least. He was, in a pathetic kind of way, not without principles. He resigned two weeks after the Proclamation was issued and returned to California, where he ended his career in an obscurity that was surely kinder to him than his brief flirtation with historical fame.

Managing The War

One bright spot for Governor Vance in 1862 was the unusually good harvest that year. The eastern section of the state alone produced some 1.5 million barrels of corn, together with sizeable amounts of pork, beef, and sweet potatoes. When Richmond did nothing to help gather or protect this bounty — despite the fact that a large portion of it would soon be feeding Robert E. Lee's army — Vance sent forth purchasing agents to buy up the goods available in the richest counties and to get the supplies moved inland, into the Piedmont, away from possible Federal raids.

The 1862 harvest also brought Vance into contact with a problem that would plague his administration throughout the war: the shortage of salt. In an age when there was virtually no refrigeration, only meat which had been salted stood any chance of surviving long enough to reach the armies that hungered for it.

Salt shortages had, in fact, been a problem during the Revolutionary War, and it was that historical reminder which prompted the state to create the office of salt commissioner. The man in charge was John Milton Worth, and he suffered numerous setbacks before getting his system into production — most notably the loss of a saltworks in Morehead City which had turned out 100 bushels of the precious stuff per day. The lucrative private salt trade was centered in Wilmington, and it was there that Worth established his most extensive saltworks. By the time Vance got his first report from Worth, in October 1862, the combined public and private saltworks in Wilmington were producing about 2,000 bushels per day.

An outbreak of yellow fever in Wilmington almost ruined the program, killing a hundred people a week (including Worth's 17-year-old son). Vance continued to demand production quotas from Wilmington, even while the disease was tearing through the city; salt was too precious for anything to interrupt its flow. Vance even visited the city himself, in early December 1862, and implored the private salt company owners to stabilize their prices in return for additional labor, transportation, and guaranteed purchases from the state treasury. In January 1863, when the commander of the Wilmington defenses, General Whiting, impressed the salt crews to dig earthworks, Vance intervened and demanded that Whiting release the saltworkers and recruit his laborers from other counties.

Despite stoppages caused by conscription, disease, military necessity, and periodic Federal raids and bombardments, the saltworks at Wilmington remained in production until the city itself fell in 1865. The works were self-supporting and even paid a profit to their investors. Vance's constant personal attention to this strategic matter was yet another example of his understanding of the economic dimensions of the war and was probably, along with Worth's diligence, the single most important factor in the success of the salt program.

As the war dragged on, however, Governor Vance sometimes became afflicted with tunnel vision. Occasionally he saw things entirely from the North Carolina point of view and adopted policies which ran counter to the interests of the Confederacy. His refusal to support the completion of the Greensboro-Danville Railroad link is the best example of this shortcoming. Had Vance cooperated with the project, the line would have been opened for business in the early spring of 1863 rather than the late spring of 1864. There is no doubt that earlier completion would have strengthened the overall Confederate posture.

Until the defeat at Gettysburg, after which the age limit for conscription was raised to 45, Vance even tried to raise a separate North Carolina army to defend the coast. As governor, Vance would have been de facto commander-in-chief of the army. Originally planned to be ten regiments strong, the projected force was later pared down to 7,000 men. But even 7,000 proved too large a number to raise; by mid-1863, there simply weren't that many eligible men left in the state, and the cost of supporting such a private army was more than the depleted state treasury could handle.

Vance toyed with the idea of mobilizing the militia, of calling for a genuine levee en masse, but he never actually did. He always drew back at the last minute, fearing that the strain on the state's economy, of supporting both conscription and total mobilization, would do more damage than the normally quiescent Yankees the mobilized troops were intended to defend against. Instead, he replaced the old militia system with the Home Guards, comprised of "all white male persons who are exempt by law from service in the Confederate Army, between the ages of eighteen and fifty years." The indifferent (when not actually pathetic) results that were obtained when the Home Guards actually went into battle late in the war would seem to indicate that the idea of a levee en masse was more dramatic as a gesture than it was practical as a military option.

Still, it would be wrong to insist, as some historians have, that Governor Vance always acted out of simple parochial motives. The strategic value of North Carolina was undervalued by Richmond, and the state's defenses were badly served by the Confederacy. Both the risks and the opportunities available on the coastal front were poorly understood. If Zebulon Vance tended to act in North Carolina's interests first and foremost, then it must be said that by doing so he often acted in the best interests of the Confederacy as well.

Conscription, Desertion, And Rampaging Cavalrymen

To be sure, the feudin' and fussin' between Raleigh and Richmond had started before Zebulon Vance became governor, but it escalated seriously in the year following his election. It centered around a few persistently troublesome topics: conscription, desertion, taxation, Richmond's prejudicial treatment of North Carolina, the conflict between civil rights and centralized authority, and the redress of grievances that often stemmed from such conflict.

The most persistent and bothersome problem derived from the Confederate government's policy of drafting men into the ranks (conscription) — a procedure which seems familiar and merely irritating to modern citizens, but which seemed shockingly drastic and severe to many North Carolinians in 1862, when the policy was first promulgated.

At the beginning of the War Between the States, recruitment was strictly voluntary, and for a while, volunteers were enough; nobody expected the war to be as long, as bloody, and as hungry for flesh as it turned out to be. When the supply of hot-blooded short-term volunteers began to dry up, longer-term enlistments were encouraged by means of a $50 bounty (an inducement left over from the days of the Revolution).

Even this second wave of voluntary enlistments was not enough to feed the cannon. The Conscription Act of April 16, 1862 allowed the Confederacy to draft all white males between the ages of 16 and 35, and it also automatically extended all volunteer terms of service to three years, beginning with the date of enlistment on each man's record. Following the slaughter at Sharpsburg, the age limit for conscripts was raised to 45, but President Davis didn't actually call up the older men until after Lee's defeat at Gettysburg in July 1863. Still later, after Braxton Bragg (Jefferson Davis's favorite general, a man who did far more damage to the Confederate Army than he ever managed to inflict on the Federals) suffered his humiliating defeat at Chattanooga, the age limit was readjusted again to include all white males under 50. The harshness of this last draft was somewhat ameliorated by the provision that the youngest and oldest class of men could only serve in the Junior and Senior Reserves.

Nobody, in any state, really liked the idea of conscription. It was against American tradition and it interfered with too many people's lives — including people of wealth and position who found it inconvenient to serve. For a time, therefore, the odious practice of "substitution" was permitted. If you had the money, you could simply hire someone else to go fight for you. Throughout the Confederacy, a total of 60,000 men were hired out as surrogate soldiers for a going rate of $5,000 each. Governor Vance led the states' outcry against this aspect of conscription. Indeed, it gave rise to his famous description of the conflict as "a rich man's war and a poor man's fight."

New War Department regulations were issued in 1863, after the abuses of the system had become so gross that even the Richmond bureaucrats could no longer ignore them. The new regulations made all those who had hired substitutes eligible for conscription. This was fine, as far as it went, but it did nothing about existing substitution contracts, and the resulting lawsuits clogged up the court systems in every state in the Confederacy.

Conscription hit North Carolina especially hard. Most of the state's farms were owned and worked by men who were prime candidates for the draft. Conscription effectively stripped the state of most of these men, leaving the farms under the care of women, children, and grandfathers. Editor William Holden of the *Raleigh Standard* attacked the laws vigorously in his newspaper: "Such a power was never before claimed or exercised in this country. If claimed and exercised now, it will be done in violation of the spirit of the Constitution, and in derogation of the rights of the States."

Vance didn't like conscription any more than Holden, but as he had stated from the start of his administration, he saw its necessity and promised to make the system as fair and as tolerable as humanly possible. He made a special effort to see that the necessary duties of enforcing conscription were performed by North Carolinians who were sympathetic to the local population, not by outside agents thrust upon the state by Richmond. Outside conscription agents were regarded by both Vance and the general populace as a brutal plague. In one letter to Jefferson Davis, Vance went so far as to describe the Confederate agents as "men unprincipled, dishonest, and filled to overflowing with all the petty meanness of small minds dressed in a little brief authority."

Vance's more humane methods of enforcement worked, as the numbers tell. North Carolina supplied one-fourth of the total number of conscripts who served in the Confederate Army — about 21,000 men. Yet Richmond continued to elbow its way into state affairs, and the Davis administration continued to treat Vance, and North Carolina, with distrust and prejudice. It is likely that Vance's policy of compassionate enforcement would have yielded even larger numbers of troops, and without the social and legal upheavals that sometimes took place, if Richmond had not kept throwing obstacles in the governor's path.

One of Richmond's most frequent complaints, and one of its most common excuses for sending its own agents to scour the North Carolina countryside, was that Vance exempted an inordinate number of men from the draft. That was true. But then, Vance alone among Confederate governors was trying to expand his state's industrial and agricultural production, feed Robert E. Lee's army with its harvests, and supply all of its own regiments (one-sixth of the entire Confederate Army) with food, clothing, arms, and medical supplies. To keep this supporting infrastructure operating, not to mention the system of state railroads on which so much of the war effort depended, Vance needed an ample supply of trained technicians and administrators, and he was determined to keep them from being drawn into the great cannon-fodder apparatus being run by Richmond.

Just before his inauguration as governor, Vance had spoken in Asheville about making the state "too hot to hold" shirkers, and he was deadly serious. He tried to organize the process of conscription by ordering the state's militia officers to round up all the reluctant conscripts in their home districts, and then to see to it that they were processed at the central training base near Raleigh (commanded by Colonel Peter Mallett). Vance soon learned that Confederate agents were already widely abroad in the state, vigorously snatching men into the ranks. Vance protested to Richmond: No one who was not a North Carolina citizen should be given authority to induct North Carolinians. The government's heavy-handed tactics were making it hard for him to fill his quotas.

Another problem was that no records of forced enlistments were being forwarded by Confederate agents to Raleigh. As a result, the state's own officers came in and combed areas that had already been hit hard by out-of-state enforcement officers. This only reinforced the people's detestation of the conscription laws.

One reason why the issue was so thorny was Richmond's insistence that the enlisting officer on the scene had the authority to determine whether an individual had to serve or could claim exemption. Since Vance depended on exemptions to fill critical jobs on the home front, he felt that exemptions should be a matter of state policy, one his own people were willing and able to handle. It almost goes without saying that the Confederate agents — ignorant of Vance's strategic plans and anxious only to get their own quotas of warm bodies into the pipeline to Virginia — tended not to exempt anyone possessed of the requisite number of arms and legs.

Not that potential conscripts didn't come up with every possible excuse to claim exemption. Men hacked off fingers with axes, dropped stones on their feet to break their toes, scaled and infected their skin to produce loathsome sores, and baldly claimed that they suffered from venereal diseases. One examining surgeon described a draftee who claimed to have "a confliction of diseases as great as any man ever had." One dark-skinned man claimed to be exempt on the grounds that he was part Negro. A great number of men simply ran away into the woods (if they lived in the Piedmont) or deep into the hills (if they lived in a mountain county). And in several cases, when men learned the conscription teams were in the neighborhood, they donned women's clothing and worked out in the fields, hoping they wouldn't be called over for a close inspection when the authorities happened by.

As months passed and the abuses of the conscription system became more flagrant, and Richmond did nothing to curb them, Vance's correspondence with Jefferson Davis became more colored by frustration and barely suppressed anger. Davis, a remote and chilly man who was irritated by displays of emotion, grew impatient with the correspondence and eventually came to regard Vance as a nag. And Vance, in truth, sounds like one in some of his letters. Relations between the two men, never cordial to begin with, grew more formal, more strained, and more openly antagonistic.

One of the Richmond authorities Vance butted heads with most often was General Samuel French. General French was in charge of manpower on the Petersburg front, where battle-thinned regiments had an insatiable appetite for fresh bodies. North Carolina was considered part of French's operational command. French had spent time in the state and had even planned some vigorous counterstrokes against the Federals on the coast before being recalled — as was every general who tried to improve the coastal situation, sooner or later — to the main front in Virginia. French was therefore not unsympathetic to Vance's position and needs, but he was a Jefferson Davis appointee and was loyal to his master. This was usually incompatible with North Carolina's interests.

The worst bone of contention between Vance and French had to do with the right of North Carolina recruits to select the regiment in which they wanted to serve. Vance, until recently a regimental commander himself, had promoted this right early in his term of office as a means of stimulating enlistments. Men tended to sign up in larger numbers when promised that they could serve with their friends and relatives. Vance had cleared the matter first, in personal discussions, with Jefferson Davis. At the time, he had seemed to receive Davis's blessing. And why not, in view of the fact that voluntary enlistments shot up some 300 percent after the policy was publicized?

Yet not too long after his chat with Davis, Vance discovered that Major Mallett had received orders to send all recruits straight from Raleigh to General French in Petersburg. Vance promptly fired off an angry protest to Richmond: "What the exigencies of the service may be, I do not know; they must be great indeed to justify bad faith toward the soldiers on the part of the government. If such is to be the policy, as I do not wish to become a party to such transactions, I shall countermand the orders to my militia officers and leave him [Mallett] to hunt up the conscripts as best he can."

To Mallett himself (an officer caught frustratingly in the middle), Vance wrote: "It is an outrage to deceive them [the recruits] in this way. I desire to sustain the Confederate Government with all my power, but certainly don't intend to assist it in duping the soldiers...."

The situation was greatly aggravated in October 1862 when a party of some 100 men arrived to sign up, citing as their inducement the promise that they could serve with the units of their choice. It happened that these recruits were from what Vance described as a "lukewarm" section of the state, so it was vital for them to be treated fairly if pro-Confederate sympathies were to be strengthened in that region. Instead, the men's pleas were ignored and they were swept up, willy-nilly, in General French's net and parceled out like "chattel property."

In his letter protesting this, Vance had the youthful temerity to lecture Jefferson Davis — one of the most experienced politicians in America — on the politics of running a state at war. He reminded the President that North Carolina could remain a bulwark of the Confederacy only with the support of the majority of citizens who were pro-Union before Fort Sumter. The dedicated secessionists were still the same minority group they had always been, and high-handed impressment policies were not likely to generate more of them.

If conscription were to work in North Carolina, Vance told Davis in no uncertain terms, it would have to be enforced by the governor's administration — with sensitivity toward local conditions, and with the support and cooperation of Richmond, not its antagonism. Then, in what West Point graduate Davis must have taken as a personal insult, Vance discussed the alternative in these words: "If on the contrary, West Point generals who know less of human nature than I do of military service, are to ride roughshod over the people, drag them from their houses and assign them, or rather consign them, to strange regiments and strange commanders without regard to their wishes or feelings, I must be compelled to decline undertaking a task which will certainly fail." He concluded by saying that, while he had little detailed information about how conscription was progressing elsewhere in the South, "a very general impression prevails that this State is doing vastly more than its share."

Vance's little dig must have made Davis wince, but he chose to reply in gentlemanly, though essentially empty, phrases. It seems clear from the tone of his remarks that he could not sympathize with Vance's argument, and that his patience with Vance and his ethical punctiliousness was growing thin. Harmonious assignments for new recruits might be desirable, Davis replied, and he would try to permit them whenever he had the luxury of doing so, but Governor Vance must surely realize that emergency conditions sometimes got in the way of such niceties.

Starting in April 1863, Vance began to receive numerous complaints that General D.H. Hill, commander of the Department of North Carolina, had taken personal control over the conscription process in many regions of the state and was grabbing numbers of men who held legitimate state-issued exemptions. Hill loathed the "exempts," as he called them, and believed that any able-bodied man who was not shouldering a musket was, ipso facto, a coward — never mind that the man in question might be producing salt, keeping a railroad running, or helping to send tons of food to the army in Virginia. When Vance protested directly to Hill, the general fired back a defiant and nasty statement of his feelings: "I loathe war..." he wrote, "but I would be willing to charge a battery if I could get a Brigade of exempts to follow. Good would result from the charge whether the Battery was taken or not."

More confrontations arose as a result of the perception that valiant and deserving North Carolina officers were not being promoted in a manner commensurate with their service and abilities. The statistics seem to back up Vance's belief that there was an unfortunate tendency on Richmond's part to slight Tar Heel officers. The Confederate government on the whole was remarkably generous with its commissions, appointing almost 500 men to the rank of one-star general during the course of the war — several times more generals, in fact, than there were divisions for them to command. Yet of that total, only 15 were from North Carolina. That was an insulting proportion, given the scale of the state's commitment of manpower to the Confederate Army.

Consider the case of Colonel Duncan McRae, who had taken command of a brigade of the Fifth North Carolina Regiment after its original commander was killed in the Maryland campaign. McRae led the unit capably in the heavy fighting at Sharpsburg and South Mountain. After these battles, Jefferson Davis rather arrogantly relieved McRae of his command and replaced him with Colonel Alfred Iverson. Iverson, it turns out, was the son of one of Davis's prewar political cronies, and that was about his only qualification for leadership. McRae was a palpably better soldier and had considerable seniority as well.

McRae resigned his commission in a fury, stating in a letter to Governor Vance that he was doing so not only because of the insult to him personally, but also as a public protest over Richmond's heavy-handed favoritism and its insulting treatment of North Carolina officers everywhere.

Vance, of course, immediately jumped into the controversy, as did the state's newspapers. The *Fayetteville Observer* editorialized that McRae had been passed over for no better reason than the fact that he had been a Stephen Douglas supporter before the war. The paper condemned the Davis administration in ringing terms, calling the whole shabby episode just another example of the "great defect in the President's character" — his habit of settling old prewar political scores at the expense of the war effort. "Like the Bourbons," the editorial concluded, "he forgets nothing and learns nothing."

McRae had also been recommended for promotion by the likes of generals James Longstreet and D.H. Hill. The latter general, in particular, was incensed over Richmond's shameful treatment of a gallant and capable fellow officer.

After resigning his commission, McRae offered his services to Vance in any capacity whatsoever. Vance had no military command to give him, but instead appointed him a state agent for the procurement of European supplies. In that role, McRae performed competently, but the Confederacy needed such men on the battlefield, not in Europe. By all accounts, McRae was a good tactician and a born leader; his services were forever lost in the very capacity to which he was best suited.

As for Alfred Iverson, Davis's choice to replace McRae, he fought his first big engagement at Gettysburg and distinguished himself by making a bloody shambles of things — not only decimating his own men, but also imperiling Lee's entire effort with his incompetence.

There were, of course, some out-of-state officers who were extremely popular with their North Carolina troops and who became, in effect, honorary Tar Heels. But in general, the effect of putting outsiders, particularly Virginians, in command of North Carolina units, when there were already dozens of battle-tested Tar Heel colonels in line for the same openings, had a galling effect on both the soldiers' morale and on public opinion at home. North Carolinians were already smarting from the egregious slurs spat at them by some of the Richmond papers.

The McRae case was but one of dozens in which a clear pattern emerged. People who had been slow to abandon the Union, less than passionate in their espousal of secession, or who were known to have been Whig supporters before the war, were ignored, time and time again, despite their proven merits in battles or in administrative roles. Meanwhile, people regarded as Davis loyalists were promoted over them. Davis professed that he had no time to investigate the political backgrounds of the men whose promotion orders crossed his desk, but the inner circle of Davis loyalists who screened the President from so much unpleasant reality certainly did have the time. They had the dossiers, and they tended to forward for the President's consideration only the names of politically congenial men. As one of Vance's biographers expressed it: "...an officer who was a North Carolina Unionist prior to Lincoln's call for volunteers had about as much chance of becoming a Brigadier General in the Confederate service as in the army of Siam."[1]

Editor Holden stated the matter plainly in the *Raleigh Standard*: "North Carolina is badly treated. She is ignored...She is raked for conscripts with a fine tooth comb. Her troops are always placed in the forefront of the hottest battles...A large portion of her people are suspected of being disloyal...Mr. Davis would do well to bear in mind that it is the last straw that breaks the camel's back."

Holden even came right out and said the unsayable: If North Carolina did not receive better treatment from the Confederacy, she might as well leave it. Governor Vance must have gnashed his teeth when he read that part of the editorial — such statements would only serve to confirm Davis's worst anxieties about North Carolina and make him even more intractable. Holden's support had often been valuable to Vance, especially when it stirred up public opinion in favor of Vance's policies, but Holden was starting to become a real pain in the backside.

The twin problems of conscription and out-of-state officers converged and came to a head in January 1863. Colonel T.P. August, a Virginian, was ordered into the state to replace Colonel Mallett, who had been wounded a month earlier while leading some of his conscript troops in a skirmish at Kinston on the coast.

Vance again dipped his pen in molten lava to write Secretary of War Seddon, accusing Richmond of callously "wounding the sensibilities of our people by the appointment of a citizen of another state to execute a law both harsh and odious. I wish to say, Sir, in all candor, that it smacks of discourtesy to our people to say the least of it…the people of this state have justly felt mortified in seeing these troops commanded by citizens of other States, to the exclusion of claims of their own."

Concluding his letter, Vance warned Seddon that continuing this policy would only stir up the very kind of antipathy within North Carolina that Richmond was most worried about. "Having submitted in silence to the many, the many, the very many acts of administration heretofore so well calculated to wound that pride, which North Carolina is so pardonable to entertaining, it is my duty to inform you that if persisted in, the appointment of strangers to all the positions in this state over her troops, will cause a feeling throughout her whole borders, which it is my very great desire to avoid."

Colonel August — who appears to have been a thoroughly decent chap, for what it's worth — was relieved, and Mallett was reinstated as soon as he recovered from his injuries. In this instance, Vance prevailed.

He was never wholly to prevail against his worst single problem, however: desertion.

During the war, and for decades afterward, there was a persistent canard in circulation to the effect that North Carolina soldiers deserted Lee's army in greater numbers than those of any other state. Modern research has proven that to be wrong. North Carolina troops deserted in just about the same percentages as those from other states, although the absolute numbers may have been higher at times because the total number of North Carolina troops in service was higher.

The main reason this impression got started was the proximity of the North Carolina mountains to the fighting, and their convenience as a hiding place. The Smokies were a haven for deserters from the Virginia front, who simply followed the valleys south until they reached the big hills, and for deserters from the western front in Tennessee. The men who flocked to the mountains came from all the Southern states, and there were some Federal deserters as well (who had little trouble finding helpful Unionists to hide them). Once in the hills, the deserters often formed miniature bandit armies, answerable to no authority save their private chieftains. No matter how many states were represented in those bands of "bush-whackers," however, once operating they were all identified as "North Carolinians."

A terrible cycle was emerging by the end of the war's second year. First came a wave of deserters, who had to live off the land — which they did with increasing ruthlessness as supplies got harder to scrounge. In pursuit of the deserters came sweeps of militia and regulars, who often behaved with more brutality than the men they were searching for. In the upper mountain counties was an added element of hardship: large herds of horses and guard detachments to tend them. These were cavalry units sent down from Virginia to a quiet sector for recovery, and they tended to treat both the land and its inhabitants with all the delicacy of migrating locusts.

The helpless women, children, and elderly people left behind to tend the hard-scrabble farms in the mountain counties, suffering all kinds of hardship, would write imploring, heart-ripping letters to their menfolk at the front — begging them to come home and protect their land, their families, their crops. This, in turn, ignited a new wave of desertion, so the whole sad cycle refueled itself time after time, while conditions for the miserable civilians went from harsh to desperate.

Sometimes these letters were intercepted or surfaced during courts martial as evidence. Here is one that was forwarded to Governor Vance, dated January 6, 1863:

Dear brother there is a great many men leaveing the Arma at this time and I am very glad to see them comeing home but if you have any notion of leaving the arma I would like very mutch to see you comeing home you could get home very easy if you would only start but still I would advice you if you want to leave the war to go to the other side whear you can get plenty and not stay in this one horse barefooted naked and famine stricken Southern Confederacy for we have come very near naught...evry person or very near say the Southern Confederacy is bound to die and if it would I would not cry...

Here is another typical letter, this one from a soldier in the 14th North Carolina Regiment to his wife, dated May 1, 1864:

My dear companion: The 28th of last month their was three men shot in our brigade that belonged to the 4th Regiment of N.C. troops. They was tied to stakes and shot to death that way, all three shot one at a time. All three men of family, they were from the eastern part of N.C. I was close by when three were shot and I never want to see the like again. They was put to death for starting home and was taken up on the way.

Dear wife and child I wish the time was so I could come home and see you and stay with you in this world what few remaining days I have to live.

One of the most heartbreaking letters that survives was a letter to Confederate soldier Edward Cooper from his wife. Cooper had deserted, been caught, and was remanded to the mercies of a court martial. When asked to produce witnesses in his defense, the poor man simply handed this letter to the presiding officer of the court:

My dear Edward — I have always been proud of you, and since your connection with the Confederate army, I have been prouder of you than ever before, I would not have you do anything wrong for the world, but before God, Edward, unless you come home, we must die. Last night, I was aroused by little Eddie's crying. I called and said, "What is the matter, Eddie?" and he said "O, mamma, I am so hungry!" And Lucy, Edward, your darling Lucy, she never complains, but she is growing thinner and thinner every day. And before God, Edward, unless you come home, we must die.

Your Mary

According to D.H. Hill, who used to tell the story, the court was moved to weep; but not moved enough to neglect its military obligation. Cooper was sentenced to death. Later, General Lee reviewed the case and issued a pardon.

Though Governor Vance sympathized with the civilians' plight, he was sworn to prosecute the war and to round up deserters. This he did, by ordering militia units into the countryside. This brought Vance into conflict with his sometime-ally against Richmond, North Carolina Chief Justice R.M. Pearson. Pearson disputed the legality of Vance's enforcement of Confederate laws with state militia, and for a time actually hoisted Vance on his own habeas corpus.

In due time, the militia sweeps were under way again. But more effective than these often blundering operations, or than the guard patrols that the governor ordered stationed at bridges and rural crossroads, were Vance's ringing public proclamations. The first was issued on January 26, 1863. Vance was known throughout the state by now as a man of his word, and when he promised "that the wife and child [of a soldier who was serving at the front] shall share the last bushel of meal and pound of meat in the state," a surprising number of men believed him. As many as 2,000 deserters returned voluntarily to the ranks in the first 30 days following the proclamation.

One young soldier even wrote a letter of confession to the governor, recounting how he had been greeted at the gate of the family farm by "my old grayheaded father" who had, at first, wept with joy to see his son. But then his father thrusted a copy of Vance's proclamation under his nose, telling him that unless he turned himself into the army and did his duty, he would be "undone forever." The boy then sat down and wrote a letter of apology to Vance, begging forgiveness for his desertion, and asked for a safe-conduct pass so he could return to his regiment and redeem himself in action. Vance responded in kind, verbally patting the boy on the head and admonishing him to "take your father's advice...return to your brave comrades...and show by your good conduct that you desire your error to be forgotten, and that you are worthy of your lineage."

Typically, even as Vance was admonishing deserters to return to the fray, he was also chiding Richmond for fueling the problem by refusing to give the men the furloughs they had been promised when they enlisted. And he again criticized Richmond's policy of assigning men haphazardly into the ranks, rather than permitting them to serve in regiments of their choice.

Despite all these efforts to stem desertion, by mid-1863 the situation in western North Carolina had deteriorated to the point where the total number of armed desperados roaming free actually exceeded the voting population of several mountain counties.

The state of near-anarchy in the region was compounded in the winter of 1862-63, when Confederate authorities in Richmond sent down a large number of horses, including hundreds of head captured during the Fredericksburg campaign, and turned them loose to forage in the northwestern part of the state. The counties to which the horses were sent had suffered a drought the previous summer, were virtually stripped of manpower, and were on the edge of ruin. The behavior of the men assigned to guard the horses ranged from callous to beastly. Vance was already shipping emergency wagon-loads of corn from the eastern districts to this region — enough to provide a subsistence ration for some of the areas hardest hit — but the shipments were being commandeered by the cavalrymen for use as horse fodder. Vance's files contained dozens of reports of civilians who were being insulted, beaten, and even raped by oafish and frequently drunken Confederate horsemen.

"If God Almighty had yet in store another plague," Vance roared to War Secretary Seddon in a letter that deserved to be penned on asbestos paper, "worse than all the others which He intended to have let loose upon the Egyptians...I am sure it must have been a regiment or so of half-armed, half-disciplined Confederate cavalry! Had they been turned loose on Pharaoh's subjects...he would have become so sensible to the anger of God that he never would have followed the children of Israel to the Red Sea. No, Sir, not an inch!"

This sorry spectacle — of helpless, starving civilians being mistreated by the men of their own side — roused Vance as nothing else ever did. He took the extreme step of informing Seddon that unless the horse-guards and their hungry charges were removed from the state, he would mobilize the militia and clear them out at bayonet-point. He would, he threatened, "levy actual war against them."

This smoldering missive arrived on Seddon's dinner table just as the cadaverous, gloomy, secretary of war was sitting down for his Christmas dinner. After reading the letter, and sharing it with his adjutant, Seddon funereally intoned: "Can you suggest, or do you advise, a general order to avert the threatened disasters which so affect Governor Vance's imagination?" The adjutant could not; Seddon would not. He called Vance's bluff by simply refusing to respond to the threat. And Vance, of course, did not call out the militia.

DEFENDING THE CITIZEN: VANCE AS CIVIL LIBERTARIAN

Some of the prickliest correspondence between Richmond and Raleigh had to do with the offensive behavior of some Confederate agents and units sent into North Carolina to comb out draft resisters and deserters.

In an attempt to redress what he considered inexcusable outrages perpetrated against North Carolina citizens, Vance recounted to Jefferson Davis the details of several incidents. In late 1862, for instance, a detachment of Confederate cavalry went into Tyrell County on the coast and commandeered, at gunpoint, a number of horses from the inhabitants. Some of the animals were actually unhitched from plows while their owners watched in helpless indignation. When the farmers sent a delegate to Richmond to demand the return of the animals, he was thrown into jail by the very men who had stolen the horses.

In a similar incursion over in Cherokee County at the opposite end of the state, a squad of horse soldiers from Georgia seized a group of over-age citizens, chained them together like felons, marched them 120 miles to Atlanta, threw them in prison, and offered them two choices: enlist for the duration, or rot in their cells.

Other outrages were committed in mountainous Wilkes County by a North Carolina regiment sent by Richmond to scour the territory for shirkers and deserters in early 1864. While performing these odious duties, some of the regiment's men had run amok, stealing from, and in some instances beating, deserters' families and loyal Confederates indiscriminately.

The language used in all of Vance's letters to President Davis about these matters is almost generic in its tone of indignation. In response to the last-mentioned incident, for example, Vance wrote: "Was that wrong redressed? Was anybody punished for that outrage?" Respectable, law-abiding families had been rendered destitute by this type of outrage, Vance continued, and what was Richmond going to do about it? Vance had already written to the secretaries of war and the treasury seeking some sort of financial relief — tax exemption if nothing else — for the victimized families. All he had received in reply were bureaucratic run-arounds, as each official sought to "pass the buck" to someone else in the Richmond hierarchy.

"I know these things in a greater or lesser degree are inseparable from a state of war," Vance pleaded, "...but they do add to the discontent in North Carolina...prompt and kindly efforts to redress would cause these poor people to love their government and support its laws far more than the terrors of the suspension of the writ of habeas corpus and a display of force."

Jefferson Davis was not overly concerned about winning the love of poor people, however, and his reply was both sulky and defensive. He claimed he had never heard of the incidents, and he chided Vance for not sending him written reports at the time they had happened.

But Vance had indeed sent detailed written reports, through the proper chain-of-command channels. They had been acknowledged, filed away, and forgotten. That was why he was pestering Davis about the matter to begin with. And it would have been hard for these incidents to have escaped Davis's attention, because the resulting outcry had even reached the Virginia newspapers. If Davis really was unaware of what was going on, he shouldn't be — once again, his shield of bureaucrats had protected him from unpleasant realities.

"...It is difficult to understand why such acrimonious complaints should have been addressed to me," Davis replied to Vance's lashing remarks, before continuing in the testiest language he had heretofore used in his correspondence with the governor. "There are...passages in your letter in which you have so far infringed the proprieties of official intercourse as to preclude the possibility of a reply. In order that I may not again be subjected to the necessity of making so unpleasant a remark, I must beg that a correspondence so unprofitable in its character, and which was not initiated by me, may end here, and that your further communications be restricted to such matters as may require official action."

Just as Davis, an indifferent military strategist, refused to give control of the battlefield to men who knew what they were doing, so too did Davis the administrator find it impossible to deal with incidents which proved that the government in Richmond had little knowledge of, and absolutely no control over, many of the activities being conducted in its name. Instead, he struck out at the messenger who brought the unpleasant truth into his cocoon of personal dignity, displaying more passion about the punctilios of proper diplomatic correspondence than he ever would about some of the terrible wrongs that had been committed in his government's name.

Even when a certain amount of political posturing on Vance's part is taken into account, the vast and extraordinary body of correspondence between the governor and Jefferson Davis reveals a Confederate President too often out of touch with the day-to-day workings of his own administration; a President more concerned with preserving the image of his own rectitude than with treating all classes of his people fairly; a consummate politician who could not abandon the instincts of a lifetime even when they were counterproductive; and a politico who favored the careers and ideas of men who sided with him. The correspondence reveals that Davis tended to think in terms of old political controversies that, by 1864, must have seemed as if they belonged to another world — political issues rendered quite irrelevant by the exigencies of total war. Moreover, from time to time, there creeps into Davis's writing a hint of personal resentment at the vigor of Vance's thought, the loyalty Vance commanded, the efficiency of his administration, and the virility of his youthful good health.

Despite the hostility caused by the Confederate government's increasingly centralized policies, it has often been asserted that if only Richmond had kept a tighter rein over the Confederate states — if only Davis had gone all out and set up a truly authoritarian regime — the South might well have been able to achieve a military standoff. And for the Confederacy, a military standoff would have amounted to a strategic victory. However, the debate is mooted by examining historical examples. Despotic governments, it is true, often fight wars more efficiently than democracies, at least in the short run. But the win/lose statistics over the past 2,000 years come out pretty close to even.

One fact that does emerge clearly from the history of the War Between the States is that the South's armies fought with greater dash, elan, and momentum during the early stages of the conflict, when there was almost a quality of ecstasy about the volunteers' enthusiasm. But when the war turned from a romantic crusade into a protracted, grueling slugging match, and when the morale of the home front began to crumble, desertion became epidemic. It became harder and harder for a rational man to justify putting not only himself, but his family at home, in jeopardy for a cause which seemed to be almost without substance. Indeed, the validity of the struggle itself was more and more called into question in direct proportion to the heavy-handedness of Richmond's policies and methods. The more the Davis government tried to tighten its control over individual and regional liberties, the more its policies were resented. When abuses of personal civil rights became common, skepticism, in many parts of the South, gave way to outright detestation. Certainly that is what happened in virtually all of western and much of central and coastal North Carolina.

For Zebulon Vance, the issue was clear-cut. The war was first and foremost about state's rights, and if the Richmond government began to trample those rights underfoot, then the heroic sacrifices of the South were rendered meaningless. In a speech given in Boston in 1886, Vance defined "the proudest boast" of his administration: "The laws were heard amidst the roar of the cannon. No man within the jurisdiction of the State of North Carolina was denied the privilege of the writ of habeas corpus, the right of trial by jury, or the equal protection of the laws, as provided by our Constitution...."

Vance first took up rhetorical arms in defense of the civil rights of North Carolinians not long after taking office. The case concerned the fate of the Reverend Robert J. Graves, pastor of the Bethlehem Presbyterian Church of Orange County. Graves had made a trip north in the autumn of 1862, ostensibly to have his throat operated on by a New York surgeon. Upon his return to North Carolina, Graves wrote a long letter to the *Richmond Enquirer*, telling about all the warlike activity he had observed in Yankeeland.

To the authorities in Richmond, the letter sounded vaguely defeatist, but they allowed it to be published anyway. When it appeared, a Confederate soldier came forward and stated that he had been present, as a prisoner of war, when Graves had made his crossing into Federal lines. This witness claimed to have overheard Graves telling a group of Federal officers, in great detail, all about the defenses of Richmond and the progress of the gunboat *Richmond*, then under construction in the city and about which the Federals were very apprehensive.

Richmond's provost marshal, General John Winder, sent a detective to North Carolina who arrested Graves without formal charges, secretly spirited him out of the state, and then threw the minister into a cell in Richmond's dreaded Castle Thunder prison. Graves was to be tried by a military court and there appeared every likelihood he would end up on the gallows.

Graves had been arrested just after finishing his Sunday sermon, so word of the incident reached Raleigh within hours. Vance was so incensed that he had all the railroad cars in Raleigh searched, but it was too late. Thus far in his administration, Vance felt that no greater insult had been dealt to North Carolina's sovereignty than this high-handed abduction. To Vance, whether Graves was or was not a spy was almost beside the point; the man must be restored promptly to North Carolina and to its system of justice. The state's newspaper supported Vance and the General Assembly even passed a unanimous resolution demanding Graves's return.

The vehemence and unanimity of North Carolina's protest took the Richmond government off-guard. War Secretary Seddon admitted to Vance that General Winder had perhaps been overzealous, and he quickly shipped Graves back to Raleigh. The case was remanded to a grand jury, and Graves defended himself by claiming that his stories about the gunboat *Richmond* had been fabrications designed to win him safe conduct through Federal lines. There was a certain logic to the minister's claim — how much genuine information about a top-secret Confederate naval project was he likely to have picked up while serving in a rural church near Hillsborough? — so he was not brought to trial.

Besides this incident, the winter of 1862-63 proved to be a busy one on the civil rights front. In November, officers under General French's command arrested 40 civilians suspected of "disloyalty" and packed them off to the dismal confines of the Salisbury prison. Vance remonstrated to President Davis in fairly mild and circumspect language, but he was thunder incarnate in his communications with General French, for whom Vance appears to have had little use. The prisoners must either be brought to a speedy trial on formal charges, Vance instructed French, or they must be released and allowed to go home unmolested. Failing either of these actions, Vance was prepared to issue a proclamation ordering the recall of North Carolina soldiers from Virginia. The threat was probably another bluff — Vance must have been one hell of a poker player — but French was undoubtedly appalled at the thought of being held responsible for such a catastrophe, however remote it might really be. He acted quickly to have the men released.

On several occasions during 1862 and 1863, the Confederate Congress voted Jefferson Davis the power to suspend the writ of habeas corpus and to declare martial law. Davis used those powers very sparingly, however, and only in times of dire military emergency. But by early 1864, the situation was different. Until then, Davis had been given extraordinary powers only for restricted periods of time; now, the Confederate Congress was debating an act that would permit Davis to suspend the writ indefinitely, whenever he chose.

Vance suspected — not without good reason — that the new act would find its harshest application in North Carolina, where opposition to conscription was rife, deserters numerous, and disenchantment with Richmond commonly voiced. He therefore initiated a long written debate with Davis on the issues of civil and universal human rights. Vance assured Davis that North Carolinians would listen to the voice of reason and still possessed Southern patriotism. Those conditions might not last, however, if Richmond came down on the state with the heavy hand of martial law. The very situations Davis sought to correct would become wildly inflamed.

The governor went on to reiterate some points he had made before in their correspondence: that the Confederate government unjustly viewed North Carolina with suspicion because of the state's reluctance to leave the Union, and that North Carolinians had been pointedly excluded both from government positions and upper ranks in the army. "...Bitter and unrelenting criticism of your administration has been indulged in," Vance conceded, "but where and when have our people failed you in battle, or withheld their blood or their vast resources?"

Whatever his shortcomings, Jefferson Davis was a man of granitic integrity; he had no intention of using his new powers frivolously, nor was he unmindful of what would happen to North Carolina's war contribution should he try to bring the state to heel with an iron fist. At this time (February 1864), Davis was facing some of the darkest days yet in his administration. His armies were barely hanging on to their defensive positions, his options were few and dwindling, and he was being subjected to growing, often savagely personal, criticism from less generous spirits than Zeb Vance.

All things considered, President Davis was probably in no mood for a verbose civics lesson from the young upstart governor of North Carolina. Moreover, he always felt compelled to reply to Vance's letters in the same exhaustive, flowery, closely reasoned style as that employed by his correspondent. Davis's reply on this occasion ran to some 1,600 words, carefully penned in longhand, and composing it must have taken a large bite out of his already crowded day. Davis was a man of limited physical stamina by this time in his life, and he must have found it exasperating to expend so much of it in these debates with Vance.

In any event, Davis never suspended the writ of habeas corpus in North Carolina. The test case involved a man named Irvin who was conscripted, hired a substitute, and then was conscripted again when the draft ages were extended and he fell once more into the eligible pool. The War Department in Richmond ruled that Irvin had to serve. The chief justice of North Carolina's Supreme Court, R.M. Pearson, ruled that he did not, because of the original substitution contract he had signed.

There was no such thing as a Confederate Supreme Court; had there been, it is likely that Vance would have deferred to it (although the legal battle would have been stupendous). In the absence of such a supreme legal body, Vance felt justified in accepting the verdict of his own state's highest court (which Vance also did in cases in which Pearson's judgment went against his wishes). Vance butted heads again with the iron-necked Seddon, who defended his War Department's actions on constitutional grounds. To Vance, that argument was spurious because the Confederate Constitution had not, by design, created a supreme court. To underscore his determination in this matter, Vance mobilized a detachment of militia and had Irvin set free. He further issued a proclamation ordering his militia commanders to resist any attempt "on the part of any person" to arrest a conscript or deserter without due legal authorization in writing.

Vance and his chief justice were upholding one of the most cherished traditions of the American legal system: the guaranteed protection of the individual's rights against the excesses of government. No one wanted to keep North Carolina's regiments at full strength more than Vance, but he saw the protection of personal rights as a corollary to the military struggle — indeed, as the very heart and soul of the South's reasons for waging war in the first place — not as a contradiction of it.

On the whole, the Confederate Constitution was not a hastily written or poorly reasoned document. Legal scholars have, in fact, praised it for offering one or two improvements over its predecessor — such as the provision for a single six-year term for the President. The very core of its ideological structure lies in the concept of a voluntary union of states, and that's why the state supreme courts were given the highest interpretive powers. Vance was, therefore, on fairly strong constitutional grounds when he acted in defiance of Richmond in the Irvin case and several similar matters.

When Seddon's adjutant, John Campbell, wrote Vance a letter implying that North Carolina's judicial system "lent itself to the protection of deserters," Vance acidly reminded him that North Carolinians had accounted for more than half the casualties at the bloody battles of Chancellorsville and Fredericksburg. Any implication that the state had not put forth its fullest energies on behalf of the Southern cause was, to Vance, vile calumny.

Taking their cue from North Carolina's aggressive governor, the political leaders of Georgia, Mississippi, and even Virginia denounced the law which gave Davis his extraordinary powers. The entire issue was mooted, finally, when Davis's unusual authority was allowed to expire in August 1864.

Summarizing his philosophy, Vance wrote these ringing phrases: "The meanest citizen in the land" should be able "instantly to command for his protection in the commonest, simplest personal right, the entire physical and moral weight of the republic."

What, after all, had the Southern rebellion really been about, more than the desire to be left alone by what was perceived as a remote and despotic government?

HARD TIMES ON THE HOME FRONT

'...it looks like we are getting right in to war at home...neightbour against neightbour [sic]. I could nock them [the deserters] in the head with a ax just as fast as they would bring them to me and never flinch at it...I wish the deserters had to dig up Randolph [County] with their teeth and carry it off with their mouths.'

— Mrs. Jane Sugg, Randolph County resident, in a letter to her brother, dated August 8, 1864.

North Carolina was in a relatively better position to withstand economic hardship during the War Between the States than some of her Deep South brethren. When years of combat and the Union blockade began to tighten the economic screws, and when the shortage of both goods and manpower began to strain every sector of Confederate society, North Carolina was at least able to postpone the worst ravages. Unlike the Deep South states, North Carolina had never relied upon cotton as the main crop. So many farmers had found cotton only marginally profitable — in relation to the effort required to make it grow in the state's red-clay soil — that they needed little persuasion, when war broke out, to switch over to food crops.

It's difficult to paint a precise picture of the state's agricultural situation between 1861 and 1865 because the surviving statistics are local in scope, fragmentary in nature, and sometimes hard for modern researchers to interpret. Still, the major trends are readily apparent.

The coastal tier of North Carolina counties was pretty well stripped bare by the end of 1862. This region was too vulnerable to attacks from the Federal garrisons in their various coastal enclaves, and wide areas became a kind of no-man's land, their populations reduced to the merest fraction of what they had been before the war. The eastern Piedmont region, however, starting with the counties that paralleled the eastern side of the Wilmington and Weldon Railroad, remained abundant — except where local conditions were bad due to weather or foraging — until the war's end. Of course, even these areas were stripped in the last stages of the war if they happened to be in the path of Sherman's invasion.

As late as the war's last Christmas, it was still possible for some of the wealthier families in the Piedmont to throw a good party. Witness the following account describing festivities on a plantation about 12 miles west of Raleigh:

> The pretty young ladies in their beautiful homespun dresses all made up and trimmed with quantities of buttons covered with contrasting material and other pretty handmade decorations, were so charming that no wonder they "scorned to wear a bit of silk or a bit of Northern lace." The young men, in spite of the wail of the "poor ragged Confederate soldiers" managed to be all dressed up in new fresh looking uniforms all resplendent in gold lace and shiny buttons. After supper they danced the...Virginia Reel, Scotch Ramble, London Bridge, or played games, such as marching around singing, "O Sister Phebe how merry we were, the night we sat under the young June apple tree," or "When I lived in the State of Virginia, to Carolina I did go, there I saw a handsome lady O! Her name I did not know," stealing partners and other amusements enlivened the occasion. This is a true picture of Christmas in my neighborhood during the War....[1]

Production was good for much of the war, too, in the northern Piedmont, although the shortage of manpower and equipment made conditions deteriorate rapidly after late 1863. In the central Piedmont, the constant disruption of low-level partisan warfare made it difficult for the inhabitants even to survive. What little they could grow, they hoarded for their own use, or had stolen from them by one side or another during the continual outbreaks of unrest.

If there was sporadic famine in the Piedmont, there was almost total destitution in the mountain counties. In general, the farther west you went, the worse conditions you would encounter.

Food was always the main concern, of course, but it was not only food that was lacking. Clothing, medicine, paper, housing, and transportation: All of these necessities for routine, basic, social interaction were afflicted with shortages which appeared early in the war and worsened at an uneven rate.

The hardships more often seemed to be caused by a random convergence of factors rather than a direct result of any one event. Two villages in the same Piedmont county, 20 miles apart by road, might experience drastically different fortunes during the same year. One village might enjoy near-peacetime levels of quantity and quality, while its neighbor struggled at a subsistence level.

Obviously, the areas closest to the fighting fronts suffered the effects of rampant foraging and impressment earliest and most keenly. City dwellers often felt the pinch of hunger sooner than their rural cousins — when times got tough, it was common practice for the farmers simply to refuse to haul their produce into town.

This pattern shifted dramatically in the spring of 1863, when the Confederate Congress enacted a sweeping taxation program that affected income, property, and agricultural production. Under the new tax-in-kind laws, a farm family was obligated to turn over 10 percent of its production of everything — potatoes, oats, corn, rice, beans, bacon, beef, hides, everything — to agents of the Confederate government. To the rich planters, the taxes were a nuisance; to the small farmers, the effects could be devastating. Speculation, falling production due to manpower and equipment shortages, and savage inflation all made it necessary for farmers to sell more and more of their output in order to survive. Many families had been living off of about 15 to 20 percent of their output and selling everything else, just to stay afloat. The added 10 percent tax to the Confederacy meant that many people who had barely been getting by at all suddenly found themselves on the edge of actual starvation. These "tithetaxes," moreover, were often collected in a brutal and heavy-handed manner by the agents sent out by Richmond. From the spring of 1863 until the end of the war, the overwhelming majority of the pleas that came to Governor Vance were from the rural citizens most afflicted by these taxes.

In the typical rural hamlets of central and western North Carolina, the first change people noticed after the war was underway was the disappearance of all the young men who had previously done the plowing, the clerking, the hauling, the harness-making, the carpentry, and the smithing. Women, old folks, and children took on more and more of these tasks, and finally took all of them. They continued to do so even after the tools began to wear out and could not be replaced, and even after the horses and mules wore out, too, or were "impressed" to haul the caissons and ambulances of the armies. On the average small farm, there was usually a period of delicate balance when the women and older people could handle it all and still provide enough to live on, but it was the most vulnerable of balances. When drought struck, or the livestock took sick, or the plow broke, there was no help to be had. Many families had no recourse, finally, except to forage for what grew wild and seek the sporadic and generally inadequate relief made available by state governments.

North Carolina was marginally luckier, because Governor Vance had hoarded supplies and made every effort to see that they were fairly distributed. But there was little that he or his assistants could do, from the state capital in Raleigh, to make sure the supply system functioned properly. Supplies intended for, say, Wilkes County often didn't actually get to Wilkes County; they might rot in a forgotten railroad shed in Statesville, or be sold for outrageous profits by one of the speculators who leeched the distribution system at every choke point.

As always happens in times of shortage, it was the poor who felt the pain first, longest, and hardest. After two years of war, though, the burden began to spread throughout every part of Southern society. Except, of course, for the inner circle of the Davis administration in Richmond, whose members rarely suffered more than a temporary lack of good things to eat, drink, and wear. As late as the winter of 1864-65, a visitor to the Davis family dining table found such unimaginably rare delicacies as roasted chicken, fresh oysters, olives, champagne, lettuce salad, real jelly, and chocolate ice cream. Nor did Confederate cabinet members Judah Benjamin and Stephen Mallory maintain their legendary girths on a diet of parched corn and goober peas.

Along with the other Confederate states, North Carolina underwent a profound social convulsion because of these hardships.

Although the immediate effects were perhaps less visible in the Old North State than in the rigidly stratified cotton states of the Deep South, the result was ultimately the same: tremendous change to a society that had been contentedly stagnant for generations. The wealthy found themselves sharing the same hardships — though not always, of course, to the same degree — as the hard-scrabble farmers down the road.

Women felt the changes early and most profoundly. Forced for the first time to manage plantations and run small farms, most were more than equal to the challenge. Women also found themselves recruited, on however small a scale, into the work force for the first time. Much of the clerical staff at the Fayetteville Arsenal, for example, was comprised of young women, who took their pay not in worthless Confederate "shin-plasters," but in raw wool. After their workday was over, they worked the wool, by candlelight, into clothing for their families.

In addition to running the farms and keeping their families (and, to a large extent, the Army of Northern Virginia) fed, the women of almost every neighborhood in the state — urban or rural — formed sewing societies, knitting clubs, hospital aid societies, and nursing associations. They were unpaid for these labors, of course, and those who volunteered for the hospitals often worked long hours under grim conditions, but there were rewards. Just having a woman close at hand could sometimes mean the difference between life and death to a young, scared, pain-wracked soldier.

One lady in Wilmington, Mrs. Armand J. DeRosset, organized her friends into a veritable assembly line of military goods, producing so much, so efficiently, that some of the local Confederate officers used to say, "She ought to be made a general." For four years, Mrs. DeRosset's Soldiers' Aid Society not only worked in all the area hospitals, but also manufactured high-quality military goods. Canvas bags by the thousand were stitched together to build the ramparts of Fort Fisher; canteen covers, haversacks, cartridge belts, even powder bags for the giant Columbiads of the fort, were all turned out steadily and in impressive numbers.

In Hillsborough, the main railroad stop between Raleigh and Greensboro, there was an especially effective ladies' aid society. Thousands of soldiers en route to and from the Virginia front were fed and refreshed there. The Hillsborough ladies were even issued permanent passes from the head of the North Carolina Railroad to give them access to all trains on the main lines, and they spread their activities accordingly.

Another ladies' group in Wadesboro came up with a novel idea for raising funds: it put together a traveling magic lantern show and took it from village to village.

The constant work had another, personal, side as well. It gave them some emotional outlet, something to do besides just coping and worrying about whose name might appear on the next casualty list posted down at the courthouse. One day, just after the fall of Fort Fisher in Wilmington, when the hospital in Fayetteville was flooded with wounded soldiers, the chief physician found himself accosted by a tiny, frail-looking woman, hobbling down the corridor on crutches. Her name, she said, was Mrs. Kyle, and she wanted to work full-time in the hospital. When the doctor looked at her dubiously, she explained that she had a husband in the army, and she was constantly worried about him. "Doctor, I don't want any pay," she insisted, "but I must have constant occupation or I will lose my mind." The doctor put her to work. She showed up every morning at nine and stayed until dark, painfully making her way on crutches from bed to bed, changing dressings, bathing those who could not bathe themselves, reading letters to the blinded, writing letters for men who had lost a hand, emptying chamber pots, offering the comfort of her presence, and just being willing to listen. In her apron pockets she carried a prayer book, and when there was nothing more that could be done for a man, she pulled it out and prayed with him during his last moments. One morning, she encountered a man of advanced years and gray-white hair. "You are too old to be here," she chided him. "I had no sons," was the reply, "so I went myself."

Reading the many testimonials from those bitter days, one comes away with renewed admiration for the day-in, day-out courage of ordinary people suddenly confronted with chaotic conditions and the raw horror of war — things for which none of them had the slightest cultural or psychological preparation. One also comes away with a certain bemused amazement at how naturally these mid-Victorians were given to spontaneous sentimental gestures. In Raleigh, for example, in the last days of the war after the battle at

Bentonville, the city was flooded with wounded. When the hospitals filled up, the churches, public buildings, and some private homes became improvised aid stations. Men lay everywhere — on benches, church pews, piles of straw, and they were moaning, shivering with fever, delirious with pain. One young man was placed hurriedly in one of the improvised wards by litter-bearers who knew nothing about him, and he died before there was any chance to learn who he was or even what unit he belonged to. As the coffin lid was being secured, an elderly nurse happened by. She asked the burial detail to wait a minute; then she knelt and tenderly kissed the young man's forehead, whispering that her kiss was in lieu of his own mother's.

As privation took its toll in every sphere of social and economic activity, improvisation became the order of day, for everyone, regardless of sex or social strata. Buttons were manufactured from gourds and persimmon seeds, slippers from rabbit and squirrel fur, and hats from palmetto leaves, corn shucks, oat straw, and broad-leaf grasses. It was discovered that rabbit fur, mixed with a small amount of cotton and then carded, could be spun into a passable kind of ersatz thread suitable for rough-and-ready home weaving. Dyes were made from roots, bark, herbs, leaves, and some kinds of clay. Shoes were made from untreated cow hides, then blackened with soot scraped from the bottoms of iron cooking pots. For soda, ashes of corn cobs were substituted. Druggists dusted off long-forgotten manuals on herbalism, and the traditions of folk medicine enjoyed a renaissance.

When candles were in short supply, pine-knots and pan-drippings were pressed into service, the latter with a rag or string wick. Other methods of illumination consisted of sycamore balls soaked in animal fat and bottles full of grease with wicks of twisted string. Ink was made from berry juice. Soap became extremely rare and costly after the first year of the war, and various mixtures were tried in place of the real thing. A typical ersatz soap would be made from a blend of meat scraps, bones, skins, and lye, boiled down and mixed with ashes as a bonding agent. It scrubbed the dirt off, all right, but on a warm day it also drew flies.

Old dresses were dug out of attics and refurbished. Bonnets made from scraps of leftover cloth, then adorned with goose feathers or plumes snipped from the old rooster in the backyard. Women dressed in their makeshift outfits with great pride, and there was plenty of informal competition to see who could spruce up her thrift-shop wardrobe with the most imagination. Calico replaced silk as the height of fashion.

Although sewing machines weren't rare in the South in the 1860s, relatively few households possessed one, and those that did soon ran out of suitable thread — that, too, was an imported commodity. But there were thousands of old spinning wheels in attics and barns, and they were pressed into service to create the famous Southern "homespun." Homespun was made in every one of the Confederate states during the war, but the material that came from North Carolina was especially prized for its quality. The best surviving specimens of the fabric have a fineness of texture that rivals muslin. Women greatly valued their homespun dresses and wore them with patriotic pride. The homespun dress even became the topic of a popular song (to the tune of "The Bonnie Blue Flag"):

> *My homespun dress is plain I know;*
> *My hat's palmetto, too.*
> *But then it shows what Southern girls*
> *For Southern rights will do.*
> *We send the bravest of our land*
> *To battle with the foe;*
> *And we will lend a helping hand*
> *We love the South, you know.* Chorus:

> *Hurrah! Hurrah! For the sunny South so dear,*
> *Three cheers for the homespun dress*
> *That Southern Ladies wear!*[2]

When shoe leather was not obtainable, people recycled old boots, cotton-gin belts, trunk-straps, and what have you, creating hybrid fashions with leather uppers and wooden clog-like bottoms. There was a factory in Raleigh which produced a hundred pairs of such shoes per day, and sold all it could make. Its advertisements claimed the product would last "until the next war." The shoes were certainly durable, and if the insides of the wooden hulls were lined with something soft, they weren't too uncomfortable to wear. However, they did make the wearer walk with a comical, rocking, penguin-like gait which gave a slightly ludicrous appearance to a crowd of pedestrians.

One fashion accessory was literally worth its weight in gold: corset stays. When store-bought stays disappeared, and antebellum stays wore out, the ladies resorted to using handmade replacements of white oak, sometimes of hickory. Blacksmiths commanded good fees for custom-made stays. And the blockade-runner shopping in Europe who had the foresight to stock up on that intimate article could turn a tidy profit after returning home. One enterprising captain bought a thousand pairs of stays in Glasgow, Scotland. When he made it past the Union blockade and returned to Wilmington, he unloaded them in a matter of days for a profit of 1,100 percent.

North Carolina was one of the few Southern states that managed to keep its public education system going throughout the war, though in a much-reduced fashion by the end. Superintendent of Schools Calvin H. Wiley worked closely with Governor Vance to keep the system functioning. The shortage of draft-age teachers meant drastically curtailed schedules, but it was still possible for a child to learn the rudiments of reading, 'riting, and 'rithmetic in most parts of the state.

Private schools didn't fare so well. Most of the all-male institutions were gutted by waves of volunteering and then by conscription. By the end of 1863, it had become just as hard to adequately feed students as it was to feed anyone else. Here and there, some schools managed to get through the war in relatively good shape — Salem's boarding school for young ladies, for example, actually grew during the war years. Its location was deemed secure, and its steward, Augustus Fogle, had been granted a special exemption by Governor Vance so that he could serve "the daughters of the South." It was also well favored with relief supplies sent from Raleigh, including some priceless consignments of white sugar.

The Piedmont was also the site of a unique educational experiment: a series of school textbooks published specifically for the Confederacy. The schoolbooks on hand when the war broke out, of course, were Northern in origin, and were subsequently discovered to have an editorial slant which was "inimical and untruthful to the South." A new series of books was therefore designed by Professor Richard Sterling, president of the Edgeworth Female Seminary in Greensboro, with help from James W. Albright, who had edited and published a literary magazine called *The Greensboro Times* until wartime exigencies forced its suspension.

Albright's printing plant, on West Market Street in Greensboro, was given over to the production of a series of volumes known collectively as "Our Own School Books." Circulars advertising these books assured the prospective buyer that "whatever excellence or defect our books may be found to possess, we are happy to know that they are purely Southern productions, both in workmanship and material. Perhaps we offer the public the first series of readers whose compilation, paper, printing, and binding, are all wholly the product of home industry."

Not very many entrepreneurial ventures survived for long under wartime conditions, but this one actually thrived. The series acquired distributors in Richmond and in Columbia, South Carolina. Success almost ruined the operation, however, when the demand for the books became too much for Albright's printing press to handle.

A dismantled Adams Book Press — considered state of the art at that time — was located in Columbia, shipped to Greensboro, assembled, and found to be in working order. It was also found to be too cumbersome to be worked by hand. To solve this problem, a man named A.P. Boren of Pomona volunteered the services of a horse-powered apparatus he had designed for grinding sugar cane. A horse was attached to the machinery, and a young boy was hired to simply ride the animal in circles all day.

Paper shortages eventually forced later editions of the series to appear on inferior material made from raw cotton, but the books continued to thrive. On the first voyage of the blockade-runner *Advance*, Professor J.J. Ayers of the Edgeworth Female Seminary took the books to Liverpool, England, to have them "stereotyped," paying for the work with a shipment of cotton.

Several specimens of these books, in fragile condition, survive in the North Carolina Collection of the Greensboro Public Library, and they make interesting reading. Most of the contents appear typical for their time: quaint and decidedly Victorian. The ideological slant is fairly muted, mainly limited to fulsome descriptions of Southern cities and natural resources. In *Our Own Spelling Book*, though, the editors proclaim that they have followed the work of "Dr. Worcester" the lexographer who "in our judgement, approaches nearer the true English standard and accords better with the usage of our best native authors in the Confederate States, than any other...." And in *Our Own Third Reader*, there is an elaborate restatement of the so-called "Biblical defense" of slavery. It was this latter volume that prompted Federal troops to close the print shop and destroy some stocks of the books in 1865.

In places, the tone and diction of these little primers does make the modern scholar reflect that perhaps the cause of reading is almost as lost as the cause of the Confederacy. Consider this example, from *Our Own Fourth Reader*, and bear in mind that it was intended for elementary school pupils: "The special purpose we have had in view in the preparation of this volume is to facilitate the acquisition of the art of reading; while at the same time we have sought to plant the precious seeds of virtue, and to cherish and protect them in their growth, and to supply the means of moral culture, to enrich the mind with useful knowledge by making it familiar with noble sentiments and elegant diction, and to bring it into communion with many of those master spirits, that have by their works, most adorned and elevated English literature."

Schoolchildren weren't the only Southerners reading during the war. Educated people continued to read for pleasure, and the favorite novel of the period by far was *Les Miserables* — although in some of the Southern editions, Victor Hugo's passages about slavery were censored. The novels of Sir Walter Scott also had tremendous appeal. Their sagas of bigger-than-life chivalry were, perhaps, a reflection of how the South desperately wanted to view its soldiers and its cause.

Poetry poured forth by the ream. Most of it, to modern tastes, is quite dreadful, wallowing in thick Victorian sentimentality, mawkish rhyme, ornate and lead-footed conceits, and callow, drum-beating jingoism. Little of it aspired to a higher level than the sort of greeting-card verse which adorned, along with smudgy engravings of banners and cannons, the envelopes sold in Confederate stationery shops and post offices:

> *Men of the South, arise, arise,*
> *Hurl back the invading foe!*
> *The sunny land must — aye — be free,*
> *Tho blood of thousands flow.*

Shall we worship only God,
To a despot bend the knee?
No! No! Men of the South arise,
And swear you will be free![3]

All things considered, the Confederate postal service functioned with remarkable consistency in North Carolina throughout the war. The major problem was that the South did not have — astonishingly — a single paper factory until after the war began. Existing stocks of stationery and envelopes ran out by the autumn of 1861, and the mail thereafter came in a variety of homemade containers. Old envelopes were turned inside-out and recycled; letters were written on the end-papers of books, wrapping paper, and frequently on the backs of wallpaper scraps.

Official Confederate stamps were first issued in October 1861, but supplies were inadequate. Once they were used up, the process of restocking them from the central warehouse in Richmond was glacial at best. Most North Carolina postmasters simply hand-cancelled the letters or made up private stamps.

Postal riders, on horseback or in buggies, made their rounds thrice weekly. They were contract personnel who had to pay for their own and their mounts' upkeep out of a yearly salary of $500. For business transactions — the transport of money, contracts, bonds, and stock certificates — there were private express companies, much like the ones that exist today, which charged a higher rate for faster and more secure service. They were frowned upon by the authorities in Richmond, but since a great deal of the Confederacy's daily business was transacted with their help, they were tolerated.

People could live, however inconveniently, without a postal service, but they couldn't live without food. Food — or the lack of it — soon became the overriding obsession of every North Carolinian, rich or poor, rural or city-dwelling.

The first items that vanished, and stayed vanished for the duration of the war, were sugar, salt, coffee, and tea. A few months after these things disappeared, other staples, too, became hard to find. They became increasingly rare and costly as the war dragged on: meat, wheat bread, condiments of any kind, even milk.

The shortages were followed, though, by a remarkable spirit of resiliency and creative improvisation. People experimented with substitutes and ersatz concoctions, and when any of these experiments turned out to be remotely palatable, they would be formalized into recipes, given cute patriotic names, and published in the newspapers or in one of the many widely circulated wartime recipe books. A formula for ersatz coffee originally dreamed up in a kitchen in Louisiana would become the latest food-fad in Raleigh six weeks later. The object of all this experimentation was to create something that looked, smelled, and tasted as close to the real McCoy as possible. Great ingenuity — not to mention tolerance — was employed to create the illusion that a gustatory sow's ear was in fact a silk purse to the palate.

Pork, long a staple of the North Carolina diet, was the first meat to become scarce in the state. Hog fodder was being diverted to other uses, there were not enough men to butcher and cure the hogs, and there was no salt to preserve the meat properly. Beef, on the other hand, was no problem for the first year or so of the war. Large quantities were still imported from Tennessee, Kentucky, and the Mississippi region. But after those areas were either lost or cut off from the Confederacy, beef, too, became a scarce and expensive commodity. By 1864, families that managed to find an ounce of meat per day, of any kind, considered themselves fortunate.

In North Carolina, fish and fowl became the commonest sources of meat. More exotic items, such as oysters, were available only at exorbitant cost. One oyster substitute concocted in the Wilmington area consisted of egg, green corn, butter, pepper, and salt (if available), all whipped together into a batter and then fried.

North Carolina was lucky in one respect: Because of the long coastline, there was considerable fishing in the eastern counties before the war, and the shortages of seines, nets, and traps — all items which had been imported from the North before the conflict — was not as critical in the state as it was in other areas.

Another food group that quickly became scarce were the fats: butter, mayonnaise, lard, oils of various kinds. The butter shortage was the most galling of all. Amazingly, for an agricultural society, the South had paid little attention to butter production during antebellum times, preferring to import "the good stuff" from the North. The small amounts of butter that North Carolina housewives could produce was often rancid and had to be sweetened with something before it was palatable. Oil made from sunflower seeds achieved a certain popularity, but it took a lot of time and trouble to produce and was, itself, a scarce commodity.

Another problem was the shortage of white sugar. Once the Federals captured the New Orleans area in 1862, the supply of first-class sugar virtually disappeared. Tiny amounts of it got through the blockade, but only the rich and well-connected obtained any by that means.

In the case of sugar, at least, there was a prolific substitute growing throughout the South, both wild and cultivated: sorghum vulgare, a cereal grain, tropical in origin, that had been raised mainly as animal fodder. During the war, it became the sweetening agent for everything from beverages to desserts. Little sorghum mills sprouted all over the Southern landscape. It didn't take much machinery or horsepower to refine the stuff, although every batch was slightly different in taste and consistency. Sorghum was adapted for use in cookies, pies, cakes, jellies, preserves, and syrups — anything, in fact, that had called for white sugar before the war.

In some regions, notably the mountain counties, honey was also employed as a sweetener. Down in the flatlands, other naturally sweet products — persimmons, figs, watermelons — also found a myriad of new uses.

A typical dessert of the time was "molasses pie": flour, sorghum, and walnuts. A snack popular with adults and children alike was "sorghum goobers" — crushed peanuts mixed with a sweetener.

Good flour was usually unobtainable, and even when it could be found, it was exorbitantly expensive. By April 1865, a single barrel of white flour could cost as much as $1,200. Substitutes had to be found for the making of everything from bread to pie crusts. Potato flour gained some popularity, as did rice flour — although bread baked from the latter substance reminded one housewife of "brick bats."[4]

For most baking purposes, the old Southern standby, cornmeal, became the most common flour substitute. North Carolina was fortunate to have a great deal of acreage already allocated for corn. Still, by mid-1864, between the need to ship food to General Lee, the shortage of manpower to cultivate large crops, several spells of bad weather, and the ravages of foragers on both sides, there were large regions, even in North Carolina, where corn was scarce. In some mountain counties, children were sent out to scrounge stray kernels that had fallen from wagons, or that had been left in the feeding troughs used by army horses. When brought home, these filthy handfuls of rock-hard kernels were washed, dried, and ground for food.

At times when cornmeal, too, was unobtainable, numerous attempts were made to concoct dishes based on pea-meal, and even acorns. Unfortunately, these ingredients, no matter how processed or disguised, imparted a thoroughly unpleasant taste to everything they appeared in.

Fresh fruits and vegetables were available only in places where they had been cultivated before the war. Pumpkins, apples, and persimmons were dried and used in cakes, pies, and dishes for which there were no agreed-upon names. Citrus fruits were unobtainable at any price, unless one happened to be good friends with the captain of a blockade runner.

Spices and condiments were always scarce. Ingenious substitutes for flavoring included leaves from peach and cherry trees, and both the petals and leaves from rose bushes.

Next to salt, the one thing North Carolinians missed above all else was coffee. By the fall of 1861, there was no more left in the state, except for small amounts hoarded by private individuals. The lack of a good, hot, cup of coffee just seemed, on some days, a burden on the spirit too great to be borne. When tiny amounts of coffee appeared for sale from the holds of blockade runners, people who were lucky enough to obtain it went to inordinate lengths to stretch it out. Chicory was the most palatable "stretcher" ingredient. (Its use as a flavoring agent for coffee remains popular with some people even today, although it is as much an acquired taste as grits, and to those who dislike it, even more inexplicable.) The truly desperate leavened their precious coffee supplies with ground-up cereal grains or even powdered okra seeds. The latter beverage must have been about as appetizing as a cup of hot motor oil.

A mania for ersatz coffee soon gripped the state, starting in early 1862. New recipes for substitute beverages were swapped between friends like precious family secrets. Many people swore by rye — boiled, dried, ground like coffee beans, and then boiled and served

just like the real thing. "Corn coffee" had its partisans, too —
General J.E.B. Stuart was reportedly fond of it, and that gave it a
certain cachet among the more romantically inclined. Sweet-potato
coffee was also produced, and however it might have tasted as a
beverage, the leftover grounds were reported to be excellent for carpet cleaning. Dandelion roots, corn, parched rice, and cotton seeds
were also occasionally employed as coffee substitutes, with — one
imagines — dramatic gastrointestinal side effects.

Tea had never caught on in North Carolina as coffee had, but tea-
drinkers, too, searched feverishly for substitutes, using willow,
huckleberry, sage, and holly leaves as the basis for their concoctions. In the coastal counties, "yaupon tea" was made by boiling the
leaves and twigs of the yaupon tree, then adding molasses and a little
milk (if available). The medicinal properties of this beverage were
said to be exceptional; less was claimed for the taste.

Whatever "real food" appeared on the open market soared in
price, year by year. This is vividly illustrated by the following table,
based on prices at the Raleigh market:

	1862	1863	1864	1865
Bacon (pound)	$ .33	1.00	5.50	7.50
Beef (pound)	$ .12	.50	2.50	3.00
Pork (pound) . . (variable)	1.60	4.00	5.50	
Sugar (pound)	$ .75	1.00	12.00	30.00
Corn (bushel)	$ 1.10	5.50	20.00	30.00
Meal (bushel)	$ 1.24	5.50	20.00	30.00
Potatoes (bushel)	$ 1.00	4.00	7.00	30.00
Sweet potatoes (bushel) . .	$ 1.50	5.00	6.00	35.00
Wheat (bushel)	$ 3.00	8.00	25.00	50.00
Flour (barrel)	$ 18.00	35.00	125.00	500.00[5]

Despite the shortages and outrageous prices, people made do,
stubbornly, quietly, yet sometimes heroically and with good humor.
Here is what Christmas was like for one North Carolina family in
1864:

> My husband was home from the army on sick leave. It taxed our
> ingenuity, but the little ones [were] not disappointed. He was skilled

in the use of tools and made a cradle for one, a carriage for another, and a cart for the little boy, while I ransacked trunks for odds and ends to make and dress dolls. They were...rag dolls with cheeks painted with poke berries, eyes with indigo, and hair with sumach berries...our pea patch had yielded well, and we had laid by late apples...we had sorghum for candy and cakes. I had bartered a little salt for a dozen eggs...our dinner was frugal. It consisted of rice and peas...and apples. My cake was made of dried cherries, dried whortle-berries, candied watermelon, and sorghum.[6]

Amusements were simpler in those days, as the daughter of a plantation owner in Morrisville recalled:

A while before Christmas hog killing time came on, which was anticipated with almost as much pleasure as Christmas itself, especially among the little folks. You see, that meant a number of bladders to be blown up. Each child, as far as they would go, had a bladder, little colored children and all. These bladders were blown up with a reed quill, and when inflated to the fullest extent were tied tightly with a string and hung up somewhere till Christmas morning, when they were somehow brought in contact with heat, and then such loud reports!...I think the "Bladder Bustin'" on Christmas morning was our biggest and most enjoyable thrill.[7]

Governor Vance and his family tried to set a well-publicized example for the common people by serving numerous substitute and ersatz recipes at the Governor's Palace, but even Zeb drew the line at a coffee substitute made from parched rye and sorghum molasses which he described to one correspondent as "secession in liquid form...."

ANARCHY IN THE PIEDMONT — A WAR WITHIN A WAR

While the larger struggle against the North was raging on the major battlefields, a small, nasty, brother-against-brother conflict was simmering in the middle of North Carolina. There was nothing romantic about it — little, in fact, that did credit to any participant on either side — and it is a curious fact that little research was done into the subject until after the Vietnam era. America's experience with divisiveness in that conflict may have broken down the unwritten taboos governing the way historians treated — or, in this case, chose not to treat — the whole shameful episode.

The site of the disturbances is usually identified in contemporary sources as "Randolph County" or "the Randolph County area," for the simple reason that the largest concentrations of Unionists and deserters always seemed to be active in and around Randolph County. In truth, though, the phrase "Randolph County area" came to mean the whole troubled midsection of the state above Salisbury, comprising not just Randolph County, but also portions of Guilford, Chatham, Moore, Montgomery, Davidson, Alamance, Forsyth, Yadkin, and Davie counties. This area also happens to form part of North Carolina's traditional "Quaker Belt."

In addition to the Quakers, several other European-derived sects in the region also held strong pacifistic, anti-slavery, anti-secessionist beliefs. The Moravian, Lutheran, Dunkard, and German Reformed churches all helped to impart a unique grassroots attitude in these counties. Here, in the middle and upper Piedmont, one finds the "Other South" in miniature — that part of Southern culture and society which dissented from the traditions of slavery and opposed secession with deep and passionate conviction. Less than 10 percent of Randolph County's population (17,000 people, according to the census of 1860) owned slaves. The economic pattern of yeoman farmers, millworkers, and skilled laborers had more in common with New England than with the Deep South. It is no coincidence that the man behind one of the most renowned and effective abolitionist tracts — Hinton Rowan Helper, author of *The Impending Crisis* — was a Davie County native of German descent. Of growing influence in this region, too, was the Wesleyan Methodist movement, an abolitionist sect that had broken away from the parent, northern, Methodists about 15 years before the war. The Wesleyan Methodists were headquartered in Randolph County during the 1850s.

Overt Unionist opposition to the war was put down swiftly in July 1861 and again in March 1862. On the latter occasion, a blustery man named John Helton (or "Hilton," as some sources have it) was holding peace rallies and threatening to lynch prominent local secessionists. The Helton-inspired incidents took place in portions of Randolph and Guilford counties that were efficiently linked to Raleigh by both railroad and telegraph — which meant that any large-scale trouble in those parts could be reported to and countered quickly by the state government. Opponents of the Confederacy learned that lesson, too, and quietly shifted their headquarters to wilder, more remote parts of the region.

After Helton was forced to flee North Carolina in the spring of 1862, leadership of the opposition devolved to two other men: Bryan Tyson and William Owens. Tyson was a pamphleteer and a propagandist who wielded pen instead of sword on behalf of the Union cause; Owens was something else again — the closest thing the Piedmont would see to an actual Unionist guerilla commander.

Tyson (1830-1909) was a modestly prosperous individual who lived just over the Moore County side of the Moore County/Randolph County line. A handsome man gifted with eloquence (he looked a lot like Richard Burton with muttonchop whiskers), Tyson was a genuine grassroots leader, and also a mystic who claimed to have personal conversations with God. Tyson seems to have been chosen more or less spontaneously to be the spokesman for the lower- and lower-middle-class whites who opposed conscription. In his postwar writings, Tyson stressed the passion of pro-Union sentiments in his part of the state: "I was urged to start an opposition movement…I never saw people in so great a state of excitement. All that was lacking was for the stars and stripes to be planted there, with a force sufficient to defend them. [The conscripts] would have enlisted under the banner almost unanimously."[1]

Probably Tyson's most effective political broadside was a treatise entitled *A Ray of Light*, in which he argued most persuasively that the Confederacy was a doomed, arrogant, political aberration whose defeat by the industrial and populous North was inevitable. The only alternative to harsh "Black Republican" rule, Tyson argued, was compromise and the swift conclusion of a peace treaty based on the U.S. Constitution.

Tyson can be viewed either as a courageous idealist or a base traitor, depending on one's sympathies for the Confederate cause, but there is no denying that the man had the courage of his convictions. He wrote many emotional yet closely reasoned letters to Confederate soldiers, urging them to leave the army, come back to North Carolina, and work for the Unionist opposition. Enough men heeded his arguments — or reached his conclusions on their own — to change the balance of political power in the Randolph County area by the end of 1862. The Unionists, augmented by a small but growing number of deserters, became the controlling political faction in many areas of the region.

In an indirect way, President Jefferson Davis and his cronies were among the movement's strongest allies. The Richmond government consistently failed to generate any lasting sense of Confederate nationalism throughout the yeomanry of the South. It was coldly indifferent toward the economic and social needs of the lower class, and at times angered lower-class people with its heavy-handed interference. Together with its blatant, at times quite offensive, kowtowing to the interests of the wealthy plantation bluebloods, these attitudes served to further alienate the mass of dirt-farmers and small-time tradesmen from the Confederate government.

Nothing could have been calculated to offend this vital mass of people more than the abhorred conscription laws of April 1862 — particularly the clause which allowed wealthy people to hire substitutes to bear arms for them. By mid-1863, inflation, taxation, and harsh impressment laws added more burdens to those imposed by the hated conscription acts. Never had the current phrase "a rich man's war and a poor man's fight" seemed more apt, and never had the common man seen less benefit for himself and his family from the continuation of the war.

These feelings were particularly intense in Randolph County. By the end of 1862, almost 25 percent of the troops who had volunteered from Randolph County at the start of the war had deserted and returned home. By contrast, the desertion rate in neighboring Guilford County was only 9 percent, and the rate for the state as a whole was 12 percent.

As early as August 21, 1862, a notice appeared in the *Greensboro Patriot* promising a reward of $30 for information leading to the arrest of 13 deserters — all of whom were from a Randolph County unit. As an index of how rapidly the problem mushroomed, there was another notice in the *Patriot* on October 28, this time listing the names of 78 deserters from Randolph County units.[2]

The men who returned took up the life of an "outlier." The life of a deserter was not easy in any part of the state, but those who fled to the mountains at least had freedom of movement — the sparse population and rough terrain in the mountain counties made it difficult for anyone to come looking for them. The Piedmont section, in general, did not offer such impenetrable cover. However, at this time in its history, it did provide vast tracts of dense, hilly woods, and it was in the leaf-choked gullies and creek-bottom ravines of the forests that the Outliers made their nests. In the Uhwarrie hills, which cover much of western Randolph County, there was enough concealment to hide bands sometimes numbering a hundred or more.

When selecting and constructing their hideouts, the Outliers adopted a trick or two from runaway slaves. Whenever possible, a man would go to earth as close as he dared to friends and family — within walking distance, at any rate. This ensured him a steady supply of food and information. Indeed, during the first year or so of the war, a lot of men were able to spend much of their time indoors, living with family, and they took to their hidey-holes only during a militia sweep or when there were armed Confederate sympathizers in the neighborhood. As conditions deteriorated and the number of deserters increased, however, fewer and fewer men enjoyed such comparative luxury. After late 1862, most Outliers lived either singly or in small bands, almost as troglodytes, in conditions that were bleak and primitive in the extreme.

The best sites for a cave or a dugout were hillsides close to running water. Aside from the sanitation aspects, the running water was useful for washing away the tell-tale traces of dirt left over from digging. If there was no stream nearby, the leftover dirt was loaded into buckets or sacks and dragged out into the woods, where it was scattered evenly at a great distance from the cave's actual location.

These spider-hole dwellings were elaborately camouflaged to blend in with their surroundings. Usually they could be entered only through a narrow trap door covered with brush, leaves, and dead wood. Some dwellings were large enough for two or three men and even had a small fireplace, although great care had to be taken to burn only dry, relatively smokeless materials. To mask the smokey scent of their own hearths, the cave-dwellers often placed dead trees near the entrance and burned them until the logs and the surrounding ground was black and charred — so that the place appeared to have been visited by a wildfire. For additional protection, whole trees were sometimes dragged over the trap doors, leaving just enough room for one man to wriggle out. That way, no one could accidentally step on the entrance and discover what was beneath. Time and time again, during the Confederate government's sweeps through the area, militia patrols passed within ten feet of such dwellings and did not spot them.

For food, the Outliers relied on their own trapping skills (and hunting skills, too, if conditions permitted them to fire a gun), and on the generosity of sympathetic friends and family. Most families who trafficked with Outliers had their own codes — yells, whistles, hog calls, the banging together of pots and pans — which would alert their men in the woods to the presence of danger. For Outliers who did not dwell within earshot of a "safe house," other signals were devised. A certain color quilt hung over the clothesline might signal "Danger, keep away!", while another piece of linen might signify "All clear!".

For all the ingenuity that went into making these primitive dwellings habitable and hard to find, existence inside them must have been unspeakably wretched. Ice-cold tombs during the winter, sump holes full of red-clay muck during the spring and autumn rains, suffocatingly close and muggy during the summer, the caves were a refuge of desperation, a place for hunted men to crouch in fear. It is little wonder that so many of the men who were forced to live in this manner became wild, violent, and maybe a little crazy.

Naturally, the growing presence of such men exacerbated the already tense situation in the area. Pro-Confederate families and groups treated the Unionists, and especially the deserters, with contempt, anger, and finally with violence. The deserters and the Unionists naturally banded together against this coercion. They were increasingly organized and usually as well-armed as their opponents (if not better, since many deserters brought back new Enfield rifles, while most of the Home Guard* and vigilante bands were armed with old smooth-bore muskets and fowling pieces). When pushed, they began to push back.

Secessionist versus Unionist...the Piedmont conflict turned into a microcosm of the vaster civil war raging all around it. As with all partisan campaigns, however, it had elements of personalized cruelty which were absent from the battlefields where the main armies clashed. The Outliers and their Unionist allies referred to the pro-Confederates simply as "Secesh," while the pro-Confederates had a whole string of pejorative labels for their adversaries: "Lincolnites," "Outlaws," "Tories," and "Bushwhackers" are among the more common and printable ones.

There was never any common political cause, in the sense of an overriding "umbrella" ideology, between the Outliers who were strongly pro-Union to begin with and the men who were simply battlefield deserters (although a drafted pro-Union man usually showed up sooner or later as a deserter). All they really had in common was disaffection with the Confederate cause and a desire to defend themselves in an increasingly hostile environment.

Farms and homes of Outlier men were often kept under surveillance, either by secessionist neighbors or by militia men detached for that duty. As the war dragged on and the troubles in the Piedmont increased, surveillance grew tighter and opportunities to smuggle food to the men in the forest became few. Cut off from their supplies, and unable to provide for themselves by raising crops or by hiring out for wages, the Outliers survived the only way they could: by taking what they needed from their pro-Confederate neighbors. The matriarch of one well-to-do Randolph County farm came up with a novel scheme to protect the family's livestock from such foraging parties:

> ...it didn't take me long to figure out how to put a stop to that sort of stock-rustling. I called little Yancey [Cox — 15-year-old son], put him on a horse and told him to ride like mad to every Negro family in our circle and tell them to come here tonight by dusk, every one of them, and without fail, and within two hours he was back with their promise they'd be here.
>
> By dusk they came, about one hundred of them, thirteen families in all, excited, and wondering what in the world had happened; and when they had all bunched around me, I said, "I've lost twenty horses and fifty steers all in a day, and by tomorrow night [they] may take everything I've got. Now I've got a plan figured out, and if you will all help me with it we can save the plantation from ruin. I want each family of you to take home with you tonight a portion of my livestock and fowls and hide them out the best way you know; and take feed and grain to feed them, till the war is over; and when the war ends, you may keep one-half of everything you saved, for your very own."
>
> Well, sir, they jumped on it like a duck on a June bug...there was no sleeping that night. The Negro families shuttled back and forth, the men handling the stock, the women catching the fowls, and the children carrying chickens and turkeys in their arms. Grain was hauled and parceled out, and the smokehouse meat was stashed in strange places; and, finally, the tail end of the herd was driven to the back pastures to begin starving, so they would soon "look too poar" to even be wanted by the foragers.[3]

A cycle of violence settled in, a pattern as old as mankind and as fresh to modern readers as memories of the Vietnam War. Troops and posses sent out to scour the countryside for deserters were ambushed and robbed by the Outliers; in retaliation, more troops were sent in; unable to find the Outliers, the troops often vented their frustration by burning the Outliers' families' farms and houses, destroying or stealing their crops, and — in a shamefully high percentage of cases — raping the womenfolk in the bargain. Children were threatened and slapped around; grandfathers were beaten and tortured into revealing the hiding places of Outliers or family valuables. One method of interrogation that appealed to the vigilantes was to strip the pants from a captive and dangle him, bottom first, over a campfire until he talked.

Atrocity begat atrocity. Soon, pro-Confederate families were visited by night-riders intent on perpetrating retaliatory horrors. The spiral of fear and violence wound tighter and tighter. By the middle of 1863, the whole region simmered on the edge of bloody anarchy.

It was this escalation of violence that probably shifted leadership of the militant pro-Unionists from the scholarly Bryan Tyson to the dour William Owens, as grim a partisan figure as any cast up by the times. Owens, himself a deserter, owned a little farm just below the Randolph-Moore County line. From the fragmentary records that exist, it appears that he first took to the field at the head of a band of armed men in late 1862, spurred to this extreme by the enactment of new, harsh, conscription laws. The new laws would, for the first time, take men over 40 years of age — in other words, the only men still capable of running the family farms and providing for the families of the men who had been swept up by the earlier waves of conscription.

During the early period when they had momentum as well as ferocity on their side, Owens and his men held the pro-Confederate population virtually at ransom throughout much of Moore and Randolph counties. Militia men, Confederate agents, and prominent secessionist citizens were kidnapped, terrorized, and forced to swear oaths of loyalty to Abe Lincoln. One Moore County deserter, writing only a short time after he had arrived back home, left this account in a letter:

> It looks like there will be bad times in this county...Col. W. Owines [sic] and his company are taking the secesh prisoners and making them take the oath as Union men...they took Peter [Shamburger — a militia officer] and kupt him a day or two and paroled him and sent him home[.] he wont tell any thing about it at all. If he does death is his portion...you can't get a man to say he is a secessionist hear now.[4]

Another, more chilling, account of conditions in the Randolph County area appears in a letter found in the correspondence files of Governor Vance. Written in January 1863 by a Mr. James Dunn, from Little River in south-central Randolph County, the account is made even more vivid by the struggles of its ill-educated author to express what he had seen:

> But oh if you knew our Condition here you would say may the good Lord deliver them...men have been shot...some Beat [so badly] that Life has been Despaired of...Property taken Barns and Fences Burned and we tak[en] from our Familys as Prisoners and Compeled by threats not to talk nor act in any way against the Out laws...[militia lieutenant] B. Prissly was Beat till Life was Despaired of...and last week his house [was] attacked the Windows Broken [and] his Wife maimed by a rock thrown and his...Barn and Grain Burned and his house Plundered...this is only a very small part of what is going on....[5]

Governor Vance found it repugnant to resort to force of arms against fellow North Carolinians, but finally had no choice except to send troops into the area. A sweep was launched in September 1862, aimed at rounding up the deserters and draft-dodgers and returning them to duty. Two companies of regular Confederate Army troops provided the spine for a force otherwise comprised of militia units from Chatham, Randolph, and Moore counties. This force beat the bushes for two months without bagging more than a handful of suspects and without disturbing the organized bands of Outliers in the slightest. Like modern-day guerrillas, the Outliers had just faded into the woods at the first sign of an approaching force. A second expedition in February 1863, this time with cavalry, covered an even wider spread of territory, but with equally disappointing results.

By the summer of that year, the clamor of pro-Confederate families for protection had risen to a roar. Loyal Confederates in the Randolph County zone were virtually at the mercy of the armed bands that roamed their countryside. Typical of the accounts reaching Governor Vance was this one:

> A few nights ago twenty or thirty [Outliers] entered on the premises of an aged and respectable citizen of [Moore County] roused him from his slumbers, presented guns at his door and windows and said they would blow his brains out if he put his head out, forced the locks of his smoke house and corn crib, and robbed him of nearly all his bacon and a quantity of corn.[6]

This kind of wide-open pillage was bad enough, but citizens who organized against the Outliers, or who complained to the Confederate authorities, faced much worse. The next visit from the night-riders would result in barns and even homes being put to the torch. People who gave the partisans too much trouble were often the victims of brutal assassinations — a farmer riding down a lonely country road would be cut down by a volley from the nearby woods, or simply pegged in the back by a single well-placed sniper round.

A surviving letter from one of the militia commanders even says, flat-out: "Governor Vance sent a company of infantry up there [Randolph County] and they were completely whipped out..."[7], which certainly sounds like something bigger than common bushwhacking. Although there is no mention of such a battle in the official records, "we are left with the slight possibility that an embarrassing defeat of troops by deserters was covered up by the Vance administration sometime in the winter of '62 or January of 1863," according to William Auman, the historian who has done more than any other to bring these matters to light.[8]

In late April 1863, Vance applied to General D.H. Hill for help in restoring order. He needed regular troops, he claimed, because the deserter bands in Randolph County were so well armed that they "can lick my militia in a fair fight" — another hint that some sort of pitched battle might have taken place soon before.

Vance's dilemma was compounded by the fact that when he had sent militia companies after the guerrillas, the militiamen had tended to behave just as abominably as the men they were hunting. The wives and children of Outliers had been bullied, raped, beaten, and robbed; horses and fodder had been stolen; and civilians had been illegally impressed to serve the needs of the troops. Accounts reached Vance's desk of one particularly brutal group of militia who went to isolated Outliers' houses night after night, forced their way in at gunpoint, then gang-raped the wives and daughters.

It was not until late that summer that regular troops could be spared to cope with the deteriorating situation. By then, the whole region was a powder keg. Large numbers of new, bitter deserters had arrived in the area following the defeat at Gettysburg. By September, Vance estimated that there were at least 1,100 armed, organized, Outliers in the Moore-Randolph-Chatham County border area alone. So bold had Owens and his fellow partisans become that they were launching hit-and-run raids against jails where conscription resisters were being held. After shooting it out with the guards, they would free the detainees inside and thus swell their ranks even more.

Richmond, finally, was forced to act — faced, as it now seemed to be, with what amounted to open insurrection in the middle of a strategically vital part of the South. General Robert Hoke's brigade was ordered to entrain for the Piedmont. Thus began a five-month campaign that ranged from the edge of Wilkes and Yadkin counties all the way to the eastern borders of Chatham and Moore counties.

While there were no pitched battles — the Outliers wisely avoided the superior numbers and firepower of Hoke's columns — there were scores of sharp little skirmishes, mostly between Confederate patrols and bands of bushwhackers. While Hoke's men behaved with a degree of restraint, as befits real soldiers, the Home Guard units called out to assist them did not. Instead, they used the protective proximity of regular Confederate units as an excuse to settle a lot of old scores. More homes and fields were burned, more property stolen, more women abused, more children traumatized. The cycle of violence went on unabated, acquiring a terrible vitality of its own.

Some individuals became famous for their lethal efficiency as man-hunters. Two of the most notorious were Adam Brewer and Peter Garner. Brewer had been robbed a number of times by bands of deserters and seems to have been driven by motives of personal revenge more than political conviction. "This man Brewer does not belong to the servis [sic]. This is just a voluntary act to hunt down his neighbors and kill them," said one contemporary observer.[9] Garner was probably the most feared of the pair. He was described by one who had seen him in action as a "brute of a man...because he hunted down every possible recruit, he got to be called 'The Hunter.' He was hated by everybody, but detested and feared by the women of the community. He wore a big gun and a knife on his belt, and a rope hung from under his coat. He was so brazen that he walked right in without knocking and used the same language to men and women alike...I tell you, if I had been a man I believe I would have shot him down like a beef."[10]

The same witness left an account of The Hunter in action: "The very next day [Garner] discovered two young men who had slipped home from the war to see their recent brides. [He arrested them and tied them behind his horse] yelling to neighbors as he passed that they were Quakers hiding out from the war. About three miles down the road, he dragged them with his horse toward Buffalo Ford on Deep River, where the two young men were blindfolded, shot in the back, and left dying in the middle of the road...it was learned later that these two young men had once before slipped home for two days and had voluntarily gone back to their units to fight. Also, they were found not to be Quakers....”[11]

Garner and Brewer often formed a team, leading Confederate detachments into the hills and sometimes commanding their own small forces. On one such mission, they lured a one-armed man named McDonald into the woods, then made sport by seeing how many times they could shoot him without actually killing him. His screams and pleas for mercy could be heard a long distance away, but no one dared venture into the underbrush to stop the atrocity. From the number of bullet holes in the corpse, and the wild arabesques of bloody footprints in the dirt, it was apparent to those who buried him that he had been a long time dying.

In December 1864, Garner and his men rounded up two dozen teenaged boys, including 15-year-old Yancey Cox, tied them in a line like slaves, and propelled them with flicks of a bullwhip to the impressment agency in Asheboro.

From Asheboro, the boys were marched almost 250 miles to a post near Wilmington. After several days of harsh imprisonment, they managed to escape. Following an amazing odyssey along back-country lanes and across rivers on homemade rafts, the boys made it back to their old neighborhood and went into hiding. When The Hunter got wind of their presence, he resolved to bring them in dead or alive.

The boys acted first. They drew straws and chose three of their number as an ambush party, including Yancey Cox. Each lad took a musket, double-charged it with powder, crammed the barrel with no less than four lead balls, and then waited for Garner near the spot where he went out every morning to inspect his fish traps.

On this particular morning, though, Garner had his seven-year-old daughter with him. This made the boys reluctant to shoot. Garner and his daughter were forced to separate, however, in order to cross in single file a log that spanned the creek. Two of the boys fired simultaneously, hitting The Hunter with several balls. Then they ran up to where he lay dying in the middle of the stream and cut the brass buttons off his coat for souvenirs.

The Hunter's sometime-partner, Adam Brewer, was more fortunate — he appears to have survived the war.

Although there are no official records to back up the legend, there is a strong regional tradition about a black manhunter who tracked deserters in the Uhwarries and is said to have killed at least one man, near Dark Mountain. If true, it's an irony within irony...a Negro, armed as a Confederate auxiliary, stalking and killing men who were almost certainly abolitionist in their convictions.[12]

While Hoke's brigade was in the area, militant Unionist activity naturally dropped off. But as soon as that force withdrew in February 1864, the Outliers came out of hiding and resumed the pattern of violence as though Hoke had never been there. The most active band was still led by William Owens, who had survived some narrow escapes.

In April, however, Owens's luck ran out. A group of militia officers led by Colonel Alfred Pike learned the location of Owens's camp by brutally torturing the information out of his wife. Pike and his men cornered Mrs. Owens while she was washing her laundry at a spring. When the armed men surrounded her, Mrs. Owens snatched up her 12-month-old child and angrily cursed Pike and his vigilantes. Pike slapped her repeatedly until she put down the infant, then turned her over to some of his men who had been leering at the woman and promising they could make her talk.

First they hung Mrs. Owens by her thumbs, with her toes just grazing the ground. When this delicate treatment failed to loosen her tongue, she was cut down and dragged some distance. Then Pike and another man crushed some of her fingers between a couple of fence rails. That did the trick.

When Governor Vance heard of this atrocity, he asked Judge Thomas Settle, a respected state solicitor, to investigate. After interviewing Pike and some of his men, Judge Settle sent a detailed account to Vance. Far from being ashamed of his brutality, Pike seemed to relish every detail of it. When Settle criticized him for his cruelty, Pike shot back: "...if I have not the right to treat Bill Owens, his wife and the like in this manner, I want to know it! I will go to the Yankees...before I will live in a country where I cannot treat such people in this manner!"

On the day after the torture of Mrs. Owens, a posse headed by the sheriff of Randolph County mounted a surprise attack on Owens's camp and captured him. He was never successfully brought to trial, however, because the men and women who could have testified against him were too afraid to open their mouths — some of Owens's men were still at large and the word had gone out that anyone who spoke against him was as good as dead. Since the authorities, with good reason, feared an attempt by the Outliers to break Owens out of jail, it was decided to remove him to a safer location, in the pro-Confederate village of Pittsboro. There he was left to rot in jail until the final weeks of the war, when a mob broke into his cell, dragged him into the street, and lynched him.

Predictably, the election of 1864 served to turn up the heat on the Randolph County front. Governor Vance sent Home Guard detachments to secure the polling places in Randolph, Moore, Montgomery, and Chatham counties, but the worst violence took place after election day when the vote totals were published.

Naturally, the Outlier bands had supported the peace candidate, William Holden, and great was their outrage when their man got skunked at the ballot box. Only two days after the elections, a band of deserters ambushed a squad of poll guards near Carthage, killing three of them. A similar ambush near Franklinville a few days later killed four more militiamen — graybeards from the Senior Reserves. Rumors abounded that a mass of deserter troops was prepared to march on Carthage, the county seat of Moore County, and put the whole town to the torch. Militia reinforcements were hastily thrown in a ring around the town until the threat evaporated.

Reports of this new level of violence alarmed Vance. So did a report he had just received from John Worth, an Asheboro citizen who happened to be the brother of the state treasurer. Worth estimated that fully one-half of the entire Randolph-Moore-Montgomery County area was controlled, day and night, by armed desperadoes. Vance wearily organized his third major sweep against the internal enemy. This time he mobilized no fewer than 11 Home Guard battalions under the supreme commander of the North Carolina Home Guard, a most interesting character named General Collett Leventhorpe.

Born in Exmouth, England, Leventhorpe was a trained British

officer, a licensed physician, and a published author. Lured to the New World in 1842, he resigned his commission in the 14th Regiment of Foot and became a gentleman farmer in North Carolina in the late 1840s. He was a more zealous Confederate than most Confederates, and he served ardently as a colonel in the 11th North Carolina Regiment. Wounded and captured at Gettysburg, he was later paroled. Some months after his parole expired, he accepted Vance's commission. He did about as much with the raw material of the Home Guards as any man could have, although he seems to have shared his men's attitude that deserters and Unionists deserved whatever ill treatment they got. Leventhorpe survived the war, lived in pastoral contentment in Happy Valley, and died there in 1889, after a life crowded with color and excitement.

Leventhorpe mounted his two-week campaign from his headquarters in Asheboro. His Home Guard units treated the civilians in pro-Union districts with remarkable roughness. Wives, children, and grandparents were herded into makeshift prisons and fed nothing but bread and water until they divulged information about their Outlier menfolk. At least, that was what happened to the luckier ones. One militia soldier described such an operation in a letter written from Asheboro, August 29, 1864:

> ...we marchet 16 miels an back yesterday...the desrtrs shot in our men an kild one an hit a nother one in the under gaw We ar taking the fathers of the Desertrs to the Camp an trete them as prisners untill that send for ther suns to relece them. we are taking property too...we bring wiming [women] to the camp that has husbins in the wodes tell thea [till they] send for them an bring them in[.] that is the best way to Cetch them.[13]

Many barbarous incidents were witnessed and reported, some by eminent Confederate citizens who were appalled at the behavior of their own militia. Judge Thomas Settle, in tones of measured outrage, reported to Governor Vance: "I found in Chatham, Randolph, and Davidson that some fifty women in each county...some of them in delicate health and far advanced in pregnancy...were rudely dragged from their homes & put under close guard & kept there for some weeks. The consequences in some instances have been shocking. Women have been frightened into abortion under the eyes of their terrifiers."[14]

Confederate Congressman James Madison Leach had seen enough to summon both gorge and anger in his report: "...the choking and dragging some hundred yards on the ground of an old lady, skinning her knees and hips until they bled...insulting delicate women with children at their breast, cursing them and their little ones for asking for bread after having been arrested and held for days...following women [who were] obeying the calls of nature, taunting them, hissing obscene language, seizing another and dragging her by the arms and head...eating up and wasting & destroying what little that a deserter's wife or child or mother may have...some of the arresting soldiers themselves — men of property[,] character and intelligence — have detailed to me instances of horror and brutality that they were made to participate in that no decent man can contemplate without burning indignation."[15]

One vividly succinct summary of this campaign came from a soldier named Welborn who was attached to the Confederate Conscript Office. After witnessing the beating of a 76-year-old man whose son was known to be with the Outliers, Welborn wrote that, while he was all in favor of rounding up the deserters, "we can do it without such measures...surely God will not smile on such doings."[16]

There was resistance, and a number of Home Guardsmen and Outliers were killed in brisk skirmishes. Brutal or not, the oppressive tactics of Leventhorpe's expedition enabled him to obtain better results than any previous "search and destroy" mission: some 300 deserters were rounded up. But that was the only lasting result; the situation began to deteriorate again only days after the expeditionary force had disbanded.

As especially vile atrocity took place in January 1865, when three abolitionist brothers — Wesleyan Methodists named William, John, and Jesse Hulin — were captured near Dark Mountain in Montgomery County and shot down in cold blood. There is a well-preserved common grave for the three brothers in the cemetery of Lovejoy United Methodist Church in northern Montgomery County; the headstone bears the names, the dates, and a stark, one-word epitaph: "Murdered."

By the spring of 1865, many pro-Confederate families had simply given up and moved out of the contested area altogether. The bloodletting went on without cease during the war's last months. Militant

Unionists and armed deserters roamed almost at will, stealing whatever they wanted, terrorizing old enemies, and lighting the night sky with the flames of burning houses.

Desperate though he was for men, Robert E. Lee detached 500 veteran troops in March 1865 and sent them to the Randolph County area to protect the rail line and supply depots in the vicinity of Greensboro. Marse Robert gave his men unusually severe orders. The deserters, he said, "cannot be too sternly dealt with." This time, arriving by rail, the Confederates were on the scene too suddenly for the Outliers to vanish as utterly as they had on previous occasions. About a hundred deserters were caught and several were slain in sharp little firefights that flickered from one end of Randolph County to the other. One of those killed, oddly enough, was a former Federal cavalryman who had joined the Outliers. He was tied to a tree in Asheboro and executed by firing squad.

The recurring disturbances in the Piedmont were both a civil war and a guerilla war, combining the most vicious properties of both. Despite six military operations mounted to clean out the area, vast tracts of the region existed in states of near-total anarchy for months, even years, at a time. The postwar assertion by the Confederates that they had merely been fighting "bandits" and "outlaws" falls far short of explaining what really happened, and the Confederates' own barbarous behavior makes their self-righteous condemnations of the Outliers seem extremely hypocritical. In truth, there was plenty of blame to spread around on both sides. No one — with the possible exception of the philosophical and nonviolent Bryan Tyson — emerges from the historical record of these dirty little campaigns with any hero's laurels to brag about.

How many died in this war-within-a-war? The official records from units involved in the various "search and destroy" expeditions list 73 fatalities on both sides, but most of the killing did not take place during those sweeps. Instead, it took place on dark country lanes and in the yards of isolated farms, and none of the backwoods bushwhacking and midnight assassinations ever made it into any official records. An educated guess would put the real number of violent deaths somewhere between 250 and 400. The number of wounded is even harder to guess. On top of the outright casualties, of course, were the emotional and psychological scars from this fratricidal period that did not begin to fade until well into the 20th century.

Anyone who studies these sanguine and shameful events must conclude that the Randolph County War was one of the sorriest episodes in North Carolina history.

*The terms "Home Guard" and "militia" are used interchangeably, for by decree on July 7, 1863, the Home Guard was created from the old state militia system. Militia officers had been exempted from the draft at Governor Vance's insistence, so they simply changed designations, not jobs. The rank and file of the old militia units, however, had been thoroughly combed out by earlier waves of conscription, so the ranks of the Home Guard were mostly filled with men 45 years of age or older.

North Carolina's 'Andersonville' — The Prison At Salisbury

Ill-prepared for war in nearly every way, both the Union and the Confederacy were equally unprepared to cope with the practical matter of prisoners of war. First of all, it was generally assumed that, whoever won, the war would not last long enough for prisoners to accumulate in large numbers. Second, the moral and physical dimensions of the problem, and its potential to generate human suffering, were but dimly and remotely perceived — as, indeed, were all the horrors of war.

"War," to most Americans in the mid-19th century, was something that had taken place far away in barbarous Mexico in 1846, or something that had happened to Grandfather back in 1812 (and that Gramps had spent the next 40 years romanticizing). For most people, the sheer ghastliness of armed conflict came as a hideous shock. And for the incomplete, overtaxed, and frequently incompetent administrative bureaucracy trying to run the show in Richmond, the peripheral aspects of waging total war presented challenges that overwhelmed both tangible resources and good intentions.

In the early months of the War Between the States, prisoners were regularly and speedily paroled. That is, they would sign a paper agreeing not to bear arms for a certain length of time after their release from captivity. Once some sort of official exchange of parolees was worked out (*x* number of Confederates for *y* number of Federals), the parole restrictions were rendered null and void, and the repatriated men could again take up arms. On the Union side, many men chose not to return to the fight. On the Confederate side, the newly exchanged man usually had no choice — he either returned to combat duty or took his chances as a deserter.

The end result of the parole arrangement was that Federal generals found themselves fighting and capturing the same rebel soldiers more than once. On the Union side, there was no manpower shortage for the long haul, so the redeployment of former POWs was a marginal matter. For the South, however, paroled veterans were a major source of experienced soldiers. As soon as the Federals realized that this gentlemanly scheme was benefitting the other side more than their own, and was in fact prolonging the war, the whole system started to come unglued. Eventually, it was abandoned altogether. It was at this point that being a prisoner of war became not a temporary inconvenience but rather a deadly serious matter.

One of the cruel ironies of the Civil War was that it was the Union's choice to end the parole-exchange system, in the summer of 1864; and yet it was the Federal prisoners who suffered the most from that decision. By that stage of the war, the South simply did not have the resources to cope with the added burden of a permanent POW population. There was never a deliberate policy of cruelty and deprivation with regard to Yankee prisoners, but such an impression was created, and persists to a certain extent, to the present day. Clearly, there were sadists and incompetents involved in the Confederate POW effort (the program does not deserve to be dignified with the word "system"). But it can also be proven that there were men of decent impulse and Christian ethics who did whatever was within their power to treat their charges humanely.

The exchange of captured soldiers was codified in July 1862 in a policy known as the Dix-Hill Cartel. It was so named because it came about from the discussions between Federal Major John A. Dix and Confederate (then Major) D.H. Hill. Both officers drew up the protocols of their policy after a detailed study of the POW arrangement worked out with the British during the War of 1812.

The Dix-Hill Cartel was implemented rapidly and thoroughly. By the end of the summer of 1862, both sides had almost entirely divested themselves of their accumulated POWs. In fact, the only prisoners still behind the walls of the Salisbury Prison in North Carolina between July 1862 and October 1864 were deserters, political prisoners, and men charged with criminal offenses.

The Dix-Hill protocols, however, showed signs of strain within a year when reports reached Washington that the Confederates were treating captured Negro soldiers as runaway slaves. This appears to have been true only in a small number of cases where the captured Negroes really were runaway slaves, but it was enough to cloud the hitherto clear-cut moral atmosphere of the Dix-Hill Cartel. By the late autumn of 1863, the whole system had ceased to work except sporadically, and commanders on both sides predicted that it would soon be repudiated altogether.

Acting on a suggestion from General Robert E. Lee, Confederate Secretary of War Seddon issued orders to erect a large POW stockade in a location sufficiently far from the front to minimize the temptation to escape. This directive resulted in the construction of a primitive enclosure in rural Georgia called Camp Sumter by the Confederates, but known to history by the more infamous name of the town near which it was built: Andersonville. All Union soldiers captured on the Virginia front between late February and late August 1864 were sent to Andersonville. When the camp filled to overflowing, they were sent to the jails in and around Richmond. When Richmond could absorb no more, they were sent to the prison in Salisbury, North Carolina.

By 1860, Salisbury was the biggest town in the western Piedmont and, with a population of 2,500, the fifth-largest "city" in the state. It was the only site in the state with a prison camp, and that was due to simple chance.

Early in the war, on July 8, 1861, the Richmond government canvassed several states to find some existing facility that could be turned into a POW camp quickly and cheaply. Governor Clark (who had assumed office only one day before the matter landed on his desk), sent out a commission to survey the state. Greensboro and Hillsborough were considered first, but no suitable facilities could be located in those towns. A good location was scouted in Alamance, but the property owner refused to sell it for the proffered amount of compensation. Finally, the commission reported finding "a very large and commodious building" in Salisbury, one which could be had for a very reasonable $15,000. The deal was not closed until November 2, 1861, due mainly to the difficulty of finding enough guards to staff the place.

Known locally as "The Old Cotton Mill," the structure had actually been a yarn factory from 1839, when it was built, until 1847, when it was driven out of business — a steam-powered operation, it could not compete with the water-powered mills of New England. At the time it was sold to the Confederacy, it housed an obscure and impecunious Presbyterian prep school called the Salisbury Male Academy. About $6,000 to $7,000 worth of repairs and additions were needed before the place could be opened for business as a prison.

The main mill building was a sturdy brick structure of four stories (three full-sized floors and a narrower attic floor that came to a peak), topped rather incongruously by a cupola-shaped belfry. Nearby stood three other substantial brick buildings, formerly used to house the factory's employees. After the Confederate government bought the place, another 15 or so buildings of various sizes were erected to house the commandant and his staff, the commissary, the quartermaster department, and the garrison of guards. The yard surrounding the factory buildings was actually a rather pleasant spot in the beginning, with numerous groves of handsome oak trees and lots of lush green grass. One prisoner who stayed there in early 1862 later wrote that the prison reminded him of nothing more sinister than the well-appointed campus of a small college.

But it was, after all, a prison, and it was defined as such by its enclosing palisade. This wall was 12 feet high and surmounted by a catwalk paced by sentries, day and night. One Federal prisoner remembered how the sentries' pacing, which was clearly audible at night after the yard had grown quiet, seemed to measure off the passing of time. He could "distinctly hear the steady tramp, tramp, tramp of the rebel guards as they walked their beats, eagerly wishing for a chance to distinguish themselves by shooting a Yank. I could hear them cry out in genuine southern dialect: 'Post number f-o-a-h; foah o'clock, and all is well!'"*

On December 9, 1861, the new prison received its first inmates: 120 men who had been kept, until that time, on the State Fair

Grounds in Raleigh. The total inmate population rose to 300 by the end of the year, and by the summer of 1862, it had filled out to about 1,500 men. Since the prison compound offered nearly six acres of space, and since the official capacity had been set at 2,500, conditions were not too bad.

That impression is borne out by POW accounts of those early days. There was room to stroll around and socialize under the trees; there was ample, if spartan, food; and the guards were not nearly as vindictive and trigger-happy as they became after the South started losing the war. There was even a makeshift theater, complete with homemade curtains and footlights, where the inmates mounted amateur productions and held lectures. There was also, for a period of several months, a camp newspaper entitled *The Stars and Stripes in Rebeldom.* Some historians cite it as an ancestor of the *Stars and Stripes* that would become so familiar to 20th-century American soldiers in the world wars.

The most famous illustration of life in the Salisbury camp during this period is probably the earliest depiction of a 19th-century baseball game. Weather permitting, baseball was played on a daily basis in the prison courtyard. The picture shows everyone having a grand ol' time, romping around in a clean, airy, pastoral setting. The guards are shown not as threatening figures, but as smiling, benign spectators.

This same courtyard, two years later, would be a cesspool of human misery — a literal hellhole whose stench, when the wind was right, offended the nostrils of people a mile away. The pastoral oak trees were among the first casualties, chopped down for firewood.

The prison was emptied of all POWs by the end of July 1862, and from that time until the autumn of 1864, it was a backwater of the Confederacy. There was far more activity in the town of Salisbury itself, where some other abandoned buildings had been taken over by the Confederacy and turned into a foundry, a distillery (for medicinal purposes only), an office of the Bureau of Niter and Mining, and an ordnance plant that turned out horseshoes, trigger guards, projectiles for Parrott guns (rifled cannons), and sundry other hunks of iron-mongery.

In fact, conditions got bad in the town of Salisbury before they did inside the prison camp. Between conscription and the raising of

Home Guard units for active duty, so many able-bodied men had left town that all the mills in the area, with the exception of those run by the government, were standing idle. The few remaining provisions usually found their way into the hands of commissary agents who sold them, for obscene profits, to food speculators. There were some exceptions to this dismal picture — people who sold surplus grain to their neighbors at a fair market price, rather than to speculators for an inflated one — but so marginal were the supplies, and so powerful the motive of greed, that hunger had become a constant companion to the citizens of Salisbury by the spring of 1863.

In March of that year, some of the hungrier people took action. A band of some 45 women — mostly the wives of Confederates off at the front — armed themselves with hatchets and cornered one food speculator in his own store. When he refused to sell them flour at a price they could afford, the ladies marched into his storeroom and began smashing open barrels with their weapons. The speculator gave in and turned over ten barrels of flour to the women, rather than risk having his entire stock demolished by their wrathful axes. With this victory under their belts, the food-rioters tore into three more businesses and the railroad depot, netting for themselves, by the end of this busy day, a total of 20 barrels of flour. After much shouting and arguing, the loot was divided up into more or less equal shares. A week after the "Salisbury food riots," the price of flour in the region had dropped by $20 a barrel.

When the Union terminated the Dix-Hill accord in 1864, prisoners rapidly overflowed every Southern POW prison. By mid-October 1864, new POWs were pouring into the Salisbury compound. Designed to hold a maximum of 2,500 men, the place was inundated by a staggering total of 10,321 new arrivals during the fall and early winter of 1864.

These new arrivals found no chummy baseball games on grassy lawns beneath oak trees. Instead they found a barren expanse of gummy red-clay mud with every available square foot covered with improvised shelters. The brick buildings had all been turned over to the sick — except for the top floor of the factory, which was reserved for "muggers," hard-core convicts nobody wanted to tangle with. When the shelters filled up, all newcomers had to live outdoors, no matter what the weather. They simply dug "gopher holes" wherever they could and slept in them. Later, when these men were under-mined by sickness and malnutrition, several of them drowned in their holes during heavy rains, too weak to crawl out.

At the northeast and northwest corners of the yard, protected by walls of sharpened stakes, were two six-pound howitzers loaded with grapeshot. Parallel to the sentries' walkway, about six feet inside the circumference of the wall, was a sinister little trench, two feet deep and a yard wide, known simply as "the dead line." Any man who crossed that line, or who even looked like he was thinking about crossing it, could be shot dead, no questions asked. Sometimes the sentries taunted the prisoners, daring them to approach the line. And on several documented occasions, sentries extended the "dead line" rather liberally into the courtyard, killing men who were some dis-tance away — for sport, for spite, or for personal revenge (some of the guards had friends or family who had been burned out by General Philip Sheridan's men in the Shenandoah Valley). After all, in a war that claimed tens of thousands of victims, what was one more dead man?

What indeed, when inmates were dying at the rate of 20 to 50 a day? One POW in three who was sent to the Salisbury Prison in 1864 died there — an estimated total of at least 4,000 men. They died from malnutrition, exposure, gunshot wounds, "breaky-bone fever," typhoid, pneumonia, and despair. Some just walked up to the dead line and stood there, waiting for the sentries to release them from Hell, and the sentries usually obliged. A staggering 43 percent of those who died succumbed to a particularly ghastly form of perni-cious diarrhea caused by the bread they ate — because as much as one-sixth of the raw cornmeal they were given to make the bread consisted of ground-up corn cobs. The small loaves the inmates baked with this pig fodder were nicknamed "solid shot," and they wreaked terrible effects on the digestive systems of the already weakened men.

As for meat, it was supplied once a day in the form of beef offal — including ears, snouts, eyes, and entrails. Guards pushed wheelbar-rows of these scraps up inclined ramps and tipped them over into the prison yard. Starving prisoners beat each other nearly to death, fighting over pieces of intestine. This source of meat, such as it was, was supplemented on occasion by a number of gruesome recipes which went by the generic title "mouse soup."

On an average day, between 700 and 1,000 men were counted as "in hospital." The word "hospital," to modern readers, conveys images of long, gleaming corridors, rows of beds where men lie beneath clean sheets, and the businesslike smell of antiseptics. But at Salisbury Prison, where every building inside the compound was used to some extent as a "hospital," the conditions were, even by Civil War standards, nightmarish. Prisoner Booth, stunned after making his first tour of the camp, wrote in his diary that the plight of the sick was "beyond the power of language to describe."

The sick and injured lay like cordwood on floors covered with straw that had not been changed since late summer, often lying in the perpetual dampness and muck of their own and other men's urine and diarrhea. In some corridors, there was no room to step between the bodies without stepping on them as well. In less crowded areas, where the floor itself was visible, the sights were no less horrible. Booth saw so many lice swarming on the floor in one building that the very straw itself appeared to be alive and in constant, squirming motion. In another ward, where men on the very cusp of death had been stretched out, he saw lice crawling freely over the eyes and lips of men too weak to brush them off. The stench from these hospital wards hung over the entire camp like a miasmic cloud.

It seems miraculous that no major epidemics broke out. There was a close call in January 1865, however, when smallpox erupted among the garrison, rather than the inmates. Only the timely and severe imposition of a quarantine saved the prison, and probably Salisbury itself, from the ravages of a full-scale epidemic. The prison quartermaster was later cashiered for "failure to provide a pest-house."

Gangrene was a constant and dreaded companion. Gunshot wounds were almost certain to be accompanied by that purulent condition, and so, too, were many of the frostbite cases suffered by men forced to sleep outdoors in mid-winter.

Booth recorded a harrowing visit to one of the gangrene wards, where he saw men whose flesh had fallen away so completely that their sinews stood out "like shining white cords."

The prison doctors — some of them, at least — were not conscienceless monsters, but their resources had not even been adequate for the 200 or 300 men the prison had contained before the great influx of October 1864. They were helpless now before the ocean of human misery that confronted them during the worst period of overcrowding. Frostbitten limbs were sometimes amputated — with whiskey as the only anesthetic — and potions were concocted from tree bark and locally grown herbs in an effort to combat the ravages of diarrhea, but beyond that there was simply nothing that could be done.

Except for burying the dead. At two in the afternoon every day, a two-horse wagon pulled up in front of the prison's "dead house" where the previous 24 hours' worth of corpses had been collected, and began loading. Eight bodies to a load, between four and ten loads every day. The bodies were hauled to an old cornfield a couple of miles away and thrown ("like dead hogs," one eyewitness wrote) into trenches 6 feet wide, 4 feet deep, and 60 yards long. The corpses were layered three or four deep, each layer sprinkled with a few shovelfuls of dirt. On several occasions, the burial detail saw one of the "corpses" still moving feebly after being thrown into the pit. Usually, these unfortunates were too far gone even to pull out of the earth. They were left to stiffen in the cold — no worse fate than dying in the hospitals themselves, or so the reasoning of the moment went.

Captain Louis Fortescue, a Pennsylvanian who survived his ordeal at the prison, served for a time on the burial parties and left this recollection: "There is an expression on the face of a man who dies of starvation that is heart-rending to look upon. Never have I witnessed on any battlefield anything that so horrified the senses, shocked the imagination, or led the mind to such diabolical thoughts towards the enemies of my country and humanity, as the sight of these, my brother soldiers, thrown into that dead cart as nude as when born, and so covered with dirt that it was almost impossible to tell a white man from a black man."[1]

The miseries experienced by the Yankee POWs were shared in full measure by the other categories of prisoners: deserters (including a number of Federals), convicts, and civilian political prisoners. Surviving records don't allow us to assign specific numbers to these minority populations, but their total was surely in the hundreds.

By all accounts, the roughest, meanest, most incorrigible group of inmates were the "muggers" (a term applied to Confederates and Federals alike) who occupied the attic floor of the mill building. These men were doubly damned for criminal offenses as well as desertion, and the area they inhabited was known as the "Devil's Den." Prisoner Booth spoke for most of the other inmates when he described these men as "the lowest classes of humanity that ever disgraced the earth." They fancied themselves top dogs in the prison pecking order and preyed viciously on newcomers who had not been inside long enough to learn the ropes. They robbed, intimidated, assaulted (sometimes sexually), and, in several recorded instances, murdered fellow inmates for extra food, clothing, or valuables. The more law-abiding prisoners hated and feared the muggers and gave them a wide berth. Some accounts hint of retaliatory violence meted out to some of the worst muggers; it would not be surprising. Nothing would, given the degrading and violent nature of the environment. However, it wouldn't be accurate to give the impression that Salisbury Prison had an Alcatraz-like intramural society, complete with organized gangs and inmate kingpins. Men who are suffering from chronic diarrhea do not have much energy left for back-alley brawls.

Of all the groups inside the Salisbury compound, the Quaker war resisters probably fared the worst. For whatever reasons, the guards seem to have singled out their Quaker charges for particularly savage treatment. An ordinance passed in 1862 allowed members of the Society of Friends to abstain from military service provided they paid an exemption tax or hired a substitute. The hiring of substitutes was terminated in late 1863, however, due largely to the public outcry raised against the system's inequities.

Given the passions aroused by the war, it is not surprising that there were even some Quaker volunteers — albeit few for actual combat duty. During the first two years of fighting, the Confederate command showed some sensitivity toward this influential and respected sect, assigning Quakers noncombatant jobs — as hospital orderlies, stretcher bearers, workers in the saltworks, and so forth. As the manpower shortage began to squeeze Confederate resources, such niceties were more often than not dispensed with. By mid-1864, too, the Quakers had acquired a reputation as Unionists first, pacifists second — indeed, in the minds of many Southerners, the two had become synonymous. When the age limits of conscription were widened in 1864, a lot of Quakers who had been left alone the first time around were summoned to the colors. Many refused, most of them from religious rather than political convictions. The Confederate squads sent out to impress these men did not treat them gently.

Let the saga of Solomon Frazier serve to tell the story of these brave and moral men. Frazier was a Randolph County farmer who had duly paid his exemption fee back in 1862 and who therefore considered himself free of any military obligations. When several draft notices were sent to him in the autumn of 1864, he ignored them, thinking they were the product of some bureaucratic snafu. One night in December, ten armed men showed up at his home, arrested him, and marched him off to a jail in Archdale. From there, he was sent by train to Salisbury, where the Confederate administration made a strong effort to persuade him to "take up the gun." Frazier was a big, strapping man, obviously good cannon fodder.

He stood his ground on religious principles and refused. Well, then, he was told, if he would not serve in combat, he must serve right there at Salisbury, as one of the guards of the prison camp. Again, and for the same reasons, Frazier refused. His high-mindedness infuriated those who were trying to enlist him. He was cast into the stockade and told that he would remain there until he chose to bear arms for the South.

It was also decided that an example should be made of Frazier. A daily regimen of torture was started, designed to break him. On the morning of his first day inside the wall, he was subjected to two hours of "bucking down." This was a form of punishment employed by the armies of both sides. It consisted of binding a man in a sitting position, with his wrists tied together and his arms pressed down over his knees. A stout stick was then forced through the space between the backs of the knees and the insides of his elbows. The victim was utterly immobilized, subjected to intense strain and cramping. After an hour of so, all feeling would be lost in the extremities — only to return, in a rush of agony, when the bindings were untied.

That first morning in Salisbury Prison was a busy one for Frazier and his guards. After softening him up with two hours of bucking-down, he was forced, for another three hours, to march around the yard at gunpoint, carrying a heavy log. That night he slept in the open, hobbled and tied at the hands. The next morning, the torture began again: Frazier was hung by his hands for three hours with a musket tied to his right arm. When the poor man sagged under the weight, a nearby guard pricked him with a bayonet. After cutting him down, Frazier's tormentors put him back into the buck-down position, this time adding a truly sadistic refinement in the form of a bayonet tied to his head like a gag, the sharp end roped tight against his stretched lips. This he endured for the rest of the day.

Other inventive forms of cruelty included thrusting the Quaker's head into a narrow barrel and jamming it down so that he could move neither arms nor legs and thus could not sit down or even lean against something; he was left standing thus, while the guards beat on the barrel with sticks and shouted obscenities at him, for several hours. At one point in his ordeal, Frazier was even tied to a cross-beam in a blasphemous parody of the crucifixion.

Throughout his mistreatment, Frazier uttered not a single angry word to the men who were abusing him. This caused the captain in charge of breaking him to grow furious. Cursing Frazier, the officer declared that his patience was at an end: the Quaker must either agree to fight or prepare to die. Frazier's matter-of-fact reply was, "If it is thy duty to inflict this punishment on me, do it cheerfully; don't get angry about it."

At this point, the Confederate captain seemed to understand that this was no ordinary draft dodger, but a man motivated by awesome moral conviction. He tacitly admitted as much when he turned angrily away and spat over his shoulder, "If any of you can make him fight, do it; I cannot."

Two of Frazier's young guards then raised their rifles and made cocking motions. They told Frazier to make his peace with God, for he was surely about to die. Frazier returned their hostile glares with an even gaze and said, "It is the Sabbath and as good a day to die as any."

By this time, word of the middle-aged Quaker's fortitude had spread throughout the camp. Intervention by a sympathetic officer, along with an official protest lodged by a visiting Quaker minister who was too prominent for the Confederate authorities to ignore,

caused the tortures to cease. Frazier spent four more months in
Salisbury Prison, but he was no longer singled out for systematic
abuse, and he survived the ordeal with his will and his health intact.
After release, he returned to his little farm and resumed the quiet life
he had led before his arrest, having earned a place of honor in the
pages of Quaker history.

To balance this terrible picture somewhat, it must be said that the
morale of the guards during that dreadful winter was not much
higher than that of the prisoners. Their quarters were warmer and
their clothing in better repair, but their food, too, was atrocious,
their pay was low, and their desertion rate was high. There were also
some humane men among their ranks who made individual gestures
of compassion toward the inmates, smuggling in small items of food,
pieces of blankets, and even the priceless luxury of a tin cup.

The majority of the guards were very young — as young as 16 —
and they were, almost to a man, terrified of their prisoners. The
inmates didn't know it, but the palisade fence that enclosed them
was so weakened by exposure that a charge by a determined and big-
shouldered man could have punched a hole right through it in many
places. Outnumbered hundreds-to-one, there would have been little
the guards could have done to stop a concerted rush by, say, 3,000
desperate prisoners.

Fear and simple immaturity, more than actual sadism, probably
accounted for most of the unnecessary "dead line" shootings. Not a
great deal is known about the guards who were present during this
last and grimmest phase of the prison's history, but given the chronic
manpower shortage in the state, and given the fact that volunteering
for prison-guard duty was one way to avoid combat, it is probably
safe to say that the guards at Salisbury Prison were not exactly the
cream of Southern manhood. Their commandant, a Floridian
named John H. Gee, was universally described in survivors'
accounts with such adjectives as "brutal," "beastly," "hellish,"
"infamous," and "cold-blooded," although one survivor did make a
gesture of forgiveness by qualifying his description with a quote
from Shakespeare: "'God made him, and therefore let him pass for a
man.'"[2]

Given the conditions, it was probably inevitable that large-scale
violence would break out at some time or another. The pot finally

boiled over on November 25, 1864. A large group of prisoners — exactly how many one cannot say, for contemporary accounts all give wildly conflicting estimates — decided, seemingly on the spur of the moment, to attack a group of guards with clubs and rocks. After wresting the guards' weapons from them, the prisoners bayonetted two of them to death, and a third later died from his wounds. Another ten or so guards were wounded in the melee which followed.

If the prisoners, even as emaciated as they were, had really planned their break and made for several points on the wall simultaneously, forcing the guards to divide their fire, the attempt might well have succeeded. Each guard would have had time to fire one or two shots at most before the mob breached the palisade. But the uprising was poorly planned and seems to have been leaderless; the mob charged in one direction only. The scattered guards thus had time to rush to the threatened segment of the wall and concentrate their fire.

Their musketry checked the would-be escapees long enough for the camp commandant to wheel his two howitzers into position and lash the compound with several rounds of grapeshot. The revolt instantly died in a spray of blood and flayed tissue, the grapeshot cutting men down like giant shotgun blasts.

Thirteen prisoners died during those few desperate moments, and at least 60 were wounded — many of them terribly mangled by the cannon fire. One of the three men who later died of his wounds turned out to be a celebrity, or more precisely, the son of a celebrity. He had enlisted in the Union army, apparently for the adventure of it, under the name "Rupert Vincent," but he was carried on the prison records as Robert Livingstone. He was the son of the world-famous missionary-explorer, David Livingstone. Young Robert lingered for several weeks in one of the hospital wards (which testifies to a strong constitution) before expiring. Despite repeated attempts to pinpoint his burial place, it remains unknown. He joined the hundreds of others who were stacked in shallow mass graves, out in the forlorn cornfields that surrounded the prison.

Another, methodically planned, breakout attempt in January 1865 did succeed. About 100 men, in two well-timed shifts, made it out through a tunnel. They did a remarkable job of construction, apparently, for when part of the tunnel was uncovered in 1965 during excavations for a new building, it was still in good enough shape for workmen to pose inside it for the newspaper photographers.

Several hundred inmates chose to make another sort of escape by changing sides and swearing allegiance to the Confederacy. It speaks volumes for the dedication of the average POW that this practice was disdained by thousands of other men who chose to endure the hell inside the walls rather than become turncoats. The inmates thus recruited were dubbed "Galvanized Yankees" and were treated by their new rebel comrades with about the same degree of trust and enthusiasm as that showed by American soldiers in Vietnam to "converted" ex-Viet Cong. Ironically, though, it was a detachment of Galvanized Yankees, mostly Irishmen, who gave General Stoneman the only serious resistance he met during his walkover campaign in the war's final days. Under Colonel Zebulon York, they fought well enough to throw Stoneman back from one of his primary objectives: the strategic bridge over the Yadkin River, north of Salisbury.

Throughout the dismal period at Salisbury Prison, the citizens of Salisbury feared a mass prison break almost as much as the guards, but their attitude toward the inmates was one of pity and compassion. People from town would approach the prison walls and, at certain well-guarded places along the perimeter, were allowed to barter with the prisoners. The inmates crafted trinkets to use for currency — finger rings, little carvings, buttons from their uniforms — and traded them for eggs, flour, vegetables, potatoes, sorghum, tiny hunks of bacon, maybe even a plug of tobacco.

One Salisbury citizen, a Northern-born gentleman named Luke Blackmer, was revealed, many years after the war, to have spent "several thousand dollars" of his own money buying scarce provisions from surrounding farms and smuggling them into the compound. Blackmer's background was known, but his credentials as a transplanted Southerner were so good that none of his neighbors suspected his pro-Union activities. He is also known to have hidden a number of escapees in his cellar, helping them find trustworthy guides who could get them back to Federal territory across the mountains.

Perhaps the most famous good samaritan in Salisbury was a poor, elderly woman named Johnson. Mrs. Johnson's son was serving in the Confederate ranks and was thus beyond suspicion. She made regular trips to the prison's front gate, bringing baskets full of food and taking the time to actually befriend some of the lonely men inside. She became a kind of surrogate mother for several of them, and all who wrote of her after the war remembered her with intense emotion. One Federal soldier, a boy named Cox, did more than that. After the war, he returned to Salisbury to look up his benefactor. He found the old woman living in conditions of dire poverty. Using his own money, the former POW brought Mrs. Johnson back to Ohio with him, obtained a house for her, and saw to it that she lived her remaining years in comfort.

By the time General Stoneman attacked Salisbury in 1865, the prison had been emptied. General Grant, sensing that the end of rebel resistance was near, had agreed to a new prisoner exchange agreement in February. The Salisbury inmates — those who were still able to walk — marched out of their compound on February 22 and eventually were repatriated into Union hands at Wilmington.

The conditions at Salisbury Prison, and the factors which engendered them and allowed them to reach such extremes of horror and inhumanity, may be viewed as a paradigm of the whole Confederate prison apparatus. Relative to the number of men incarcerated, Salisbury was an even more lethal camp than the much more infamous institution at Andersonville. At the Georgia prison, the death rate was 28 percent; at Salisbury, it was 38.6 percent. During the five months of its worst overcrowding, it was probably the worst place in North America.

*The diarist was Benjamin F. Booth, whose comrades in the Salisbury Prison dubbed him "The Reporter." An enlisted man from Iowa, Booth was captured at the Battle of Cedar Creek in the Shenandoah Valley campaign on October 19, 1864. He kept a lucid and meticulously detailed diary of prison life, using every scrap of writing material he could find. When he was liberated in February 1865, he smuggled the diary out of the camp inside a bundle of old tenting. During his four-month sojourn in the Salisbury Prison, Booth lost 94 pounds. He published his account in 1897 in a volume entitled *Dark Days of the Rebellion*. That book is rare, having been out of print for nearly a century, but large portions of the diary are reproduced in Louis Brown's *The Salisbury Prison* (Avera Press, Wendell, North Carolina, 1980) — the definitive study of this previously neglected subject.

The "Heroes Of America"

Readers of the *Raleigh Conservative* had a shock in store for them when they picked up the issue that hit the capital's streets on July 2, 1864.

> A secret oath-bound Society, of a treasonable character, exists in North Carolina. There can be no doubt of the fact. The proof has been gradually accumulating and is now overwhelming. The names of some of its traitorous leaders are known. Their places of assemblage has [sic] been ascertained. Their channels of "communication" have been discovered...an association devised by the Yankees themselves, as a covert and cowardly means of affecting the subjugation and slavery of the Southern people.

With this page of thundering expose journalism, the *Raleigh Conservative* brought into the light of public scrutiny the most secretive, and probably best organized, antiwar movement in the Confederacy — and, not so coincidentally, struck a major political blow against the gubernatorial candidacy of William W. Holden, editor of the rival *Raleigh Standard*, who was certain to be associated with this underground movement whether he was actually a member or not.

The name of the organization thus exposed was the "Heroes of America," and it was the most coherent, effective, and elusive movement of antiwar Unionists functioning in North Carolina. Bound by rituals modeled after those of Freemasonry, the HOA "cells" employed symbolism drawn from the Biblical story of Rahab the harlot and the spies sent by Israel into Jericho (Joshua, Chapter 2). The movement chose as its emblem a scarlet cord, like the one

Rahab used to lower the spies from Jericho's walls. This was adopted as the so-called "Red String," which members of the order could wear inside their coat lapels for mutual identification. Some members placed the symbolic ornament on the edge of their window frames or on top of their doors, where couriers, or passengers along the Underground Railway to the North, could find them. For these reasons, the HOA is often identified in contemporary sources as the "Red Strings."

The exact origins of the Heroes of America remain obscure, despite the zealous research of modern historians. It appears to have been formed in early 1861 within the four-county region known as the Quaker Belt (Guilford, Forsyth, Randolph, and Davidson counties) — an area with a long history of antislavery activity and where Unionism was exceptionally strong before the war.

The social makeup of the organization is also a matter of conjecture, although its most visible members belonged to the upper middle class — doctors, merchants, clergymen, and so forth. It seems likely, though, that most Heroes were working-class whites. This can be attributed to the long-simmering resentments held by the blue-collar workers of the time against the landed gentry who ran the state's political machinery. The wealthier citizens were perceived — rightly or wrongly — as the chief instigators of the war, as well as the only people who could possibly profit from it.

Ideological positions aside, the pervasive religious pacifism indigenous to the Quaker Belt was perfect for the nourishment of a movement whose activities — while sometimes not wholly pacifistic in nature — were intended to hasten the end of the war.

In the great tidal flood of Confederate patriotism that swept North Carolina when the news of Fort Sumter broke, the north-central Piedmont remained stubbornly oriented toward the Union. And at some point either just before or just after the start of hostilities, this previously inchoate body of pro-Union emotion coalesced into an organized movement. Again, no one has been able to determine exactly when the title Heroes of America was attached to this movement, but the name was seized upon and deemed effective from the beginning — that much seems clear.

The fact that Confederate sympathizers in the northern Piedmont were organizing Home Guard companies as early as the spring of

1861 attests not to any fear of Yankee invasion, but rather to an awareness of how strong was the disloyalty in that region of the state. One landowning gentleman, attempting to organize a Home Guard unit in a locality close to the Guilford-Randolph County border, complained to Governor Ellis that he could find only four or five men in his whole district who were not openly and aggressively pro-Union.

A defiant band of Unionists, armed and organized in paramilitary style, sprang up early in the war in northeastern Davidson County. This group was under the incendiary leadership of the man named John Helton (sometimes spelled "Hilton"), who may have been an early member of the HOA. Helton openly claimed that he commanded 500 armed men and bragged that prominent secessionists in the area would soon "feel the rope."

Helton was instrumental in organizing civil disturbances in the High Point area in the late summer of 1861. The situation became threatening enough, in fact, for Governor Clark to send troops to High Point in August of that year. Helton was arrested and jailed, but this early knee-jerk reaction by the government did nothing to quell the region's Unionism. Instead, it merely forced the movement underground and gave enormous impetus to the secret-society structure of the Heroes of America.

The existence of the order was first revealed, oddly enough, by an article in the *Richmond Examiner* in January 1862. A traveler just back from North Carolina asserted that such an order existed, that it had already spread from Randolph County as far west as Wilkes County, and that its leaders were in regular contact with members of the Lincoln administration.

Meanwhile, John Helton had been released from jail on a technicality and was once more agitating in the High Point area. Governor Clark again sent troops to that city in March 1862 when he received intelligence reports about a large pro-Union rally Helton had organized. The meeting place was surrounded and a large number of prisoners taken. Helton himself — possibly warned by a fellow HOA member — escaped the net, followed the Underground Railway into Tennessee, and promptly enlisted in the Union army, where he eventually attained the rank of captain. He appears to have turned his back on North Carolina politics at this time, and his postwar trail is obscure.

There were other leaders ready to take over Helton's work, most notably Doctor John Lewis Johnson of Forsyth County — a man who may, indeed, have been one of the original founders of the Heroes of America. Doctor Johnson enlisted in the 48th North Carolina Regiment, became assistant to the regimental surgeon, and appears to have deserted at the earliest opportunity. He was repatriated by parole in September 1862. Exactly what happened during that interval of time, and exactly how close Johnson's ties were with the North, remain topics of speculation. What is certain is that Johnson worked vigorously to spread the HOA as soon as he was back in North Carolina. He took a job in a Confederate hospital in Raleigh and probably organized the Grand Council of the HOA within the city during the closing weeks of 1862.

Johnson may also have made a secret trip to the Federal-occupied towns of New Bern and Beaufort during the summer of 1863, probably to set up lines of communication between the HOA in Raleigh and the Federal enclaves on the coast, and also to sow the seeds of further expansion in some of the eastern counties closest to the enemy. He appears to have been successful on both counts. The HOA became a viable political force in those counties in the months following his purported visit.

Many of the HOA members who joined at this time later stated that one of the main recruiting tactics used by Johnson and his deputies was the promise that HOA members' property would not be destroyed in the event of a Union incursion from the coast — a promise Johnson was not likely to have given without at least verbal assurances to that effect from Federal commanders.

It is not known exactly how widespread the HOA had become by the end of 1862; it was, after all, a secret society operating in a hostile environment. But there is another reason why so little is known about it, and that derives from official policy. Both the Clark and Vance administrations encouraged self-censorship on the part of loyal newspaper editors, and most of them printed far, far less about Unionist activities than they actually knew. One of them, the editor of the *Charlotte Western Democrat*, even said as much in a letter to Edward Hale, editor of the influential *Fayetteville Observer*: "I have not published one-sixteenth of what I have heard, because I dislike for the public outside of the State to know that we have any Tories in the State..."[1]

HOA chapters communicated with the other side, passing men as well as information via the well-established Underground Railroad routes into Tennessee and Ohio. A network to the east coast was established after the Federals invaded that region in 1862. Although it started as a local phenomenon, the HOA was perfectly positioned to expand in direct proportion to the growth of antiwar feeling in the state as disillusionment and disaffection set in with the Confederate cause. When the "peace movement" began to grow, in the summer of 1863, the HOA reached its peak strength and maximum effectiveness.

Most of the smaller acts of sabotage done by HOA members went unrecorded. Hundreds, perhaps thousands, of deserters received HOA help to either hide or escape to the enemy. When Kirk's Federal cavalry raided Morganton and burned Camp Vance in 1864, they were almost certainly guided by HOA agents. Two strategic bridges in Davidson County, at Abbott's Creek and Rich Fork, were burned by HOA saboteurs, forcing Governor Vance to station Home Guard detachments on other bridges in the region.

Perhaps the most dramatic single incident, however, came in October 1864, when Doctor Johnson persuaded an entire company of Confederate soldiers to defect. This was a bold stroke, but Johnson lost his cover in the process of arranging it. He was able to flee to the North, but his wife and infant son were arrested and thrown into prison in Richmond, where the child died on November 16.

The HOA based its structure as well as its rituals on the model of Freemasonry — there were "degrees" of initiation into deeper and wider secrets. This was actually a very practical setup, since it meant that low-level members, if captured, could give only low-level information to their interrogators.

Policies of the Lincoln administration towards the HOA, from what little is known, appear to have been ambiguous in the extreme. On the one hand, the HOA was a valuable source of intelligence data from the South, and contact with its cells enabled Federal commanders to pinpoint Unionists in their vicinity who might be employed as guides or informants. On the other hand, the cause of Southern Unionists was viewed with a jaundiced political eye by many powerful men in the Republican Party. Unionism was seen as a potential conservative force in the region which might oppose some of the administration's plans for reconstruction. Hence, very little seems to have been done, from Washington at least, to encourage the growth of the HOA. It was regarded as useful in a marginal and temporary sort of way, but it had the potential of becoming a political albatross later on, so nothing was done to strengthen its powers of resistance or to encourage its members to wage open guerilla actions against the Southern war effort.

What motivated the members of the HOA to take their dangerous and treasonable political stand? Again, due to the secrecy that shrouded the order, a detailed picture of its membership simply cannot be drawn today. But from the fragmentary documentation, and the often confusing references that have survived in contemporary letters and journals, it is possible to make some guesses.

For many HOA members, loyalty to the Union was related to their hostility toward the social and political elite that ran both the state of North Carolina and the Confederacy itself. If the HOA can be said to have had any long-range political agenda, it stopped at the overthrow of the planter aristocracy — or at least, it grew very vague beyond that point. Any radical agrarian schemes that may have been discussed — and there are hints that some were, from time to time — were not enshrined in any surviving formal policy statements.

Certainly, a fairly large number of lower-class whites were attracted to the organization by the assumption (which some of its leaders surely encouraged) that their lot would improve if the power of the gentry were broken and the Confederate cause overthrown. But many more, just as certainly, joined the movement for the practical reason that, in the event of a Federal invasion, members of the HOA were more likely to be left alone, with their property intact. During the ebb of Southern morale after the defeat at Gettysburg, this inducement gained enormously. A Federal invasion, once unthinkable, had become almost inevitable.

In the spring of 1864, the Heroes of America peaked as a movement. From their power base in the northern Piedmont, the Heroes had spread their network through both the coastal and the mountainous regions of North Carolina; they had functioning cells in Virginia, Tennessee, Kentucky, Ohio, and possibly in Washington, D.C.

They actively promoted anti-Confederate ideas, fomented desertion, aided Unionists and escaped POWs to get out of the Confederacy, and were, on some isolated occasions, involved in actual sabotage.

What proved the undoing of the HOA was its sudden exposure to public scrutiny during the 1864 gubernatorial campaign. A great deal more about the HOA was known than the few hints which had appeared in the state's newspapers — until the moment when Governor Vance's political machine decided the time had come to reveal the awful truth and, as a bonus, to tar opponent Holden and the peace movement with the same brush as the treasonous secret society members. It was the old guilt-by-association ploy, and it worked, in this case, superbly. Vance was nothing if not a master of political timing.

Ironically, few modern historians believe that Holden actually was a member of the Heroes of America. And no one any longer believes the old story that he was actually the secret head of the whole organization. Even a pro-Vance newspaper, the *Raleigh Confederate*, admitted that "Mr. Holden...though not a member, is a beneficiary of the organization."

Certainly Holden was in touch with the movement's leaders, and surely they shared certain goals. But there was a taint of treason to the HOA's activities — however pure and high-minded the motives of its organizers — and Holden must have understood that any perceived association between himself and the Heroes could cut public opinion two ways.

The peace movement itself overlapped the HOA, but was not led or unduly influenced by it. Many leaders of the peace movement felt that their movement offered the only realistic hope of reconstruction on Southern terms, but the potential for social and political radicalism nascent within the HOA's lower-class orientation was almost as alarming to them as the prospect of a Yankee invasion.

It's not possible to determine what part the HOA may have played in organizing the many peace meetings held from mid-1863 until Holden's defeat a year later. One such meeting, in Greensboro in January 1864, attracted more than a thousand people. And Raleigh itself was such a hotbed of Unionism and antiwar sentiments that only the massive, visible presence of Confederate forces kept the lid on.

Still, the sudden front-page revelations about a secret Unionist society shocked and alarmed many citizens. The source of much of the published information was a man named Orrin Churchill, whom Governor Vance, or Vance's agents, had persuaded to turn "state's evidence" by promising him immunity in exchange for his "confession." Churchill recanted at great length, even going so far as to reveal the order's secret hand signals and passwords. It was very dramatic material, and it stuck to Holden like flypaper, even though there was no evidence that he was actually a member of the secret society.

By far the most electrifying revelation concerned a plot between the HOA and the Federal armies on the coast. According to this scenario, a Federal offensive inland was to be coordinated with an armed uprising in Raleigh. Some oblique references in scattered contemporary documents suggest that such a scheme might really have been under consideration. If so, it would have been bold beyond any precedent in American history; and, if the timing had been just right, it might well have worked, given the strength of both the peace movement and Unionism in Wake County.

Once Holden had been trounced at the polls, however, the furor over the HOA died down with surprising suddenness. There were no dramatic trials of the alleged leaders of the movement, no search-and-destroy missions by the militia. Much of the movement's strength, apparently, lay in its secretiveness. It shriveled in the public limelight and sank quickly into a state of moribund inactivity. It later revived during Reconstruction. Indeed, some of its members were to play important roles in the political drama that unfolded between 1865 and 1870, but for the remainder of the war itself, the Heroes of America faded from the stage.

At the height of its strength, the organization embodied a surprisingly strong and widespread grassroots discontent on the part of the small farmers and working-class people of North Carolina. One cannot help but wonder what V.I. Lenin could have fashioned from such raw material. Looking back on the movement today, it is impossible to label the movement's members as either "heroes" or "traitors"; but their very existence, in such substantial numbers, tells us a great deal about the complexity of the internal political situation in North Carolina during the Civil War.

THE PEACE MOVEMENT AND THE ELECTION OF 1864

As the summer of 1863 ripened and the "dog days" approached, North Carolinians of every political persuasion followed General Robert E. Lee's invasion of Pennsylvania with mounting apprehension. No one devoured the newspaper dispatches more avidly than Governor Zebulon Vance. Vance knew enough about grand strategy to sense what was at stake — the Confederacy was rolling the dice with history itself.

Vance also followed the newspaper accounts with a certain amount of personal frustration. He had been trying, ever since his election the previous year, to get an accredited North Carolina war correspondent attached to the Army of Northern Virginia, but Lee had fended him off time after time. Lee had little use for civilian correspondents, and probably would have booted out the Virginia correspondents he already had, if he could have done so without causing an unholy row back in Richmond. The battle reports that drifted back to the North Carolina press were therefore mostly reprints of dispatches written by correspondents who were prone not to even mention the exploits of North Carolina regiments. Or, when they did mention the state's regiments, they often belittled them in comparison to regiments from other states. It was the old North Carolina/Virginia antipathy once again.

For these reasons, the newspaper accounts did little to prepare the citizens of North Carolina for the reality of what was happening in Pennsylvania during that July of 1863. When the casualty lists began to appear — hideous in their length, portraying the virtual extermination of unit after unit — it quickly became obvious that North Carolina's troops had suffered terribly at Gettysburg.

After the battle, Vance received a heartbreaking letter from Major Samuel MacDowell Tate, acting commander of the Sixth North Carolina Regiment, written in pencil from Hagerstown on July 8. Tate's letter recounted the true story of what had happened during the fierce assault on Cemetery Ridge on July 2. Lee had been flailing about for two days, looking for a place to drive into the Federals' strong line, but he had failed to come up with any innovative tactics for creating one. He was not in good form for this battle. But on July 2, the Sixth North Carolina, together with the North Carolina units commanded by General Robert Hoke and the valiant "Louisiana Tigers" of Hay's brigade, actually shattered the Union line near its center. They overran the Union artillery batteries there and virtually handed Lee the break he had been searching for. But at that moment — one of the pivotal moments of the battle — General Jubal Early had failed to support the attack. The golden opportunity was lost when strong Federal reinforcements converged on the salient and drove out the attackers after savage fighting.

Tate wanted Vance to know the truth, he said, because only the force spearheaded by the North Carolinians had succeeded that day, and the after-battle reports of the many regiments which had not done so well were unlikely to mention that fact. As for the cannon they had overrun, Tate made a prophecy: "This battery will be credited to Early's Division — see if it don't."

Vance could do nothing but gnash his teeth. The habit of belittling the achievements of North Carolina regiments was too deeply ingrained in Lee's correspondents to be disturbed by anything as inconvenient as facts. Lee thought Vance was hypersensitive about this and denied that his Virginia officers indulged in historical distortions when writing up their after-battle reports. Vance was indeed hypersensitive about it, and with plenty of good reasons. Even the "official" reports of some engagements were written up by the officers *after* the distorted press accounts had been printed, and they were clearly modeled on those newspaper accounts — exactly the reverse of how things were supposed to be done.

One of North Carolina's ablest and bravest officers, General Johnston Pettigrew, died in the Gettysburg campaign. Vance marched in the funeral procession through the streets of Raleigh on July 29.

The mood in North Carolina changed after Gettysburg. Even people with no deep knowledge of military affairs could sense that an irrevocable turning point in the fortunes of the South had been reached. Resignation replaced faith, and cynicism about the Confederate cause — always strong in some areas of the state — began to spread. Yet the majority of the state's people, taking their cue from Vance himself, put their losses behind them, tightened their belts, and in some sectors of the wartime economy, actually increased production.

As the autumn of that pivotal year drew to a close, Governor Vance found himself facing the most delicate and complicated political crisis of his administration. It is possible to sense in him — for the first time since his career began — a faltering of the will, a pervasive mood of doubt and confusion. He was still, after all, a very young man for the kind of responsibilities that had swamped his office.

In less than a year he would stand for reelection. The greatest threat to his chances, and to the internal stability of the state, was the growing power of the peace movement and the direction in which that once-inchoate philosophy was being steered by the politicians who had joined it.

Vance's original constituency, the bloc that had voted him into office in August 1862, had been comprised of old-time Whigs, disaffected Democrats (now organized into the "Conservatives"), and a smattering of former Know-Nothings. All of these people were opposed to some Confederate policies, and some were opposed to all Confederate policies. Many of them had voted for Vance out of the belief that he would be a strong bulwark between them and the "despotism" of Richmond. And so he had proved to be, if not always in the sense his supporters had originally envisioned. But Vance had never claimed to be the standard bearer of an anti-Richmond movement, and his disagreements with President Jefferson Davis were always over specific, individual problems, never with the idea of the Confederacy's right to exist in peace.

The first year of Vance's administration had been relatively untroubled by domestic political wrangling, but that began to change not long after Gettysburg. A number of powerful Conservatives began to publicly articulate their dislike of the Davis administration and their belief that the South should sue for peace. The latter attitude, over a period of about six months, gradually coalesced into the idea that North Carolina should seek a separate peace, if the rest of the Confederacy would not go along.

Leading the voices of dissent was Vance's powerful sometime-ally, William W. Holden, the outspoken and intellectually brilliant editor of the *Raleigh Standard*, the most influential newspaper in the state. Holden had thundered in print against conscription, against the impressment of supplies, and against the way North Carolina was treated by the Richmond papers. In these matters, Vance agreed with the editor, and even made use of his paper as a platform for arousing public support for Vance's own squabbles with Richmond. But when Holden actually came out and said the unsayable — that North Carolina should give serious thought to leaving the Confederacy — he stepped over the line as far as Vance was concerned.

Holden went too far out on a limb when he made that declaration, and he pulled away from it quickly. But the lid had been opened, and one of Jefferson Davis's worst fears about North Carolina had popped out into the daylight. The tone of political debate in the state permanently shifted.

Throughout the summer of 1863, Holden continued to lash out at the Richmond administration and to demand that the South, and North Carolina in particular, search for an "honorable peace." He was somewhat fuzzy about just what kind of terms would constitute an honorable peace as opposed to the other kind, but most readers interpreted his remarks to mean reunion with the United States and reconstruction. Holden was not playing Don Quixote here; he sincerely believed that he was voicing the opinion of the majority of North Carolina's people.

In August 1863, there were signs that Holden and his supporters had indeed tapped into a wellspring of popular discontent. Nearly 100 public meetings were held, mostly in the central and western sections of the state, to pass resolutions demanding that peace negotiations be undertaken. The timing of these "spontaneous" rallies, and the unmistakable similarity in the wording of their resolutions, strongly indicated a hidden but highly effective organizing effort on behalf of the Holdenites. Typical of these resolutions was this one, passed at a rally in Surry County: "That in our opinion, under the circumstances, the best thing the people of North Carolina could do would be to go in for the 'Constitution as it is, and the Union as it was.'"

By publishing full accounts of a dozen or so of these meetings, and giving maximum publicity to their resolutions, newspaper editor Holden was busily laying the groundwork for the as-yet-unannounced gubernatorial candidate Holden, and several astute editors quickly figured out what he was up to. As the editor of the *State Journal* expressed it: "If Gov. Vance cannot see the drift of all this, if he will not see that Holden's objective is to shelve him at the expiration of his first term and become a candidate himself, we can't help it."

Vance knew perfectly well that Holden had crossed over from editorializing to covert political activism, but he was seemingly paralyzed by his own doubts. What if Holden was right? What if the majority of North Carolina's people did want what Holden said they wanted? Should he then align himself with Holden and add his voice to the clamor for an end to hostilities, even if it meant compromising the ideal of Southern independence for which he had fought so hard? Or should he make a clean break with Holden and take a stand in opposition to the peace movement that was gathering behind his leadership? More than idealism was at stake here. Many of Vance's most powerful supporters in the 1862 election were flirting with ideas similar to Holden's, and if Vance lost their support, he might well lose the upcoming 1864 election.

The delicate political situation in North Carolina was starting to have a deleterious effect on the whole Confederate war effort. No small number of captured deserters claimed that Holden's editorials in the *Raleigh Standard* had helped crystallize their discontent into action, and the conviction grew among Lee's officers that Holden and his editorial allies — most notably J.L. Pennington, publisher of *The Daily Progress* — were responsible for fomenting desertion and bad morale. Not only that, but feedback from the Yankee press indicated that the North was drawing encouragement from the peace movement and was overestimating the amount of dissension in the Confederacy. Holden and his supporters were operating in a gray area somewhere between dissent and treason.

Opposition to Holden was voiced in many state newspapers, and some of it was decidedly personal. Not content with labeling him a traitor, the *State Journal* called him "a desperate and despicable blackleg," while another paper tossed around such adjectives as "unscrupulous," "crafty," and "vulgar." A Petersburg editor went even further, declaring in print that Holden's parents had never been legally married.

Concern over the harm Holden was doing motivated former North Carolina governors William Graham and David L. Swain to have a long talk with the editor in late summer, 1863. They could not dissuade him. Neither could Vance, who was gradually becoming tainted by his former association with Holden. Holden's paper, after all, had at one time been the "official" organ of Vance's political apparatus. After a lengthy conversation with Holden, Vance wrote to a friend, on July 26, 1863: "He pretends, and may be really of [the] opinion, that 4/5ths of the people are ready for reconstruction & says he is only following the people, not leading them...."

Nevertheless, Vance still believed, as the summer drew to a close, that he could in time persuade Holden to shift his course and give up the peace movement platform entirely. Meanwhile, Vance himself was under growing pressure to repudiate Holden publicly, to make some sort of dramatic gesture, in print or in a public forum, that would draw a clear and unambiguous line between himself and the rogue editor of the *Raleigh Standard*.

One of the voices which rang loudest in Vance's ear was that of E.J. Hale, editor of the influential *Fayetteville Observer*. Hale had long tried to reason with Holden in print and had finally given up. Now he was urging Vance, in letters of increasing passion, to disavow Holden and the *Raleigh Standard*. Vance replied to one of Hale's letters on August 11, 1863, assuring the Fayetteville editor that a "split with Holden is decreed by the Gods — I have made up my mind to it and am preparing for it any day — tho' I don't intend to 'precipitate' it...He is for submission, reconstruction, or anything else that will put him back under Lincoln and stop the war...."

Vance composed a long (17-page!) letter about Holden and the peace movement which he intended to submit for publication. It would have been as dramatic a break with Holden as his advisers had been urging, including as it did such statements as this: "I can only look upon propositions of peace coming from us, no matter how pure and patriotic the motive which induces them, as involving national dishonor, ruin, and disgrace." Or this, clearly aimed at Holden himself: "There may be a designing few who desire to take advantage of the suffering and patriotic many to lead them into this inevitable ruin with hopes of peace."

But having drafted this ringing rhetorical blast, Vance waffled about actually issuing it. He even showed it to Holden, who thought it (not surprisingly) "very extreme and violent." He also showed a copy to former governor Graham, who thought it unnecessarily strong. Other advisers and friends voiced completely different opinions. Vance listened to all of them, partially agreed with most of them, and for a long time did nothing except put the letter back in his files.

September came, and Vance was still paralyzed. "God knows, I desire to do my duty…but this matter is one of great delicacy and a mistake might be fatal," he wrote despairingly to a friend in late August.

During a conference at the Governor's Palace on September 2, former governor Graham again attempted to change Holden's course, debating with him for three solid hours "like a revivalist wrestling with an unbeliever."[1] Vance even offered to maintain a strict and neutral silence about the peace movement if Holden would agree to disassociate himself from it. Holden remained adamant.

Acting on Graham's advice, Vance issued a lukewarm proclamation on September 8. He was stern and authoritative when asking the people to obey the laws and not resist conscription, but noncommittal when addressing the peace movement, letting it go by simply asking the people to "abstain from assembling together for the purpose of denouncing each other…and to avoid seeking any remedy for the Evils of the times, by other than legal means" — a statement so guarded and nebulous that many readers didn't really understand what he was talking about.

Almost as soon as the proclamation appeared, Vance expressed his displeasure with it. It did not draw as clear a line between himself and Holden as he needed to draw. Instead of warning people away from the peace movement, and admonishing them not to support the growing clamor for a statewide convention to discuss separate negotiations, Vance tip-toed around those subjects so cautiously that they were scarcely in focus at all.

The problem was not just the confusing and contradictory advice Vance was receiving, nor his sense of personal obligation to Holden for past favors. He also drew back from the break because, so far, most of Holden's provable activities, and all of his statements in print, were, in Vance's eyes, sheltered by the principle of freedom of speech. Vance shrank in genuine horror from initiating any action that could be interpreted as a blow against that sacred institution.

Others were not so hesitant. While Vance had been hemming and hawing, backing and filling, Confederate loyalists had been screaming for Holden's head on a pike. Petitions were being sent to Richmond demanding that Holden be hung for treason. An official sent to North Carolina from Richmond reported that "military repression" might be needed in North Carolina, if the peace movement gathered any more momentum and if Vance did not act to quash Holden.

"Military repression" came to Raleigh on the night of September 9, 1863, when a lynch mob of Confederate soldiers descended on Holden's home. Not finding him there, they proceeded to the offices of the *Raleigh Standard*, battered down the doors, and ran amok. Trays full of type were dumped into the street, furniture was smashed, and kegs of printer's ink were bashed and splashed all over the walls. Only the printing presses were spared, perhaps because there was little the mob could do to the hulking machines with their bare hands.

Vance had been told about the mob while the soldiers were still on their way to the newspaper office. Mounting his horse, he rode to the scene but arrived too late to do anything more than give the men a characteristic lecture on the meaning of freedom of the press. The mob listened politely, gave the governor three cheers, then happily returned to the train station. Vance went home and discovered that Holden had sought shelter there. Holden thanked Vance for his intervention; Vance gave the trembling man a stiff drink of brandy.

Retaliation followed the next morning, when a gang of Holden supporters broke into and thoroughly wrecked the offices of the *State Journal*, an important pro-Confederate organ. This time, the presses were reduced to scrap iron, for the pro-Holden mob had remembered to bring along some sledge hammers. Again, Vance saddled his horse and rode to the scene, where he managed to convince the Holdenites to disperse without further violence.

Raleigh was as tense as a bowstring that morning. Church bells were ringing, the streets were full of aimless, angry crowds, and more anti-Holden Confederate soldiers were passing through town with every hour. The ingredients were on hand for a major civil disturbance; Vance could smell it in the air. Exhausted and red-eyed from a tense and sleepless night, he cabled Jefferson Davis and told him to send priority orders forbidding any Confederate soldiers from entering the city, closing the message with a note of panic: "If you wish to save North Carolina for the Confederacy, be quick!"

Vance blamed the outrages of September 9 on General Benning, commander of the Georgia unit that was passing through Raleigh that night on its way to the front in Tennessee. General Benning had been asleep in his railway carriage at the time Holden's paper was being trashed. Benning angrily denied that his men had instigated the trouble, and he tried to blame the whole affair on some North Carolina troops who had hitched a ride on his train before it got to Raleigh. Letters and newspaper accusations flew like arrows for weeks after the incident, and what really happened remains cloudy to this day. Both Georgia and North Carolina troops were in the streets that night, so the truth — as usual — probably lies somewhere in the murky middle.

Jefferson Davis was a bit slow to take action; Vance had cried wolf too many times before. As a result, things almost boiled over again on the afternoon of September 11, when several hundred Alabama troops rampaged through the streets of Raleigh, threatening to burn down Holden's house and promising violence to the governor if he tried to stop them. Vance rode down to the depot and found an Alabama officer with his wits about him who offered to take a more disciplined detachment into town and round up the rowdies. This was done before any fires were set or government officials tarred and feathered, but it was a close call. For a while, Vance had entertained images of the capital city going up in flames.

Now he sent another telegram to Richmond, one which reflects his raw-nerved state at the moment: "This thing is becoming intolerable. For 60 hours I have traveled up and down making speeches alternately to citizens and soldiers, without rest...engaged in the humiliating task of trying to defend the laws and peace of the State against our own bayonets. Sir, the means of stopping these outrages I leave to you. If not done, I shall feel it a duty which I owe to the dignity and self-respect of [North Carolina] to issue my proclamation recalling her troops from the field to the defense of their own homes."

This time, Davis acted promptly, issuing stern orders that pertained to every unit of rebel troops passing through or near Raleigh. Three days later, Vance was able to wire the President that law and order had been restored and no further incidents had been reported.

Holden caught his breath, rallied his supporters, and resumed publication in October, as feisty and as contentious as ever. But when the sun went down, he slept in hiding, often with a loaded revolver near his hand. And on November 4, when Congressional elections were held, the peace movement showed its muscle by electing several of its men to the Confederate Congress — five, in fact, out of a total of ten candidates. When the election results were announced, the *Richmond Enquirer* once more clucked its tongue over the state of politics in North Carolina: "What an unaccountable people! They fight to defend their homes, and then they send a man to Congress because he says they have defended them 'long enough.'"

By December 1863, Holden's statements had grown very bold indeed for a man who had been fleeing an angry mob only two months earlier. The last issue of his paper to appear before New Year's Day carried this inflammatory statement: "The only power that can close the war, is the power that made it, that of the sovereign States; and the states can speak authoritatively only in Convention." This call for a convention, with its echoes of the original move to secession, was a new ingredient in Holden's strategy. Clearly, the matter to be debated at such a conclave could only be the prospects of a separate, negotiated peace. Moreover, Vance — who had eyes and ears all over the capital — soon learned that the issue of a convention would be the litmus test for his own reelection. If Vance ran on a platform that included a call for a convention, Holden and his papers would support him; if not, they would fight him.

It was at this point, in the early days of 1864, when he realized what sort of game Holden was playing with the convention gambit, that Vance was finally moved to an open break. "The convention is to be my test," he wrote to editor Hale in Fayetteville, "and I am to be beaten if I oppose it." To his avuncular mentor, former governor Graham, Vance spelled out his opinion of the convention scheme in no uncertain terms: "I can not of course favor such a thing...I will see the Conservative party blown into a thousand atoms and Holden and his understrappers in hell...before I will consent to a course which I think would bring dishonor and ruin upon both state & Confederacy!"

His emotions and his thoughts were still in turmoil. For a time, he agonized over whether he should even run for reelection. In a January 2 letter to another long-time friend and adviser, President Swain of the University of North Carolina, Vance expressed his personal anguish on paper in a way he could not do in public:

> The final plunge, which I have been dreading and avoiding, that is to separate me from a large number of my political friends, is about to be made. It is now a fixed policy of Mr. Holden and others to call a convention in May to take N.C. back to the United States...the agitation has already begun...I can never consent to this course. Never. But should it be inevitable and I be unable to prevent it...believing that it would be ruin alike to State and Confederacy, producing war and devastation at home, and that it would steep the name of North Carolina in infamy and make her memory a reproach among the nations, it is my determination to quietly retire to the army and find a death which will enable my children to say that their father was not consenting to their degradation. This sounds no doubt, a little wild and bombastic, not to say foolish, but it is for your eye only. I feel, sir, in many respects as a son towards you....

After discussing the chances of the Confederacy, and concluding that historically "many people have been worse off, infinitely, and yet triumphed," Vance, by the end of the letter, had answered his own pleas for advice and resolved on the course best suited to him, both psychologically and politically. "My inclination is, to take the stump early and to spend all my time and strength in trying to warn and harmonize the people. If I go down before the current I shall 'perish if it must be so/At bay, destroying many a foe.'"

Although it was fired through the medium of private correspondence, Vance had just triggered the first shot of the 1864 gubernatorial campaign.

Holden soon fired a salvo of his own, one that was much more public. In the January 19 issue of his paper, Holden attempted to tie Vance's reelection bid even more closely to the issue of peace negotiations: "If Gov. Vance should go with the people who have honored him by placing him where he is, he will be reelected...but if he should oppose the views and wishes of those who made him Governor, he will be defeated. That is all." Holden had obviously acquired a higher opinion of himself since the mob violence of September. At that time, he claimed to be speaking for only four-fifths of the electorate; now he claimed to be the spokesman for "the people" as a whole.

Another series of "spontaneous" peace rallies erupted across the state, resulting in another rash of high-minded resolutions and a deluge of petitions to the governor's office, most of them demanding a new convention.

There was now a strong process of polarization at work in the state. Vance, in spite of all his feuding with Richmond, had gradually emerged as a monolith of commitment to the Confederate cause. Holden, also gradually, had become the point man for all the old pro-Union, antiwar factions that had been so strong and so influential in North Carolina before Lincoln's call for troops.

Vance, in the course of his long wrangles with Richmond, had erected a number of legal and procedural precedents which safeguarded North Carolinians from many of the worst authoritarian tendencies of the Confederate government. But as passionately as he upheld civil rights — including William Holden's — Vance now regarded the peace movement not only as a source of perfidy and dishonor, but also as a source of anarchy from within. The antiwar, pro-Union movements had never entirely gone away, and in the Quaker Belt of the Piedmont, by this stage of the war, those sentiments were strong enough and deep enough to have engendered conditions bordering on low-level guerilla war. After the double catastrophes of Vicksburg and Gettysburg in July 1863, every idea and activity that tended to pull the state away from the Confederacy had simply grown stronger. And as the voices of the peace movement became more clamorous, Zeb Vance, almost by default, moved closer and closer to the policies of Richmond.

Alarm over the peace movement was perhaps the main thrust behind the Confederate Congress' decision to suspend the writ of habeas corpus for any person arrested for "advising or inciting others to abandon the Confederate cause, or to resist the Confederate States, or to adhere to the enemy." This extraordinary legal measure took effect in February 1864, precipitating an extended written argument between Vance and Jefferson Davis. It also forced William Holden to shut down his newspaper, at least temporarily.

In the midst of the intellectual chill created by the suspension of the writ, Vance began to plan his reelection campaign. With typical audacity, he chose to make his first speech right in the heart of the most disaffected section of the state, in Wilkesboro. It was a watershed address, for it marked not only the official start of his campaign, but also his first open, public, repudiation of the peace movement.

Vance was the hottest ticket in town that February 22, 1864, and some 2,000 people showed up to hear him speak. At least one aspect of the speech, a concert by the famous Johnny Reb Band from Salem, was a rousing success. Vance's speech, however — with its insistence that if North Carolina took itself out of the war by means of a special convention, things would get worse, not better — met a decidedly cool reception. Immediately after the story of the Wilkesboro appearance got around, Raleigh gamblers began putting their money on Holden.

Ironically, the best press coverage Vance received was from Richmond. Rather cunningly, Vance had made sure there was a reporter from the *Richmond Enquirer* on hand in Wilkesboro, one who could take shorthand. As a result, long verbatim excerpts from his speech were accurately reprinted in the capital city of the Confederacy. The Richmond paper's editor lauded the speech as being worthy of Patrick Henry — extravagant praise indeed from a Virginian — and Vance, from that point on, found his campaign trailed by a helpful reporter from the *Enquirer*, a newspaper that had been his nemesis on many occasions.

His stock rose to the sky in late March when he toured the North Carolina regiments in General Lee's army, starting at the encampment south of the Rapidan River, near Orange Court House. With General Longstreet's corps absent in Tennessee, more than half of the Army of Northern Virginia now consisted of North Carolina troops: some 65 regiments in all, organized into 13 brigades. Vance started his tour on Lee's right flank, where Ramseur's North Carolina brigade was in position, then worked his way across the line. For some of these visits and speeches, Lee and General J.E.B. Stuart were also present, as were soldiers from other states who were drawn by Vance's reputation as a great orator, together with large flocks of local civilians and a host of political small-fry.

The winter had been long and dreary, punctuated by chilling rains, and the North Carolina troops were restless. The peace movement was widely talked about, desertions were commonplace, and men returning from the home front brought back tales of widespread hunger and deprivation. In early 1864, the flame of enthusiasm was fluttering low in the Army of Northern Virginia.

By all accounts, Vance's tour had a tremendously tonic effect on everyone involved, from the generals to the lowliest privates. Always a dependable orator, and always inspired by the feedback of an enthusiastic crowd, Vance surpassed himself and spoke with a tongue of fire. At the end of one especially stirring rhetorical cadenza, interrupted at the proper moments by rebel yells and cheers, one observer noted wryly that it was too bad Lee hadn't planned to start an offensive that very day — the men were ready to storm Washington at bayonet point. A visiting editor from Fayetteville, who would have occasion later in his career to hear both men make numerous speeches, later wrote that if you measured Zebulon Vance's abilities by this front-line tour, he was even more effective than the famed British orator William E. Gladstone.

It is unfortunate that none of his speeches from this tour survived in its entirety. Like all great speakers, however, Vance was a "plunger," sensing the mood of a crowd and flowing with its current until he could shape it in his own direction, so it's likely that much of his speaking was spontaneous on each occasion. Some fragments were recorded, and one specimen illustrates the man's uncanny sense of tact and timing. Fuss though he would with Jefferson Davis, complain though he did about the way Virginia's soldiers received preferential treatment from the Confederate press and bureaucracy, Vance had nothing but the deepest respect for the valor of that state's combat troops. And on one occasion, when large numbers of them

were present in the audience, he altered his verbal course and
praised them so extravagantly that the North Carolina troops standing nearby started to get restless. Instantly sensitive to the mood-
swing of his audience, Vance silkily turned the moment around by
saying that, yes, Virginians were born leaders and Carolinians were
always glad to follow; "and it was well we did follow you, and keep
close to you, too, for if we hadn't, all those big battles around Richmond would have been mere skirmishes!" Cheers all around.

The week-long tour was climaxed by a grand review — the only
one Robert E. Lee ever staged for a civilian — in which virtually the
whole Army of Northern Virginia, ragged and decimated but still
unconquered on the field of battle, marched past in the chill light of
the Virginia spring. Vance stood, deeply moved, on the same
reviewing stand as Generals Lee, Stuart, Early, Ewell, Hill, Hampton, Gordon, and Fitzhugh Lee...probably the greatest concentration of sheer military prowess ever gathered in one place since the
last time Napoleon conferred with his marshals before Waterloo.

Vance certainly accomplished his goal of raising morale and
demonstrating his commitment to the Confederate cause, even if
Lee's generous assessment of the tour seems hyperbolic ("Governor
Vance's visit was the equivalent of a reinforcement of 50,000 troops"
— a remark overheard and recorded by Surgeon General Warren).
Vance had done much to offset the weariness and depression that
had settled in the bones of North Carolina's soldiers during that dismal winter. And, though there is no doubt that Vance's primary
motive for going to Virginia was exactly what he said it was, the tour
and its attendant headlines did nothing to hurt his chances of reelection back in North Carolina.

Meanwhile, William Holden made one of the least surprising
announcements of his career by openly declaring himself a candidate for governor. He also declared the search for an "honorable
peace" as the main plank in his platform. But by then, Vance had
outmaneuvered Holden so that the editor's long agitation for a
peace-seeking convention was made to look like a cynical move to
further his own political career. Holden, in turn, tried to portray
Vance as having sold out the best interests of North Carolina in order
to further the policies of Richmond. In his own speeches, Holden
drove home the litany of North Carolinians' discontent: conscrip-

tion, impressment, taxation, economic exhaustion, despotic treatment at the hands of Richmond — all the things that Vance had labored mightily to correct or at least soften.

Vance campaigned by doing what he did best: hitting the stump. He traveled to every part of the state in a whirlwind whistle-stop speaking tour: Taylorsville, Statesville, Salisbury, Fayetteville, Asheboro, Greensboro, Graham, Lexington, Snow Camp, Salisbury, Lincolnton, Marion, Asheville, Hendersonville, Morganton, Lenoir, Charlotte, and even Davidson College. The crowds were good and by now were enthusiastic — the chilly reception of the Wilkesboro speech was ancient history. Sometimes, when Vance was speaking on two consecutive days and the distance between stops was not too great, he would be followed from one town to the next by hundreds of people.

Modern readers, used to the streamlined, manipulative speeches of television-oriented politicians, should remember that in mid-Victorian times political orations were not just prepackaged propaganda, but also a form of mass entertainment. People came to rallies expecting to be amused, moved, and carried along by a great speaker in the way a music lover is swept up by a great concerto soloist. "Symphonic" would not, in fact, be a bad way to describe Vance's style of public speaking. A typical Vance address was from 90 minutes to two hours long, and was overflowing with anecdotes, rhetorical cadenzas and flourishes, delicious asides, and witty improvisations. In all America, there was probably no one better at this sort of thing than Zebulon Vance.

The more he spoke, the more he refined his argument. He stated his platform simply and clearly: supremacy of civil over military law...protection of the writ of habeas corpus...obedience to the law by citizens...no submission to the enemy, but a willingness, always, to seek honorable negotiations...no counter-revolutionary state conventions...unswerving opposition to despotism, whatever the source.

To leave the Confederacy, Vance told his audiences, would be to make North Carolina an independent country, a rebel within the rebellion. At that point, the Confederate government would almost certainly have to declare war on the state, while at the same time she would be threatened from east and west by the enemy she was now engaged in fighting. Put in those terms, Holden's idea of a separate peace did not look so much desirable as deadly, and the whole spectacle of secession-within-secession appeared both dishonorable and slightly absurd. Rather than helping the state secure an honorable peace, Holden's proposals would almost guarantee she would be laid waste and would have to sue for respite under conditions of humiliation and helplessness.

The voters heard what Vance was saying, and they ate up the way in which he said it. The army vote went for Vance six-to-one — not surprising, in view of the fact that many Holden supporters were abused, intimidated, and threatened with dire reprisals if they did not vote for Vance. Vance himself surely had no hand in these dirty aspects of the campaign, but he did not hesitate to claim the votes, however they were obtained.

He would have won anyway, for the civilian vote was 44,856 for Vance and a pathetic 12,647 for Holden, who carried only three counties, including Randolph — seat of the worst anti-Confederate activities in the state.

It was the sweetest victory of Vance's political career. On August 5, in a private letter, he permitted himself to crow just a little: "My competitor, a bold and popular demagogue, made the issue distinctly of peace on terms less than independence and I have beaten him worse than any man was ever beaten in North Carolina."

"Their Rude Hands Spared Nothing But Our Lives..."

Mrs. Croaker was a Kinston native known for her sharp tongue and quick repartee. A Federal chaplain visited her house, not long before Sherman arrived in that part of the state, and attempted to engage her in pious conversation. She should not despair, he told her, for Sherman's Yankees were coming to bring freedom to the oppressed — God's gift to the enslaved. "That may be so," Mrs. Croaker replied, "but if it is, then the Devil himself came to bring the gift." The chaplain smugly repeated the already cliched (and inaccurate) "War is Hell" motto attributed to General Sherman. Mrs. Croaker snorted with indignation: "Sherman ought to know about his native customs — Hell is his home town!"

— from a story told by Mrs. John Anderson, in her compilation volume North Carolina Women of the Confederacy *(Fayetteville, North Carolina, privately printed, 1926).*

"A drunken soldier with a musket in one hand and a match in the other is not a pleasant visitor to have about the house on a dark, windy night, particularly when for a series of years you have urged him to come, so that you might have an opportunity to perform a surgical operation on him...."

— General Henry Slocum, commander of Sherman's left wing during the Carolinas campaign.

General William Tecumseh Sherman's approach was viewed as the inhabitants of a medieval city would have viewed the encroachments of the Black Death; as Egyptian farmers would have viewed a thunderhead of locusts sweeping over the desert; as the inhabitants of Christian Europe had once viewed the onslaught of Attila the Hun. He was the very Devil himself, Satan incarnate, Tecumseh the bloody-handed. The horrors visited upon Georgia had already become legend…but that had been Georgia. Now, as those same horrors began to devastate South Carolina, the people of North Carolina scanned their morning papers for the latest telegraphic dispatches of Sherman's progress, following on their maps as the fat blue arrows of his columns inched up the Eastern seaboard, leaving the proverbial "howling waste" in their wake.

Sherman's concept of warfare was essentially 20th-century "total war," in which all of the old Napoleonic rules were cast away and the constraints of Victorian sentimentality were simply ignored as irrelevant hypocrisy. The essence of his strategy was as brutal in its simplicity as it was in its execution. Make war not just on the enemy's army, but on the whole of the enemy in all dimensions. Ravage the enemy's entire way of life: his economy, his society, his culture, his state of mind. Bring war, in all its pitilessness and terror, to the doorsteps of his homes; rub the civilians' noses in the blood and misery; destroy the enemy's ability and will to fight from within his own borders.

Nearly a century later, that strategy would be executed by waves of heavy bombers darkening the skies over enemy territory; in the 1860s, the only way to accomplish the task was to invade the enemy's territory.

News of what he was doing to the Southern homeland would undermine the Southern armies as surely as a whole season of battlefield defeats, Sherman reasoned, and he was absolutely right. His strategy offended and outraged every existing stereotype of how a warrior was supposed to behave, but there is no evidence that he was a cruel or sadistic man. He had carefully studied the problems of winning this war, had correctly divined the nature of his enemy, and had applied a cold, rational calculus to his planning. By visiting the South with the full horror of the conflict, by unleashing his army in a policy of calculated barbarity, he could measurably shorten the war and save not only time but thousands of lives...on both sides. It was a harsh, flinty arithmetic, but its equations balanced, and things worked out more or less as he envisioned they would. He did not expect to be loved for it, and he was not.

"War...is war, and not popularity seeking," he growled. The South had started this thing and its people, he felt, bore a collective responsibility for allowing the killing to begin in the first place. He embarked on his campaign not because he derived any pleasure from it, but because it seemed to be the fastest, surest, most economical way to bring the whole bloody business to an end. And for all the bloodthirstiness that was accrued to his army, Sherman's March turned out not to be an especially bloody campaign — at least, not compared to General Grant's persistent thrusts in Virginia. Relatively speaking, Sherman won his victories on the cheap. His concept of maneuver, of indirect pressure against the enemy's economy and mindset, was very economical in terms of casualties. He used movement, sheer movement, with the elegance and deftness of Frederick the Great.

Curiously enough, the only way the South could have countered his 20th-century strategy of total war would have been to adopt another modern tactic: people's war, such as the one waged 80 years later by Mao Zedong. Sherman's marauding army would have been very vulnerable to a genuine levee en mass. But he had read both the South's condition and its psychology correctly. The Confederacy never got its military act together sufficiently to give him serious resistance — not until he reached North Carolina, and by then it was too late.

It is interesting to speculate how history might have changed if the whole countryside had risen against Sherman after the fall of Atlanta. His foraging parties, some of them two or three days' ride from the main columns and seldom numbering more than a hundred men, were especially vulnerable to hit-and-run tactics, for they were a long way from help if they got cut off. If the South had possessed the unity of purpose and strength of will to mount a people's war, Sherman's free-floating columns could have been bled white by Viet

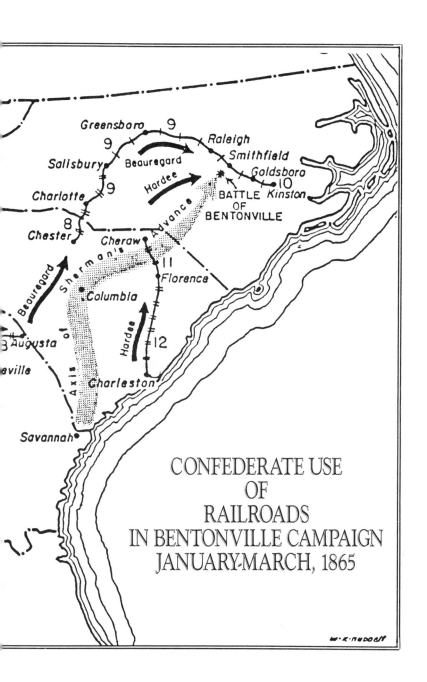

Greensboro 9

Salisbury Beauregard

Charlotte 9

Hardee

Raleigh

Smithfield

Goldsboro

10

BATTLE Kinston

OF

BENTONVILLE

Chester 8

Cheraw

Advance

Sherman's

11

Florence

Columbia

Beauregard

Augusta

Axis of

Hardee 12

eville

Charleston

Savannah

CONFEDERATE USE
OF
RAILROADS
IN BENTONVILLE CAMPAIGN
JANUARY-MARCH, 1865

Cong-style attacks. There were, of course, isolated instances of ambush and murder against the Yankees, but for the most part Sherman's "bummers" preyed on a populace more supine than defiant. What would have happened if half of his foraging parties, during just one week, had ventured into the boondocks and never returned? Sherman would have been in serious trouble in a matter of days.

When the dramatic "March to the Sea" climaxed at Savannah, Georgia, on December 21, 1864 (the city having fallen to Sherman with contemptible ease), General Grant fully expected Sherman to revert to conventional military thinking and embark his 60,000 men, by sea, to rejoin the main effort in front of Richmond. Sherman, too, had in mind a linkup with Grant. But he proposed to march overland, northward by way of the Carolinas, to finish gutting the midsection of the Confederacy as he advanced. By exerting this kind of cruel, grinding pressure on the heartland, Sherman argued, he would be assisting Grant just as effectively as if he were throwing his corps against the lines at Petersburg. Grant was at first reluctant to abandon his more conventional strategy, but Sherman's ideas had borne such fruit up to this point, and his arguments were so persistent and so full of conviction, that Grant finally agreed to the plan. His decision was made somewhat easier by the news of General Hood's trouncing at Nashville, a bloodbath that obviously had knocked the Army of Tennessee out of action for a while.

Sherman laid his plans carefully before cutting loose from the coast. He was going for the jugular: the crucial rail junction at Goldsboro, North Carolina. Once that was in his hands, Robert E. Lee's main supply line would be severed. On the way to Goldsboro, he would visit his wrath on the capital of South Carolina and on the vital arsenal at Fayetteville, North Carolina. After taking Goldsboro, he would march northwest and occupy the capital city of Raleigh, thus cutting out the political hearts of both Carolinas and almost certainly knocking them out of the war.

There were risks. Once he left Savannah, he could expect no more shipments of supplies until he touched the sea again on the Cape Fear River in lower North Carolina. He took enough wagons only for essential military basics: powder, shot, medicines, hardtack, salt, and coffee. For the rest of his supplies, he would, again, "live off the country." He organized numerous parties of outriders to bring home the bacon, or, as his orders delicately put it, "to forage liberally on the country." Conscious that many Northerners, too, had been upset about the stories of atrocities that had accompanied his drive through Georgia, Sherman issued strict orders to regulate the activities of his "bummers." And then he looked the other way.

On the day he left Savannah, Sherman's army numbered slightly more than 60,000 men, accompanied by 2,500 wagons and several hundred ambulances. If the entire army had traveled by the same road, the resulting column would have been an unmanageable and vulnerable 25 miles long. That was the main reason why Sherman customarily divided his force into two wings and issued orders for each corps within those wings to march, if possible, on a separate road. But they were also ordered to march not so separately that the corps could not support one another if anybody ran into trouble.

Sherman had spent a good part of his prewar army career stationed in South Carolina, so he knew what the roads would be like between Savannah and Goldsboro this time of year: awful. The progress of his columns depended on the efforts of his combat engineers — called, in the military parlance of the time, "pioneers" — to make the muddy roads passable by employing a technique known as "corduroying." This involved cutting down hundreds of trees, stripping their branches, and then laying them across the muddy parts of the roads, at right angles to the direction of march. It might take several layers of logs to hit bottom and create a firm roadbed, but eventually the roads would be made passable, after a fashion, for the heavy wagons and artillery. The infantry, poor sods, were usually ordered to march parallel to the roads, not actually on them, to avoid the wear and tear of thousands of feet.

A sergeant from the 123rd New York, Rice C. Bull, left a vivid description of what it was like to move an army over these roads during the rainy season:

> ...we made slow work of it. The road was cut up by the wagons and artillery and in places was impassable. On the surface of the road, the mud looked smooth and like varnish; but when the mules and wagons moved along, they found holes two feet deep. The wagons would sink to the wheel hubs and the mules would be helpless. The whole brigade was set at the job of getting the wagons through the slough. In many cases the mules had to be taken from the wagons, logs had to be brought and placed across the road, the wheels

> pried up with long levers, ropes hitched to the wagons, and then
> a hundred men, pulling and pushing, yelling and swearing, would
> after a while get the wagon out of the mire and on higher ground...we
> kept at this work until ten-thirty that night and made in six and one-
> half hours' time a march of one and one-half miles.[1]

The "March Through the Carolinas" began on the last day of December 1864, but didn't really gather steam until mid-January. By February 12, Orangeburg, South Carolina had fallen. From Orangeburg, the army descended on the capital city of Columbia. The city fell, without any significant resistance, on February 17. There was, unfortunately, quite a lot of liquor stored in the capital, and — as soldiers will do — Sherman's men sniffed out its location. For a lot of thirsty Federals, it had been a long time between drinks. Things got out of hand, as did the flames from some burning cotton bales. Beyond control of their officers, some of whom were also deep in their cups, hundreds of men ran amok, looting and torching. By morning, the capital of South Carolina had been burned to the ground, and a ripple of terror from that event sent a shudder running northwards, over the state line. Sherman more or less shrugged the incident off with one of his c'est la guerre comments: "I never ordered it, and never wished it, [but] I have never shed any tears over the event."

His army marched out of the smoldering city on February 20. The inhabitants lined the streets, hissing, booing, cursing, and spitting at the regiments as they passed. Many of the soldiers shamefacedly avoided looking at the civilians — others were too hung over to care.

The last stop on the South Carolina side of the border was Cheraw, which also suffered mightily from plundering and arson. While taking a breather at Cheraw, Sherman received word that his old adversary, General Joseph E. Johnston, was back in command and was scraping together the remains of the Confederate military establishment to oppose him somewhere in North Carolina. After ruefully admitting that for once the Confederates had done something smart by recalling Old Joe, Sherman reflected soberly that the big battle he had hoped to avoid was now a virtual certainty. Johnston, he knew, had not been called back just to preside over a complacent surrender. Somewhere up ahead, he would make a final stand with every man he could find.

Since before the new year, the people of North Carolina had been preparing themselves psychologically for the arrival of Sherman — they seem to have assumed all along that Sherman would not embark his army at Savannah, but would continue his sweep through the South. And as Sherman's army approached the state, his strategy had a side effect that was more telling than he had foreseen. Hundreds, perhaps thousands, of North Carolina soldiers deserted Lee's ailing army in Virginia and headed back to their home state. They were determined to do whatever they could to protect their homes and families from the scourge that was about to descend on them.

Sherman, on the other hand, fully expected to find North Carolina swarming with Unionists who would be eager to see the state out of the war and who would provide him with valuable assistance as he moved north. Just before the main body of his army crossed the state line, he issued revised instructions to his corps commanders and foraging parties, orders which reflected his beliefs about North Carolina's political climate. Here is an excerpt of the orders issued to General Slocum, commander of the left wing: "All officers and soldiers of this command are reminded that the State of North Carolina was one of the last states that passed the ordinance of secession, and from the commencement of the war there has been in this state a strong Union party. Her action on the question of secession was undoubtedly brought about by the traitorous acts of other states, and by intrigue and dishonesty on the part of her own citizens. The act never even met the approval of the great mass of her people. It should not be assumed that the inhabitants are enemies of our government, and it is to be hoped that every effort will be made to prevent any wanton destruction of property, or any unkind treatment of civilians."

Further efforts were also made, again for political more than humanitarian reasons, to curb the worst excesses of the bummers. Officially, there could be only one foraging party per division, commanded by "reliable officers," who would be held "strictly accountable for the conduct of their men." Only horses and food were to be taken. Private dwellings were strictly off-limits, as were personal valuables. It is possible that, because of these orders and the general awareness of them that percolated through the ranks, the outrages against civilians in North Carolina were marginally fewer and their perpetrators more often called to justice than was the case in Georgia or South Carolina. However, you can't tell that from the accounts of those who received visits from the bummers, all the way from the border to the capital.

Issuing temperate orders was one thing; enforcing them was another. There may have been only one official foraging party per division, but there were always plenty of unofficial ones roaming through the woods and along the back roads for several miles on both sides of the Federal columns. Likewise, it was fit and proper to hold the foraging parties' officers responsible for their actions; but those same officers, as often as not, were also responsible for reporting the outrages in the first place. And many bummer parties were controlled by no one, answerable to no one, and afraid of no one.

Sometimes, foraging parties ran into lurking bands of rebel cavalry. When that happened — in a hundred little mud-spattered gunfights deep in the pine groves — there was no quarter, no mercy, and frequently no prisoners. But for the most part, the bummers went unregulated and unchecked, either by army discipline or armed resistance. They went where they pleased, took what they wanted as well as what they needed, and treated anyone who was in their path according to their mood at the moment.

An inhabitant of Fayetteville penned this description of the foraging detachments at work: "There was no place, no chamber, no truck, drawer, desk, garret, closet, or cellar that was private to their unholy eyes. Their rude hands spared nothing but our lives...Squad after squad unceasingly came and went and tramped through the halls and rooms of our house day and night...they killed every chicken, goose, turkey, calf, and every living thing, even to our pet dog. They carried off wagons, carriage and horses, and broke our buggy, wheelbarrow, garden implements, axes, hatchets, hammers, saws, etc., and burned the fences. Our smoke house and pantry, that a few days ago were well stocked with bacon, lard, flour, dried fruits, pickles, preserves, etc., now contain nothing whatever except a few pounds of meal and flour and five pounds of bacon. They took from old men, women, and children alike, every garment of wearing apparel except what he had on, not even sparing the napkins of infants, blankets, sheets, quilts, etc...such as did not suit them to take away, they tore to pieces before our eyes."[2]

The first units to enter the state were the regiments of Sherman's eccentric and choleric cavalry commander, General Judson Kilpatrick. One detachment of Kilpatrick's men ran into some of Joe Wheeler's cavalry at a flyspeck hamlet called Phillips Cross-Roads, and they were very roughly handled in the exchange. Only the timely arrival of some Federal cannon — to which Wheeler could make no reply — saved Kilpatrick from a nasty little defeat.

The first town inside North Carolina to feel the invaders' wrath was Wadesboro. On the same day as the fight at Phillips Cross-Roads, some other units from Kilpatrick's command tore through the town like a cyclone. Legitimate objectives were destroyed first — a gristmill, a tannery, and a big Confederate stablery — and then the civilians were set upon. Barns, storehouses, and private homes were broken into at gunpoint and looted not only of food and clothing, but also of watches, silverware, jewelry, and family heirlooms. The town's wealthiest citizen, an elderly man named James Bennett, was accosted on the front porch of his house by some of Kilpatrick's men, who demanded that he give them his watch and money. Bennett could not, because an earlier group of Yankee horsemen had already relieved him of those articles. When he attempted to explain, one of Kilpatrick's men cut him short by shooting him down in his own front door.

Wheeler raced Kilpatrick for the crossings of the Pee Dee River and won. He struck back at the invaders on March 7, just outside of Rockingham. There, with a small detachment of men, he bushwhacked a party of foragers from Sherman's left wing, killing or capturing 35 of them. Wheeler's colleague, the fiery and swaggering Wade Hampton, conducted a stubborn rear-guard action inside Rockingham itself, skirmishing house to house against Kilpatrick's advance guard and keeping the Federals out of town for half a day before weight of numbers forced him out.

Sherman himself, at this time, was busy moving his army over the Pee Dee and organizing the march for his planned thrust toward Fayetteville, some 70 miles to the northeast. The country the Federals were entering, between the Pee Dee and Cape Fear Rivers, was wild and sparsely populated. Flat, sandy, pine-forested wilderness was pocked with bogs, creeks, and black-water ponds scummed with the bodies of moribund insects. The region had long been cultivated as one vast turpentine plantation and was dotted with tiny wooden factories where tar, rosin, and turps were tapped from the lofty pines.

The first day the Federals moved into this wilderness, they were impressed by its vast stillness, by the solemn, regular spacing of the trees in the pine barrens, and by the brooding, eerie silences that hung like vaulted ceilings above the creak and chink of their passage. To Captain Daniel Oakey, of the Second Massachusetts Volunteers, it seemed quite lovely: "...we marched into that grand forest with its beautiful carpet of pine needles. The straight trunks of the pine trees shot up to a great height, and then spread out in a green roof, which kept us in perpetual shade."[3]

That night, the view changed dramatically. Some bummers had discovered that a match held up to the resin-pits on the trees in the turpentine plantations would produce a spectacular fire. Whole forests were put to the torch on either side of the invaders' columns, producing phantasmagorical infernos. Tall, slender spirals of fire would shoot up from the point of ignition and engulf the entire length of the pine. The smoke from thousands of burning trees united overhead to form a dark, roiled, fire-streaked ceiling, held aloft by writhing pillars of flame. To the men in Sherman's columns, it was like marching through a cathedral in Hell.

Confederate General Joseph E. Johnston was a better general than he usually had a
chance to be. General Sherman respected him, and at Bentonville, Johnston gave
Sherman his roughest opposition since Atlanta.

Union General William Tecumseh Sherman — "the concentrated essence of Yankeedom," one colleague called him. Not by nature a cruel man, he believed that the quickest route to victory lay in waging "hard war."

Governor Zebulon Vance at about age 28. A hypnotic speaker and a great storyteller, Vance was one of the finest political leaders of the South.

Union General Judson Kilpatrick strikes a characteristic pose in 1863. Although described by one contemporary as "weasel-faced," Kilpatrick campaigned through North Carolina in the company of a beautiful young woman.

The enigmatic but fascinating Judah P. Benjamin, Confederate secretary of state, was described by one contemporary as "keg-like." As the Davis caravan left Greensboro, Benjamin recited lugubrious poetry by Tennyson.

Stephen R. Mallory, the very able Confederate secretary of the navy, who penned a Dickensian account of life on the run with President Jefferson Davis.

John C. Breckinridge, Confederate secretary of war, who thought Sherman was "a hog" because the general would not share his bourbon.

An overall view of the grounds and buildings of the Salisbury Prison as it appeared before it became hideously overcrowded and littered with dying men.

Yankee prisoners enjoy a baseball game on the grounds of the Salisbury Prison, sometime in 1862. This is the first known depiction of a baseball game in America.

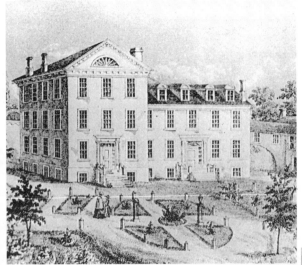

On the grounds of the Edgeworth Female Seminary in Greensboro, the Guilford Grays received their battle flag on a warm May afternoon in 1860. In March 1865, the school was filled with wounded from the Battle of Bentonville.

Kilpatrick's men "foraging" for loot and provisions. Such scenes were common during Sherman's March, although North Carolina got off more lightly than South Carolina — a state which Sherman considered directly responsible for the war.

Sherman's artillery struggling to advance through the boggy terrain in the lower part of North Carolina. This sketch gives a good idea of the "corduroy" roads Sherman's engineers were forced to build.

Sherman's columns advancing through the pine-barrens and swamps of southeastern North Carolina. At night, groves of turpentine-rich trees were set afire, providing a Satanic illumination to the scene.

Sherman's troops skirmishing with the Confederate rear guard in the streets of Fayetteville.

Sherman's men occupying the Fayetteville Arsenal. (From a contemporary sketch.)

Sherman's army moving out through the streets of Fayetteville, a city which the Yankees found "offensively rebellious."

Another view of the Fayetteville Arsenal.

The Battle of Bentonville: Union General Mower's division of the 17th Corps charges the Confederate left.

Climax of the Battle of Bentonville: Johnston's men try to storm the 20th Corps' line. This scene, viewed from the Federal artillery position in front of Harper House, is essentially accurate, although the elevation is somewhat exaggerated and the fields were probably more wooded.

While Sherman and Johnston discussed surrender terms inside the Bennett house, Kilpatrick and Confederate General Wade Hampton — the two rival cavalry commanders — engaged in a spirited debate outside.

The earliest known photograph of the Bennett house, near Durham, where generals Johnston and Sherman negotiated the end of hostilities.

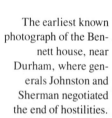

Following the surrender and parole of Johnston's proud but haggard little army, Confederate knapsacks and accouterments were collected in a warehouse in Greensboro.

JOE JOHNSTON TAKES COMMAND

When you look at the faded daguerreotypes, you can see why his men called him "Ol' Joe" — he looks as if he had emerged from the womb middle-aged. He had the same soldierly bearing as Robert E. Lee — that, too, is apparent from the old photographs — but there's no hint of Lee's calm in his eyes.

Ol' Joe's eyes were dominated by a vast, lofty forehead, the type of forehead that phrenologically inclined Victorians associated with a powerful intellect. In this case, they would have been right, because Johnston's forehead enclosed one of the finest military brains of the age.

But by 1865, General Joseph E. Johnston's eyes were pools of stoic bitterness, and the weight of his brow threatened to crush the rest of his features. His eyes, deeply ringed and pouched by the strain of warfare and by the shame of his public banishment by Jefferson Davis, peered outward from a reservoir of pain: deep, sorrowful, compelling. His cheeks were sunken, and his bushy Van Dyke beard and sideburns had turned grizzled and thatchy. In earlier pictures, when he was a Mexican War cavalier, his eyes seemed clear and full of youthful vigor; his mouth, framed by that same beard, had a warm, almost sensual cast. By 1865, that mouth had grown thin and pinched, incised with anger, frustration, and grief at the way both his own career and his beloved Army of Tennessee had been used up and thrown away by his commander-in-chief in Richmond. By the last winter of the war, Joe Johnston was haggard, inside and out, and it showed.

In the opinion of the average Confederate soldier, Johnston ranked as a leader of men right up there with Marse Robert. Both men were hero-worshipped by their armies to an extraordinary degree. Confederate veterans certainly had ample opportunity to become familiar with Ol' Joe's leadership, because at one time or another he commanded every Confederate force east of the Mississippi. On more than one occasion, he commanded more men than Lee.

Johnston and Lee were matched contemporaries, born only 15 days apart in 1807. Both were Virginians. Both graduated from West Point in the class of '29, Lee second in his class, Johnston thirteenth.

After serving in the Black Hawk War and the Seminole campaigns, Johnston temporarily left the army in 1837 to follow a career as a civil engineer. But when, a year after his resignation, he was offered a commission as a captain in the Topographical Engineers, he changed his mind and resumed his military career.

Both Johnston and Lee saw major combat for the first time during the Mexican War in 1846. Both men attracted attention by their bravery and competence, both earned three battlefield promotions, and both were wounded — Johnston twice, in fact, at Cerro Gordo and again during the assault on Mexico City. During his lifetime of military service, Joseph E. Johnston would be wounded no less than ten times.

Although Johnston wasn't widely recognized for his actions at First Manassas, he was the man primarily responsible for the stunning Confederate victory at the war's first major battle (Pierre Beauregard got the credit, and did nothing to disown it). Johnston's troubles with Jefferson Davis stemmed from that battle, for in the list of promotions to full general published afterward, Johnston was fourth on the roster, despite his seniority and his importance in the victory. He was as proud a man, in his own way, as Jefferson Davis was in his, and so he wrote a letter of protest to the Confederate President. He didn't intend for the letter to become public, but it did, thanks to the machinations of Richmond politics, and it earned him a verbal slap on the hand from Davis.

Both men then backed off, and Johnston thought the matter was over and done. He was not a man who held grudges, and did not become so until too many of them were forced upon him. Jefferson Davis, on the other hand, suckled whole litters of grudges, and he continued to resent Johnston even after the promotion affair had seemingly blown over. How much this rather trivial tiff had to do with their later public falling-out is a matter of conjecture, but it should be noted that Johnston was absolutely right in every point his original letter raised with Davis — he should have been promoted ahead of the others, including Lee.

Worse trouble followed in September 1861 when Davis, with typical insight, named Judah P. Benjamin as his secretary of war. Benjamin had about as much expertise in the field of military science as he did in neurosurgery. He immediately began flinging his weight around, issuing bombastic directives and taking experienced career soldiers to task, treating them as though they were all personal and political enemies. His behavior and manifest incompetence disrupted the entire Confederate war effort. At one point, General Stonewall Jackson — not a man given to melodramatic gestures — tendered his resignation rather than serve under Benjamin.

Benjamin also seemed to bring out the worst in his patron, Jefferson Davis, who backed him to the hilt even when Benjamin was issuing directives so patently irrational as to be virtually treasonous. It was Johnston's lot to fight constantly with Benjamin, more than any other Confederate general, for the simple reason that at the time Johnston was commanding the biggest army. Benjamin's capacity to wreak mischief was greatest in the sphere of Ol' Joe's responsibility. Benjamin took an instant dislike to Johnston and constantly poisoned Davis's ear with complaints about him. One can see, week by week, the deteriorating tone of Davis's letters to Johnston. The language goes from frigidly correct to arrogant, testy, and finally downright snide.

Fortunately for the Southern cause, Benjamin was shuffled sideways in March 1862 to the post of secretary of state, a position more suited to his limited talents, if only because men did not get killed as a result of his orders. His replacement, George W. Randolph, was more diplomatic and better versed in military affairs. By that time, however, the relationship between Davis and Johnston had been permanently damaged.

Johnston was severely wounded during the Battle of Seven Pines (Fair Oaks) in May-June 1862. This brought Lee into command of the army, which he renamed the Army of Northern Virginia. Seven

Pines was not one of Johnston's better performances as a general, but he did about as well as Lee did a month later in the very similar Seven Days' Battles. Both men were still learning their trade, and both were finding out just how incredibly difficult it was, in the days before electronic communications, to control large armies in a complex engagement. When comparing Seven Pines to the Seven Days' Battles, historians have judged Johnston's flawed performance much more harshly than Lee's, but a dispassionate study of both battles suggests that the aura of Olympian reverence which surrounds Lee to this day, and does not cling at all to Ol' Joe, is the only explanation for the prejudicial treatment. There was no significant difference in the way either general handled his troops in the two battles.

When Johnston had recovered from his wounds — and for a while there was doubt that he would even live, much less return to active duty — he was appointed commander of the Department of the West, an immense theater of war which included portions of Louisiana, Georgia, and North Carolina, and all of Tennessee, Alabama, and Mississippi. To defend this vast area, Johnston mainly had the armies of General John Pemberton, in Mississippi, and of General Braxton Bragg, in Tennessee. Because of the great distance between his headquarters and Richmond, Johnston rarely had a chance to confer with Jefferson Davis personally; they communicated almost entirely through letters, and no flicker of warmth can be discerned on the part of either man.

The breaking point between the two men came during the Vicksburg campaign (although its most dramatic fallout would not occur until much later). Davis expected a signal miracle from Johnston: the rescue of besieged Vicksburg. Johnston undertook his orders with some confidence, but when he arrived at Jackson, Mississippi to take command of what had been billed as a "relief force," he found only 12,000 men — totally inadequate for the job. The only chance of saving the beleaguered city was for its commander, Pemberton, to attack Grant from one side while Johnston simultaneously struck from another. Alternatively, if they couldn't pull off that trick, Johnston formulated a plan for Pemberton to secretly abandon the city altogether, unite the two armies, and then turn on Grant with their combined strength. With this numerically adequate force, they stood a chance of beating Grant out in the open or maybe even bagging him inside the city.

But for political reasons, President Davis wanted Pemberton to hold the city to the end; and for Davis, apparently, political reasons were a more important consideration than saving the besieged army. Pemberton's professional instincts and good sense told him to follow Johnston's plans, but his orders from Richmond told him to sit tight. The resulting strategic muddle presented the Confederate president with the worst possible result. On July 4, 1863, the day after Lee's shocking defeat at Gettysburg, the Confederacy lost both Vicksburg and the army bottled up there. The Union soon controlled the entire length of the Mississippi River, splitting the Confederacy in two.

Johnston's next major responsibility was to replace Braxton Bragg as commander of the Army of Tennessee after Bragg's humiliating defeats near Chattanooga. Given the closest thing in eastern America to a genuinely impregnable fortress — Lookout Mountain — Bragg should have been able to hold his position, Masada-like, for months, perhaps even years. Well-led and properly motivated, a troop of Boy Scouts armed with rocks and slingshots probably could have held the mountain for a week or two. Bragg somehow managed to lose it in one day, and followed that disaster with another, almost as grotesque in its avoidability, on Missionary Ridge. Despite the high esteem Jefferson Davis still had for his old buddy Braxton, the outcry over this needless catastrophe was so loud that Bragg simply had to be sacked.

But having for once listened to good counsel in replacing Bragg with Johnston, Davis would not thereafter leave Ol' Joe alone to fight his campaign. Clamoring always for Johnston to take a stand, for "action," Davis just could not, or would not, see that Johnston was fighting Sherman in the only way that made a lick of strategic sense. Sherman's army greatly outnumbered Johnston's, and Sherman could whip him in a stand-up fight without half trying. Johnston's plan, therefore, was to fall back as slowly as he could, stretching Sherman's supply lines, forcing him to disperse his forces more and more with every mile, and wearing him down by turning and offering resistance wherever and whenever the terrain favored the Confederates. At the same time, Johnston was always waiting for Sherman to slip up and leave some portion of his force vulnerable to a sudden counterattack.

Students of military history will discern that this is basically the same strategy Lee was using against Grant in Virginia late in the war; Lee got praised for it, but Johnston got axed. Lee won credit for being a "fighting general," and Johnston was vilified for being timid, even cowardly. Actually, the only difference between the campaigns both generals were fighting at this stage of the war lay in their respective opponents. Grant was always coming after Lee; Grant was never reluctant to accept battle, the way Sherman was, even if it was on Lee's terms. The result was more or less continuous fighting and enormous Federal casualties. But Sherman preferred maneuvering to fighting, so the campaign between Johnston and him resembled a chess game rather than an alley brawl.

Nevertheless, Johnston managed to bring Sherman to battle on several occasions — notably in the battles of Resaca, New Hope Church, and Kenesaw Mountain — and usually drew more blood than he shed (Sherman lost 3,000 men in one morning at Kenesaw Mountain). And slowing Sherman down was just as important, in Johnston's opinion, as killing his troops. Ol' Joe had a good grasp of the political dimensions of this war, and of the impact battlefield events could have on them. He knew that if neither Richmond nor Atlanta had been captured by the time the elections rolled around in November 1864, there was a chance that the war-weary Northern voters would turn Abe Lincoln out of the White House. And that, for the South, would be even more of a victory than a battlefield defeat of Sherman.

It is curious, ironic, and a bit pathetic, that Jefferson Davis — the consummate career politician — was so blind to that aspect of Johnston's strategy. Sherman knew what Ol' Joe was doing, and it worried the devil out of him. Grant, too, thought that Johnston's handling of the strategic withdrawal toward Atlanta was both wise and masterful. In any event, Johnston planned to turn and give battle when he reached Atlanta, unleashing his army like a coiled spring.

He never had the chance. Just as Johnston's policy of conserving his army was about to pay off, Jefferson Davis summarily removed him from command on July 17, 1864. Citing again the need for "action," Davis gave the army to the valiant but bloodthirsty General John B. Hood. Soon Davis had all the action he could ask for.

Brave, Hood certainly was; smart, he was not. He seemed to have one and only one tactical solution to any situation: Fix bayonets and charge. Which he did, with most of his army, instead of waiting behind Atlanta's formidable defenses until Sherman — who was himself under intense political pressure to capture the city before the election — was bled and winded and ripe for a counterstroke. Had Johnston fought the Atlanta campaign, win or lose, Sherman's March to the Sea probably never would have happened.

Instead, Hood was soundly defeated by Sherman and managed to lose Atlanta in record time. Next, he left Georgia to the mercies of Sherman's bummers and struck north against General George Thomas in the disastrous Franklin/Nashville campaign. Sherman didn't bother to follow, preferring instead to cut a 60-mile-wide swath to Savannah. At Franklin, under Hood's command, the Army of Tennessee lost 6,000 men in a futile attack against Union forces. Soon afterward, at Nashville, Hood's men mounted repeated frontal attacks with incomparable bravery against deeply entrenched Federals. Union forces threw them back and captured 10,000 Confederates, shattering the Army of Tennessee beyond repair.

Johnston, meanwhile, was in official disgrace and professional limbo, although his case was angrily defended by most Southern newspapers and other Confederate generals. Embittered at his treatment, and heartsick over the ruination of his beloved army, Johnston languished until early 1865. At that time, he donned his uniform one more time at the request of the one man he could not refuse: his old friend, Robert E. Lee. Finally doing what it should have done a year earlier, the Confederacy had designated Lee commander-in-chief of all Confederate forces. Lee's first official act in that capacity was to recall Joseph Johnston to duty.

Johnston took command of all Confederate forces south of Virginia and east of the Mississippi on February 25, 1865. His directive from Lee was simple, but simply impossible — "concentrate all available forces and drive back Sherman." Even carrying out the first part of the order was hopeless. General Wade Hampton, in a postwar essay on the Bentonville campaign, accurately assessed Johnston's situation when he wrote, "It would scarcely have been possible to disperse an army more effectively."

Johnston set up his first headquarters in Charlotte, North Carolina, where he formally took command from the loyal, but sick and dispirited, Pierre Beauregard. Aside from Beauregard and a few other officers who happened to be in the neighborhood, he had no staff, no supplies, and no army. His first step was to issue a plea for all absent soldiers to rejoin their units, wherever they happened to be.

Looking at the map, Johnston saw the Federals' grand strategy with utter clarity. Sherman would continue his march north and overwhelm whatever resistance was left in North Carolina, effectively taking that wavering state out of the Confederacy. Then he would unite with Grant, and together they would annihilate Lee, no matter how brilliantly Lee managed to fight or maneuver.

Looking at his own far-flung and shrunken resources, Johnston must have felt a sensation of futility. The task of stopping Sherman was clearly beyond his means, yet for the sake of his own and his army's honor, Johnston began to move with such decisiveness that he created the illusion something could still be done. Whether Johnston in his deepest heart really thought he had a chance seems doubtful. That he accomplished as much as he did, given his burden, is a testament to his granite strength of will.

Under his command were the battered and demoralized remnants of the Army of Tennessee, some very good cavalry under Generals Wade Hampton and Joseph Wheeler, and the scattered scraps of little garrisons strewn all over the map of southeastern America. Even if he managed to get every man together in one place in enough time to oppose his old enemy, the odds would still be greatly against him. And given the condition of the Confederacy's railroad system at this time — what was left of it after Sherman got through bending half the rails in Georgia and South Carolina — just getting his new command together would prove a herculean task. Six months before, there had been a thousand miles of railroad track in Georgia. Sherman had burned and bow-tied nearly half of that.

General Hardee was coming north from Columbia, by way of Florence and Cheraw — where the railroad ended — with 11,000 men, but a lot of them were former members of the Charleston garrison, and they weren't used to this kind of hard-marching campaign. Stewart, Cheatham, and Beauregard were shepherding the remnants of the Army of Tennessee toward a planned concentration at Fayetteville, but the trains moved sporadically. And after every one of the numerous stopovers, more and more men disappeared. Men just waited until they came to the station nearest to home and walked away.

There was plenty of opportunity to desert. What was left of the Army of Tennessee moved by rail through the Deep South: Tupelo, Meridian, Montgomery, Columbus, Macon, Midgeville, and Augusta. From Augusta to Chester, South Carolina, they had to leave the trains and march on foot until they reached Charlotte. Hardee's men had to march from Cheraw to Smithfield, keeping just out of reach on the western side of Sherman's left wing.

To expedite movement north of Charlotte, Beauregard asked the authorities in Richmond for permission to widen the tracks; the rails running north from Salisbury were a different gauge than those running from Chester to Salisbury. But that meant severing the connection between the main North Carolina rail system and the Western North Carolina line that ran from Salisbury to Morganton, and Governor Vance refused to allow it. The Confederate secretary of war (John C. Breckinridge, now) tried to lean on Vance, but couldn't budge him. So strong was the doctrine of states' rights even in this eleventh hour that Richmond could not force Vance's cooperation.

Beauregard, who had planned and executed this far-flung rail effort about as well as anyone could have at this stage of the war, suggested Smithfield as a good point of concentration. By then, it was clear that Sherman would get to Fayetteville before the Confederates possibly could. Smithfield was chosen, then, for this reason, as well as its proximity to the force Braxton Bragg was leading westward from Wilmington.

General Johnston headed for the eastern part of the state on March 4, while Beauregard remained in Charlotte to hustle the troops forward as fast as possible. On March 6, Johnston passed word for the newly arriving units to concentrate on Goldsboro rather than Smithfield. The next day, learning that Sherman was about to enter Fayetteville, he changed the orders back to Smithfield again.

But however good Beauregard was at improvising, and however good Johnston was at stirring up morale and confidence, both men were fighting nightmarish logistical problems. Johnston was at the narrow end of the funnel, and the chaos back along the railroad line compounded with every passing hour. Whole brigades of men piled up at the Salisbury bottleneck, where the track gauge changed. By March 11, 120 carloads of men, guns, and wagons clogged the over-burdened freight yard. Over where Johnston faced Sherman, only 500 men per day were getting through by rail.

It was during that first hectic week in March, too, that Johnston learned none of his troops had been paid for months. He forcefully protested to Richmond, asking that four months' pay be sent down immediately. He was told, rather sheepishly (and rather inac-curately), that the Confederate treasury was out of funds. Nor could Richmond do anything about provisions. Johnston turned to Gover-nor Vance for wagons, horses, and food, and some supplies — exactly how much cannot be determined — were delivered from the stocks the governor had been hoarding against the day when central North Carolina would become a battleground.

On March 6, Johnston received word that Union General J.M. Schofield's men were almost at Kinston. It was vital that Schofield be checked, even for a day or two, but the only reinforcements John-ston had available to send to Braxton Bragg were commanded by D.H. Hill, whom Bragg had sacked after Chickamauga. Hill thoroughly detested Bragg — and not just because Bragg had sacked him. "I beg you to forget the past in this emergency," Johnston wrote to Hill. Hill swallowed his pride, dutifully reported to Bragg, and together they turned at Kinston and took a fair-sized bite out of Schofield's fur.

Johnston and Lee were also conferring by letter on the strategic possibilities of Lee retaining half his army to shield Richmond and sending the other half south to join Johnston for a do-or-die attempt to crush Sherman. After Sherman was eliminated, they could turn and face Grant with everything the Confederacy still had. It was a bold, even visionary strategy, but also a desperate one. It appealed to the gambler in Lee, and he ruminated on it for a few days before concluding that, even if Jefferson Davis did permit such a risky move, the condition of his troops, and of the decrepit railroad system needed to move them, would make the operation all but impossible.

Lee now realized what a bricks-without-straw task he had set for Johnston by ordering him to "drive back Sherman." Lee waffled, in fact, between urging Johnston to make a "bold and unexpected attack" on Sherman and warning him to be cautious in preserving the last viable rebel army south of Virginia. "If you are forced back from Raleigh," Lee wrote, "and we be deprived of the supplies from East North Carolina, I do not know how this army can be supported. Yet a disaster to your army will not improve my condition, and while I would urge upon you to neglect no opportunity of delivering the enemy a successful blow, I would not recommend you to engage in a general battle without a prospect of success."

Joseph Johnston was reunited with the survivors of the Army of Tennessee at Smithfield. The men cheered him; the general was moved near to weeping. Observing Johnston at close range for the first time, a young aide at General Stewart's headquarters described the grizzled old warrior as "surprisingly social...[he] endeavors to conceal his greatness rather than to impress you with it. I expressed to him the joy the Army of Tennessee manifested on hearing of his restoration to command. He answered that he was equally as much gratified to be with them as they were at his coming, but he feared it 'too late to make it the same army.'"

Maybe so, but it was close enough to the old army for Johnston to decide, only a few days later, to do what Lee had first urged him to do, then cautioned him against doing: "a bold and unexpected attack."

GENERAL KILPATRICK IS SURPRISED

All of General Sherman's army had crossed into North Carolina by March 8, 1865. The day before, his left wing under command of General Slocum tore up and bent the rails along nearly a mile of the Charlotte-Wilmington Railroad — a token gesture at best. Since the fall of Wilmington in January, the line had ceased to have much importance. A depot and some repair shops at Launrinburg were also burned.

During his first week in North Carolina, Sherman would be more troubled by the weather than by Confederate resistance. He had enjoyed exceedingly good weather, in fact, until the start of the second week in March. Beginning on March 8, the customary and long-delayed spring rains began. The long, heavy, sodden downpours pushed the normally treacherous Lumber River into flood status, then saturated and finally flooded the low-lying swamps on either bank of the river. The next week of the campaign was characterized by what Sherman later described as "the damndest marching I ever saw."

Cannon and supply wagons were all but immobilized after sinking into mud above their axles. Extra mules had to be hitched to each wagon, and when the mules could do no more, brute manpower was enlisted to push, pull, or — it seemed — cuss the wagons into motion again. War correspondents who accompanied the columns claimed that no group of men in their combat experience could match Sherman's teamsters when it came to colorful, inventive, tenacious swearing. The dripping pines rang with oaths and raucous braying as burly men, soaked to the skin and bathed in mud to the waist, lashed their mules without mercy in the downpour: *Crack!* —

231

"Gee-up, you lop-eared son of a bitch!" — *Crack!* — "God *damn* your black, military heart!" — *Crack!* — "I said *move*, you mother-less bag of dung!" — *Crack!*

Lumberton was raided on March 9, and despite the new orders pertaining to the treatment of civilians, the same old story of rob-bery, intimidation, and terror was played out again in that village and others in the region.

General Judson Kilpatrick had taken most of the Federal cavalry across the Lumber River on the night of March 8 and had encamped at a place called Monroe's Cross-Roads, up in the panhandle of Cumberland County, northwest of Fayetteville. During the day, his men had caught up with some stragglers from Hardee's retreating command and captured a few of them. From questioning these men, Kilpatrick learned that his old nemesis, Confederate cavalry com-mander Wade Hampton, was in the vicinity, making for Fayetteville. After studying his map, Kilpatrick positioned each of his three brigades to cover one of the three roads Hampton would have to use. The arrangement was roughly triangular: the routes of the roads allowed Kilpatrick to put each brigade within supporting distance of the others. One of them, surely, would intercept Hampton and pin him down long enough for the others to join in.

Judson Kilpatrick was a character. The Civil War produced numerous interesting "supporting players" on both sides, and none was more controversial in his own time than Kilpatrick. He was an impetuous, even reckless commander, throwing his men into dan-gerous spots time and time again, and then fudging on his after-battle reports to absolve himself of blame for anything that went wrong. But things did go wrong, so often and so bloodily, that by the start of the March to the Sea, he had already acquired the nickname "Kil-cavalry." One Federal officer who campaigned with him and did not care for the experience described him simply as "a frothy braggart with no brains."

Sherman knew Kilpatrick's faults, but weighed them against his virtues and decided to use him anyway. When General Grant advised Sherman not to appoint Kilpatrick as his cavalry commander, Sher-man wrote back: "I know Kilpatrick is a hell of a damned fool, but I want just that sort of man to command my cavalry on this expedition."

Kilpatrick's zeal had been equal to his task — particularly his passion for wreaking devastation. The man simply enjoyed setting fires. At the beginning of the march through South Carolina, Kilpatrick issued large bundles of matches to his men, and prophesied: "In after years, when travelers passing through South Carolina shall see chimneys without houses, and the country desolate, and shall ask, 'Who did this?', some Yankee will answer: 'Kilpatrick's cavalry.'"

Because of his depredations in South Carolina, a blood feud had developed between Kilpatrick and Wade Hampton. The two cavalry commanders were always trying to get the drop on each other, sniffing out each other's columns and looking for a chance to settle old scores. On several occasions, when isolated detachments of Kilpatrick's men fell into the hands of Hampton's patrols, they were shot down without mercy. How many times this happened will never be known, because Hampton preferred not to discuss it and Kilpatrick habitually lied on his casualty reports.

Kilpatrick was a small, cocky bantam-weight, full of coiled-spring energy that sometimes had a manic edge to it. Although one historian dismisses his physical appearance with the adjective "raccoon-faced," he still managed to cut quite a figure with his flaming red sideburns, elegantly tailored uniforms, and rakish black felt hat. He knew how to pose for a camera, too; in most of his wartime photos, he manages to look like a diminutive and slightly too thin-lipped incarnation of John Wayne.

Kilpatrick was nakedly ambitious and spoke airily of one day running for President of the United States. Those hopes were dashed after he staked his whole career on a reckless cavalry raid on Richmond in late February 1864. No less a personage than Abraham Lincoln himself had helped sponsor the raid. The President followed events closely as Kilpatrick first enjoyed the success that sometimes attends mad audacity, and then suffered the failure that usually comes to those who press their luck foolishly.

Kilpatrick's command, finally, was cut to pieces just outside of Richmond after the raid. Among the officers slain was the 21-year-old son of the respected and influential U.S. Navy officer, John A. Dahlgren, inventor of the bottle-shaped Dahlgren gun found on many U.S. warships. On young Dahlgren's body were papers indicating that Kilpatrick's ultimate objective had been to burn the city of Richmond to ashes and to kill Jefferson Davis and his Confederate cabinet. The bloody failure of the raid, and the uncivilized nature of Kilpatrick's orders, created a scandal in the newspapers. Lincoln was displeased. Kilpatrick was booted out of the main theater of war and transferred to Sherman's command.

During his months with Sherman, Kilpatrick imbued his entire command with a spirit of aggressiveness and headlong energy that fit in perfectly with Sherman's concept of how things ought to be done. If other Federal officers considered Kilpatrick a conceited and bloody-minded popinjay, his own men had mixed emotions. It is true that he sometimes squandered their lives, but just as often, his reckless desire to close with the enemy gave them easy victories. Kilpatrick looked after his boys, too, making sure they had good mounts, plenty to eat, fine, spiffy uniforms, and plenty of good old-fashioned plunder to fill their saddle bags.

There was one aspect of Kilpatrick's character, though, that filled some of his men with envy and resentment: his insatiable zest for sexual indulgence. Though a strict teetotaler when it came to booze, Kilpatrick was thoroughly and flagrantly given to lechery. Not even the rigors of Sherman's campaign could keep him from satisfying his appetite. For a while, up in Virginia, Kilpatrick and General George Custer had enjoyed a menage a trois with a bountifully endowed camp follower. And at some point during his stay in Columbia, South Carolina, Kilpatrick had managed to persuade another lady of easy virtue to accompany him on the rest of the campaign. When there were no pressing military matters to tend to, Kilpatrick rode with this woman in a wagon, his head reclining on her ample and shapely lap. A somewhat embarrassed enlisted man was at the reins of the wagon, and, for at least part of the trip, a captured Confederate officer was forced to walk behind their conveyance — where he was tortured by the scent of the lady's perfume and by the sight of her lascivious nibbling on the Union general's ear.

The lady in question was named Marie Boozer; regarded as one of the great beauties of Columbia, Miss Boozer was 19, a Unionist, and well to do. She was also quite experienced — she had just left her fourth husband at the time Sherman's army arrived in South Carolina. Kilpatrick had wooed her away from a veritable horde of Federal suitors by giving her, among other things, her own private cavalry escort. By the time Kilpatrick's command was ready to move on, Marie Boozer had become the general's mistress, and she would invariably share his bed at the end of each day's ride.

And so it was on the night of March 10, when Kilpatrick decided to make camp with Colonel George Spencer's brigade. Spencer's men were encamped near Monroe's Cross-Roads, just north of Solemn Grove, a rural post office on the Morganton Road a bit west of the present-day boundary of Fort Bragg.

At twilight, General Butler's division of Wade Hampton's Confederate cavalry discovered clues on one of the Fayetteville roads that a large body of horsemen had recently happened by (it's nearly impossible for a large body of horsemen to go anywhere without leaving "clues"). Shortly after this discovery, Butler's men surprised a squad of Federal cavalry and took them all prisoner without firing a shot. Thanks to this stroke of luck, and some skillful interrogation of a Union officer who mistakenly rode into Confederate lines a short time later, Butler was able to give Wade Hampton a detailed picture of Kilpatrick's position and strength.

The more he learned, the more Hampton must have salivated at the opportunity fate had handed him: his old enemy, caught (literally) with his pants down. Hampton could not have asked for a better situation. Kilpatrick, eager to forget the rigors of the day's ride in the arms of his lady, had retired to his quarters — a white frame house belonging to Charles Monroe, for whose family the crossroads was named. Kilpatrick hadn't even bothered to post pickets on one side of his encampment. Behind the clearing where the Federals had pitched their tents was a broad, meandering creek with extensive rain-swollen swamps on either bank, and Kilpatrick had assumed that he was safe from being pestered in that direction.

He wasn't. Carefully working their horses through the quagmire, Butler and a detachment of hand-picked men were able to get close enough to smell the food cooking over the Yankees' campfires. They carefully noted the details of Kilpatrick's careless bivouac. Although a small patrol of skilled men could sneak close on the swampy flank, it was, as Kilpatrick had surmised, impassable for a force large enough to attack him with any hope of success. Nevertheless, from their vantage point, Butler's men were able to determine that the side of the Federal camp facing the Morganton Road was also bereft of sentries and was wide open for an assault. Butler returned to the Confederate camp and reported what he had seen to Wheeler and Hampton. All three cavalrymen then made their plans, with an unusual degree of confidence and elation.

Butler would lead the attack, at dawn; Wheeler would move through the woods behind him and strike the enemy encampment from the rear. A third, smaller detachment, under the leadership of one Captain Bostick, was instructed to charge straight for the house where Kilpatrick was sleeping — or whatever — and then surround the building and hold it until reinforced. Hampton wanted the bastard alive, if possible. Meanwhile, during the night, more of Hampton's men would engage in continuous skirmishing to mask the noise made by the movements of the forces designated for the attack.

The woods around the Monroe house were full of moving horsemen that night. On several occasions, Union and Confederate troopers intermingled, sometimes not realizing what had happened until a sudden flare of torchlight revealed an unfriendly uniform riding close at hand.

Butler's men were in position well before daylight and maintained strict discipline. No fires, no conversation, each man responsible for the silence of his own mount. During the march, there had been considerable ribald speculation over the physical attributes of Kilpatrick's lady friend — by this time Marie Boozer had become something of a legend to the Confederates as well — and numerous wagers had been made regarding who, if anyone, would get the first and closest look at her.

Finally, the wet, slow, grainy light of a soggy lowland dawn percolated through the pines, providing enough light to ride by. Silent as ghosts, the Confederates mounted their horses, drew their sabers, and cocked their cap-and-ball revolvers.

In a thundering charge, they swept out of the forest like nocturnal demons, taking the enemy camp completely by surprise. Not a single picket challenged the Confederate cavalrymen as they crashed into the ring of smoldering campfire ashes and began slashing tent-ropes with their blades. There simply was no resistance, at first — just a mad dash for safety as sleep-drugged Yankees flapped out of their tents like panic-stricken geese and ran for the woods. All around them, rebel horsemen whooped and hollered and fired their pistols, as often into the air as at the fleeing Federals.

The men detached to nab Kilpatrick got to within 20 yards of the house when the general himself appeared, clad only in his boots and nightshirt. "Little Kil" had been slumbering in his lady's arms when the first rebel yells pierced the warmth of his dreams. With visions of his entire military career going up in smoke, he hurried downstairs, gallantly leaving the lady to fend for herself. As he reached the vestibule of the house, a fierce-looking cavalryman in a suspiciously ill-fitting Federal uniform reined in his horse, brandished a huge pistol, and shouted, "Where is General Kilpatrick?"

Kilpatrick may have been sleazy, but he wasn't slow. Spotting another officer riding off on a distinctive black mount, he thrust out a finger and replied, "There he goes, on that black horse!" The excited Confederate in the Yankee uniform gave a yelp and spurred his horse in pursuit. Kilpatrick then leaped onto the back of the nearest unoccupied horse and galloped for the trees.

His female companion, meanwhile, was awakened not by the general's familiar snoring but by the brutal "Whap!" of carbine rounds punching holes through the wall of the bedroom. Still befogged with sleep, the fair lady — and by all accounts, she was rather fair — stumbled downstairs to the front door. Clad only in her abbreviated sleeping attire, Marie Boozer appeared on the vestibule like a white apparition.

Standing there in the middle of a furious firefight with a glazed expression on her face, she stared at the carriage that had brought her here. Its horses were nowhere to be seen, and she obviously wondered how she was going to escape to safety.

The answer appeared in the form of a dashing Southern cavalryman. He galloped over on his horse, dismounted, courteously bowed, and escorted the lady to the protection of a nearby ditch. Let no one underestimate the power of Southern chivalry to flourish under adverse conditions. (It is also probable that this gentleman collected on a good number of wagers, once he was back in camp with his comrades.)

Kilpatrick located most of his scattered brigade milling around crazily about 500 yards back in the swamp. Fortunately for Kilpatrick, many of them had the presence of mind to grab their lever-action Spencer carbines as they fled. Luckier still, the Confederate attack bogged down right after its initial success. Wheeler's men had difficulty moving through the bogs and could not support Butler as planned. And a lot of Butler's men, startled by the apparent ease of their victory, had stopped to plunder the enemy camp and liberate some Confederate prisoners, rather than chase Kilpatrick into the trees and finish him off.

The turning point in the battle came after about 30 minutes of intense combat. Kilpatrick's artillery commander, a lieutenant named Stetson, crept up close to the spot where the Confederates were frantically trying to harness some horses to the abandoned Union guns. So hot was the fighting, so great the noise and confusion, that no one saw Stetson single-handedly pivot one of the field-pieces around toward the thickest concentration of rebel infantry near the farmhouse. He then loaded the big gun with a huge charge of grapeshot and fired at a range of only 20 yards. The effects of the blast were so terrible that the entire Confederate advance reeled back from the carnage.

Meanwhile, Kilpatrick, now fired-up and eager to redeem what was left of his dignity, if not his reputation, hastily organized a counterattack. Making maximum use of the firepower thrown out by their Spencer repeating carbines, his men drove the disorganized rebels away from his artillery. Then they swiftly turned the cannon around and began ripping the encampment with grapeshot. Unequipped with either artillery or repeating rifles, the Confederates were driven out of the camp almost as quickly as they had overrun it.

Kilpatrick's official casualty return listed about 20 men killed and 80 wounded, as well as a fairly large number of men taken prisoner. But then, this was a general who lied about his losses when he won a battle. It strains credulity to assume he was being honest on the occasion of his worst professional humiliation. Realistically, he probably lost half again as many killed and wounded as he admitted. As for the number of his men taken prisoner, Kilpatrick admitted to losing 103 men, but Wheeler claimed to have taken 350 (as well as liberating more than 150 Confederates). General Joe Johnston, in his official summary of the action, estimated Yankee POWs at 500. Take your pick.

About 80 Confederates were killed and perhaps twice that number wounded, virtually all during the Yankee counterattack — grim testimony to the deadliness of the Spencer repeating carbine in a close-range firefight.

Among the Confederate dead were several teenaged boys, cadets from The Citadel, the famed military school in Charleston, South Carolina. They had slogged all the way from Charleston only to die with their backs against a blackwater swamp in the middle of nowhere.

Strategically, the encounter amounted to a Confederate victory, since it cleared the road to Fayetteville and enabled Wade Hampton to accomplish his original purpose, which was to join with Hardee's infantry there.

But the raid earned its place in history for different reasons, of course. The episode of the Yankee general and his Southern lady quickly passed into Civil War folklore. After the war, with people still snickering about it, Kilpatrick fiercely maintained that he had actually awakened at dawn, as was his custom, to make sure his horses were being properly fed. In mocking this far-fetched excuse, one Confederate veteran of the raid replied in print that Kilpatrick must surely be the only general since Joshua to leave a warm bed on a cold morning for the sake of his horses.

News of the incident, doubtless much embroidered with vulgar detail, spread quickly through the ranks of Sherman's army. It soon acquired its own name: not "The Battle of Monroe's Cross-Roads," nor even the more poetic and evocative "Battle of Solemn Grove," but simply "Kilpatrick's Shirt-tail Skedaddle."

And what happened to the lady? Marie Boozer stayed with Kilpatrick until Fayetteville, where she declared that she had endured enough of this rude existence. She then took the first available ship — the Union tug Davidson — down-river.

The rest of Marie Boozer's life resembles the plot of a bad bodice-ripper. She married a rich Yankee (her fifth husband), left him in a divorce case that made scandalous headlines, and then married a French count and became a gilded social butterfly until her fortunes again plummeted. After a while her trail becomes obscure, although it appears that she traveled to the Far East and plied her skills as a courtesan there until she died. Her exact fate is unknown, but there are several colorful legends. According to one, she finished her days as the favorite concubine of a rich Chinese warlord, who fattened her until she weighed 300 pounds and then had her hamstrung to prevent her from leaving him. According to another, rather operatic, set of rumors, she became the mistress of the prime minister of Japan, until she somehow angered him and was beheaded.

Hard Fighting At Averasboro

Because of its arsenal, Fayetteville was one of the prime military objectives in the whole southeastern Piedmont, and the Confederates planned to make Sherman fight for it. That's why General Wade Hampton was moving there with his cavalry to help set up the defenses.

As things turned out, there was a fight, all right, but not the kind Hampton had been hoping for. Just after dawn on March 11, the commander of Sherman's right wing, General O.O. Howard, sent one of his aides, a captain named Duncan, to scout the roads to Fayetteville. With an escort about the size of a company, Duncan probed the back roads and successfully located an unguarded route into the city.

Secure in the belief that the Federals were at least a day's march behind them, Confederate General Butler and one of his aides had decided to catch up on the sleep they had lost while planning their attack on Kilpatrick. They were deep in slumber inside a private home when Captain Duncan and his troop rode in; worse than that, their clothes, including their underwear, were soaking in a washtub in the backyard, where a Negro woman was preparing to scrub them out. They were roused by a panicky sentry who ran into the bedroom yelling "The Yankees! The Yankees!"

Stark naked, both officers bolted from their beds and donned the only items of clothing at hand: hats, boots, and overcoats. They rushed out the back door, leaped on their horses, and fled. Butler later admitted that the incident had given him a certain grudging sympathy for Kilpatrick.

Wade Hampton had an even narrower escape. Alerted by one of his scouts, Hampton had only a couple of minutes to respond to Duncan's sudden appearance. Indeed, if Duncan had not halted his men a block or two away to regroup his formation, he almost certainly would have captured Hampton and won himself a dandy promotion. But Hampton, on this occasion, lived up to his own best legend. With only two or three minutes' warning, he rallied all the Confederates within shouting distance — a grand total of seven — drew his saber, and led them in a mad charge against an enemy who outnumbered them ten to one.

Startled by this demented tactic, Duncan's troopers bolted, probably convinced that Hampton's entire command must be just out of sight behind the berserkers bearing down on them. They wheeled their mounts about and galloped around a corner, only to find themselves suddenly jammed together as they tried to funnel into the narrow country lane that had led them into town in the first place. Hampton and his tiny band crashed into them from behind. A furious melee erupted, with pistols and swords flashing at point-blank range. Before the Federals managed to extricate themselves and flee back into the woods, Hampton's men had shot or hacked to death 11 of their number, in addition to capturing a dozen more. One poor Yankee was nearly decapitated by a sword stroke. The Confederates lost one horse.

Invigorating as this little victory was (Hampton boasted about it until his dying day, claiming he had killed two of the Yankees with his own hands, which he probably did), it was small change indeed compared to the subsequent loss of Fayetteville and its arsenal. Federal reinforcements followed hard on the heels of Duncan's hapless scouting party and flooded into the southern part of the city before the Confederates could organize a coherent defense. After the arsenal district fell, and after some vigorous house-to-house skirmishing, Hampton saw no point in wasting any more men on that side of the Cape Fear River. The Confederates withdrew to the northern bank and prepared to burn the bridge by igniting the enormous heaps of pine rosin that had been piled against its wooden trestles.

Sherman's Fourth Division (17th Corps) provided the main force

in the capture of Fayetteville. The Fourth Division arrived complete
with a brass band, which played an impromptu concert during the
skirmishing. At one point, the band roared out such a loud fortis-
simo that it terrified the horse of a nearby Federal officer. The high-
strung animal bolted and for some reason headed straight for the
Cape Fear bridge. Observing this one-man charge, and thinking it
was a gallant attempt to storm the bridge before the rebs could burn
it, some Federal infantry joined the attack, cheering bravely. Both
horse and men, however, were brought up short as the bridge
erupted into a wall of fire.

When General Sherman entered Fayetteville, he was in a scratchy
and thunderous mood. He was used to taking these little Southern
cities without a fight, and he was visibly upset at the sight of Duncan's chopped-up men lying in the mud at the edge of town. When
word spread through Fayetteville that Sherman was preparing to
demolish the town's textile mills — the only source of employment
for hundreds of local residents — the owner of the largest milling
company approached the general's headquarters, along with several
members of the town council, and begged him not to inflict this
additional hardship on the region. Sherman heard the man out
without uttering a single word, his face chiseled from basalt. Then
he quietly growled, "Gentlemen, niggers and cotton caused this war,
and I wish them both in Hell. On Wednesday, these mills will be
blown up. Good morning."

When General Howard rode up to Sherman and reported that there
was still a pocket of snipers on the south side of the river, Sherman
angrily snapped, "What unit are they from?" Howard replied, "I
think they are Texans." Sherman ordered, "Well, then, shoot some
Texas prisoners." Taken aback by the general's unusually vitriolic
mood, Howard stammered, "We haven't got any Texans." Sherman
barked back, "Then shoot some others...I will not have my men
murdered!" Then he strode tensely off. As far as is known, Howard
chose to ignore the order.

Just before Sherman's arrival, the Confederates had managed,
with great difficulty, to dismount some of the gun-making machines
from the arsenal and hide them in a nearby coal mine. A substantial
quantity of muskets, shot, powder, and accessories also had been
loaded onto wagons and sent to Greensboro. So by the time Sherman

occupied the arsenal, it was no longer functional. Still, he wanted it destroyed, and he wanted it destroyed in a spectacular and admonitory manner. "I hope the people at Washington will have the good sense never to trust North Carolina with an arsenal again," he remarked as he issued orders for the demolition. His engineers tore down the buildings and blew up the pieces, and the blasts were so powerful that the city felt gripped by an earthquake and several nearby houses burst into flames.

While the arsenal was being prepared for demolition, an elegantly dressed and obviously prosperous civilian approached Major Byers, the officer in charge of the work, and identified himself as Mr. Edward Monagan. Monagan had come to lodge a complaint with General Sherman about looters on his property. Byers expressed doubt that the general would have time to listen. Monagan disputed that: He and Sherman were old friends, he said, comrades from West Point days. He then regaled Byers with several raunchy stories that lent the ring of truth to his claim. "He'll be pleased to meet me," Monagan insisted. "You just watch Sherman's face when we meet."

At that moment, Sherman rode up, having finished a quick inspection tour of the town. Monagan approached the general with open arms, ready to embrace him. And Byers, watching closely, did in fact see a sudden flush of genuine pleasure on the general's normally saturnine features. Then it utterly vanished. Sherman drew himself up stiffly and his eyes grew cold.

"We were friends, weren't we?" Sherman said in the frostiest voice he could summon.

"Oh, yes," responded Monagan. "You shared my friendship and my bread, too, didn't you?"

"That I did," replied Sherman. Now his voice began to shake. "You have betrayed it all. Betrayed me...betrayed the country that educated you for its defense. And here you are — a traitor — asking me to be your friend once more, to protect your property...to risk the lives of brave men who were fired on from houses here today...Turn your back on me forever. I won't punish you, only go your way. There is room in this world even for traitors."

Shaken, Monagan turned and left. Sherman took a seat on the front steps of the arsenal. Someone brought him lunch. Byers was close enough to observe that the general's hand trembled when he brought the bread to his mouth, and that, at one point, as he raised his head and stared in the direction of Monagan's departure, his eyes filled with tears.

Sherman's engineers got busy and erected two pontoon bridges over the Cape Fear River. The day after the city was secured, on Sunday, March 12, the Federal armed tug Davidson arrived from Wilmington — the first contact Sherman's army had with the outside world since leaving Savannah. On her decks were sacks of mail, the first letters from home any of his men had received since before Christmas. The effect of the little ship's arrival was electric. Sherman instantly shed his black mood and mingled with the troops as they whooped and cheered. Then he went to the town hotel, sat down at a desk and got busy. He wrote ten official dispatches and a letter to his wife, Ellen. In his letter, he foresaw that the Confederates would make a stand soon, and that there would be serious fighting. He also predicted the outcome, without any hesitation: "I can whip Joe Johnston, unless his men fight better than they have since I left Savannah. The same brags and boasts are kept up, but when I reach the path where the lion crouched I find him slinking away."

Sherman was anxious to press on with the campaign, to get it all over with, but he was forced to dally in Fayetteville long enough to gather fresh horses and mules from the surrounding countryside. After robbing the area of its fresh animals, he had no intention of leaving for the civilian populace even the worn-out horses and mules the army had used all the way from Georgia. Instead, about a thousand of the animals were herded into a big field on the banks of the Cape Fear and boxed in by men with rifles. Then the shooting started. As soon as the scent of blood filled the air, the animals went wild, plunging and kicking and braying with raw terror as the bullets thudded pitilessly into their crowded ranks. For days afterward, the river was choked with swollen corpses floating downstream, and the stench of the hundreds of rotting animals left on the banks was loathsome and suffocating. Finally, the sickened townspeople got together and burned them in massive heaps, leaving a stink that persisted for days.

Before moving on, the general also shed the enormous "tail" of refugees and liberated Negroes that had gathered in the wake of his army, growing daily, all the way from Georgia — anywhere from

20,000 to 30,000 "useless mouths." These people were organized into a separate column, given a small armed escort, and sent off toward Wilmington.

General Slocum left a colorful description of the sad refugee column:

> It was natural that these poor creatures, seeking a place of safety, should flee to the army and endeavor to keep in sight of it. Every day, as we marched on we could see, on each side of our line of march, crowds of these people coming to us...bringing with them all their earthly goods, and many goods which were not theirs. Horses, mules, cows, dogs, old family carriages, carts, and whatever they thought might be of use to them were seized upon and brought to us. They were allowed to follow in rear of our column, and at times they were almost equal in numbers to the army they were following. As singular, comical, and pitiable a spectacle was never before presented.
>
> One day a large family of slaves came through the fields to join us. The head of the family, a venerable Negro, was mounted on a mule, and safely stowed away behind him in pockets or bags attached to the blanket which covered the mule were two little pickaninnies, one on each side. This gave rise to a most important invention, i.e., "the best way of transporting pickaninnies." On the next day a mule appeared in the column, covered by a blanket with two pockets on each side, each containing a little Negro...Very soon old tent-flies or strong canvas was used instead of the blanket, and often 10 or 15 pockets were attached to each side, so that nothing of the mule was visible except the head, tail and feet, all else being covered by the black woolly heads and bright shining eyes of the little darkies. Occasionally a cow was made to take the place of the mule; this was a decided improvement, as the cow furnished rations as well as transportation for the babies.
>
> Old stages, family carriages, carts and lumber wagons filled with bedding, cooking utensils...with men, women and children loaded with bundles, made up the balance of the refugee train. As all the bridges were burned in front of us, our pontoon-trains were in constant use, and the bridges would be left but a short time for the use of the refugees. A scramble for precedence in crossing the bridge always occurred. The firing of a musket or pistol in rear would bring to the refugees visions of [Confederate] guerrillas, and then came a panic. As our bridges were not supplied with guard rails, occasionally a mule would be crowded off, and with its precious load would float down the river.[1]

With military necessities taken care of, and a bit of time on their hands, Sherman's men proceeded to give Fayetteville a working-over that would linger bitterly in the town's memory until well into the 20th century. The pillaging went on only for a few days, but it was so widespread that Sherman finally had to bring in three brigades of infantry to restore order. In the outlying farms beyond the city limits, the looting and vandalism were even worse than in town, where the officers curbed at least the most flagrant abuses. People were beaten (and a few actually tortured) to make them reveal the whereabouts of their valuables; two or three were killed outright; and a number of farm buildings were wantonly burned.

James Evans, whose plantation lay close to Fayetteville, recorded these fearful times in his diary:

> March 13, 1865 — clear, over 1,000 Yanks in my house during the day and niggers in vast numbers, in the yard and outhouses, stole all my provisions and a large amount of other things, all my cattle, horses, mules, buggy wagons, hogs...
>
> March 14, 1865 — very cloudy. Thousands of Yanks in the yard and house all day...
>
> March 15...thousands of Yanks in house and yard and field, plantation entirely covered with them, from one side to the other....[2]

Vast quantities of food were found in and around Fayetteville, and virtually all of it was hauled off when the soldiers departed. Women and children, as well as a fair number of paroled Confederate officers, had to beg for meals at the Union commissary. By the time the last troopers marched over the pontoon bridges, it was as though a plague of locusts had descended on the little city. Most families were left with only a few days' worth of subsistence rations, if that much, and only a single grist mill was left in working order.

One thing Sherman did not find in Fayetteville, or anywhere else along his route, was much of that pro-Union sentiment he had expected among the common people of North Carolina. He might have found it in some measure, a few weeks earlier, had he visited the state quietly and as a private citizen. But coming as a destroying conqueror, he had brought into the state the very thing that had driven rational North Carolinians to accept secession in the first place: an invasion. Against the physical and brutal fact of his army's presence on North Carolina soil, the fine points of peacetime political theory counted for nothing. Even people who would have described themselves as pro-Union only a few weeks before were driven to hatred by the spectacle of ruin and destitution left behind by the enemy columns.

"Thus far we have been disappointed," wrote one of Sherman's aides, "in looking for the Union sentiment in North Carolina about which so much has been said. Our experience is decidedly in favor of its sister state; for we found more persons in Columbia who had proved their fealty to the Union cause...than in all this state put together. The city of Fayetteville was offensively rebellious...."[3]

Most of Sherman's army had crossed the Cape Fear River by the end of March 15. Although the campaign so far had not been without its rigors and surprises, on the whole it had gone according to plan. Confederate resistance, though occasionally spirited, had been more of a nuisance than an obstacle. Sherman was in good spirits now. Next stop, Goldsboro.

Of course, he did realize that his march so far had been blessed by the dispersal and disorganization of his enemy. By now, though, enough time had passed so that surely Joe Johnston would have been able to assemble some kind of army. Somewhere on the road ahead, Johnston would stand and fight. Sherman believed it was likely to happen in front of Raleigh, but just the same, he would have to proceed more cautiously now than he had been required to do since leaving Columbia.

As he left Fayetteville, Sherman organized his army in the following fashion. Kilpatrick's cavalry once again acted as the advance guard, moving up the main plank-covered road that roughly paralleled the eastern bank of the Cape Fear River, passing through Averasboro (a little village that no longer exists, having been bypassed by the railroad after the war; the nearest existing town is Erwin). Behind Kilpatrick followed four divisions of the left wing, traveling light. Behind them came the bulk of the wagons and artillery, escorted by the remaining two divisions of the left wing. And finally, General Howard's right wing followed a more easterly and direct route toward Goldsboro, with two-thirds of the troops stripped down for action while the other third brought up the rear with baggage and supplies.

Not far ahead of Kilpatrick was Confederate General Hardee's rear guard, comprised of Wheeler's cavalry. Hardee's force had never been very large, and by March 15 it had dwindled to just under 6,000 men. Hardee had lost a brigade of South Carolina militia that

had been ordered home by their governor, and desertions had
siphoned off hundreds more. Nevertheless, Hardee elected to dig in
and fight at Averasboro. He was not motivated by any deluded hopes
of seriously checking a force five times his size, but by a sound military reason — he needed to find out how much of Sherman's army
was following him, and the surest way was to make the enemy come
at him deployed for battle.

He chose good ground, positioning his men on some elevated terrain in front of the junction of the Smithfield-Averasboro Road. This
defensive position was flanked at a distance by the Cape Fear and
Black Rivers, and flanked more closely by swamps and woods that
were largely impenetrable, thanks to their density and to the briar
thickets that obstructed movement nearly as well as barbed wire. In
front of this position were open fields of fire. The Confederates furiously began digging two lines of entrenchments. A strong line of
skirmishers, also partly entrenched, was placed 300 yards in front of
the position.

Hardee's infantry were the men of Taliaferro's division. The skirmish line was manned by the brigade of the Charleston blueblood,
Colonel Alfred Rhett. For once, the Confederates had some significant cannon: their front line contained several large-caliber guns
manned by crews from the Charleston coastal artillery. These crews
were expert gunners and their fire would take a heavy toll of the
enemy, but they were also virgins when it came to this kind of combat, and most would die in the next 24 hours. Hardee's regular field
artillery was deployed in his second line of entrenchments.

The battle started on March 15 when the two armies made contact
at a place just over the Cumberland County line known as the Gypsy
Pine. For more than a century, gypsy caravans had parked around
that pine tree, holding fairs and tribal conclaves, and plotting nocturnal raids on the barnyards of local plantations. Local legends claim
that when the cannons first roared on that rain-misted day, the apparition of a gypsy girl was seen above the tree, outlined against the
murky sky and seemingly holding a wand. It is a curious fact that,
although all the trees around the Gypsy Pine were mangled by shrap-
nel and Minie balls, not a single round struck that particular tree.
And never again, after the battle, were the gypsies seen to camp
beneath it.[4]

Kilpatrick's main column ran smack into the Confederates at about three o'clock in the afternoon. After a brisk exchange of gunfire, he managed to drive the Confederate skirmishers out from the open fields back into their gun-pits. But that's about all Kilpatrick could do — Hardee's gunners made the open field a lethal zone. During the ensuing stalemate, Kilpatrick ordered his men, by brigades as they came up, to deploy on either side of the initial point of contact and erect breastworks of their own. The Confederates attacked Kilpatrick's line several times during the late afternoon, pressing him hard, occasionally coming to within pistol range of his entrenchments. By twilight, Kilpatrick managed to get a few cannon of his own into action, and they enabled him to hold his own, just barely.

In the last hour of daylight, Slocum hustled forward Colonel William Hawley's brigade of 20th Corps. Hawley's men spent the evening and a good part of the night struggling to get into position.

The fighting started again at first light on March 16, when Kilpatrick sent the Eighth Indiana Cavalry at the Confederates' right flank. They succeeded in driving the pickets before them and penetrating the skirmish line at some points, but they weren't strong enough to assault the rebel breastworks on their own and were soon compelled to retire to Union lines.

No sooner had this opening round of fighting died down than Taliaferro's division came howling out of the morning mists like demonic specters. They launched a furious attack on Hawley's lines that shook the whole Federal position. On the right flank, where Kilpatrick's men were down to their last few rounds of ammunition, Taliaferro's men used excellent tactics, advancing by fire more than by the bayonet. They came within an eyelash of turning the whole Union flank.

Fortunately for the Federals, the timely arrival of another division of 20th Corps (Williams's) restored the situation. The reinforced Federal infantry surged forward in a counterattack that seemed to gather force as it went. The first Confederate line bent, cracked, and finally disintegrated. The rebels ran for the rear, flinging down knapsacks and rifles, and abandoning a large number of wounded as well as most of the Charleston artillery.

An officer with Hawley's division, Captain Oakey of the Second

Massachusetts, left this description of the Federal attack on that day: "It was a wretched place to fight. At some points we had to support our wounded until they could be carried off, to prevent their falling into swamp water, in which we stood ankle deep...No ordinary troops were in our front. They would not give way until a division of Davis's corps [actually a brigade] was thrown upon their right while we pressed them closely. As we passed over their dead and wounded, I came upon the body of a very young officer, whose handsome, refined face attracted my attention. While the line of battle swept past me, I knelt at his side for a moment. His buttons bore the arms of South Carolina...we were fighting the Charleston chivalry."[5]

The Federal assault then began to suffer greatly from the well-handled artillery in Hardee's rearmost line of entrenchments. These field batteries spat out such blistering fire that some survivors later described it as the hottest bombardment they endured during the entire campaign. The 129th Illinois lost 20 men to the barrage in a space of minutes and was forced to seek shelter in the abandoned Confederate trenches.

Kilpatrick was now instructed to withdraw his horsemen from the firing line, replenish their ammunition, and then mass them on the extreme right of the battlefield. Once they were reorganized and in position, he was to probe for a way around the Confederate flank on that side.

It didn't take long for his scouts to report back with news about a passable track that led in exactly the right direction and that did not seem defended. Kilpatrick sent the Ninth Ohio down the road first. They rode only a few hundred yards before they were struck by a blast of fire from the woods a few feet away on their left. A rebel brigade from McClaws's division had been executing a mirror-image flanking maneuver in the opposite direction and had run into the cavalry at right angles. The Ohioans fell back and regrouped, and a stalemate ensued in that part of the battlefield.

Taliaferro's third line held all afternoon, despite repeated stubborn attacks by the Yankees. Early that night, Hardee decided that enough was enough, and ordered a withdrawal. Under cover of some desultory shelling by rebel guns, he withdrew his small army without further incident. The Union troops spent a restless night, soaked by hard, cold rain showers and tormented by the cries of wounded men who had lost their way in the swamps and were drowning in quicksand.

An extraordinary account of the Averasboro fighting, and its gruesome aftermath, exists in a letter written about a month later by 18-year-old Janie Smith to a friend in Bladen County. Like most Confederate households, the Smith family no longer had any proper stationery, so the girl wrote on flyleaf paper torn from books and on the back of several strips of wallpaper:

Where Home Used to Be April 12, 1865...At daylight on the 16th [of March] the firing was terrific. The infirmary was here and — oh! it makes me shudder when I think of the awful sights I witnessed that morning. Ambulance after ambulance drove up with our wounded...The house, every barn and outhouse were full, and under every shed and tree the tables were carried for amputating the limbs...the blood stood in puddles in the grove; the groans of the dying and the shrieks of those undergoing amputation was horrible. I can never forget it.

...We were kept busy making and rolling bandages and sending nourishment to the sick and wounded.

It was about nine in the morning when the courier came with orders for us to leave. Then was my trial, leaving our poor sick and suffering soldiers when I could have been relieving them some. As we passed the wounded going to the woods, they would beseech us: Ladies, don't leave your home. We won't let the enemy fire on you. But orders must be obeyed and to the woods we went. Imagine us all and Uncle John's family trudging through the rain and mud to a ravine near the river.

The firing continued incessantly up and down the line, all day, when about five in the evening the enemy flanked out right, and the firing was right over us. We could hear the commands and the groans and shrieks of the wounded...a short time later we were ordered home...General Wheeler took tea here about two o'clock during the night after the battle closed, and about four o'clock the Yankees came charging, yelling and howling...

The palings did not hinder them at all. They just knocked them down like so many mad cattle. Right into the house, breaking open drawers and cursing us for having hid everything. They stuck Pa with a bayonet to make him disclose something. Sis Susan was sick in bed and they snatched the very pillows she was lying on. They would catch the little biddies in the yard and just squeeze them to death. They left no living thing on the place except one old sick hen.

They didn't burn the house, but the blacksmith shop was set on fire and into the flames they threw every plow, tool, etc., on the place.

One impudent dog came up to me and said, "Good morning, girls. Why aren't you getting breakfast? It's late."

I told him servants prepared "breakfasts for Southern ladies." He went away muttering something about them not waiting on us any more.

The house was so crowded with them all day we could hardly move — and of all the horrible smelling things in the world, the Yankees can't be beat. I don't believe they have washed since they were borne. The battlefield does not compare with them in stench....If I ever see a Yankee woman, I intend to whip her and take the very clothes off her back.

...I can dress amputated limbs now and do most anything in the way of nursing the wounded.

I am really attached to the patients in the hospital and feel so lonely now that so many have left or died. My favorite, a little black eyed boy with the whitest brow and thick curls falling on it, died last Sunday....[6]

When General Hardee withdrew with his remaining Confederates, he left behind one of the more colorful prisoners of war ever to land in Sherman's hands: the handsome, dashing, and hopelessly arrogant Colonel Alfred Rhett. The son of Confederate Congressman Barnwell Rhett, young Alfred had until recently been commander of the rebel garrison at Fort Sumter. And he was enormously vexed that he had been taken alive, and under rather embarrassing circumstances. He had blundered into a four-man patrol of Kilpatrick's scouts and had mistaken them for Confederates. When one of them demanded that he surrender, Rhett drew himself to his full height and imperiously replied, "Do you realize who you are talking to, suh?"

"I don't give a damn who you are," was the blunt reply. "I'm taking you back."

Rhett glared right back at the Yankee who had spoken, who happened to be Captain Theo Northrop, Kilpatrick's best patrol leader. Rhett told Northrop, "You'll watch your language when you speak to me, offisuh! General Hampton will hear of this!"

Northrop rode up to Rhett, drew a huge Navy Colt from his holster, cocked it, and pointed at the colonel's head. Rhett gulped and raised his hands, then permitted himself to be led back to General

Kilpatrick. Kilpatrick thought Rhett was a vain little prig, strutting around in his elegant, gold-braided uniform and his glossy, hand-tooled jackboots; what Rhett, the snooty Charleston aristocrat, thought of the vulgar and feisty little Irishman can only be imagined. Rhett was quickly relieved of his fancy boots. As one of the guards tossed him a battered pair of mud-covered brogans in exchange, Kilpatrick laughed at the Confederate colonel's obvious discomfiture. "They'll feel better on the march tomorrow, Colonel," he sniggered. "You won't be on horseback...you'll be riding shank's mare." Some of Little Kil's officers gambled for the fancy boots, but when they discovered that nobody could stuff his feet into them because of their petite size, they gave them back to their owner.

Sherman was present during the fighting at Averasboro, and some Northern newspapers described him "directing the battle under warm fire." Actually he did no such thing; Patton-like heroics were not old "Crazy Billy's" style. As was his custom, he left the tactical decisions to his corps and division commanders, fully confident that they would, as usual, do the right thing at the right time. The general himself, according to a somewhat scandalized aide who was with him, spent most of the battle "lying around in the woods" and listening to stray bullets splash through the leaves overhead.

Depending on how one likes to define these things, the engagement at Averasboro could be looked upon as a "large skirmish" or a "small battle." Every participant who wrote about it, whichever side he was on, agreed it was a very hot fight. One Illinois private who participated in the attack that cracked Hardee's main line stated flatly, "I never saw the dead so thick on the field before."[7] It was costly for both sides: Slocum and Kilpatrick reported a total of almost 700 casualties. Hardee probably lost slightly more than 600.

More important than the losses inflicted on Sherman was the delay caused by Hardee's determined stand. Hardee had halted half of Sherman's whole left wing for about 48 hours. This caused Slocum's entire formation to straggle and created a much greater than intended gap between his two corps and Howard's right wing, which was still marching steadily towards Goldsboro, ignorant of the battle that had developed to the west.

It was this dispersion, confirmed by Hardee's reports, that gave General Joe Johnston the chance he had been praying for.

BENTONVILLE: THE LAST REBEL YELL

On March 18, 1865, not long after he had established his head-quarters at Smithfield, General Joseph Johnston received a dramatic dispatch from Wade Hampton, his bellicose cavalry commander. Hampton, who was about 12 miles to the south near the tiny hamlet of Bentonville, reported that Sherman was near and contact was imminent.

Johnston wasn't really ready to tackle Sherman yet. The Army of Tennessee had been so incredibly fragmented and scattered that it had taken Johnston from February 23 until about March 12 just to get them all together in the same state — no small accomplishment, given the condition of the railroads over which some of the soldiers had journeyed, and the torn-up, devastated countryside through which others had marched in South Carolina. Ben Cheatham's division, potentially one of the best units in Old Joe's inventory, was entangled in the unbelievable railroad bottleneck at Salisbury; it wouldn't be available in time. As for the other regional units nominally under his command, they were still scattered in ineffectual packets from Kinston all the way back to Charlotte.

The largest single coherent force Johnston had in the field on the morning of March 18 was Hardee's corps of two divisions (7,500 men). Hardee had stayed as close to Sherman's advancing columns as he dared, but with so few men, staying close was about all he could do — at least until March 16, when he offered battle at Averasboro.

Studying Sherman's moves, Johnston figured that his adversary, after brushing aside Hardee's resistance, would do one of two things: move on Raleigh, or turn east and move on Goldsboro. When Johnston received intelligence that the left wing of Sherman's army had turned east, toward Bentonville, he understood that Sherman intended to go for the rail junction and supply depots in Goldsboro — a more tempting military objective than Raleigh with its politicians.

Cavalry reports reaching Johnston on March 17 informed him that Sherman had again split his army into two marching columns, both heading for Goldsboro, but separated by a considerable distance due to the layout of roads in that part of the state.

Johnston had been pondering how his ragtag force of 21,000 men could hope to challenge Sherman's battle-hardened army of 60,000. Now, on March 18, after studying the maps and conferring with Hampton, who had arrived to discuss the options personally with Johnston, it was possible to discern the glimmer of a possibility.

It was Wade Hampton who formulated the basic plan. They worked out the details together, but the execution and responsibility fell on Ol' Joe's shoulders. Win or lose, it would be thought of as "his" battle. The scheme was based on two factors: First, Sherman's tradition of dividing his army into two permanent columns, designated the left and right wings; and second, the layout of the roads they were marching on. The left wing, which had been roughly handled for a few days at Averasboro, was commanded by General Slocum and consisted of the 14th and 20th Corps. Hampton had pinpointed its location: two miles below Bentonville, on the Goldsboro pike. The right wing, commanded by General O.O. Howard, consisting of the 15th and 17th Corps, was known to be farther east and south, although exactly how far was not known with certainty.

Looking at their maps, Hampton and Johnston figured that Howard was at least a full day's march beyond Slocum, too far away to support him. The same maps seemed to indicate that Hardee could engage Slocum at Bentonville after a not-too-strenuous half-day march. Unfortunately for Hampton and Johnston, the maps were wrong — as usual. Howard was actually much closer to Slocum.

Even without that knowledge, Ol' Joe knew the odds against him were formidable. Slocum's wing alone, which included Kilpatrick's cavalry, outnumbered him by about 10,000 men. Johnston needed to fall on Slocum like a thunderbolt, crush him rapidly, and then redeploy his troops against Howard's wing, which would surely change direction and come at him as soon as Sherman realized what was going on. The whole plan hinged on that short period when Slocum would be alone and, presumably, taken by surprise. Johnston figured he would have a day to wreak whatever damage he could on Slocum before having to deal with Howard. Even without the knowledge that Howard was considerably closer than he was thought to be, Ol' Joe was taking one hell of a gamble.

But it was the only plan that offered even the slightest flicker of hope. Johnston was bound, by orders and by honor, to give it a try — another such opportunity might never arise. He must have known, from the start, that there was at best a one-in-a-hundred chance of success; and he must also have known that, if by some miracle he did pull it off, his name would go down in the history books alongside that of Hannibal.

What a motley army he had to work with! Hardee's men were proven, steady, reliable, but few...too few. The First Tennessee, which had started the war as a gallant regiment with 1250 men, now numbered 65; the 13th Tennessee, once a thousand-strong, now mustered 50 men. And the survivors of Hood's tenure over the Army of Tennessee were as drained physically and emotionally as the survivors of the Somme would be a half-century later. Hood had bled that once-superb army almost to death with his reckless and profligate attacks during the Franklin/Nashville campaign a few months earlier, and the survivors were burned-out shells of what they had been a year before. Still, in the breasts of many of those old veterans, there burned a stubborn determination to resurrect their army's honor and reputation from the ashes of its galling defeats. They yearned to prove that the Army of Tennessee was still, by God, the same army that had given the Federals blow-for-blow at Shiloh.

Among Johnston's other resources was the audacious and tactically savvy young General Robert Hoke, back in North Carolina with his splendid division from the Army of Northern Virginia. As for the others, well, they didn't inspire much confidence: out-of-shape garrison troops from the now-fallen coastal defenses; artillerymen who had spent the past two years in stale garrison duty in backwater positions all over the state; and a brigade of virgin teenagers belonging to the North Carolina Junior reserves. These were the troops Johnston had to hurl against one of the meanest, leanest, toughest armies ever fielded by the United States.

Johnston could at least draw some comfort from the quantity and quality of the leadership he would have on hand for the coming battle. In additon to the hotspur Hoke, he had Lafayette McLaws, A.P. Stewart, Wade Hampton, Hardee, and J.E.B. Stuart's successor, Joe Wheeler. Of course, there was also Braxton Bragg, but Ol' Joe could be excused, perhaps, if he chose to regard Bragg as a potential liability rather than an asset. Bragg would be commanding Hoke's forces, and there was nothing Johnston could do about that except pray. Still, Bragg had not done badly at Kinston, not so long ago; maybe, in the twilight of his checkered career, he had finally learned something about managing a battle. In sum, then, Johnston had a veritable galaxy of military talent and experience. In fact, there were almost too many prima donnas on the same stage, especially considering that the supporting cast — the troops under their collective command — was so uneven in quality and experience.

Johnston probably did not dare hope for a victory of sweeping decisiveness; by this stage of the war, one-sided routs were rare. When the going got tough, both sides had long ago learned how to dig in rapidly and rely on the considerable defensive power of their rifles. Tactics had not kept pace with technology — a really decisive blow could be dealt by an attacker only when he got close enough to physically disrupt the enemy's formations. And that was hard to do. Defensively, artillery could inflict terrible punishment at great distances on men caught in the open, but it was only marginally useful to the attacker. Explosive shells were not yet powerful enough, nor accurate enough, to rip significant holes in a fortified line. And in the new age of rifled barrels and Minie balls, accurate and lethal at ranges of up to half a mile, few attacking formations could survive long enough to bring their bayonets into play. Pickett's charge at Gettysburg had proven that. For all these reasons, virtually all battles now were struggles of attrition that rarely resulted in clear-cut victories for either side.

Still, if Johnston could hurt Slocum badly enough to force Sherman away from Goldsboro, he would at least win a consolation prize, for there were provisions and clothes in Goldsboro that Sherman needed badly. If Sherman could be turned away from Goldsboro, his army would be hungry. He would also be prevented from linking up with the two additional corps of Federal troops, under Generals Terry and Schofield, that were moving inland from Wilmington and New Bern. Merely preventing the junction of these forces would constitute a strategic victory for the Confederates, because otherwise Sherman's army would total nearly 100,000 men...and there were not enough soldiers left in the whole Confederacy south of Virginia to oppose such a horde.

So the strategy was agreed upon: Johnston would try to overwhelm Slocum's left wing and disrupt the imminent Union linkup at Goldsboro. As for what he would do afterward, if he managed to do that much, Johnston would worry about that later.

Wade Hampton's cavalry moved out on March 18 and took up skirmishing positions across Slocum's route. The fighting was spotty and inconclusive, but Slocum had no choice except to deal with it. Hampton succeeded in delaying the Federals long enough for Ol' Joe to reach Bentonville with most of his command that same evening. Hardee, with his two divisions, had begun his day's march too far away to reach Bentonville and had encamped five miles north and west of the hamlet.

During the day's skirmishing, Hampton had been sniffing out the enemy's dispositions. That night, he reported what he learned to Johnston. Orders went out to the various Confederate units.

As the morning of March 19 dawned, the Confederate line found itself on no defensively strong terrain; there wasn't any. Between the Cole and Harper houses, the landscape consisted of some open fields belonging to the Cole plantation, but most of the territory, especially south of the Goldsboro pike, was thick, tangled, briarchoked "blackjack" pine forest, liberally laced with patches of swamp. Except for an elevation east of the Harper house, the entire area was relatively flat, except where it was depressed by swamps or furrowed by creeks. There were too few roads, so many of Johnston's units had to struggle through thickets and bogs, and therefore were winded or exhausted before they even got into position. As Johnston put it in his memoirs, "the deployment of the troops consumed a weary time."

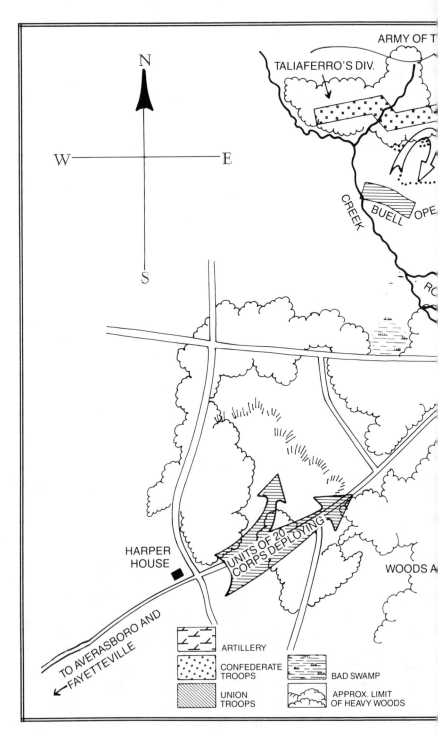

ARMY OF T

TALIAFERRO'S DIV.

CREEK

BUELL OPE

RO

N

W E

S

HARPER
HOUSE

UNITS OF 20
CORPS DEPLOYING

WOODS A

TO AVERASBORO AND
FAYETTEVILLE

ARTILLERY

CONFEDERATE
TROOPS

UNION
TROOPS

BAD SWAMP

APPROX. LIMIT
OF HEAVY WOODS

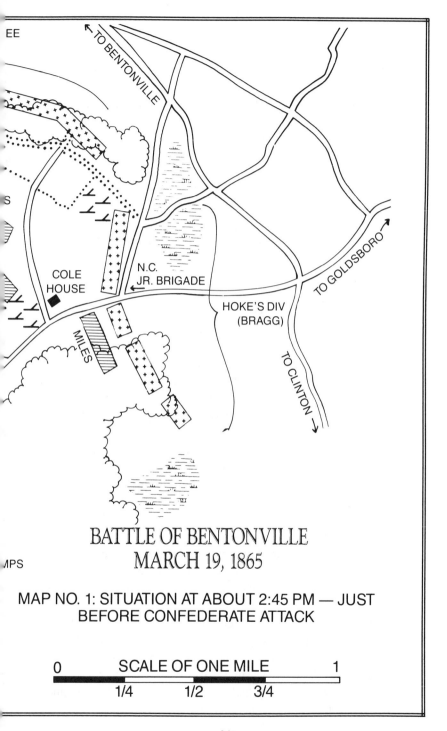

EE

S

COLE
HOUSE

N.C.
JR. BRIGADE

HOKE'S DIV
(BRAGG)

TO BENTONVILLE

TO GOLDSBORO

TO CLINTON

MILES

BATTLE OF BENTONVILLE
MARCH 19, 1865

MPS

MAP NO. 1: SITUATION AT ABOUT 2:45 PM — JUST
BEFORE CONFEDERATE ATTACK

0   SCALE OF ONE MILE   1

1/4   1/2   3/4

Appropriately enough, given the sense of desperation that marked Johnston's whole strategy, the Confederate line ended up resembling a huge question mark. Its tail crossed the Goldsboro road, and its curved portion was north and west of the road. At the bottom of the question mark, on the Confederate left, was Hoke's division, now nominally under Bragg's control. The lower-middle section of the question mark was occupied by Hardee's two divisions, positioned more or less parallel to the northern fork in the Goldsboro road. The upper curve of the question mark was held by Stewart's corps. Part of Johnston's cavalry screened the front above the tip of the question mark, north of the creek that meandered through planter Cole's property.

The Confederates could now see advancing toward their lines hundreds of Federal soldiers from Sherman's 14th Corps (whose commander, ironically, was named General Jeff Davis) deployed in skirmish formation across the fields. Despite the awesome sight, Joe Johnston's little army was fired up and rarin' to go. Maybe it was the presence of so many famous Confederate officers; maybe it was the urgency many of the veterans felt to redeem their Franklin/Nashville defeats; maybe it was the chance to strike back at Sherman for the first time, really, since the fall of Atlanta; or maybe they just had no idea how badly the odds were stacked against them.

Slocum's men definitely weren't expecting the kind of battle they were about to get. Sherman wasn't anticipating any serious resistance this side of Raleigh. In fact, Sherman wasn't even on the field that morning; he had departed the left wing right after breakfast, eager to ride ahead and personally hasten the linkup with Terry and Schofield. He didn't get very far when he heard cannon fire behind him. He was about to return when a messenger arrived. Slocum had run into some stubborn dismounted cavalry pickets, the messenger said; nothing serious, nothing he couldn't handle. Sherman saluted and kept on riding.

The point unit of Slocum's force was Brigadier General William Carlin's division of 14th Corps. Like the Confederates, Carlin's men, too, were in good spirits. The morning was beautiful, and they had finally left behind the swampy, torturous, rain-flooded part of the state through which they had been slogging, knee-deep in mud, for weeks. Following the usual hardtack-and-coffee breakfast,

Carlin's men swung out onto the Goldsboro road, expecting to enjoy
as pleasant a day's march as a day's march ever was. Nearby were
some peach orchards, and their spring blossoms perfumed the warm
air, blending with the by-now familiar smells of the pine woods.

Carlin's men hadn't gone far when they came under vigorous fire
from what they assumed were dismounted cavalry. This kind of skirmishing happened somewhere along Sherman's march nearly every
day, and usually didn't amount to much. A few nuisance volleys
from Confederates in the woods would be answered by a few rounds
of cannon fire from the Federals. These little affairs-of-honor
usually ended with few or no losses on either side.

This time it was different. These dismounted horse soldiers, if
that's what they were, fired methodically and fell back slowly, tree to
tree, seemingly undeterred as more and more bluecoats appeared on
the road and in the surrounding fields. Carlin's forward elements
deployed and unleashed a few volleys of their own. This was usually
the signal for the Confederate skirmishers to fade away; this time
they didn't. Instead, they just kept firing and falling back without
noticeable haste. Observing their unusual behavior, one Yankee
soldier remarked, "Those men don't drive worth a damn!"

Slocum ordered Carlin to clear the road, but by ten o'clock it was
clear that Carlin had run up against something tougher than a stubborn cavalry patrol. He had, in fact, run into Hoke's infantry, at the
lower end of the "question mark." Hoke's line was firmly
entrenched behind the rail fences that marked one edge of Cole's
plantation.

If all went according to plan, Joe Johnston's question mark would
now turn into a razor-sharp sickle. Stewart's corps, already poised
so that its right extended beyond the head of Carlin's force, was prepared to fall on Carlin's left while Carlin was pinned down by his
firefight with Hoke. There was one major problem, however:
Hardee had not yet arrived to take his place in the battle line. And
when Hardee did arrive, his units were used to reinforce weak parts
of the Confederate line, resulting in some confusion over just who
commanded which part of the line. In general, it may be said that
Hardee was in control of the right, and Stewart the center. For the
moment, though, until Hardee showed up, it was all Stewart's show.

Carlin's foremost brigade had reached the vicinity of the Cole house when Hoke's artillery opened fire from the north, opposite the house.

There were three brigades in Carlin's division. General H.C. Hobart's brigade, stung by the artillery fire, moved forward and to the left, toward the Confederate right, lured in that direction by the shelter of a tree-covered ravine. Carlin ordered another of his brigade commanders, General G.P. Buell, to advance around Hobart's position and probe the Confederate line, hoping to find some gap through which Hoke could be outflanked. Buell probed, found no gaps, and took up position on Hobart's left, extending the Federal line along the creek-bed ravine. The third of Carlin's brigades, led by Colonel David Miles, fanned out on the south side of the Goldsboro road and repeatedly attacked Hoke's positions, but made no headway.

Slocum was still under the misapprehension that he was facing cavalry. Stronger and more determined than usual, and well-equipped with cannon for a change, but still just a crust of resistant cavalry. So he did not send for help. Instead, his 14th Corps commander, General Jeff Davis, ordered Buell's brigade to attack, supported by the rest of Carlin's division.

Buell ran into a chainsaw. As one young Federal officer described the attack: "The Rebs held their fire until we were within 3 rods of the works when they opened fire from all sides and gave us an awful volley. We went for them with a yell and got within 5 paces of their works...I tell you it was a tight place...Men pelted each other with Ramrods and butts of muskets...[we] were finally compelled to fall back...[we] stood it as long as man could stand and when that was no longer a possibility, we run like the duce...."[1]

Now Slocum was getting a fair idea of what was actually up there, behind those smoke-shrouded pine trees. He and Davis were discussing the situation when an excited, sweaty officer ran up and pantingly confirmed what Slocum had already surmised: "Well, General, I have found something more than cavalry — I find infantry entrenched all along our whole front, and enough of them to give us all the amusement we shall want for the rest of the day!"

Slocum ordered another of his divisions — Morgan's — to advance and take up position south of the Goldsboro road, probably hoping Morgan could find a way around Hoke's right flank. He also sent another messenger after Sherman, this time carrying a more accurate estimate of the size of the enemy and the scope of the developing engagement.

By 1:30 in the afternoon, Slocum's situation was deteriorating. Carlin's division was industriously building breastworks, but it was still strung out in a single, vulnerable line. Buell was on the left and Hobart's regiments on the right, almost to the grounds of the Cole house. Sensing that his greatest peril loomed on the right, Slocum hurried forward the closest element of 20th Corps, Robinson's brigade, ordering him to take position behind Carlin's right flank. Miles's brigade was now athwart and south of the Goldsboro road. Morgan's division was to the right of Miles's, on the Federals' right flank, opposite Hoke, with two brigades in line and one in reserve. Slocum's right flank was therefore in a much better position than his left, where Carlin was hunkering in his ravine. Morgan's men began digging in, flinging up log breastworks in quick order.

The real weakness in the Union line was at the point where Hobart and Buell were pinned down. Hobart had recklessly pushed one of his regiments too far forward, exposing it to flank attack. Two of Robinson's regiments had been kept back near the Harper house, where 20th Corps was hurriedly deploying, and he simply didn't have enough men to plug the hole and still maintain his own unbroken front. Slocum sent an engineer officer forward to suggest to Carlin that he fall back, put the creek between his men and the rebels, and link up with Robinson to form a continuous and protected line. Carlin dallied, however, either because he wasn't convinced of his danger or because he was simply unwilling to give up ground his men had already paid for in blood.

There was a growing mood of alarm on the Federal left now. The Confederates were under good cover, pouring out volleys of fire at anything that moved, and they had savagely repulsed Carlin's first attack. Rumors began to fly that the Confederate force numbered 30,000, maybe 40,000. Somehow, word had started going around, too, that Robert E. Lee himself had come down from Virginia to take the helm for this engagement. That rumor unnerved far more Yankees than the wild exaggerations of Confederate troop strength.

Things were going Joe Johnston's way, better than he had dared hope. He had pinned down and virtually isolated 10,000 Yankees on the Federal left; he had achieved local parity, if not superiority, of numbers; and he had the advantage of better position and better morale. At this point, however, things began to go awry.

Miles and Morgan were pressing their Union forces hard against Hoke's line, and Braxton Bragg sent an urgent plea to Johnston for reinforcements. Johnston sent him McLaws's division, the first of Hardee's two divisions to reach the field. The results of this unforeseen redeployment were typically Braggian. McLaws arrived to find that Hoke had already repulsed the attacks, leaving McLaws with nothing much to do except stand around. But the absence of McLaws's division considerably weakened the power of the counterstroke that Hardee and Stewart were preparing against the Yankee left. Worst of all, shuffling McLaws's troops had cost Johnston time. By the time Johnston got his men reorganized and formed up for the attack, most of Slocum's 20th Corps had reached the battlefield, and the improvised breastworks Carlin's men were building had progressed from flimsy to substantial.

By 2:45 p.m., Hardee's truncated force was in position. The extreme right of the Confederate line, the sickle's "point," was given to Taliaferro's division. Next came two divisions of Cheatham's old corps, now commanded by W.B. Bate. The center of the sickle blade was given to D.H. Hill, with three divisions. On his left was W.W. Loring's division, eaten away now to a mere 500 men. Opposite the Cole house was most of the Confederate artillery under Atkins, supported by E.C. Whithall's division. McLaws's division, of course, was still being retained by Bragg, who had placed it across the Goldsboro road.

The distance between the Confederates' front rank and Carlin's breastworks was about 600 yards. The attackers formed into two lines, and advanced with the sort of fire and elan that had made the Confederate army so formidable...once. And now, for the next proud hour, it would be as it had been during the glory days. There were the famous commanders — Hill, Hardee, and Stewart — out in front, urging their men forward, swords blazing in the sunlight. There were the old shot-torn battleflags, borne aloft in triumph for one last time. There, on the peach-scented breeze, came the skin-tightening, goose-pimpling, banshee-wail of the Rebel Yell — the poor man's bagpipes. To the Yankees crouching dry-mouthed behind their fallen trees and piled-up stones, it seemed the very picture of battlefield terror, a flash of deja vu back to those early campaigns, when the Confederates' reputation for invincibility had been more than the burned-out bluff it had been since Gettysburg.

There was a lull at this moment over on the Confederate left, which gave the men in Hoke's (Bragg's) lines a chance to watch the action now beginning on their right. To them, the distant Confederate attack was clear enough to resemble an epic engraving from the pages of *Harper's Weekly*, an engraving that came thundering magically to life. That last victorious Confederate charge carried a palpable air of something already legend — something that seemed to have materialized from the pages of some great historical saga. Feeling a chill as they watched it unfold, the men in Bragg's lines who observed the attack knew they were witnessing a thing out of its proper time, a living anachronism. "It looked like a picture," one eyewitness later wrote, "and at our distance it was truly beautiful...[but] it was a painful sight to see how close their battle flags were together, regiments being scarcely larger than companies and a division not much larger than a regiment should be."[2]

The Confederate attackers advanced now over the corpses of Carlin's men who had been struck down in the first Federal attack; the faces of the corpses were already turning black in the hot sun. Halfway to Hobart's line, the attacking formations were struck by heavy fire. Gaps appeared in their lines, and the formations wavered. Then the Confederates seemed to pull themselves together and reform, and the attack kept going.

The assault went straight for the gap in Hobart's lines as though drawn by a powerful magnet. General Hardee himself was one of the first men to hit the enemy line. After ordering the men behind him to follow at the "double-quick," Hardee spurred his horse into a steeplechase jump and soared majestically over the Union breastworks. D.H. Hill's men went through first, a howling gray wave tipped with steel. Then they linked up with Taliaferro's men and outflanked Buell's exposed position.

Hobart's men crumbled first. Buell's men had no choice then but to pull out or be overwhelmed. They threw away their rifles, knapsacks, canteens, caps, and cooking pans, and ran, pell-mell, for the rear.

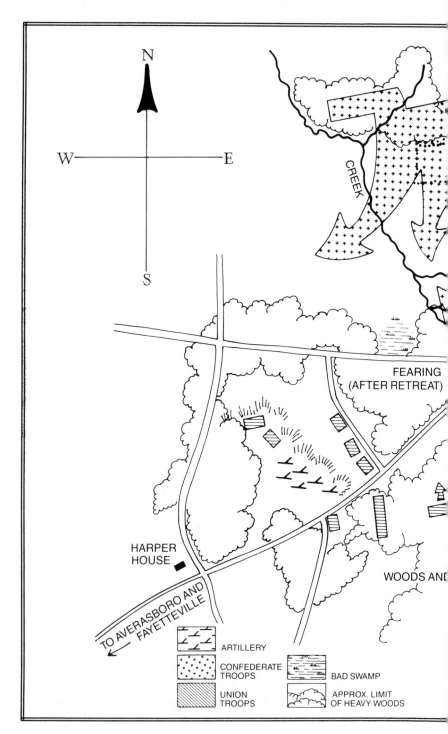

N

W——E

S

CREEK

FEARING
(AFTER RETREAT)

HARPER
HOUSE

TO AVERASBORO AND
FAYETTEVILLE

WOODS AND

ARTILLERY

CONFEDERATE
TROOPS

UNION
TROOPS

BAD SWAMP

APPROX. LIMIT
OF HEAVY WOODS

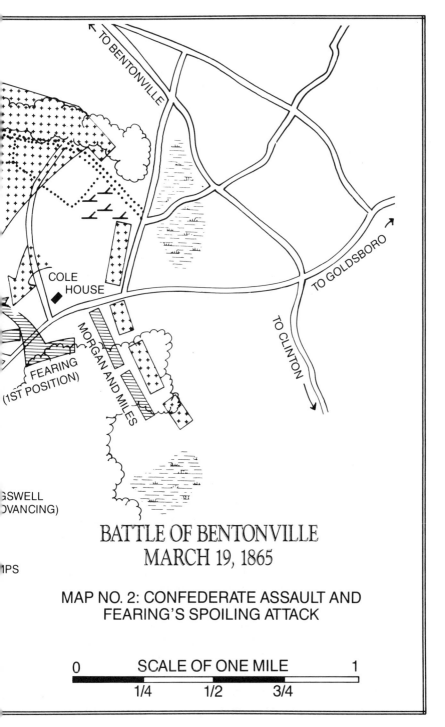

TO BENTONVILLE

TO GOLDSBORO

TO CLINTON →

COLE
HOUSE

MORGAN AND MILES

FEARING
(1ST POSITION)

GSWELL
DVANCING)

PS

BATTLE OF BENTONVILLE
MARCH 19, 1865

MAP NO. 2: CONFEDERATE ASSAULT AND
FEARING'S SPOILING ATTACK

0	SCALE OF ONE MILE	1
	1/4 1/2 3/4	

A young lieutenant named Brown, who was with Buell's brigade, later praised General Carlin's courage as he watched his position collapse: "[He] was cool...as ice. When the Rebs got around us, so as to fire into our rear, he turned to the boys: 'No use, boys,' and started back. The Regiment followed and...it was the best thing we ever did. For falling back, we met a line of Rebs marching straight for our rear and in 15 minutes more we would have been between two lines of the buggers...We showed the Rebs as well as our side some of the best running ever did."

Just minutes after the Confederate attackers had crashed into Carlin's breastworks, they had caved in the entire Federal left. Sweeping through and around the confused fragments of Buell's and Hobart's brigades, the Confederates easily overran Robinson's line, some 300 yards farther on. The broken remnants of all three distressed units — Hobart's, Buell's, and Robinson's — fell back in disarray toward the fortified lines being established by the newly arrived units of 20th Corps. The Confederates even captured three Federal cannon in the advance. Observing the route north of the road, Miles drew his brigade inside Morgan's lines south of the road and tried to position it to meet any new Confederate threats.

To the Federal officers standing on the elevations in front of the Harper house, the broad, partly open battlefield that stretched before them had become a spectacular sight. It was a vast, pine-forested plain, swarming with amoeba-knots of dusty blue uniforms, wheeling horses, lurching caissons and cannon, officers yelling and gesturing in attempts to restore order, wounded men staggering through the haze. Far off, across the open fields near the Cole plantation, rippling and surging lake a wave, came that thin tide of gray-clad attackers, their flags violently bobbling spots of blue and red, accenting the colors of the red-clay dust and pine needles. Thrumming above this entire panorama, like an invisible ceiling over all the roiling movement, could be heard the oscillating, beehive tones of Minie balls whizzing in all directions: *Zooooooooo!* and *Bzzzzzzzzzz!* and *Vmmmmmmmmmm!*, sometimes punctuated by a flat-of-the-axe *Whock!* as one of those fat lead projectiles buried itself in flesh.

With the Federal left flank shattered and in flight, and the Federal right unsupported and shaken, now was a good time for Bragg to unleash Hoke's division. Predictably, Bragg did nothing. McLaws's division of veteran troops, which Bragg had begged for earlier that day, received no orders at all. They simply milled around restlessly for most of the day, completely wasted.

Jeff Davis, the 14th Corps' commander, moved now to check the Confederate flood on his left. He ordered Morgan to deploy his reserve brigade (Fearing's) and counterattack the axis of the main Rebel thrust. Davis rode up to Fearing while the latter officer was dressing his men for a charge. "Advance to their flank, Fearing!" Davis shouted. "Deploy as you go. Strike them wherever you find them! Give them the best you've got and we'll whip them yet!"

Fearing's men who had been within earshot of that dramatic exchange went into battle shouting, "We'll whip 'em yet!" Fearing led them bravely. He smote the straggling Confederate flank with some effect, checking its momentum and even pushing it back in places. But then fresh Confederate troops came rushing down the Goldsboro road and struck Fearing on his own right flank. Fearing himself was hit and seriously wounded. In sudden danger of being cut off and hacked up piecemeal, his brigade wisely pulled back some 300 yards and formed a defensive line with its right flank on the roadway. The focus of the battle then shifted elsewhere and Fearing's men got a breathing spell; they had done exactly what was asked of them.

But Fearing's withdrawal, however necessary, had opened a route across the road toward the rear of Morgan's line. Three of D.H. Hill's Confederate brigades crashed through the spotty resistance and struck the rear of Morgan's improvised entrenchments.

Robert Hoke, who was watching all this and who had a sense of tactical timing second to no other Confederate general, was almost beside himself. He approached the dour and sickly Braxton Bragg and begged for permission to take his division into the breach created by Hill's advance. This would reinforce a clear Confederate chance to roll up Morgan's entire position from its most vulnerable point. If any man in the Confederate Army could have done it, it was Hoke; his men were charged with adrenalin, and together with Hill's troops, they would have been irresistible. A coup de grace to Morgan, crushing the entire Federal right, would have given Joseph Johnston his only real chance to sweep the field and turn Bentonville

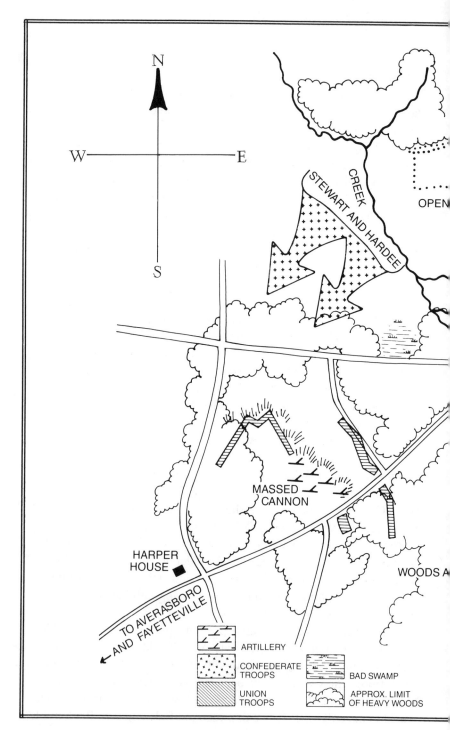

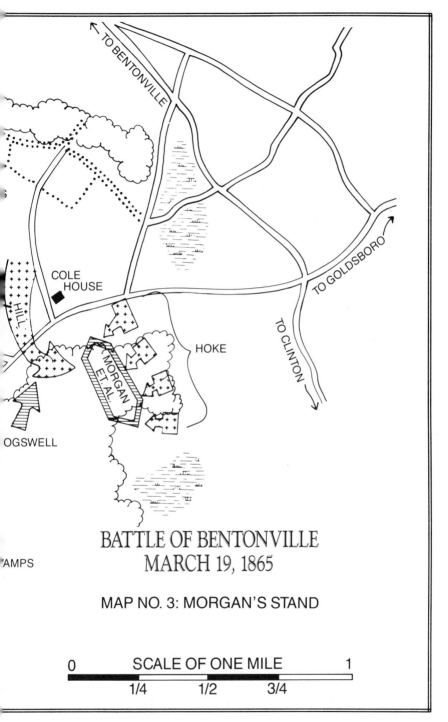

TO BENTONVILLE

TO GOLDSBORO

TO CLINTON

COLE
HOUSE

HILL

HOKE

MORGAN
ET AL.

OGSWELL

AMPS

BATTLE OF BENTONVILLE
MARCH 19, 1865

MAP NO. 3: MORGAN'S STAND

SCALE OF ONE MILE

0   1

1/4   1/2   3/4

into a startling Confederate victory.

No, Bragg ruminated; sounds too risky. Better just launch a frontal attack instead, to keep Morgan occupied.

Morgan's men had, in fact, been occupied for several hours. They had been industriously strengthening their fieldworks and raising respectable walls of brush, sharpened tree limbs, fence rails, and earthen parapets. All of these fortifications were facing Hoke's lines, and all were designed to do just one thing: stop cold the exact sort of attack Bragg had just authorized.

So what might have been a swift, economical, and decisive stroke degenerated instead into a gutter brawl. Morgan's men, now entirely surrounded, and fighting from both sides of their breastworks simultaneously, resisted the Confederate attacks furiously. In some places, the defenders formed two ranks. The rear rank loaded while the front rank fired, and the discharged muskets were passed back and exchanged for freshly loaded ones fast enough to maintain a continuous rolling fire. Rifle barrels grew so hot that they seared the skin of the men who handled them.

General Hoke's troops, instead of pouring through that temporary hole and crashing into the weakest part of Morgan's perimeter, now dashed themselves head-first against his strongest defenses. They suffered wicked casualties: 600 men killed, wounded, or captured. One of Hoke's units, the 36th North Carolina, opened its frontal attackes with 267 men; in ten minutes of desperate combat, it lost 152 of them. Once again, Braxton Bragg had managed to wrest defeat from the jaws of victory.

The battle became a wild and merciless fight between individual groups of infantry. Veterans of the Virginia front were reminded of the butchery at Cold Harbor. At one point, some Texas troops broke into Union General Vandever's perimeter, but the smoke and confusion were so great that Vandever didn't know the new arrivals were Confederates. Then he heard an unmistakable Southern drawl calling out for him and his men to surrender. "You go to Hell!" screamed several Federal soldiers. With a yell, Vandever's men charged over their own breastworks, toward what had been their rear, and attacked the Confederate intruders with rifle butts, bayonets, picks, and even rocks.

Observing Morgan's men fighting for their lives, General Jeff

Davis remarked to one of his aides: "If Morgan's men can stand this, all is right; if not, the day is lost." He was right. He had committed every single man in his corps, including his personal headquarters guards.

At 4:30 p.m., the turning point of the battle came with the arrival of Cogswell's brigade of 20th Corps. Though exhausted by a forced march, part of it through a boot-sucking swamp, Cogswell's men hurled themselves at Hood's brigades, who by now were even more tired. After some fairly vigorous resistance, the Confederates were forced to break off their attack on Morgan's rear and retire back to the Goldsboro road.

The final phase of the day's fighting began at about five o'clock. The original Confederate attacking force, minus the three of Hill's brigades that had turned south to strike Morgan, had regrouped and caught their breath. Fearing's attack, though repulsed, had disorganized the Confederates and sapped some of the steam from their advance. Still, given their successes of the early afternoon, the officers felt there was still a reasonable chance to sweep on and crack the line that Slocum's 20th Corps had been fortifying on the elevated terrain half a mile in front of the Harper house. The day could still be won.

On the Federal side, General Jeff Davis had put to use every minute of time he had been given since the first of 20th Corps — Hawley's brigade — had arrived at about two o'clock, too late to reinforce Carlin and Robinson. Robinson's men, after falling back in disorder before the rebel onslaught, had reformed alongside their two sister regiments that had been held back earlier that day. Robinson's command now held a line with its right anchored on the Goldsboro road. Carlin's winded and demoralized troops were collected, reformed, and placed in reserve — where most of them were glad to be. Additional units of 20th Corps, including Kilpatrick's cavalry, took up positions on Hawley's left. This extended the Union line and deepened it, in some places, to a double line.

Urged on frantically by their officers, the Federal infantry had fortified their positions. In the two to three hours between the time these units were put into line and the time they came under attack, their position had become a strong one. Rail fences had been dismantled and turned into breastworks, holes had been dug, and boul-

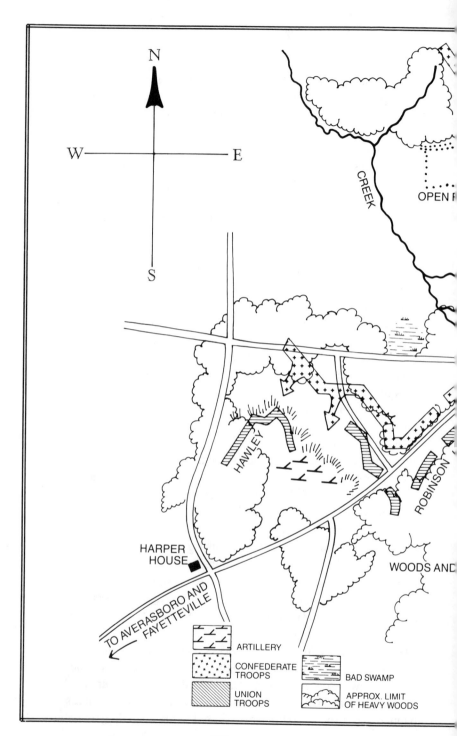

N

W——E

S

CREEK

OPEN F

HAWLEY

ROBINSON

HARPER
HOUSE

WOODS AND

TO AVERASBORO AND
FAYETTEVILLE

ARTILLERY

CONFEDERATE
TROOPS

UNION
TROOPS

BAD SWAMP

APPROX. LIMIT
OF HEAVY WOODS

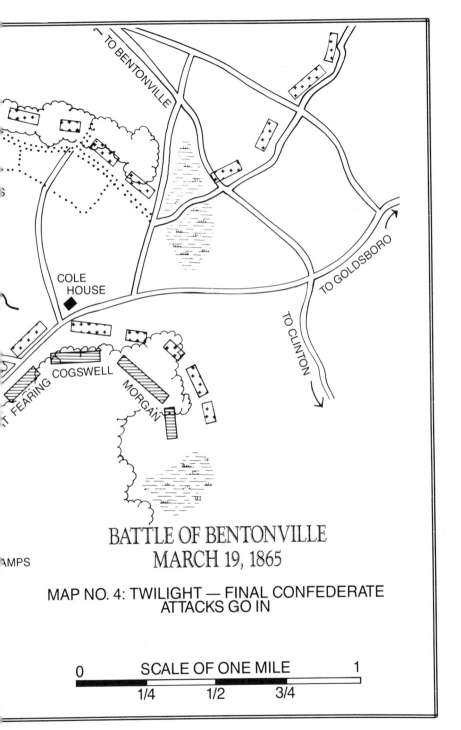

TO BENTONVILLE

COLE
HOUSE

TO GOLDSBORO

TO CLINTON

FEARING COGSWELL

MORGAN

BATTLE OF BENTONVILLE
MARCH 19, 1865

MAP NO. 4: TWILIGHT — FINAL CONFEDERATE
ATTACKS GO IN

AMPS

0   SCALE OF ONE MILE   1

1/4   1/2   3/4

ders, earth, and tree trunks had been piled up. All of this faced the wooded fields where the Confederates were now dressing their lines for a renewed onslaught.

Between Robinson's left and the right flank of Hawley's line was a 400-yard gap of open, rising terrain, covered by a strong line of Federal artillery. Anticipating that this gap would be the aiming point of the Confederate assault, the Federal artillery commander ordered his crews to cram their pieces with double loads of canister. Some gun crews had even wrapped handfuls of Minie balls in scraps of rag and stuffed them on top of the canister loads.

When the Confederates attacked, they walked into a hurricane of lead. The double- and triple-loaded cannon blasted forth such a volume of fire that pine trees were stripped not only of all their limbs, but of their bark as well. But men persisted where trees could not. The Confederates charged no fewer than five times, each time weaker and more faltering, suffering bigger and bigger gaps in their formations.

The last attacks hit at sundown. McLaws's division was finally committed, just in time to take part in the final action. The blood-red light of the sunset, filtering through the torn and burning pines, partly obscured by thick banks of reeking smoke, lent the scene a surreal and Hellish cast. On this all-but-forgotten battlefield, the Army of Tennessee gave its last measure of devotion to the Confederate cause, shed its last forlorn effusion of blood, and proved for one final time what it had proven a hundred times before: that in the age of field entrenchments and rifled muskets, sheer valor was a debased currency.

The Confederate attacks finally petered out with the last daylight, and the survivors retreated to essentially the same lines they had held that morning. In those final five attacks, General Johnston had lost nearly 600 men.

For both armies, the night of March 19 was a time to dig in and reposition for what was expected to be a second round of fighting the following day. Sherman's right wing had finally been ordered to countermarch toward Bentonville, and by nightfall its leading elements were a little more than 20 miles to the east.

All day long, Sherman had remained under the impression that Slocum was still up against cavalry detachments and nothing more.

Slocum's second, more urgent, dispatch did not catch up with Sherman until after dark. When the dispatch rider pulled up at the general's tent, he found Sherman clad in nothing but a red flannel nightshirt. Without bothering to change, a cold cigar clamped in the corner of his mouth, Sherman strode around his tent giving the orders that would send the right wing's units into position the following day, his feet kicking up small clouds of old campfire ashes.

Even at this point, Sherman was reluctant to ride back to Bentonville. He was damned if he would get his whole army sucked into a general engagement, not if he could help it, not this close to the end of the whole bloody campaign. Even when he did return to the front, he intervened only a few times with direct orders. Generally, he was content to let Slocum fight the battle pretty much on his own, as he had been doing very capably so far.

Johnston's battered army, meanwhile, retired a mile or so to the rear of the positions it occupied on the morning of March 19. The Confederates extended themselves in a fishhook-shaped line covering the road through Bentonville. Aware that General Howard's right wing was surely marching on them by now, Johnston sent Joe Wheeler's cavalry out to delay the Union force as long as possible.

By dawn on March 20, Sherman's 15th and 17th Corps were united and marching westward down the Goldsboro pike. Wheeler's men, dismounted and fighting cannily behind successive lines of improvised breastworks, slowed the advance so effectively that Howard's first division did not reach the Bentonville front until midday.

By late afternoon, Sherman's entire army was together again, although some of Howard's units, after forced marches of 20 miles or more, were too winded to be of much use for the moment. There was some fighting in the afternoon, as Howard's point division tangled with, and pushed back, some of Hoke's men close to the Goldsboro road.

Johnston now occupied a U-shaped front across the road south from Bentonville. At his rear was the rain-swollen Mill Creek, and the only bridge across that creek was in Bentonville. Johnston's right flank was held by Taliaferro's division and the much-diminished regiments of Hill and Bate. His center was held by the divisions of Loring and Walthall, and his left by Hoke's and McLaws's divisions. The extreme flanks were screened by the cavalry of Hampton and Wheeler.

Facing Johnston's right flank was the Federal 20th Corps, now up to full strength and deeply entrenched. The hardfought 14th Corps was next in line, on the south side of the Goldsboro road, facing the Cole house. Opposite Hoke was the newly arrived Union 15th Corps, with three divisions in line and one in reserve. On the Federal right flank was the 17th Corps, in a similar formation.

March 20 was a day that saw both armies jockeying for advantage. Still, there was some intense skirmishing, as recorded in the following account by a member of the 100th Indiana:

> ...We were hurried up, part of our Regiment was deployed as skirmishers under command of Major Headington. Col. Johnson kept the rest of the Regiment close up. The Johnnys sent a lot of Cavelry around our flank, thinking they would capture our skirmish line which was well in advance. We were driving the Johnnys rapidly. They had a little 3-pounder gun on the road and would stop and fire it sometimes. We were perhaps 80 rods away. Some of our boys had been firing at the men with the gun, but could not seem to have much effect.
>
> Then Capt. Pratt called me to try it with my Henry rifle. I got as close as I dared, for they were firing at us with their small arms too. By that time they had the gun limbered up and were starting away with it, but I was close enough now so I could see them good. The rider was on the rear mule. I pulled up my rifle, thinking I would shoot him which I could easily have done as his whole body showed plainly above the mule. Just as I was going to fire, something seemed to say to me: "Don't kill the man; kill the mule," so I dropped my rifle a little and shot the off mule just behind the fore leg. He went down and that delayed them so much that we got the gun...
>
> While we were resting[,] the little gun we captured was brought back to where we were and Captain Pratt told Col. Johnson how we got it. The Colonel thanked me before all the boys and I felt pretty good. I am glad I shot the mule instead of the man.[3]

Also on March 20, the Cole house and its outbuildings were occupied by Union snipers, who picked off a few of Hill's men before the Confederate artillery shelled the buildings to pieces.

Johnston knew he had shot his bolt as far as offensive action was concerned. To attack Sherman's reunited army under these conditions would have been suicidal. He did hope, however, that Sherman could be induced to attack him and thereby forfeit some of his numerical advantage.

But Sherman didn't take the bait. As far as he was concerned, the whole Bentonville episode had been a nasty diversion, little more. He was far more interested in linking up with Schofield and Terry in the east. Once he had done that, he would be invincible, far beyond the reach of anything Johnston might hope to do with his little army. Sherman expected that Ol' Joe would wait until darkness, then slip away across the Mill Creek bridge.

At sunset, a drenching rain began to fall. Like Sherman, the confederate troops also were expecting Johnston to order a retreat. When the order didn't come, they spent a wretched night huddled in their flooded gun-pits.

In a dispatch to Slocum, written that night, Sherman expressed vexation over Johnston's intentions: "I cannot see why he remains...I would rather avoid a general battle if possible, but if he insists upon it, we must accommodate him."

The morning of March 21 found Ol' Joe's men wringing out their socks in the trenches. The Federal 15th Corps maintained steady pressure on Hoke and McLaws that morning, overrunning a forward line of foxholes and retaining control despite several vigorous Confederate attempts to retake the lost ground.

The day's hottest action, however, took place on the Union's far right flank. Union General J.A. Mower of the 17th Corps managed to turn the rebel left flank with two of his brigades. Mower's attack developed well. By four o'clock that afternoon, his men had overrun two lines of entrenchments and were getting dangerously close to a point from which they could bring the Mill Creek bridge under fire — and thus endanger Johnston's only line of retreat. At one point, very briefly, they endangered Ol' Joe himself, as some determined skirmishers probed to within 50 yards of his headquarters.

But Mower's very success was his undoing. He didn't realize, until it was almost too late, that he had pushed his men almost a mile beyond the nearest Federal support. A brigade of Confederate infantry checked Mower frontally. A short time later, the Eighth Texas Cavalry, dashingly led by General Hardee himself, crashed into Mower's left flank. Wheeler's cavalry, not far behind, struck Mower to the right of Hardee, all but cutting off Mower from Union lines. The Texans in particular charged with tremendous spirit, some riders holding the reins in their teeth and firing pistols with both hands.

Now Wade Hampton, always riding to the sound of the guns, put himself at the head of yet another cavalry brigade and led them full-tilt against Mower's right flank. Mower hastily and prudently withdrew to his starting point in the Federal lines, where Sherman ordered him to stay.

The cavalry versus infantry action had been especially hot. Just how hot can be judged from Hardee's remark to a bystander, as he came back, sweat-drenched, from the field: "That was Nip and Tuck, and for a time I thought Tuck had it!"

Sherman was later criticized for not throwing more men behind Mower, reinforcing his early success. However, that would have brought on the general engagement Sherman was still hoping to avoid. Possibly, such a move would have turned Mower's localized advance into a major breakthrough. Just as possibly, it would have resulted only in heavier Union losses. As it was, Mower had run into a virtual hornet's nest of aggressive Confederate cavalry, had just made it back to friendly lines by the skin of his teeth, and had lost 150 men for his trouble while inflicting only small losses on the Confederates.

Against the tactical success of ejecting Mower and saving their line of retreat, the Confederates had to balance the blow to morale that befell one of their best commanders. When the fighting started, General Hardee's 16-year-old son, Willie — who had joined the Texas outfit only a few days before — had kissed his father, waved gallantly, and charged into the thick of the action. Within minutes, he was struck and gravely wounded by a bullet. Following the battle, Confederate General Stephen Lee wrote a letter to Union General O.O. Howard, commander of Sherman's right wing, describing what had happened to Willie Hardee. Lee thought Howard would want to know — before the war, when both Hardee and Howard had been on the staff of West Point, Howard had been Willie's Sunday school teacher, and Willie had been Howard's favorite pupil. Willie survived the agonizing ride back to Raleigh, but died there. He was General Hardee's only son.

With the repulse of Mower's impetuous attack on March 21, the Battle of Bentonville came to an end. Both armies spent a miserable night in their holes, unable to light campfires due to the heavy downpour that sloshed over them hour after hour. Word came to General Johnston that Union General Schofield had finally reached Goldsboro, which meant that Sherman's army would be powerfully augmented yet again within the next 24 hours. There was no reason for Johnston to remain where he was any longer. Except for Mower's men, none of Sherman's divisions had tested the Confederate defenses, and Mower, alone, had come perilously close to undoing Johnston's whole line. Clearly, it was time to retire, to keep the army intact and hope for another opportunity in the future.

By two o'clock in the morning on March 22, all the Confederate wounded had been moved across Mill Creek, except for about a hundred critically injured men who were left either in Bentonville or in a makeshift hospital that was set up at Harper's house; half of those would die in the next few days. A colonel in the Ninth Ohio Cavalry left a graphic description of the scene inside the improvised hospital: "A dozen surgeons and attendants in their shirt sleeves stood at rude benches cutting off arms and legs and throwing them out of the windows, where they lay scattered on the grass. The legs of infantrymen could be distinguished from those of the cavalry by the size of the calves, as the march of 1,000 miles had increased the size of the one and diminished the size of the other."[4]

By dawn, Ol' Joe and his valiant little army had vanished, leaving only their empty, muddy fieldworks and some overlooked corpses. Sherman made no attempt to follow him. He knew he had nothing, really, to fear any longer, now that he was about to link up with the Federal columns from the coast; Johnston would not dare attack him again.

Thus ended the largest battle ever fought on North Carolina soil, as well as one of the least decisive. Sherman was not deterred from what he had planned to do all along: proceed to Goldsboro to rest and refit, then link up with the coastal columns. He had been delayed only about 72 hours, to no appreciable material gain for the Confederates. Nor did Sherman decide anything by occupying the field and driving Johnston away. Ol' Joe's army survived, and though it was essentially powerless as an offensive force, it could still be a tough nut to crack in defensive positions.

Even if Johnston had prevailed against Sherman's left wing, there was probably nothing he could have done to prevent the linkup at Goldsboro. And even if Sherman had lost the entire wing, he would still have commanded, with Howard's, Terry's, and Schofield's units, a force three times bigger than Johnston's.

Slocum had been in serious trouble for a while on March 19, but he never lost his nerve or his wits. Basically, all he had to do was dig in and hold out until Sherman sent help. If the Confederates had been able to overwhelm Morgan's surrounded forces on the Union right, and then had concentrated all their power against the 20th Corps, they might have won an upset victory at Bentonville; but in the long run, little would have been changed by it. By this stage of the war, the disparity between the two sides, in numbers and resources, had become just too great.

That Johnston did not win more than a face-saving draw on March 19 can be laid — along with so many other sins — at the feet of Jefferson Davis's favorite general, Braxton Bragg. By demanding re-inforcements (McLaws's division) when he didn't really need them, and then doing nothing with them all day, Bragg was responsible for delaying the main Confederate attack for more than an hour and robbing it of some of Johnston's best troops. Later in the day, by not unleashing Hoke's and McLaws's men to exploit D.H. Hill's break-through into Morgan's rear, and then by ordering Hoke to mount frontal attacks on Morgan's entrenchments, Bragg virtually guaran-teed both Morgan's survival and unnecessary Confederate casualties.

Otherwise, considering that Johnston's tattered forces had never fought together as a unit, and considering that many Confederate troops were fighting that day under leaders who were strangers to them, or known only by reputation, Johnston and his officers acquit-ted themselves well. Hardee galvanized his men wherever he lead them; Hoke, though chained down by Bragg, was his usual steadfast self. Hampton and Wheeler handled their small cavalry forces bril-liantly.

And the men...the men were magnificent. Although Bentonville is today almost a forgotten battle, and was virtually ignored even at the time because of the dramatic events taking place simultaneously in Virginia, it was as hard-fought and as bloody (relative to the number of men engaged) as any engagement in the war. One old veteran, describing Taliaferro's assaults against 20th Corps on the afternoon of March 19, later said, "If there was a place in the battle of Gettysburg as hot as that spot, I never saw it."

If the men performed well, so too did the boys. There was a unit of teenaged Junior Reserves attached to Hoke's command, and Hoke had nothing but praise for their performance: "...they held a very important part of the battlefield in opposition to Sherman's old and trained soldiers, and repulsed every charge made against them...Their conduct in camp, on the march, and on the battlefield, was everything that could be expected of them, and I am free to say, was equal to that of the old soldiers who has passed through four years of war."[5]

Confederate losses for all three days of fighting totaled 2,606 (although one-quarter to one-third of that figure represents men taken prisoner). Officially, Union losses amounted to 1,527 — but that figure seems too low. Every official tabulation of losses for this battle is different, sometimes considerably different. For instance, Johnston's actual headcount of Yankee prisoners amounted to 900. It seems nearly impossible — given the ferocity of the fighting and the fact that on March 20 and 21, Sherman was attacking and Johnston defending — that the Federals could have suffered only 700-odd killed and wounded. Johnston let the matter go by simply saying that "from the appearance of the field" and from his discussions with enemy officers, both immediately after the fight and later on, after the war, he reckoned that Sherman suffered about 4,000 casualties — though a portion of that estimate must be regarded by historians as wishful thinking.

However you figure it, in terms of actual harm done, Bentonville came out about even, with both sides losing at least 2,000 men killed or wounded. Johnston had done all that any general could have done under the circumstances: the plan had been sound, and the execution of it unflinching, if imperfect. Honor, at least, had been saved — Sherman had not faced such determined opposition since the fall of Atlanta. His march through North Carolina would not go down in history as a walk in the sun.

"CALL FUR STONES FROM THE VASTY DEEP" — THE LAST MONTHS OF THE VANCE ADMINISTRATION

At the time Zebulon Baird Vance was reelected governor of North Carolina in August 1864, survival had replaced victory on the Confederate agenda. General Robert E. Lee and his battered Army of Northern Virginia was holding the vastly superior Union forces of Ulysses S. Grant at bay at Petersburg with a combination of bluff and brilliantly improvised defensive tactics; General John B. Hood and the Army of Tennessee was struggling hopelessly against General Sherman's columns in front of Atlanta; and thousands of men were deserting the sagging Confederate cause every month — many of them eventually roosting in the North Carolina mountains, where they did far more harm to the populace than the Yankees ever did.

Vance's top priority was to replenish the dwindling manpower of North Carolina's regiments. In August he issued a proclamation, giving every deserter in the state an ultimatum. If they returned to their units within 30 days, all would be forgiven; otherwise, he promised, "the utmost power of this State will be exerted to capture them or drive them from the borders of a country whose high honor and spotless renown they disgrace by refusing to defend." Vance also warned that magistrates who refused to prosecute deserters and shirkers could find their draft exemptions removed and themselves in the Petersburg trenches shouldering a musket.

Several thousand men, in fact, did return to their units, and a sizeable number were rounded up and shipped back under guard by the militia. But the manpower shortage was beyond any Band-Aid solutions. Vance even tried to get the state legislature to approve sending Home Guard units to General Lee — a dubious reinforcement indeed — but the measure never got very far. And by the final weeks of 1864, the attention of the entire state was focused on internal defense, not on what was happening around Richmond. The U.S. Navy was about to send everything it had against Fort Fisher, the stubborn bastion that had protected the vital blockade-runner port of Wilmington throughout the war (and that had earned the nickname "Gibraltar of the South" in doing so).

Again, as on every previous occasion, Richmond met the threat against North Carolina's seacoast with half-measures. The Confederate government sent only a handful of troops and placed them under the command of perhaps the least-qualified general in the entire Confederacy: Braxton Bragg. Dismayed that the fortunes of the last important Confederate seaport should be placed in such feeble hands, Governor Vance made a personal tour of inspection late in the year. He found the fortifications adequate and manned by enthusiastic garrisons, but he found Bragg in his usual state of gloomy passivity, in command of a pathetically small reaction force of infantry, and without any good plans to counter the amphibious attack the enemy was certain to launch. On his return from Wilmington, Vance issued a proclamation calling for volunteers, and he rather bombastically added: "Your Governor will meet you at the front, and will share with you the worst."

But as the old Southern colloquialism had it, "that dog don't hunt no more." The public's attitude was vividly summarized in an anonymous open letter to Vance, issued in response to his call to arms. The letter was couched in such extravagantly shaggy English that the author was most likely "putting on" the governor. Here it is, with some of its minstrel-show spelling parenthetically corrected for the modern reader:

> You say we are kowards if we don't kum. That's purty hard to take, but I'd rather take it than git a ball in the belly! Sur, you sing Sams [psalms] to a ded hoss when you kall on us fellers at home tu pitch in. I seed a feller not long since talkin about volunteerin, and the nabers all said he oght to be sent to the lunytick assylum, kase he was krazy...Guverner, if you'll give me a fat bumproof Offis [bomb-proof office], I'll kum a-kitin, but if you don't do this, call fur stones from the vasty deep, but not fur this chile.[1]

Apparently, Vance could no longer get much mileage from such phrases as "high honor and spotless renown." As a final desperation measure, he permitted the formation of what was called the "Junior Reserves." In the closing months of the war, the Junior Reserves became the largest single brigade in the Confederate Army in North Carolina. It was formed, however, from beardless youths of 16 and even younger, and commanded in some instances by lads of 17 and 18.

The story of the Virginia Military Institute cadets at the Battle of New Market has been told countless times, and a fine yarn it makes, too, but the Junior Reserves — "the seed-corn of the Confederacy," as Vance called them — deserve to be remembered as well. There were ten times as many of them in General Robert Hoke's division at Bentonville than there were VMI cadets at New Market. According to the laws which created the Junior Reserves, they were supposed to serve only within North Carolina, but large numbers fought under Hoke in Virginia before returning to the state in time for Johnston's final stand.

These boys were first inducted at their regional and county recruiting centers, then sent to Raleigh, where Vance, if other duties were not pressing, always tried to welcome each detachment with a few kind and inspiring words. At Camp Holmes, they were instructed in the rudiments of drill and discipline, trained how to load and fire percussion-cap rifles, and were equipped — as much as was possible — with either carbines or undersized muskets. Their junior officers (in modern nomenclature, platoon and squad leaders) were 17 and 18 years old. The senior commanders were usually older veterans, often men who had recuperated from wounds but were not quite in shape to go back to the meat-grinder outside of Petersburg.

The spirit and valor of these adolescent warriors, and their record of steadiness under fire, would have done any veteran unit proud. They were a telling argument in favor of Governor Vance's policy of maintaining full democratic rights within the state. After four years of deprivation at home, and four years of seeing their older brothers and fathers killed or maimed, these youths would never have responded to a despotic central power as they did to the paternalistic fervor of Vance's proclamations.

The Juniors' in-state baptism of fire came at Fort Fisher, Wilmington, in late December 1864. Despite a noisy and spectacular assault by an amphibious force led by Union General Butler, the garrison smartly repulsed the first attacks. They were not so successful on January 13 when the Federals returned and unleashed one of the heaviest naval bombardments of the 19th century, followed by a vigorous land assault. While Braxton Bragg — who was actually positioned to the *rear* of the attacking force with 5,000 battle-hardened veterans of Lee's army — fretted and fussed and finally did nothing, the garrison of Fort Fisher was overwhelmed after a desperate Alamo-style defense. Wilmington's other defensive works were easy pickings once Fort Fisher was neutralized, and the last, most important Confederate link with Europe was in enemy hands by the end of February.

Following this signal defeat, and with the specter of Sherman's columns inching their way northward toward the state line, despondency seemed to grip the civilian population. Governor Vance was inundated with petitions and pleas from every corner of the state, begging him to take action personally to find a way to end the suffering. Typical of the letters that crossed the governor's desk was this one, anonymous but eloquent in its untutored fashion, dated January 10, 1865:

> For the sake of the sufering women and children, do try and stop this cruel war. here I am without one mouthfull to eat for myself and five children and God only knows where I will get something now you know as well as you have a head that it is impossible to whip the Yankees, therefore I beg you for God sake to try and make peace on some terms, and let they rest of they poor men come home and try to make something to eat, my husband has been killed, and ef they all stay till they are dead, what in they name of God will become of us poor women and children?[2]

Curiously, the state's newspapers continued to beat the drums of unfounded military optimism. The *Fayetteville Observer* still clung to the bankrupt hope that England and France would recognize the Confederacy, the *Charlotte Democrat* advocated last-ditch resistance, and the *Raleigh Confederate* somewhat hollowly urged people to "hold out yet a while longer and all will be well."

Meanwhile, over at the *Raleigh Standard*, editor William Holden was crowing his I-told-you-sos and already angling to position himself for the governorship when Vance's regime was forced out of Raleigh. Nor did the state legislature echo the newspapers' empty rhetoric: Convinced that the war was in its final days, the lawmakers were busily exempting blacksmiths, millers, railway employees, and other skilled persons from military service, so they could remain alive until the return of peace.

As late as Valentine's Day, 1865, Vance was still trying to pump up the waning fires of resistance in the state. In a proclamation dated February 14, he adumbrated the horrors of Federal occupation: destruction and confiscation of private property; whole families reduced to penury and starvation; a veritable forest of Confederate leaders dangling from the victors' gallows (no doubt, and with some reason, the governor saw himself among them). Then he closed with yet another tintinnabulation of rhetoric: "Great God, is there a man in all this honorable, high-spirited and noble Commonwealth, so steeped in every conceivable meanness, so blackened with all the guilt of treason, or so damned with the leprosy of cowardice, as to say, yes, we will submit to all this!"

In an editorial written in response to Vance's proclamation, Holden quietly reached out with a sharp pin and punctured the gubernatorial hot-air balloon by quietly reminding his readers that "if proclamations could have defeated our enemies, they would long since have retired with trailing banners...."

Ten days later, the Confederate Bureau of Subsistence asked Vance to issue an appeal for supplies from the public. The official Confederate supply service — a baroquely inefficient apparatus in its best days — had simply collapsed under the strain of military pressure, deteriorating railroads, bankrupt coffers, and the halt of supplies from Europe. Vance responded with a generosity that future historians would sometimes overlook, pledging one-half of the state's food supply and putting himself and his family on short rations to set an example.

Like everyone else in the state, Vance watched the approach of General Sherman with a sense of great foreboding. As report after report came in of the savagery visited by Sherman's men upon South Carolina — culminating in the burning of Columbia — Vance could not help but contrast the way Sherman chose to wage war with the scrupulous attention Lee had paid to civilian rights and property during his invasion of Pennsylvania. During that campaign, the strongest complaint lodged by the local population had been that some of General Longstreet's men milked their cows without permission. Historically minded fellow that he was, Vance also contrasted Sherman's behavior with that of Lord Cornwallis, another invader of the Carolinas nearly a century before. Vance cited an order Cornwallis had issued from Beatties' Ford in January 1781: "It is needless to point out to the officers the necessity of preserving the strictest discipline, and of preventing the oppressed people from suffering violence at the hands from whom they are taught to look for protection."

But there was something else about Sherman's march that disturbed Vance as much, if not more, than the Union Army's callous disregard of civilian property — the docility with which the South's population was submitting to the barbarism. After contemplating Sherman's iron-handed style of waging war, Vance was perhaps the first observer to suggest the correct form of resistance: mass guerilla warfare. In several letters and numerous conversations, Vance admitted that the South's manpower resources were scant in some of the areas ravaged by Sherman. But he maintained that there were still enough able-bodied people, and enough firearms of one kind or another (not to mention scythes, pruning hooks, and pitchforks), to have inflicted great hurt on Sherman...had there been any strong will to resist.

Instead, Vance lamented, "not a bridge has been burned, not a car thrown from its tracks, nor a man shot" by the very people whose homes were being pillaged. All along Sherman's route, as soon as any organized Confederate troops left an area, resistance collapsed and the inhabitants supinely accepted their harsh treatment. What this proved to Vance was a cold realization indeed. "It shows," he wrote, "what I have always believed, that the great popular heart is not now, and never has been in this war. It was a revolution of the Politicians...not the People; and was fought at first by the natural enthusiasm of our young men, and has been kept going by state and sectional pride, assisted by that bitterness of feeling produced by the cruelties and brutalities of the enemy."

On his more despairing days, Vance could see that the end was coming to this great and bloody adventure, and he later described the mood with typical rhetorical cadences. "In kaleidoscopic array, each phase swept across the stage, as storm-clouds are driven across the sky, culminating in that moral darkness of men ungoverned by law...All these things, and more, I witnessed among my own people in these unhappy times; from the day when the first company of volunteers went forth amid the plaudits of the people, as to a festival, down to that dark hour when I saw the last regiment of beardless boys, the 'seed corn' of our hopes, pass through the unprotected capital of our state."[3]

That last sentence is almost certainly a reference to the final review of the battered Army of Tennessee, staged in Raleigh on April 4, 1865. That pathetic yet moving spectacle is best described by an eyewitness, Captain B.L. Ridley, a member of General Stewart's staff, who recorded the event in his diary:

> I witnessed today the saddest spectacle of my life, the review of the skeleton Army of Tennessee, that but one year ago was replete with men, and not filled with the tattered garments, worn out shoes, barefooted, and ranks so depleted that each color was supported only by thirty or forty men. Desertion, sickness, deaths, hardships, perils and vicissitudes demonstrated themselves too plainly on that old army...the march of the remnant was so slow — colors torn and tattered with bullets — it looked like a funeral procession. The countenance of every spectator was depressed and dejected, and the solemn, stern look of the soldiers was so impressive — oh! it is beginning to look dark in the east, gloomy in the west, and like almost a lost hope when we reflect upon that review today![4]

Despite fervent arguments from advisers, Vance did not want to be the man who started separate peace negotiations with the Federals. In his reelection campaign he had taken a strong stand against separate negotiations. If someone else initiated the peace process, Vance was willing to swing behind it and lend his weight; but he was opposed to taking the first plunge. As long as Richmond was determined to continue the struggle, Zebulon Vance was pledged by honor and oath to support the Confederate cause.

But that did not mean blind faith and inactivity while waiting for a miracle. Taking his cue from what had happened in Columbia, and knowing how close Sherman was to Raleigh, Vance took steps, beginning on April 10, to pack and ship the more valuable state archives to the hamlet of Company Shops (modern-day Burlington). He also ordered the state warehouses around Raleigh to be emptied and their contents cached in depots back down the main railroad line.

The latter action, and the startling amounts of food, clothing, and medical supplies involved, was later brought up by Vance's political opponents and subjected to the worst possible interpretation: that the governor had been hoarding while Lee's army was barefoot and starving. In truth, Vance never — not once — refused to send supplies requested by Lee. Indeed, until the fall of Richmond, Lee's army was still drawing at least 60 percent of its supplies from North Carolina.

His actual motives for stockpiling and then dispersing such comparatively large quantities of stores suggest several other, more reasonable, interpretations. At the time Vance ordered the dispersal, there was still a very real chance that Lee would retreat down the line of the Greensboro-Danville Railroad, link up with General Johnston at Greensboro, and either fight a last stand in North Carolina or withdraw into the interior of the state for a partisan campaign. Either way, those supplies — the fruits of Vance's industrialization campaign on the home front, as well as his industrious blockade-running activities — would have been crucial. Alternatively, if the Richmond government should suddenly capitulate, those supplies would go a long way toward easing the destitution of North Carolina's returning veterans and their families.

It should also be remembered that in the final months of the war, a great deal of what was supposed to be shipped from North Carolina to Virginia never got there, for reasons beyond Vance's control. Vance was at the wide end of the supply funnel; Lee's army was at the narrow end. In between lay the tangled tentacles of one of the least efficient and most ill-managed military services in history, the

Confederate Quartermaster Corps.

As Zebulon Vance rode out of Raleigh at midnight on April 12, 1865, he could at least take some pride in the knowledge that North Carolina's troops had stood firm with Robert E. Lee until the end. During the final days of the Appomattox campaign, at Sayler's Creek, when a Confederate collapse seemed imminent, a gray-clad column suddenly appeared. Its arrival to join the Army of Northern Virginia was a timely answer to Lee's prayers, and it made ready to shore up the rebel line.

"What troops are those?" called Lee to the nearest officer.

"Cox's North Carolina brigade," was the reply.

Lee removed his hat, waved it at the grim-faced veterans, and cried out in an emotion-choked voice: "God bless gallant old North Carolina!"

ENDGAME – THE
FALL OF RALEIGH

On March 22, 1865, General William Tecumseh Sherman finally linked up with the Union troops under General Terry at Cox's Bridge, North Carolina. On the following day he entered Goldsboro and met with General Schofield and his Federal forces. Sherman's augmented army was now invincible.

By March 25, the first train from New Bern arrived, bearing much-needed supplies and much-appreciated sacks of mail for the Union armies. The march that had begun at Christmas back in Savannah was now officially concluded, its primary objective reached and taken. All of Sherman's larger strategic objectives had also been accomplished: He had united his command with those of Generals Terry and Schofield, forming an irresistible army too large for General Joseph E. Johnston ever to challenge again; he had opened communications with supply bases on the coast and with his superiors in Washington; and he had cut a punishing swath, 30 to 60 miles wide, through both Carolinas.

In terms of the difficulty of the march and of the resistance encountered, it had been much tougher than the famous March to the Sea from Atlanta to Savannah. In later years, Sherman always insisted that the march through Georgia had been "child's play" compared to the Carolinas campaign. But it was the first march that captured press attention and the public's imagination, and it would forever remain the feat of arms for which Sherman was best remembered, while the events in the Carolinas would remain largely unknown. Even today, most general histories of the Civil War gloss over the battle of Bentonville in one or two vague paragraphs.

The contrast between Sherman's lean, mean, raggedy army and

the comparatively sleek, well-dressed Union troops that marched in from the coast was extreme and somewhat amusing. By this stage of the campaign, Sherman's men actually looked worse than the Confederates they were pursuing. Many of his men were barefooted, or wore torn, flopping rags of leather, sometimes tied to their feet with string or thongs. It was rare to see an intact pair of trousers, for most of the pants legs had worn to a frazzle and had been cut off at the knee, so that whole companies appeared to be clad in mud-colored Bermuda shorts. On their heads, Sherman's men wore whatever outlandish pieces of headgear they had created or liberated along the way: ancient tricorn hats from the 18th century, tall stovepipe hats of crushed silk, or simply colorful buccaneer's bandannas. Some men still had coats, invariably full of holes and patches; some had coats with no sleeves, and others marched only in their louse-infested shirts. Sherman had scheduled a grand review through the center of Goldsboro, but the contrast between his formations of armed hobos and the spit-and-polish of the men in the coastal columns was so ridiculous that he cut the affair short after only two regiments had marched past.

Sergeant Rice C. Bull, of the 123rd New York, recorded a telling glimpse of the difference between Sherman's men and Terry's when they encountered each other at a bridge over the Neuse River:

> The troops at the bridge were colored men, and they made the mistake of thinking when they first saw us that we were also Negroes. This was not surprising as we were certainly as black as they were. We had had no soap for weeks and were completely covered with greasy black that could not be removed by water alone. While in the matter of our complexion we might resemble our colored comrades, in other ways we presented a strange contrast. Their uniforms were new and well fitted, bright and clean, and their shoes were black, new, shining; their guns were the latest Springfield model and almost sparkled with brightness.[1]

But when the supplies started rolling into Goldsboro, Sherman's men once again found themselves under strict orders to clean up and maintain a more conventional soldierly appearance. New clothing was issued, delousing operations were undertaken, and beards and hair were trimmed.

Goldsboro itself was not unduly molested by the Yankees. Indeed, they seem to have found it an unimpressive place compared to Fayetteville, which had surprised them with its size and gracious architecture. But little Goldsboro, wrote one private in the 103rd Illinois, "don't amount to anything." There were some serious depredations committed by Yankees in the surrounding farmlands — only this time they didn't go entirely unpunished. (In fact, two of Sherman's men were executed by firing squad — one for rape, the other for murder.) This was a sure sign that the high command figured the fighting was just about over.

Satisfied that his army was refitting at a proper rate, Sherman embarked for the coast on March 25. He traveled from New Bern to City Point, Virginia by boat for a strategy conference with General Grant. Sherman badly wanted to be in on the kill in Virginia, and thought that, in view of all the hard marching his men had done, they deserved a share in that final glory. But it was not to be. Grant didn't need any help to finish off Lee's tattered army, and he politely but firmly rebuffed Sherman's attempts to share in his triumph. Only if Grant should fail in his end-game moves against Lee would there be any chance that Sherman's troops could arrive in Virginia in time to take part in the headline-grabbing surrender.

While at Grant's headquarters, Sherman also held discussions with another visitor, President Lincoln. Lincoln told Sherman that his sole concern was to get the nation reunited as smoothly and as rapidly as possible. Retribution was not on his agenda, and neither was the enslavement of the South. As for Jefferson Davis, Lincoln strongly hinted that he would gladly look the other way if Davis wanted to slip out of the country and go into voluntary exile. Beyond these liberal generalities, Lincoln did not give Sherman any specific instructions as to what sort of surrender terms he should demand from General Johnston and the Army of Tennessee. This oversight would have unfortunate consequences in a couple of weeks.

By March 30, a somewhat crestfallen Sherman was back in Goldsboro, organizing his men for the final push on Raleigh. The first ten days of April were given over to resupply and reorganization. With an army now mustering almost 90,000 men, Sherman felt that his old two-wing structure had become too cumbersome to administrate. He therefore divided his army into a three-wing configuration (left, center, and right), the wings commanded by Slocum, Schofield, and Howard, respectively. Once the railroads were back in working order, supplies came through in a steady flow from Wilmington and Morehead City, although the hard-working quartermasters could not keep up with the demands of such a large army. Kinston therefore was designated a supplementary supply base. Steamboats hauled food, ammunition, and clothing up from Beaufort and New Bern to Kinston, where it was loaded onto wagons, driven across town to the railroad station, and loaded onto trains for Goldsboro. The Neuse River was still not an entirely secure supply line, however, as Sherman discovered on April 5 and 7, when enterprising raiders from the 67th North Carolina Regiment captured and burned two steamers and two barges loaded with commissary stores.

By April 5, Sherman deemed the resupply efforts successful enough to warrant the issuance of Special Field Order No. 48, the directive that set in motion the final movements of the war. Order No. 48 clearly spelled out the army's objective: to link up with the Army of the Potomac somewhere near Petersburg. The order was obsolete before it had been read, for on April 6 came the electrifying news that Richmond and Petersburg had, at long last, fallen to Grant's army. Sherman instantly amended his orders, making the capture of Raleigh, and the cornering of Johnston's Army of Tennessee, the final objective.

News of Richmond's fall was greeted with cheers and music and volleys fired into the air. Sherman permitted the men to blow off some steam — figuring they had earned it many times over — and coolly laid plans for the march on Raleigh. The various columns moved out in the direction of the state capital on April 10, via Smithfield, Pikefield, Beulah, and the south bank of the Neuse.

Meanwhile, General Johnston had used the breathing spell to reorganize his winded little army. Morale was surprisingly high for a brief period after Bentonville. The general impression in the ranks was that they had given "Crazy Billy" Sherman a painful bloody nose and that — in their own minds at least — some of the accumulated gloom of previous defeats had been washed clean by the blood they had shed in that engagement. Several thousand troops arrived to reinforce Johnston's army, squeezed through the railroad bottlenecks between Raleigh and Charlotte. Johnston also received a considerable amount of supplies — he was actually stronger now than he had been before the fight at Bentonville. A grand review was staged on

April 4 in front of Governor Vance, and although the thin, haggard ranks of the Army of Tennessee made a less-than-cheering spectacle to some observers, they created a noisy stir of affection from the crowd of civilians; it had been a long time since these men had been cheered by the ladies.

But morale plummeted cruelly, never to recover, on April 5, when the first rumors began to circulate about the fall of Richmond. Due to the confusion surrounding that event, Johnston never received formal notification that the capital of the Confederacy was being abandoned. He was still in the dark about General Lee's situation when he received word from his cavalry, on April 9, that Sherman was preparing to march again. In that interim of only five days, spirits had crumbled in Johnston's army. Hundreds, possibly thousands, of men had taken the news of Richmond's fall as their cue to desert the ranks. Others, though, were resolved to fight to the end, such as young Walter Clark of the "Junior Brigade." Clark wrote to his mother after learning of the fall of Richmond: "While I am able to service I intend to stand by the cause while a banner floats to tell where Freedom and freedom's sons still support her...."

Both armies were in motion again on April 10. Sherman's 20th Corps encountered some stubborn resistance at Moccasin Creek on the road to Smithfield. The Sixth North Carolina Regiment and the First South Carolina Cavalry skillfully defended the crossings, their flanks guarded by impassable swamps. The skirmish ended when the 123rd New York charged boldly across the charred "stringers" of a burned-out bridge under sharp fire, and secured a bridgehead on the Confederate side of the waterway.

Moccasin Creek was a fairly hot skirmish. One observer who lived near the disputed crossing, a Mr. Atkinson, counted more than a dozen dead Federals near the bridge alone. One of the final casualties of the engagement was a young New Yorker named William H. Toohey, shot while fording the stream alongside the damaged bridge. Toohey had fought through every major engagement since Chancellorsville without a scratch, and he was very likely the last of Sherman's soldiers to die in combat on the road to Raleigh. The Confederate defenders, led by South Carolina cavalier John Logan Black, suffered no more than a half-dozen killed. Among them was one unfortunate man who was shot through the heart when a loaded rifle — possibly his own — fell from where it had been stacked and discharged in his direction.

By the end of April 11, Smithfield was firmly in Union hands, and news had reached Sherman that Johnston had retired his whole army to Raleigh, not intending to make a stand anywhere east of the city. That same night, Sherman received word of Lee's surrender to Grant at Appomattox. That news rocked the Federal encampments like an earthquake. Sherman addressed a proclamation to his troops: "Glory to God and our country, and all honor to our comrades in arms...a little more labor, a little more toil on our part [and] the great race is won...." To General Grant, after expressing his congratulations, he wired: "I hardly know how to express my feelings, but you can imagine them. The terms you have given Lee are magnanimous and liberal. Should Johnston follow Lee's example, I shall of course grant the same."

An orgy of rejoicing erupted in the Federal encampments. Officers broke out their hidden supplies of booze, brass bands played all night, rifles and pistols were fired into the air, men danced, cheered, toasted, and wept for joy. Perhaps it was really all over now except for the formalities; perhaps, now, it was safe to believe that there would be no more big battles.

Or would there? Would Johnston follow suit and surrender at Raleigh? Or would be continue to withdraw ahead of Sherman and perhaps disperse his forces into the Southern interior, either for the purpose of waging protracted guerilla warfare or to reunite his units into a coherent army at some predetermined location beyond Sherman's reach? If Johnston chose either of the last two courses, the war might not be coming to an end at all, but rather might be entering a new and even grimmer phase. After having marched through so much of the South, Sherman knew too well how ideally suited was the interior of the Confederacy for partisan resistance. His only recourse, in view of the consequences hanging in the balance, was to press Johnston hard and hope that Old Joe followed Lee's example.

He therefore issued orders on April 12 for his columns to cut loose from their slow-moving supplies and forge ahead, rapidly but with all due caution. Slocum's wing was designated to move directly on Raleigh by the shortest and straightest route, with General Kilpatrick's cavalry again forming the advance guard.

In Raleigh, meanwhile, the government of North Carolina was
frantically trying to wrest the best possible result from the unpalatable situation. On April 8, former governor David L. Swain, president of the University of North Carolina at Chapel Hill, took matters
into his own hands by writing to his friend, former governor William
A. Graham. Swain suggested that they both travel to Raleigh and discuss with Governor Vance the ways and means of obtaining peace
for the state.

Graham, who had recently discussed those very topics with
Vance, declined to make the trip. But Graham invited Swain to stay
overnight at his home in Hillsborough on April 9 for a heart-to-heart
discussion.

On April 10, Swain presented their plan to Governor Vance: Vance
should convene the state legislature and compel it to pass a resolution calling for an end to hostilities. A special convention should be
called for this extraordinary occasion — just as one had been called
for the issue of secession. Let the legislature appoint specially
empowered commissioners to negotiate with the enemy, and have
them report back to the convention. In other words, take the initiative now, in the hope of getting better terms than would be offered
later at the invader's pleasure.

Of course, there was a very good chance that Sherman would be in
Raleigh before this rather ponderous plan could get rolling; in that
case, Swain suggested, the governor should go ahead and send a special commission directly to Sherman and ask him to halt hostilities
until the state's peace initiative could produce results, one way or the
other.

Vance pondered these points and replied that he thought it would
be best to put the second part of the scheme into effect first — that is,
approach Sherman. The plan would have Vance's approval if he, in
turn, could obtain the blessing of General Johnston.

Johnston didn't see how it could hurt. Let Vance stay in Raleigh
for a day or two and open communications with Sherman; if the
Union general treated the delegation with respect, then as far as
Johnston was concerned, Vance might as well see what sort of terms
Sherman was willing to put on the table.

The most obvious choices for the special team of envoys were
former governors Swain and Graham themselves — men of prestige,

dignity, and vast political experience. Besides, it had been their idea in the first place. Graham agreed and arrived in Raleigh on the morning of April 12. After breakfasting together, the two ex-governors and the soon-to-be ex-governor repaired to the capitol, closeted themselves, and drafted a letter to their adversary. It was a hasty job — there was little time to lose, for Vance was reasonably certain that April 12 was probably going to be the last day Raleigh would remain in Confederate hands. Their letter read:

> Understanding that your army is advancing on this capital, I have to request, under proper safe conduct, a personal interview, at such time as may be agreeable to you, for the purpose of conferring upon the subject of a suspension of hostilities, with view to further communications with the authorities of the United States, touching the final termination of the existing War. If you concur in the propriety of such a proceeding I shall be obliged by an early reply.

While all this was taking place, President Jefferson Davis had reached Greensboro and had wired General Johnston to meet him there for a council of war. In Johnston's absence, General Hardee commanded the rebel forces around Raleigh. It was therefore Hardee who wrote the safe conduct pass for Swain and Graham. Together with Surgeon General Warren and a pair of military aides, the two ex-governors boarded their special train at about 10:30 in the morning on April 12. Word of their mission had spread through the city on the wings of wartime rumor, and from the streets came hisses and cries of "Traitors!" as the delegation departed.

Not too far beyond the city limits, the train was flagged down by Confederate cavalrymen; the delegation had reached the front lines, in a matter of minutes. The horsemen were in Hampton's command, and when the peace delegation was presented to him, the burly, bearded cavalier snorted in derision. He thought the whole scheme was crack-brained. Even now, characteristically, Hampton was anxious to fight the Yankees, not dicker with them. Still, General Hardee's and Governor Vance's signatures carried enough weight to convince him to let the delegation go forward. First, however, he drafted his own dispatch to Sherman, requesting that Sherman name a time and place for the first conference in his reply. Both Swain and Graham added personal notes of their own, and a courier was immediately set out, under a flag of truce, for Federal lines.

The special train resumed crawling eastward. About two miles beyond Hampton's front, things started to get a little crazy. A cavalryman rode up and breathlessly informed the official party that they were hereby ordered to return to Raleigh — General Hardee's safe conduct pass had been canceled. The commissioners refused to accept a verbal order to that effect and insisted on either hearing it from Hampton's own lips or seeing it in writing above the proper signatures. But they did agree to halt the train and wait for clarification.

It came, a few minutes later, in the form of General Hampton himself. Hampton confirmed the new orders, then read a new dispatch he had written to Sherman: "Since my dispatch of half an hour ago, circumstances have occurred which induce me to give you no further trouble in relation to the mission of ex-governors Graham and Swain. These gentlemen will return with the flag of truce to Raleigh."

Hampton then admitted that it might no longer be possible to return to Raleigh without some difficulty, as he had reason to believe that some of General Kilpatrick's Union cavalry were now between them and the state capital. For that reason, he had taken the liberty of preparing a note for Kilpatrick, begging him to be so good as to let the train and its passengers return to Raleigh unmolested. Having delivered himself of all these messages, Hampton doffed his hat to the two elderly dignitaries and rode off in a cloud of dust — only to find himself surrounded by Kilpatrick's men and forced to go into hiding until nightfall, when he successfully broke free and made it back to Raleigh.

Swain and Graham correctly surmised that news of their mission had traveled up the chain of command and had incurred the wrath of whatever was left of the Confederate government. Crestfallen, the erstwhile peace commission allowed the engineer to reverse the train. Slowly, they began to move back toward Raleigh. They had gone just a bit more than a mile when, once again, they were stopped — this time by a strong patrol of Kilpatrick's cavalry. The Union horsemen ordered them down at gunpoint, told them they must be presented to General Kilpatrick at his headquarters, and then — in the words of one of the delegates — "piled down on them like wild Indians" and relieved them of their watches, jewelry, and cash.

Discipline (if not all of the stolen property) was restored with the arrival of the Federal detachment's commander, Brigadier General Smith Atkins. Atkins, a dashingly handsome young man from Illinois, treated the governors with much courtesy. He must have made a good impression, for he ended up marrying Swain's daughter a mere six months after the close of hostilities.

Atkins brought the peace delegates to Kilpatrick, who blustered and huffed and cursed and threatened to detain them as prisoners of war, despite their age, station, and safe conduct passes. He also "lectured them [Swain and Graham] considerably about law and political science, concerning which probably no two persons in the United States were better informed."[3]

After hectoring them and throwing his weight around for an hour and a half, Kilpatrick finally ordered the delegates taken to a farmhouse a mile or so behind Federal lines. On the way, the Confederate party was taunted, jeered, and cursed. Much fun was made of the spectacle presented by the two venerable gentlemen in their long-tailed antebellum coats and tall beaver hats. The whole experience, said one member of the delegation, was "irritating almost beyond endurance."[4]

A short time later, Kilpatrick talked with them again. This time, now that the skirmishing had ended in front of his positions, he was more civil-tongued and expansive of mood. So they had come to see General Sherman, eh? Well, see him they would, just as soon as their locomotive could be fired up again.

That took some doing, as Kilpatrick's men had doused the fire in the boiler, pulled off the throttle lever, and amused themselves by waving guns at the engineer and robbing him of all of his personal effects.

Finally, with several dozen Yankee soldiers hitching a ride on top of the railroad cars, the peace train pulled out once more. Now, as they passed through regiment after regiment of enemy troops, the delegates found themselves being cheered lustily. Word of General Lee's surrender in Virginia was still the number-one topic of scuttlebutt among the soldiers, and the two elderly gents in the frock coats were obviously viewed as a surrender delegation sent by General Johnston.

When they were finally introduced to Sherman, the delegates found him surprisingly amicable and willing to enter into peace discussions. Whatever other charges could be lodged against old Tecumseh, he would prove himself, on this occasion and numerous others in the near future, to be a man of his word. He had promised the Southern people that, when the war was over, he would treat them with fairness and honor. He now set the tone for his future actions in the letter he dictated to Governor Vance:

> I have the honor to acknowledge the receipt of your communication of this date, and inclose you a safeguard for yourself and any members of the State government that choose to remain in Raleigh. I would gladly have enabled you to meet me here, but some interruption occurred to the train by orders of General Johnston, after it had passed within the lines of my cavalry advance, but as it came out of Raleigh in good faith, it shall return in good faith, and will in no measure, be claimed by us. I doubt if hostilities can be suspended as between the army of the Confederate Government and the one I command, but I will aid you all in my power to contribute to the end you aim to reach, the termination of the existing war.

Sherman also enclosed in the same dispatch a signed order designed to protect the governor and all state property, provided there was no resistance in Raleigh.

By this time, it was getting late in the day and the commission members were feeling the accumulated fatigue of all their travel and excitement. Sherman gave them an excellent supper, complete with a band concert, and donated the spare bunk in his own tent to Graham. The other members of the party spent what seems to have been, by all accounts, a surprisingly agreeable night. Swain bunked with a Major Hitchcock, whose mother, it turned out, had been a schoolmate of Swain's many years before.

Back in Raleigh, tensions were mounting. Governor Vance had expected the commissioners to be back in the city by nightfall, but late in the day he received word that they were being detained by Sherman. Vance had already pressed his luck by staying in the city until dark, for the last Confederate troops covering the city — the rear guard of General Robert Hoke's division and some of the ubiquitous rebel cavalry — were preparing to pull out. As the sun was setting, Vance drafted a message to Sherman, informing him that the mayor of Raleigh, William Harrison, had been instructed to surrender the city without resistance. He also asked Sherman to ensure the protection of the capitol, the state museum, the hospitals, and the city's charity wards.

Vance then busied himself overseeing the departure of the last carloads of government records and supplies. The last Confederate train left Raleigh at about 9 p.m., but Vance lingered until midnight, reluctant to leave the city and all that it symbolized both to himself and to the people he had governed so vigorously for so many strenuous months. Finally, with nothing more to be done and the danger of capture growing by the minute, Vance armed himself with a revolver, mounted his horse, and rode out to Hoke's encampment a few miles west of the city. With him were two volunteer escorts — his official military aides had vanished during the day, and he was furiously angry about their desertion, muttering dire threats of revenge as he made the tense nocturnal journey to Hoke's lines.

Mayor Harrison was ill and depressed by the prospects of what might happen the next morning, but he dutifully laid plans to lead a delegation of men, before dawn, to surrender the city to Sherman.

As morning dawned on April 13, 1865, the peace commission breakfasted and made preparations for their return to Raleigh. Five miles from the city, they were again halted by General Kilpatrick, who could not refrain from lecturing them again on the importance of giving up the capital without a fight. If he encountered resistance, the strutting little general swore, waving his fists, he would "give you hell!"

A mile from town, the commission could see flames rising from the railway depot. It had been looted and torched by some of Confederate General Wheeler's stragglers.

Just west of the depot, the tracks were blocked, so the delegation got off the train and walked, following Hillsborough and Fayetteville Streets. The town was eerily silent. Houses and stores were closed and locked. One inhabitant, Cornelia Phillips Spencer, remembered that hushed morning: "The very air seemed shriveled. In the brief interval that elapsed from the retreat of her protectors to the arrival of her foes, the beautiful city of Raleigh stood under the outstretched arms of her noble oaks...stood with folded hands and drooping head, in all the mortal anguish of suspense, in a silence that spoke, awaiting her fate."[5]

As they walked through the near-empty streets, the commissioners tried to stop some of Wheeler's stragglers from looting the shops on Fayetteville Street, but they found themselves arguing with desperate and reckless men. "Damn Sherman and the town too!" one of them cried.

The government buildings were deserted. At the state capitol, they found one dutiful Negro servant who was zealously guarding the keys, entrusted to him by Governor Vance himself. Wheeler's men had already done what Vance had begged Sherman not to do: the capitol was thoroughly trashed. Records, documents, and maps lay everywhere. The glass cases in the museum rooms had been smashed and their exhibits vandalized. Inside the assembly hall, it was found that someone had upended a bottle of ink over a marble bust of John C. Calhoun and scrawled a message on the statue's base: "Father of Secession."

The by-now thoroughly depressed peace commissioners decided that Graham should proceed to Hillsborough, where Governor Vance was rumored to be, while Swain would remain at the capitol to do whatever he could to smooth the transition to Federal occupation. All around them, the capital city of North Carolina — abandoned and vandalized by its own soldiers — waited silently for the invaders to reach its streets.

Mayor Harrison and his delegates had shouldered their burden and gone out to seek Sherman just after daybreak. The sky had been curdled with dark, low clouds, and friend and foe alike were drenched with chill spring rains as they drew near one another. A mile outside of Raleigh, the mayor and his men encountered General Kilpatrick, who was pepped up and full of beans at the prospect of taking the surrender of a secessionist capital. The mayor formally surrendered the city, and Kilpatrick's protection was sought for the property and civilian population.

Kilpatrick was inclined to be merciful that morning, and he seemed to be enjoying himself hugely as he rode into the handsome and mannerly city with banners streaming and bands playing. Moments after he came in sight of the capitol, however, his mood turned bloody and murderous.

At the appearance of Kilpatrick's column, the last Confederate stragglers had quickly ridden out of town — all except for one man, a wild young lieutenant from Texas named Walsh. The lone Confederate drew his revolver, shouted "God damn them!", and let fly with five shots in the direction of Kilpatrick. But the Union general was a good hundred yards away and escaped unharmed.

Kilpatrick was, however, enraged. A squad of Federal horsemen quickly overtook and overpowered Walsh and dragged him before his intended target. Walsh begged for five minutes' time to compose a farewell letter to his wife; Kilpatrick refused. The young man was immediately hung.

Kilpatrick then cooled off, satisfied that he had been attacked by a lone fanatic and not a treacherous rebel ambush party. He assured Swain, who was watching the young Texan's execution with open-mouthed horror, that he would take no reprisals against the city on account of the incident. And, aside from cutting down the Confederate flag on the capitol grounds, he was as good as his word. In fact, Kilpatrick didn't linger in Raleigh for much longer than it took to string up his assailant. Instead, he pushed his men forward, hoping to get a crack at the retreating Wheeler. One regiment of Federal cavalry stayed in the city to maintain order until Sherman's main force arrived.

By eight o'clock in the morning, Sherman had arrived in Raleigh and set up his headquarters in the governor's mansion. The building had been stripped of its furnishings and other amenities, and one of the general's aides found the place "musty [and] almost uninhabitable." From there, Sherman wired Grant that he had taken the capital city, and that he now intended to march on Asheboro and Charlotte, hoping to forestall any attempt by Johnston to keep his army intact by withdrawing south and west.

Sherman also quickly organized a grand review through Raleigh. Surgeon General Warren recorded the spectacle in his usual fulsome style: "As I listened for hours to the tread of those countless legions, so complete in their equipment, thorough in their organization and admirable in their discipline...I could but feel a profound admiration for the genius which had perfected such a mighty instrument of destruction and conquest, and a supreme realization of the heroism and fortitude of the ragged, half-starved and completely unorganized army which for four years of unequal conflict had defied its power, and had finally succumbed, not so much to its prowess as to the force of circumstance and the laws of nature."

One by one, Sherman's divisions reached their assigned bivouac locations in and around Raleigh. The weather moderated as the day wore on. The city's stately trees were filled with mockingbirds, singing lustily, and the city itself, except for the state buildings and the smoldering railroad station, had a pleasing, peaceful aspect. Once the marching stopped, Sherman's men began to luxuriate in the North Carolina spring and in the prospect of imminent peace.

One of his regiments pitched camp on the grounds of the State Lunatic Asylum. Thinking they were about to be freed, the patients lined the windows and shouted wildly, imploringly, at the nearby Federal soldiers. One man in particular made a stirring speech, claiming that he had been imprisoned here only because he was a Union man and his secessionist enemies had sought to punish him by incarceration. Impressed by the fellow's eloquence, one of the Federal officers sought out an administrator for the asylum and made inquires. The unjustly imprisoned "Unionist," he learned, was perhaps the most dangerous and violent inmate in the entire asylum.

ALL
THINGS CONVERGE AT
GREENSBORO

The war swept over Greensboro in a wave of human suffering on the night of March 19, 1865. Hospital facilities in Raleigh were quickly overwhelmed by the number of wounded men pouring in from the battle at Bentonville, so there was nothing to do but subject the overflow to the agony of an additional bumpy train ride to Greensboro.

Greensboro's women turned out en masse to deal with this tide of pain as well as they could, bringing whatever food and medicines were still available in the town. When these supplies ran out, they gathered bouquets of spring flowers and placed them beside the cots and pallets of the maimed and dying. Improvising, the ladies divided Greensboro into districts, and delegations of women from each district took responsibility for nursing and feeding the men in their part of town. Edgeworth Female Seminary — where the gallant Guilford Grays had received their silken banner only four years earlier — was turned into a makeshift hospital; so was the Guilford County Court House and the First Presbyterian Church.

Until the spring of 1865, war had been a distant thunder, and armies only moved through Greensboro, not toward it. Greensboro's main importance had been as a way-station on the vital North Carolina Railroad; it was located about equidistant between the two important terminals of Goldsboro and Charlotte. The town's importance greatly increased when the long-delayed rail line to Danville was opened in 1864. Greensboro became the site of numerous warehouses and storage depots, containing Confederate foodstuffs, cloth, medical supplies, and ordnance.

Guilford County's large population of Quakers assured the existence of strong antiwar, antislavery opinion. Indeed, the vote against secession in February 1861 had been 2,771 against and only 113 in favor. But, like the rest of the state, the people of Guilford County succumbed to patriotic fever after President Lincoln's call for troops and Governor Ellis's ringing denunciation of that call to arms.

Next to the courthouse, the social center of Greensboro (and much of Guilford County) was the prosperous First Presbyterian Church. In April 1862, in a bellwether turnabout of sentiment, the membership of that church had voted to turn their building over to the Confederate government for the duration of the war. The ladies of Greensboro turned much of the property into a cottage factory where barrels of old linens and quilts were converted into bandages, and where carpet scraps were made into bedding. The church bells also went to war: they were dismantled and melted down, then cast into bullets.

The ubiquitous Greensboro Ladies Soldiers' Aid Society published appeals from the hospitals in Virginia: "Let the people of Greensboro again respond & to the best of our ability aid in alleviating the sufferings of those noble & heroic defenders of our homes and liberties...Bandages and rags are particularly desired; also wines, jellies, & everything needed by the sick — donations of money will also be received and appropriated for the benefit of the hospitals."

Confederate soldiers passing through Greensboro on their way either to the North Carolina coast or to the Virginia battle lines most likely encountered the Ladies Aid Society in the form of a dedicated band of canteen workers. The volunteers offered what meager comfort and refreshment they could: a bit of bacon and cornbread, milk, and a bit of sorghum sweetener (coffee had run out early in the war and was simply unobtainable).

For four tiring years, the women of Greensboro faithfully met the troop trains, devoted to their duty by the thought that, somewhere else in the Confederacy, some other compassionate souls might be extending the same kindness to their own sons, husbands, and brothers. Sometimes, indeed, the trains brought back a wounded loved one. The women who met the trains never knew, from one day to the next, what ghastly and heart-wrenching discovery they might make.

And it got to them. One of the women was Mary Watson Smith, whose husband Jacob — formerly the pastor of First Presbyterian Church — was serving at the front as a chaplain. Mrs. Smith remembered the experience: "In this labor of love so freely given for four long years, our women carried a heartache that never lifted, for husbands, sons, brothers, lovers and friends on the firing line, not knowing what a day or even an hour might bring forth, as casualties fell pitiless here and there."[1]

Throughout the war, Greensboro's citizens avidly followed the news from the front. The entire town seemed to stay awake on the night following the Second Battle of Manassas, the menfolk pacing the streets, women keeping vigil at home, with their friends, waiting for the news...waiting for the casualty lists to be published.

Now, in 1865, as March gave way to April, the once-placid little town was flooded with misery from several directions. The city's normal population of about 2,000 doubled, then tripled, then practically became lost among the successive waves of people who converged there. First came hundreds of refugees from the towns that lay in Sherman's path. Then came the hundreds of wounded from Bentonville. Then came General Beauregard's Confederate troops — and the first rumors of Stoneman's Yankee cavalry incursion into North Carolina.

Anyone who could read a map could see that Greensboro was a likely target. Beauregard fretfully began to organize some sort of defense for the town. He ordered that all able-bodied men who passed through Greensboro on the trains must be mustered into the town's garrison. On April 11, General Johnston promised to send a thousand men as reinforcements, and he instructed Beauregard to throw up some entrenchments and battery sites "with all possible speed. Sherman will not give us much rest."

Those first days of April were chaotic. Hundreds of additional wounded and sick men were transported to Greensboro from Richmond. Confederate units arrived each day and made their bivouac in and around the city, now the official rallying point for what was left of Johnston's Army of Tennessee. In the west, Stoneman was riding roughshod over approximately one-third of North Carolina, consuming and destroying tons of carefully hoarded supplies and carrying off all the remaining horses. On the Virginia front, Grant was harrying Lee without mercy. And from the east marched the invincible and terrible Tecumseh. The citizens of Greensboro could draw but one chilling conclusion: the last major engagement of the war was shaping up right in their own front yards. A vast convergence of forces seemed to be gathering just over the horizon, all aimed at the once-peaceful little city.

The streets were knee-deep in mud, torn up by the incessant lines of horses, wagons, gun carriages, and ambulances. At night, campfires sparkled like a necklace around the city. Drums rapped in the pine woods, and bugles etched their bronze patterns against the soft spring sky. Great armies hemmed in the city; the last dramatic acts of the war were about to be played out, and this was the stage that history had chosen for them. The local newspaper, the *Greensboro Patriot*, had a loquacious columnist who went by the nom de plume of "Athos" (probably a prominent citizen named James Cole), and he left numerous vivid if hyperthyroid accounts of those tumultuous days. In one column, Athos said the nervous tension gripping the town was so intense that many once-placid citizens were seized by insomnia, and that some men walked fretfully up and down the streets all night long.

Whatever food was left in Greensboro was stored mainly in the guarded Confederate and state depots. The majority of Greensboro's inhabitants faced a limited and depressing menu: cornbread, spring onions, turnips, and some scraggly greens.

With each passing day in April, the temporary population of Greensboro continued to grow by the hundreds: wounded from Richmond, elements of Johnston's retreating army, large numbers of deserters from both fronts, civilian refugees. By the end of the first week of April, there may have been as many as 50,000 people crowding into Guilford County.

Soon there would be a few more, very important, people: President Jefferson Davis and his Confederate cabinet.

Davis yielded Richmond to the enemy on April 2, 1865. He had already sent his wife Varina and their children south to Charlotte. The long-dreaded telegram from General Robert E. Lee, announcing that his defensive lines had been ruptured beyond repair, came to Davis's desk at about 10:30 a.m. on April 2.

The arrival of Varina Davis and her family in Charlotte on that day had been taken by the skittish citizens of that town as a sign of Richmond's imminent collapse — as indeed it was. The house that had been rented for the presidential family turned out to be utterly barren of furniture, and the people of Charlotte, on the whole, turned out to be singularly inhospitable. While Mrs. Davis was forced to wait in her railroad car for her quarters to be made habitable, a mob of stragglers and deserters reviled her and cursed her husband.

The Confederate President, meanwhile, had contacted his cabinet members and told them that the hour of departure was finally at hand. Accompanying the Confederate leader in his flight from Richmond would be the following officials:

* Judah Benjamin, secretary of state: Exceedingly gifted in some areas, abysmally ignorant in others, Benjamin was something of an enigma to his contemporaries and remains so to this day. He could be unctuous or urbane as the occasion demanded, and he frequently masked his inner feelings with an expression of bland, smiling, optimism. After provoking a storm of controversy during his brief tenure as secretary of war — often because he was simply carrying out the half-baked military schemes of President Davis — Benjamin had functioned capably enough as secretary of state. A good after-dinner speaker, perpetually found chomping on a cigar, he was a portly gentleman whom one contemporary described as "keg-like."

* George Davis, attorney general: One of the few North Carolinians to win a high position in Davis's administration, Davis was respected for his eloquence, quickness of mind, and inordinate good looks. At the time of the fall of Richmond, he had been a cabinet member for only about a year.

* John Reagan, postmaster general: Reagan had made some interesting and effective efforts to reform this notoriously poor government service, and, although the mails were still dreadfully slow, they usually did get through. A big, barrel-chested man, Reagan was one of the original movers and shakers of Texas politics.

* Stephen R. Mallory, secretary of the navy: Moon-faced and affable, with a quick, almost Johnsonian wit, Mallory was a superb conversationalist and social lion. He was known, in better times, for serving the best mint juleps in Richmond. He had also been a first-rate navy secretary. Thanks to his imagination and ability, the Con-

federates' seagoing arm had been vigorous and progressive, experimenting with torpedoes, mines, submarines, and ironclads.

*George A. Trenholm, secretary of the treasury: He could do little, during his term in office, to halt the collapse of the shaky Confederate financial system. By April 1865, there was nothing more he could do but oversee the movement out of Richmond of what little was left of the treasury. On the day Richmond fell, Trenholm was so ill that he had to be taken to the train in an ambulance.

*John Breckinridge, secretary of war: A strapping young Kentuckian whose features were largely hidden behind a Yosemite Sam mustache, Breckinridge joined the Davis party in Greensboro after a harrowing horseback escape from Richmond, just ahead of the entering Yankees. During that ride, he and his escort were forced to fight their way through an enemy cavalry patrol — giving Breckinridge the distinction of being the only man in American history to lead troops in combat while holding a cabinet post.

Each man met the crisis of confederacy's waning days in his own way, of course — Benjamin with his perpetual smile-mask, Mallory with phlegmatic irony and detachment — but one thing was uppermost in the minds of all: the examples furnished by history of what usually happened to those who had led failed revolutions. If caught, most of these men fully expected to be hanged. Or, at the least, they expected to be imprisoned for the best part of whatever remained of their lives.

Davis's train reached Danville, Virginia at about four o'clock in the afternoon, April 3. The trip from Richmond to Danville, 140 miles, had taken 18 nerve-twisting hours. But in contrast to the sullen and grudging welcome Mrs. Davis had received in Charlotte, the people of Danville gave Davis and his men a heartening demonstration of patriotic fervor. In fact, they gave every indication of being willing to have their city serve as the new capital of the shrinking Confederacy.

Davis sought out the most likely military man on the scene and asked him to take command of the Danville garrison. That man happened to be the bold and enterprising Admiral Raphael Semmes, who had commanded the legendary raider CSS *Alabama* with such audacity that he had singlehandedly almost ruined the North's maritime insurance industry. Here, at least, was one soldier whom Davis

could count on to fight to the last breath. Davis impulsively
bestowed on Semmes the highest rank in his power to confer, thus
giving Semmes the curious distinction of being the only man in
recorded military history to hold the ranks of general and admiral
simultaneously. Semmes promised to do his best, but he was able to
round up only 400 men. By the time he had managed to find shovels
for them and set them to work digging trenches, the traveling medicine show that was now the Confederate government had moved on
down the line.

After he had arrived in Danville, Davis had anxiously awaited
word from General Lee, doing his best to convince himself, and
those around him, that no news was good news. The last report he
had received from Lee, dated April 5, indicated that the tactical situation might be stabilizing. That delusion was shattered on the evening of April 8 by the appearance of a hard-riding courier from Lee's
headquarters, who informed Davis in no uncertain terms that the end
was very near.

Still, this was only a verbal report, and one that was at least 24
hours old...might not Lee have managed to pull off another one of
his celebrated defensive miracles? No, not this time. News of the
surrender of the Army of Northern Virginia at Appomattox reached
Davis on the afternoon of April 10.

Davis barely had time to recover from the initial impact of this
news before he received word that Union General Stoneman was
heading east with 6,000 cavalry, brushing aside the pitiful opposition
of whatever brave but hopelessly outgunned Home Guard units
dared to block his path. According to "Athos" in the *Greensboro
Patriot*, it was about this time when Stoneman, or one of his men,
attempted one of the hoariest ruses in history, telegraphing ahead to
Greensboro and asking if President Davis had arrived yet — and if
so, was he adequately defended. The Greensboro telegraph operator
didn't fall for the trick, however, wiring back that no, Davis was not
in town yet, but Joe Johnston was, with most of his army. Thus it was
that Stoneman's cavalry came close to Greensboro, but refrained
from actually attacking the city.

In Danville, however, it was thought that Stoneman might already
be threatening the railway line south. If Davis wanted to avoid capture, he would have to abandon the pleasant surroundings he had

found at Danville. In truth, the environment was no longer so pleasant — Danville's patriotic enthusiasm had collapsed like a pricked balloon at the first rumors that Stoneman was in the neighborhood.

Before leaving, Davis telegraphed General Johnston and ordered him to meet the presidential party in Greensboro. It took several chaotic hours to repack the government's papers and the cabinet's personal effects, and the train didn't leave until midnight. The track to Greensboro was in foul condition, and the train had to crawl along through intermittent rain squalls, fearing to outrun its feeble headlight. At an average speed of four miles per hour, it was almost noon on April 11 before the train pulled into Greensboro.

On their way in, the Davis party crossed a trestle bridge over Reedy Fork Creek; not long afterward, some raiders from a regiment of Pennsylvania cavalry attacked the bridge, drove off the Home Guard detachment, and burned it down. Exactly how long after Jefferson Davis's crossing was the bridge destroyed is a matter of some debate — "just minutes," according to some accounts, "about an hour," according to others. Either way, it was a close call. When told of the incident, Davis merely shrugged, and dryly remarked: "A miss is as good as a mile."

"LIKE SNOW BEFORE THE SUN...."

By the end of April 1865, Greensboro and its environs were inundated by events and people. At the beginning of March, the town had a population of about 2,000 citizens; by the end of April, there were almost 100,000 refugees, soldiers, and stragglers crammed into the city and in the Guilford County hamlets scattered around its outskirts.

First had come the refugees from eastern North Carolina, fleeing before General Sherman's army; then came the survivors from the battle of Bentonville; then thousands of hungry and desperate and sick men from General Lee's surrendered Army of Northern Virginia, following the rail line south in hopes of finding food at the big government depots known to be in the Greensboro area; then came General Johnston's Army of Tennessee, numbering more than 40,000 men by now, moving into Guilford County between April 16 and April 27; and finally, as April waned, the Federal occupation forces of nearly 30,000 soldiers arrived. There was also the population of Camp Stokes, a prison for deserters located just north of Greensboro's city limits, which had been augmented by a few hundred Yankee prisoners captured in the fighting east of Raleigh.

Conditions were chaotic and sometimes violent. The citizens of Greensboro, having heard many tales from refugees who had been steamrollered by earlier Sherman advances, had long ago hid their gold and silver. By mid-April they were also busily squirreling away hams and bags of grain. In the panic-stricken days just before Johnston's surrender, when it was assumed that Stoneman's Yankee cavalry might arrive at any minute, some of the precious commissary stocks positioned in and around the city were destroyed or looted. In McCleansville, just east of Greensboro, the destruction of one mound of goods made a sorry spectacle indeed: "A carload of shells exploded, barrels and barrels of molasses and of whiskey were burst open. Hungry women dipped up molasses from the gutter in buckets. Hopeless men lapped up the liquor like dogs."[1]

During mid-April, especially during the five-day period when Greensboro was the ad hoc capital of the Confederacy, attempts were made by General Beauregard and his deputies to organize the incoming stragglers into some kind of coherent defense force for the town. Unfortunately, any group of men they rounded up would skeedaddle into the woods again as soon as the authorities' backs were turned. No one wanted to fight the Yankees any more, except for cavalryman Wade Hampton and a handful of hard-core zealots. No one saw any point to it — the main thing in life now was to find a mule that could be stolen and a few days' worth of food to cram into one's knapsack.

The supply of horses and mules remaining in private hands dwindled rapidly. Some were taken at gunpoint by men who had become, to all intents and purposes, simple desperadoes. Others were "impressed" by Confederate soldiers claiming to represent President Jefferson Davis — any complaints should be referred to that gentleman. He received complaints, all right, by the score, and he suffered genuine anguish upon learning what sort of acts were being committed in his name, but there was absolutely nothing he could do about it. The roads were clogged with thousands of soldiers, some legitimately paroled, most just deserters, and the Confederacy had no one to spare to protect the civilians who were in their path.

Commissary depots were set upon by men driven by fierce hunger and utterly unrestrained by any shred of military discipline. The faithful chronicler in the *Greensboro Patriot*, that eloquent gentleman who signed himself "Athos," witnessed and described a number of violent incidents that took place when the parolees from Lee's surrendered army swept into town. They were, Athos plainly stated, little more than rabble: "Some on foot, some on horseback, some nearly famished for want of food, others barely able to totter along from disease."

Athos described how one band of desperadoes attempted to storm a quartermaster depot left in charge of a major named S.R. Chisman. Brushed aside in the first rush, Chisman seemed to have been trampled by the mob as they poured into the warehouse and began to ransack the place. Suddenly, Chisman appeared once again, brandishing a torch in one hand and a keg of gunpowder in the other. He promised to blow everyone sky-high if order was not instantly restored. It was.

In an even more violent incident, a mob stormed another depot and was furiously pillaging everything that wasn't nailed down when a detachment of the 45th North Carolina arrived, double-timing down the street with fixed bayonets. The captain in command barked an order for the mob to disperse. The leader of the mob, a gigantic Kentuckian from Wheeler's cavalry, cursed the captain and fired a pistol at him. The captain responded by steadily raising his own revolver and shooting the man dead, then ordering his men to fire a volley. When the smoke cleared, the mob had fled, leaving four of its number dead on the floor.

In another part of town, General Beauregard himself had to take command and protect a supply depot with artillery charged with grapeshot.

The situation at one point became so bad that Major Sloan, chief quartermaster of North Carolina and a man of advanced years, went to Governor Vance, who had just arrived in town, and begged to be replaced. Vance appointed a Greensboro native, James R. Cole (whom many local historians think may have been "Athos"), to guard the remaining $2 million worth of stores. Cole went out to recruit someone who had what it took to handle the mobs, and found him in the person of a handsome young Mississippi officer named Major Brantly.

"Will you obey orders to the letter?" Cole asked Brantly.

"I will," replied the major.

"Take 300 men on whom you can rely...post them around the warehouse...and allow no one to enter without my permission," ordered Cole.

Brantly surrounded the main quartermaster depot with two rings of bayonets. When the mob arrived, it was preceded by a phalanx of women as a ruse to get past the guards. Brantly was made of stubborn stuff, however, and this tactic didn't work. In a voice loud enough to carry to the crowd, he ordered his men to shoot anyone who tried to get in.

"We want some of them goods!" the women screamed.

"You can't have them," Brantly replied.

"Why don't you distribute them?" the mob demanded.

"We are distributing them — to the soldiers," said Brantly. Then, having had enough of this badinage, Brantly again ordered, "If anyone attempts to break your line, shoot him on the spot!" Seething and cursing, the mob gradually dispersed.

Such were the conditions in Greensboro when President Jefferson Davis and his cabinet arrived on April 11. The town was swarming with wild soldiery, and the civilian population was sullen and undemonstrative. At least, that's the impression left by three men who kept diaries of this time: Navy Secretary Stephen Mallory, Captain John T. Wood, and Burton Harrison, President Davis's executive secretary. As Mallory put it, they found "doors closed and latch strings pulled in" when they arrived in Greensboro. Other descriptions of the town were "cold," "unconcerned," "a hole of Unionism." One diarist swore that the most common greeting addressed to them by the citizens of Greensboro was "How long are you staying?"

It seems most unlikely that all three men would have put their heads together, compared notes, and then systematically conspired to blacken Greensboro's reputation without good reason — and blackened it certainly was, throughout the South. So many tales were told about the town's cold-shouldering of the President and his men that newspapers as far away as Georgia editorialized about the collective shame of the population. Even one of Davis's modern biographers, after sifting through the records, felt compelled to describe Greensboro as "a city that disgracefully refused hospitality to the little band."[2]

A considerable body of local documentation, on the other hand, suggests that the diarists and those who picked up the scent from them may have overstated the case. Certainly, the town was edgy — expecting, with good reason, that it was about to become the site of a major battle. And, to be sure, the strong antebellum Unionist slant of Guilford County was reviving as Confederate fortunes waned. But it is also doubtful, by this time, that Davis and company would have been welcomed with brass-band enthusiasm in any town that lay along General Sherman's presumed route of march. The pep-rally atmosphere that had greeted the refugees in Danville was a fragile and short-lived phenomenon, evaporating at the first news of General Lee's surrender. The contrast between that illusory welcome and bitter new realities accounts for some of the bad feelings in Greensboro.

Numerous individuals, out of patriotism or simple human compassion, did befriend, shelter, feed, entertain, and console members of the Presidential party; but the town as a whole was not overjoyed to see them arrive and not unhappy to see them go. Greensboro's self-appointed chronicler, Athos, published what surely must stand as the townspeople's consensus view of Jefferson Davis:

> The people of Greensboro had never agreed with Jefferson Davis in his political sentiments. But when he became head of the Confederacy and leader of the South in the great struggle, they followed him and gave their whole support to his government. They rejoiced at his success, for it was theirs, and sorrowed over his failures or errors, for they suffered. When victory turned against us and hope fled from our borders and our chief left his capital a defeated and sorrowing old man, we sorrowed with him and for him, and our respect and admiration for his great a noble qualities were heightened and increased when we saw how nobly and manly his bearing was under the accumulation of misfortune such as rarely been borne by mortal man.[3]

In those phrases can be discerned sympathy for Davis's predicament, an almost abstract admiration for the way he bore his burdens, a gentle reminder that many of the South's woes were traceable to Davis's own stiff-necked policies, and, above all, a vast emotional distance between the Greensboro observers and those passionate states of mind that Davis engendered in the hearts of Confederate zealots. In short, Greensboro treated Jefferson Davis as though he were a once-prominent citizen who had, through his own mistakes, contracted leprosy: One felt sorry for the fellow, but one did not want to get close enough to scrutinize his sores.

One thing is clear — there are almost as many differing accounts of Davis's stay in Greensboro as there were eyewitnesses to write them. Athos started the hoary legend of Davis choosing to sleep in a "leaky railroad car" rather than in any of the homes whose owners

offered invitations. One account has him staying at Blandwood,
former governor John Morehead's estate in the center of town;
another has him residing at the Britton Hotel.

But there's really no reason to doubt Davis's own account, which
clearly states that he stayed in a house on South Elm Street which
was rented and occupied by Colonel John T. Wood. Wood's landlord
panicked, however, when he learned that Davis was staying on the
premises — figuring that the Yankees, when they arrived, would
burn it down in reprisal. Wood refused to evict his own President
and superior officer, but Davis appears to have vacated on his own
accord in order to spare the landlord's feelings — a gesture of
characteristic "good breeding" on the President's part.

Davis was almost certainly invited to stay at Blandwood, but
apparently declined to do more than have tea there, for the same reasons. When other private citizens opened their doors to him, Davis
declined, arguing that, if he did accept these gestures of hospitality,
Sherman's men might retaliate against his hosts in the future. So, for
at least part of the time he was in Greensboro, the President of the
Confederacy did indeed sleep in a leaky railroad car — although it
was at least a passenger car and not a boxcar, as has sometimes been
said.

The Confederate cabinet, meanwhile (with the exception of the
gravely ill Treasury Secretary George Trenholm, who was recuper-
ating at Blandwood) also spent its entire time encamped in and
around a Pullman car which had seen better days. There wasn't
much in the way of official duties for these gentlemen to attend to,
and after the morning "councils of war" — as Davis persisted in
calling them, long after the term had lost any meaning — most of
them killed time by strolling around downtown, flirting with the
ladies in the fashionable College Hill district, or just sitting around
on the railroad siding, drinking. Their car, in fact, became known as
the "Cabinet Bar," and anyone who dropped in for a chat would have
a demijohn opened in his honor. Doubtless, the number of guests
increased as the word got around — good whiskey was hard to come
by in those days, and the Confederate government still had a supply.

Secretary Mallory, whose writing style had a distinctly Dickensian turn now and then, put it this way: "The 'Cabinet Bar' was,
however, during those dreary days at Greensboro, a very agreeable

resort. Like true men of the world its distinguished hosts did the honors to their visitors with a cheerfulness and good humour, seasoned by a flow of good spirits, which threw rather a charm around the wretched shelter and made their situation seem rather a matter of choice than of necessity."

Aside from its plentiful supply of booze, the Confederate cabinet made do with a fairly sparse inventory of amenities: some spoons and utility knives, and a couple of tin cups to share among them. Meals were cooked with the help of a single Negro servant over a fire beside the railroad tracks. (This location, still a railroad siding and still in downtown Greensboro, would, a century later, acquire a certain measure of local fame as "Hamburger Square," haven for some of the most grizzled winos in the Southeast. Many a humble Sterno campfire has blackened the ground there since the Confederate cabinet first encamped on the spot.)

Mallory, a portly, chin-whiskered gentleman who bore a striking resemblance to actor Ned Beatty, left a vivid and good-humored account of life inside the "cabinet's boxcar," as it was called by its residents:

> The times were sadly out of joint, just then, and so was the Confederate government. Here was the astute Minister of Justice, a grave and most exemplary gentleman, with a piece of half-broiled "middling" in one hand and a hoe-cake in the other, his face bearing unmistakable evidence of the condition of the bacon. There was the Secretary of State, busily dividing his attention between a bucket of stewed dried apples and a haversack of hard boiled eggs; here was the Postmaster General, sternly and energetically running his bowie knife through a ham, as if it were the chief business of life, and there was the Secretary of the Navy courteously swallowing his coffee scalding hot that he might not keep the venerable Adjutant General waiting too long for the coveted tin cup...Secession, foreign intervention and recognition, finance and independence, the ever recurring and fruitful themes of discussion, gave place to the more pressing and practical questions of dinner or no dinner, and how and when and where it was to be had; and to schemes and devices for enabling a man of six feet to sleep upon a car seat of four.[4]

Aside from Davis himself, the only cabinet member who enjoyed any true comfort in Greensboro was the ailing Treasury Secretary Trenholm. Trenholm was met — "effusively," in the words of diarist Harrison — at the train station by former governor Morehead. Trenholm was immediately taken to the Morehead family manse, the elegant Blandwood estate, located just a few blocks from the railroad siding where the cabinet was bivouacked. Harrison rather cattily suggested that Morehead's motive in showing such hospitality was to persuade Trenholm to redeem some of the former governor's Confederate bonds in gold. Although it's possible that this matter was discussed, it would have been completely out of character for the genteel and courteous Morehead to badger a sick friend under his own roof.

If Jefferson Davis ever loosened up long enough to enjoy a toddy with his cabinet, it is not recorded. There was an unmistakable aura of eroded tragic grandeur about Davis which stirred the hearts of those who had never even sympathized with his policies. Restless and cramped in his railroad car quarters, he was spotted at odd hours of the day and night, striding in a grim, preoccupied manner up and down the streets of Greensboro — a thin, gauntly handsome man whose six-foot frame was flattered by the frock coats he habitually wore. He seemed sustained only by that same fierce and unyielding pride which had been both the greatest strength and the greatest weakness of his leadership. Those who spoke to him on the street, whether common soldier or community leader, were treated with the full measure of courtesy and dignity for which this tragic gentleman was famous.

And as he strode the wooden sidewalks of Greensboro during those verdant spring days, Davis's mind — not unlike Adolf Hitler's during his final days in the Fuhrer bunker — revolved endlessly around desperate schemes to salvage, even now, some vestige of military hope and political legitimacy. Davis held meetings to that effect, referring to them wishfully as "councils of war," manipulating distant or nonexistent regiments as though they were still his to command. In truth, there were no military options left for him, and in some part of his mind, he must have realized that.

Upon his arrival in Greensboro, Davis had been met by General Beauregard, then in charge of the city's defenses, such as they were. Relations between the two men had not always been cordial, but on this occasion, sensing the gravity of the hour, both were on their best behavior. When Beauregard informed Davis that General Johnston was on his way with the Army of Tennessee, the President scheduled a preliminary meeting for that afternoon and a full-scale "council of war" for the next day, April 13.

When Johnston arrived in Greensboro on the morning of April 12, he went first to meet with his old comrade in arms, General Beauregard. While awaiting a summons from Davis, the two generals spent about two hours comparing notes on what they had seen and heard. Both men reluctantly reached the same grim conclusion — the South had no military cards left to play.

The generals' first Greensboro meeting with Davis and his cabinet took place in a 12- by 16-foot upstairs room in the house that Colonel Woods was renting. Present with Davis were Navy Secretary Mallory, Secretary of State Judah Benjamin, and Postmaster General John Reagan.

Both generals had assumed that Davis had called them to the meeting to seek their advice about how to terminate hostilities as expeditiously as possible. Now, to their mutual astonishment, the Confederate President launched into a monologue concerned with far-fetched and utterly impractical strategic schemes for prolonging the war. General Johnston felt his old contempt for Jefferson Davis rising back on a wave of incredulous resentment. Did this man really believe the Confederate Army was still a viable military entity? Evidently, he did. As Johnston acidly remarked in his memoirs, "The President's object seemed to be to give, not to obtain, information."[5]

Davis monopolized the floor without once opening the "discussion" to his generals. He plucked from thin air a deluded scheme to field a whole new army comprised of deserters and draft evaders, without explaining how men who had given up on the Confederate cause when it was still vigorous might now be persuaded to risk their lives again when it was on its deathbed. With this unlikely force, Davis proposed to march all the way to Alabama — God knows how, given the difficulties he would encounter just in marching to Charlotte, a mere 90 miles away — and join forces there with the small armies of General Kirby-Smith and General Richard Taylor. After delivering himself of this pipe-dream, and seemingly having exhausted his eloquence, Davis abruptly terminated the meeting. The two visiting generals retired in a state of dazed disbelief.

Later, Johnston and Beauregard polled the cabinet members who were present at the meeting. Only Judah Benjamin — who had managed to alienate both generals during his brief tenure as secretary of war — volubly sided with Davis, displaying to the last both his loyalty to his master and his continued ignorance of military realities. Writing about the event years later, Joseph Johnston still expressed amazement at what he called "the intransigence of the occult Jew."

April 12 must have been an emotional roller-coaster for the Confederate President. It was probably on that day, and probably right after the morning conference with Johnston and Beauregard, that Robert E. Lee's son, Captain Bob Lee, Jr., arrived in Greensboro. Captain Lee expressed his own continued confidence in the Confederate cause in tones of such enthusiasm that, briefly, a wintry smile was seen on Davis's thin lips. That smile vanished quickly, though, for even as young Bob was waxing enthusiastic about the prospects for continued resistance, another officer arrived and handed Davis a detailed, written account of the surrender at Appomattox.

Davis began silently to weep. Until that moment, he had continued to nurture some faint hope that the news of Lee's surrender might turn out to be just another dreadful rumor. But here was tangible proof that the catastrophe was real. The other men in the room withdrew tactfully, leaving the shaken President alone with his grief.

Secretary of War John Breckinridge also rejoined the Presidential party on April 12, bringing further details of the surrender in Virginia. Later that night, after supper, Beauregard, Breckinridge, and Johnston, along with several other interested parties, including Navy Secretary Mallory, held a grim conclave. Comparing their personal observations, all three generals came to the conclusion that the Confederate Army was finished and that further resistance would do nothing but spill blood needlessly. As Johnston bluntly summarized it, "Gentlemen, we are at the end of our row."

Mallory urged Johnston to state his feelings just that plainly to Davis at the full-dress conference scheduled for the following morning. Johnston at first demurred — the earlier meeting with Davis had unnerved him and convinced him that the President had lost touch with reality altogether. Instead, Johnston suggested that Davis might pay more attention if one of his own political appointees brought the matter to a head. Mallory agreed to do so, but said that Johnston's opinion — as commander of the only sizable Confederate force still in the field — was the one that really counted.

Thanks to Mallory's vivid notes, it is possible to reconstruct the dramatic conference of April 13 in some detail. President Davis began the session, as was his habit, with an amiable, anecdotal bit of conversation or reminiscence that was totally unconnected with the agenda — a custom that was endearing in more relaxed times, but that all present found very irritating under the present circumstances.

Eventually, however, Davis did get around to the main topic under consideration. He turned to generals Johnston and Beauregard and asked them to give their professional opinions of the overall situation. Even as he gave them the floor, however, he made it clear that he wanted to hear something optimistic: "Our late disasters are terrible," he admitted, "but I do not think we should regard them as fatal. I think we can whip the enemy yet, if our people will turn out...whatever can be done must be done at once...."

There was a tense, expectant pause. Johnston, still anxious and reigning in his emotions, gradually understood that everyone was waiting for him to speak. After several strained moments had passed, Davis prodded him: "We should like to have your views, General Johnston."

Very well, then, Johnston must have thought, you shall bloody well have them. As though a dam had broken inside him, Johnston unleashed his feelings in sharp, choppy, staccato sentences, openly colored with contempt for Jefferson Davis. His words crashed into the room like projectiles:

> My views are, sir, that our people are tired of the war, feel themselves whipped, and will not fight. Our country is overrun, its military resources greatly diminished, while the enemy's military power and resources were never greater, and may be increased to any extent desired. We cannot place another large army in the field, and cut off as we are from foreign intercourse, I do not see how we could maintain it in fighting condition if we had it.
>
> My men are daily deserting in large numbers, and are stealing my artillery teams to aid their escape to their homes. Since Lee's defeat, they regard the war as at an end. If I march out of North Carolina, her people will leave my ranks. It will be the same as I proceed through South Carolina and Georgia...I shall expect to

retain no man beyond the bye road or cow path that leads to his home. My small force is melting away like snow before the sun....

There was a roaring silence when the general finished. Jefferson Davis had taken the whole barrage with his head down, gaze fixed absently on a scrap of paper which he kept folding and unfolding; no flicker of emotion disturbed his stone-carved features. At last, in a grave but even voice, he said, "What do you say, General Beauregard?"

"I concur in all that General Johnston has said," Beauregard replied.

There was another long silence. Still, Davis's expression did not change. Finally, he said, "Well, General Johnston...what do you propose?"

Johnston proposed that Davis exercise "the only function of government still in his possession" and open peace talks immediately.

Still Davis balked. He polled the cabinet and found, much to his visible annoyance, that every man except Judah Benjamin agreed with the generals. With the heaviest reluctance, every word sounding as though it were being dragged from him with iron hooks, Jefferson Davis finally gave permission for Johnston to contact General Sherman about, first, a cease fire, and then a negotiated surrender. Davis then dictated the letter for Johnston's signature:

> Maj. Gen. W.T. Sherman, Commanding U.S. Forces:
> General: The results of the recent campaign in Virginia have changed the relative military condition of the belligerents. I am therefore induced to address you in this form of inquiry, whether, in order to stop the further effusion of blood and devastation of property, you are willing to make a temporary suspension of active operations, and to communicate to Lieutenant-General Grant, commanding the armies of the United States, the request that he will take like action in regard to other armies; the object being to permit the civil authorities to enter into the needful arrangements to terminate the existing war.
> I have the honor to be, very respectfully, your obedient servant,
> J.E. Johnston General

After the conference of April 13 was finished, the despairing Jefferson Davis wrote to his wife in Charlotte: "I will come to you if I can — Everything is dark — you should prepare for the worst by dividing your baggage so as to move in wagons...I have lingered on the road and labored to little purpose...." He gave the letter to a mounted officer and ordered him to deliver it in Charlotte. There was no possibility now of reaching that city by mail — word had come that Stoneman's men had torn up the tracks between the two cities. Varina Davis, in fact, had already left Charlotte and had gone by rail to Chester, South Carolina.

Johnston barely had time to obtain Davis's permission to negotiate before he ran out of troops altogether. Whole companies were walking away, hourly. Before Johnston had arrived in Greensboro, Sherman outnumbered him 12 to 1; by the time Johnston left Greensboro, the odds had become about 15 to 1.

All the way from Greensboro to Danville and eastward to Raleigh, there flowed a river of gray-clad men, all hungry, all desperate, most of them beyond any discipline save the threat of naked force. Johnston discovered how bad things were when he learned that his horse and those of his headquarters staff had been stolen during the conference with President Davis. Scenes of anarchy were witnessed on every hand. On one Greensboro street, a group of ex-soldiers turned viciously on their superiors. With drawn guns, they cornered several officers on horseback. One man shouted, "You damned sons of bitches have rode long enough — git off before I let some daylight through ye!" The officers meekly dismounted and watched their horses ride off under new owners.

When word spread through town that the railroad line was severed both north and south of Greensboro, the prices of horses, mules, and wagons tripled in a few hours. The animals obtained for the presidential party were but one step away from the glue factory. Nevertheless, the presidential caravan was ready to move by the morning of April 15.

The unpaved roads, as always during the Piedmont spring, were abominable, and the creaky, ill-sprung wagons were strained almost to breaking by the weight of the files, personal effects, and treasury funds they were carrying. Davis and Benjamin rode in wagons, while the other cabinet members rode on horses or mules. The rest followed in wagons and ambulances. Some cavalry troops rode escort. All in all, the convoy looked less like a procession of state than a caravan of country tinkers on their way to find work.

Just outside of Greensboro, the group meandered onto the wrong road, but they were soon corrected by a teenage boy named Bumpass, who was startled to learn that the stout gentleman who leaned down from a worn-out country wagon to ask directions was none other than the Confederate secretary of state. After obtaining directions to the Salisbury road, Benjamin chatted with the lad for a few moments and learned that young Bumpass was out hunting rabbits as an alternative to starvation. "All our men are in the army," the boy explained, "or comin' home ragged and hungry...." On further inquiry, Benjamin learned that the only thing the boy and his family subsisted on were garden greens, an occasional cup of corn meal, and rabbits. Then the lad sang for the Confederate cabinet a rhyme that had become popular in the Greensboro area:

Rabbits hot and rabbits cold,
Rabbits young and rabbits old;
Rabbits tender and rabbits tough —
Thank the Lord, we had rabbits enough!

The Conversations At Bennett's Farm

The last recorded skirmishes of General William Tecumseh Sherman's Carolinas campaign occurred on the afternoon of Friday, April 14, at Morrisville and at the Atkins plantation on New Hope Creek, about eight miles from Chapel Hill. At the Atkins plantation, the rear guard of General Wheeler's Confederate cavalry destroyed the bridge over the rain-swollen New Hope Creek, and then some of the troops lingered behind to take pot-shots at the pursuing Yankees. They fired on the blue-clad soldiers of Smith Atkins's brigade, which nevertheless established a bridgehead by floating across the creek on tree trunks. In both skirmishes, a handful of men died — no one knows exactly how many.

Among the wounded from those last insignificant firefights was a young man from Selma, Alabama who was brought to Chapel Hill and nursed with great tenderness, and almost adopted, by the citizens of that green and tranquil college town. He clung to life for several days, until after the town had passed into Federal control, and then he seemed to sense that the end was near. Cornelia Philips Spencer, a prominent resident, was on hand when the boy died. She recorded his last moments: "He resigned himself to die with child-like patience, asking for a favorite hymn and begging the lovely girl who had watched him with a sister's fidelity, to kiss him, as he was dying...he was laid to rest in the garden, and perhaps as bitter tears of regret and despair fell on that lonely grave as on any during the war; for the war was over, and he and the rest had died in vain."[1]

Wheeler's cavalrymen held Chapel Hill until Sunday, April 16.

Mrs. Spencer got a good look at them, as well as their leader, and judged them a mixed lot indeed. The majority, she thought, remained "true and gallant" to the last. For General Wheeler she had nothing but praise, but many of his men, she admitted, had become as dangerous to the civilians as Sherman's bummers — "utterly demoralized, lawless, and defiant." They were men who knew their cause was lost, who had gone for months with nothing to eat but sorghum, boiled peas, and a little parched corn, and who had not been paid a cent — not even in Confederate money — for more than a year. Even a commander as respected as General Wheeler couldn't keep such men from indulging in some looting of their own before Sherman's troops beat them to it.

The last rebel cavalry left Chapel Hill on Sunday afternoon. From her front yard, Mrs. Spencer watched them go and recorded the mood of the scene with her gifted, novelist's eye:

> We...waved our last farewell to our army. A few hours of absolute and Sabbath stillness ensued...The groves stood thick and solemn, the bright sun shining through the great boles and down the grassy slopes...all that nature can do was still done with order and beauty, while mens' hearts were failing them for fear, and for looking after those things which were coming on the earth.
>
> We sat in our pleasant piazzas and awaited events with quiet resignation. The silver had all been buried — some of it in springs, some under rocks in the streams, some of it in fence corners, which, after the fences had been burned down, was pretty hard to find again...There was not much provision to carry off — that was one comfort. The sight of our empty store-rooms and smoke-houses would be likely to move our invaders to laughter. Our wardrobes were hardly worth hiding — homespun and jeans hung placidly in their accustomed places. But the libraries...the buildings of the University — all minor selfish considerations were merged in a generous anxiety for these. So we talked and speculated, while the very peace and profound quiet of the place sustained and soothed our minds. Just at sunset a sedate and soldierly-looking man, at the head of a dozen dressed in blue, rode quietly in by the Raleigh road....[2]

The graduating class of the University of North Carolina at Chapel Hill in that spring of 1865 was comprised of a single senior, by the name of W.C. Prout. Total enrollment, in all classes, was no more than a dozen. Of all the Chapel Hill graduates who qualified for military service during the years 1861-65, approximately one man in five died in combat.

General Joseph E. Johnston's initial dispatch to Sherman (dictated by Jefferson Davis on April 13) was sent by way of General Wade Hampton's headquarters, where a Confederate captain named Lowndes carried it across the lines to General Kilpatrick's headquarters at Morrisville. While they waited for Sherman's response to the dispatch, Lowndes and Kilpatrick had a man-to-man chat, amicable at first, then increasingly acrimonious as the subject turned, inevitably, to military engagements of the recent past. Kilpatrick, still smarting over the embarrassment he had suffered at Monroe's Cross Roads, swore to Lowndes that the battle would have turned out differently if he hadn't been taken so completely by surprise — a logical assumption, though quite irrelevant, considering that the object in war is to take the enemy by surprise if possible. Lowndes then issued a bizarre challenge to Kilpatrick in the name of Wade Hampton: Let Kilpatrick pick 1,500 Yankee cavalrymen, and Hampton pick 1,000 of his rebel cavalry, and then let them meet somewhere and fight it out with sabers only. When Hampton heard about the challenge, he heartily agreed with it and even drafted a fairly insulting duelling invitation to Kilpatrick. Historians may be permitted a twinge of regret that this medieval scenario was never played out — the war ended too soon — for it would certainly have provided a rousing climax to the long-running feud between the cavalry forces of the two armies.

While his cavalry commander was fantasizing about revenge, General Sherman was eagerly reading Johnston's letter. He replied quickly and in a temperate vein:

> I have this moment received your communication of this date. I am fully empowered to arrange with you any terms for the suspension of hostilities between the armies commanded by you and those commanded by myself, and will be willing to confer with you to that end. I will limit the advance of my main column, tomorrow, to Morrisville, and the cavalry to the university, and expect that you will also maintain the present position of your forces until each has notice of a failure to agree. That a basis for action may be had, I undertake to abide by the same terms and conditions as were made by Generals Grant and Lee at Appomattox Court-House, on the 9th instant, relative to our two armies; and, furthermore, to obtain from

General Grant an order to suspend the movements of any troops from the direction of Virginia. General Stoneman is under my command, and my order will suspend any devastation or destruction contemplated by him. I will add that I really desire to save the people of North Carolina the damage they would sustain by the march of this army through the central or western parts of the State.

Sherman sent the reply back to Kilpatrick and urged him to deliver it speedily. But Kilpatrick turned the matter over to his staff and rode off to Durham's Station on business of his own, so Sherman's answer did not reach Wade Hampton until sundown of April 15. Johnston received the note on the morning of April 16 and immediately hurried to Greensboro, only to find that Davis and his unwieldy caravan had already departed for Charlotte. Time being of the essence, Johnston proposed to Sherman that they meet on the following day, April 17, at a point equidistant between Hillsborough and Durham's Station.

Sherman meanwhile had informed General Ulysses S. Grant and Secretary of War Edwin M. Stanton, in Washington, of all developments up to April 15. He proposed to offer Johnston generous terms and clearly spelled out his belief that North Carolina was ready to rejoin the Union and should be permitted to do so without penalty or retribution.

On Monday morning, April 17, Sherman was boarding his train for Durham's Station when he was handed a stunning top-secret dispatch informing him of the assassination of President Abraham Lincoln, who had died Saturday morning. Sherman feared that this tragic news would spark rage and disorder in his army at a very delicate moment, so he swore the telegraph operator to secrecy and went on with his preparations as though nothing had happened. His train arrived at Durham's Station at 11 o'clock. Kilpatrick met him there at the head of a nattily dressed escort of cavalry, and the procession rode out to greet their opposite numbers, white flag at the point.

Riding in the opposite direction was another man with a white flag: General Hampton's personal orderly, Wade H. Manning, who found the task onerous indeed. Behind him were generals Hampton and Johnston with a small staff, all escorted by members of the Fifth South Carolina cavalry.

Sherman's party had ridden about five miles when the Confederates' white flag came into view. Now, for the first time, the two old adversaries rode forward to meet one another face to face: Sherman in a dusty coat and pants, his beard straggly and uncombed, his reddish hair tangled in a most unmilitary fashion; and Old Joe, dressed in his best gray uniform, all buttons fastened, his peppery beard and sideburns neatly trimmed. Their initial handshake was almost an afterthought — these two men knew each other intimately, from a dozen battlefields. Then they introduced the members of their respective staffs. Sherman gestured to the rural landscape around them and asked Johnston if he knew of any place conveniently close where they might retire for their discussion. As it happened, Johnston had seen a tidy little farmhouse just a ways back down the road; perhaps they could go there.

This was the modest log home of farmer Daniel Bennett. The two commanders were met at the door by a surprised Mrs. Bennett, who, when she learned of the business at hand, willingly turned over the main house to them and took her four children off to one of the outbuildings.

A reporter for the *New York Herald* happened to be present when the two generals were standing around waiting to enter the farmhouse. He left a good description of the side-by-side contrast between the two men: "General Sherman smoked his cigar with his hands stuffed in his pockets as usual — on the whole looked at ease and master of the situation. Johnston on the other hand, was taciturn and looked haggard and care-worn, but still maintained the dignity of the soldier and gentleman, as he certainly is."[3]

Bennett's farmhouse was sturdy, neat, unpretentious: a large downstairs room with an attic above, a bed, two tables, a desk, and some chairs. There was a drop-leaf table on the west side of the room and a candle table near the center. It's likely that Sherman sat at one table and Johnston at the other.

No witnesses were in the room, but both generals recorded essentially the same account of what transpired. According to Sherman's account, he showed Johnston the telegram containing the news about President Lincoln; Johnston was dumfounded and expressed the hope that the Confederacy would not be held responsible for such an atrocity. Johnston, however, does not describe his own reaction to Lincoln's assassination, other than to write that this was "the greatest possible calamity for the South." But since the news must have been a total surprise to Johnston, it seems safe to rely on Sherman's account — it is unlikely that Johnston took the shocking news quite as calmly as he implied.

Once the actual talks commenced, it was clear that Sherman had abandoned the mask of ferocity behind which he had ravaged the South. Having bent all his energies to the swift and brutally efficient defeat of the enemy, he could afford, at this pinnacle of military supremacy, to be both gracious and sympathetic.

Johnston explained that he had come to seek a cease-fire; Sherman had supposed that he was there to discuss surrender terms. The armistice, Johnston said, was to create a breathing space during which the "civil authorities" on both sides would have time to work out a settlement. Sherman demurred at that point. The Union did not recognize the Confederacy as a legitimate government, so consequently the South's "civil authorities" also were unrecognized.

Sherman made a counterproposal: surrender on a purely military basis, using the Appomattox terms as guidelines. Johnston agreed that any further combat between his army and Sherman's would be simple "murder." Now Old Joe moved a chess piece of his own: Lee, he reminded Sherman, had been compelled to surrender to Grant when surrounded, at bay, and without further military options. His own army, however, remained intact (although he neglected to mention, of course, how small that "intact" part had become) and was still three or four days' march ahead of Sherman. Therefore, Johnston wanted more specific guarantees from Sherman about the welfare of his men and the safety of their personal property. Johnston actually went much further than he was authorized to, asking that Sherman give assurances that the Southern states might be allowed to rejoin the Union with all of their prewar rights intact.

If he could obtain sufficiently generous terms, Johnston hinted, he might be induced to arrange the surrender of virtually all Confederate forces still left in the field. When pressed by Sherman, Johnston admitted that, given the chaotic condition of communications, he was not in actual control of the units in Florida, Georgia, and South Carolina — but he supposed that, if he insisted, President Davis could and would arrange for the agreement to cover them as well.

Shrewdly or luckily, Johnston had struck a most responsive nerve in Sherman. Sherman was being presented with a chance, in effect, to reunify the entire nation with one document, one stroke of his pen. The boldness of the act, the historic sweep of it all, inflamed Sherman's imagination. He could go down in history not just as a bearer of wrath and destruction, but also as a visionary bringer of peace and healing. The conversation became, on Sherman's part, frankly emotional. In addition to the historical and political considerations, Sherman was also aware that if Johnston's army did escape and opened a guerilla campaign in the interior, Sherman would be held accountable, because he had not vigorously pursued Johnston after Bentonville to crush him in another big engagement.

The discussion moved on to details of the terms the rebellious states might obtain once they had again submitted to Federal authority. There was one sticking point: amnesty for Jefferson Davis and his Confederate cabinet. Sherman was not so sure he could deliver on that point, so the talks wound down inconclusively. Still, both generals decided they had made a good deal of progress for one day. As they rose to leave the room, they agreed to meet again the following day.

When the two commanders emerged from the house, they looked preoccupied but not unhappy. Without more than perfunctory words to their respective entourages, they both mounted and rode off in opposite directions. Their men had spent the two-hour interlude fraternizing pleasantly — in most cases. Cavalry commanders Kilpatrick and Hampton had spent the whole time sullenly glaring at each other, trading insults, and bragging about their martial prowess.

When Sherman got back to Raleigh, he decided to issue a Special Field Order breaking the news of President Lincoln's death and assuring his men that the crime was not to be blamed on the Confederate army. He also took precautions to increase security in the city, lest the dreadful news trigger another Columbia-type rampage. Shrewdly, Sherman inserted into the same Special Order an official confirmation that peace talks had started between himself and General Johnston, so that anger at the bad news would be somewhat offset by relief that the end of the war was near.

A small band of angry men carrying torches was turned back at the city limits by armed guards, and most of the population of

Raleigh spent a fretful night filling fire buckets, but nothing much happened aside from the burning of an abandoned building on the outskirts of town, and even that was probably accidental.

During the night of April 17, Sherman conferred with his corps and divisional commanders. All of them agreed that, if necessary, they could easily beat Johnston's ragtag army in a stand-up fight. But one troublesome possibility kept cropping up: If the talks collapsed, would Johnston still seek an honorable surrender, or would he order his men to disperse into the countryside and form guerilla bands? That prospect worried Sherman very much — the country between Durham and the mountains was fairly well-roaded and there was no way his men could surround Johnston in time to prevent him from dispersing, should he choose to order such last-ditch resistance. Naturally adept at guerilla warfare, even a few thousand armed and zealous Confederates could wreak chaos over a wide region, prolonging the war for months, maybe years. Such a strategy, in fact, was very much in Jefferson Davis's mind at that moment — if only as a means to buy more favorable terms at the peace table.

Sherman found his officers in agreement with his own conviction: the conflict must be brought to an end. The men in Sherman's ranks already felt that the war was over, and indeed won. It would be very hard indeed to get them back into a combative mood at this point — the edge was already gone. Someone even suggested that Sherman arrange for a ship to spirit Jefferson Davis and his cabinet off to Nassau, if it would help bring hostilities to a close.

General Johnston spent his night two miles east of Hillsborough at the home of a Doctor Dickerson. He wired General John Breckinridge and requested his presence at the next day's discussions with Sherman. As the Confederacy's secretary of war, Breckinridge could be enormously useful in convincing Davis to agree to whatever terms might be finalized at the second meeting.

Breckinridge, accompanied by Postmaster General John Reagan, who came along out of curiosity, reached Wade Hampton's headquarters in Hillsborough before dawn, April 18. When they discovered that Johnston had no written copy of the terms already discussed with Sherman, Reagan offered to draft one. He lingered behind to work on the document while Johnston and Breckinridge saddled up and rode toward Bennett's farm. A courier would bring the document to the negotiations as soon as Reagan finished writing it out.

On the morning of April 18, Sherman rode to Bennett's farm with Kilpatrick at his side, and the contrast between the two Union generals was dramatic. "Little Kil" was bedecked in a crimson sash, adorned with gleaming belts, mint-bright buttons, and a polished saber. Sherman looked a little like a hobo with his frayed old coat flapping in the breeze and his battered, black, felt slouch hat pulled down over his grizzled head.

Like the first meeting, the second conference was characterized by dignity and cordiality on the part of the principles. Johnston's opening gambit was to assure Sherman that, yes, he did have legal authority to surrender all Confederate armies still in the field, east of the Mississippi. He then asked Sherman what assurances he could give that the political rights of his men would be respected after a surrender. Citing General Grant's terms to Lee and Lincoln's Amnesty Proclamation of 1863, Sherman assured Johnston that full citizenship rights would be restored as soon as his men laid down their arms and swore an oath of allegiance to the United States of America.

At this point, Johnston thought he needed someone capable of giving legal advice. He suggested that Breckinridge join them, not in his capacity as a representative of the Confederate government, but rather as a major general of the Confederate Army. Breckinridge was summoned and entered the house. A few moments passed. Then Sherman appeared at the front door again and called for his saddlebags. The men waiting outside assumed this to mean that an agreement was ready to be signed.

What it really meant was that Sherman was thirsty and his bourbon was in the saddlebags. Breckinridge, a Kentuckian, was exceedingly fond of his state's most famous beverage, and he greeted the appearance of the whiskey bottle with unfeigned joy — when invited, he helped himself to a stiff drink. Thus lubricated, Breckinridge commenced to eloquently lecture Sherman on the subject of international law and precedent with regard to rebellions. Amused but impatient, Sherman waved him into silence after listening for nearly ten minutes and drawled, "See here, gentlemen, who is doing this surrendering anyway? If this thing goes on, you'll have me sending an apology to Jeff Davis."

Not too long after that remark, a courier arrived from Hillsborough with Postmaster Reagan's draft of the terms discussed at the previous day's meeting. Sherman read through them and announced that they were "too general and too verbose." Then he sat down and scribbled out a new version that, to the unprejudiced eye, seems every bit as verbose. While he was composing this document, he got up, ambled over to his saddlebags, and made ready to pour himself another cup of whiskey. Breckinridge perked up, thinking he was about to be offered another round, too; he leaned over to the window and rid himself of a plug of chewing tobacco in preparation. But Sherman, completely preoccupied with his composition, took no notice of Breckinridge. Instead, he poured himself a generous toddy and slipped the bottle back into its resting place. Breckinridge was aghast at this breach of manners, and sulked throughout the rest of the meeting.

When Sherman's pen finished scratching through the warm, dusty silence, he handed the document to Johnston. Fearing the worst, Old Joe was agreeably surprised to find that the new terms were every bit as generous as the ones he had hoped to obtain. The agreement called for:

* Both armies to remain in place; if either army planned a move, notice in writing should be given to the opponent 48 hours in advance.

* All Confederate forces still in the field would be disbanded and disarmed in an orderly manner.

* Officials of state governments in the Confederacy must take new oaths of allegiance to the United States.

* Federal courts would be reestablished in the states "with powers as defined by the Constitution and the laws of Congress."

* The citizens of the rebellious states would be guaranteed their political rights and franchises, as well as all rights of personal property, as conferred by the Constitution.

* No reprisals would be exacted for anything done during the heat of war; the inhabitants of the rebellious states would not be disturbed, so long as they refrained from hostile acts and obeyed the laws.

* As soon as the Confederate armies had disbanded, obtained paroles, and turned in their weapons, a general amnesty would take effect and the rebel soldiers would be free to pursue their peacetime lives once more.

There was really no meaningful difference between this document and the terms that Reagan had drafted, only a different arrangement of words. So — just like that — the two generals signed, shook hands, and parted. Sherman went off to convince Washington that this was a good treaty, and Johnston went to convince Jefferson Davis that it was the best deal they would ever be offered.

Once the two Confederate generals were out in the yard, Johnston asked Breckinridge for his first impression of William Tecumseh Sherman. "Oh, he's bright enough," responded Breckinridge, "and a man of force...but Sherman is a hog! Yes, sir, a hog! Did you see him take that drink by himself?"

Johnston excused Sherman's rudeness on the grounds that he was, after all, preoccupied with ending the bloodiest war in American history. Breckinridge would not be mollified.

"Ah! No Kentucky gentleman would have taken that bottle away. He knew how much we needed it — needed it badly!"

When an interviewer asked Sherman about the incident some years later, he thought for a moment and then replied with a chuckle: "Well, I don't remember it, but if Joe Johnston says it happened, then it's true. Those fellows hustled me so, I was sorry for the drink I did give them!"

In such a manner did Sherman keep his promise to "befriend the South" once it was militarily defeated. Indeed, no defeated army could have asked for more magnanimous terms than Sherman offered on that April day: recognition of existing state governments, reestablishment of Federal courts, a guarantee of political and private rights, and so on. It was a virtual restoration of the status that the Southern states had enjoyed before hostilities broke out. Indeed, these were the sort of terms that Jefferson Davis had been willing to wage guerilla war to obtain. Thus, through generosity, Sherman had pulled the fangs of the worst-case scenario that had disturbed his thoughts for weeks. The provisions, the language, the particulars of this agreement, were all Sherman's — and therein lay the problem.

In extending recognition to existing state governments, for instance, he went far beyond anything that even Lincoln is known to have planned.

It seems never to have entered Sherman's mind that his terms would not only be rejected by Washington, but that he himself would be castigated bitterly, for years to come, for having the audacity to show such generosity to unrepentant rebels.

The mood in the North was not charitable, but vindictive — at least, among the men who now held political power in Washington after Lincoln's assassination. It was not enough that the rebels should be humbled and beaten in battle; they must also be punished, ground under the conqueror's heel. General Grant was ordered to Raleigh to keep a tighter reign on things, but he discreetly kept out of Sherman's way, for he shared Sherman's distaste for politicians and his contempt for men whose desire to wreak vengeance against a beaten foe seemed to increase in direct proportion to the distance they had stayed from the actual fighting.

Grant brought with him to Raleigh an order directing Sherman to end the cease-fire at noon on April 26 — after which he must either attack Johnston or at least begin maneuvering against him. Sherman dutifully informed Johnston that their agreement had been scuttled by the politicians and gave him 48 hours' notice that Union forces would be on the move.

Things were now getting complicated indeed. On the afternoon of April 24, Jefferson Davis had wired Johnston that he approved of the terms of the agreement signed at Bennett's farm on April 18. But before Johnston could pass this along to Sherman, he received the bad news from Sherman that hostilities would recommence in 48 hours unless an agreement could be reached on the same terms concluded between Lee and Grant. Johnston forwarded the new message to Davis. On the morning of April 25, Davis's alarming response arrived on Johnston's desk. Davis ordered Johnston to disband the infantry without surrendering, then order the men to meet again at some safe interior location. The cavalry, meanwhile, was to be organized into one large force and dispatched south to escort the President and his cabinet to...well, to wherever.

But Joseph Johnston had had enough. To obey these desperate instructions would be to prolong the misery, the killing, the hunger, the anarchy. And where would he get these phantom armies? In the four days since the armistice was signed, at least 4,000 of his infantry had simply walked away, along with half as many cavalrymen. Hampton could probably persuade some of his fire-eaters to keep fighting, but the infantry, once dispersed — Johnston had no doubt about it — would never reassemble again for the purpose of fighting. Eighty percent of them would head straight home, never to budge again. Certainly not for Jefferson Davis.

So Johnston, violating a lifetime of military discipline and professional habit, disobeyed a direct order from his commander-in-chief. Ignoring Davis's telegrams, he wired Sherman instead, requesting yet another meeting at the farmhouse.

Union General Schofield was on hand for this session, since he would be assuming command of the region after Sherman's departure. Schofield — by most accounts, a decent sort of man — assured Johnston that he would take all reasonable steps to see that the paroled Confederate soldiers had enough food in their knapsacks to keep them from turning into robbers as they headed home. With that consideration put to rest, a simple agreement was speedily reached. Under the terms of the Military Convention of April 26, Schofield agreed to help Johnston's men find transportation, agreed to permit each unit to retain one-seventh of its arms for self-protection until it reached its home state's capital, and agreed that both officers and enlisted men could keep their private property. With Sherman and Grant backing him up, Schofield was as good as his word, and in the coming days he managed to provide a quarter-million units of rations for the departing Confederates (in addition to the vast quantities of goods they had already looted from Confederate depots) and a fair number of wagons to help carry them home.

A storm of abuse erupted over Sherman's head when the vengeance-hungry Northern press got to work on the story of his original peace negotiations with Johnston. One of Sherman's most implacable foes in the new Andrew Johnson administration, War Secretary Stanton, even accused Sherman of "allowing Davis to escape," hinting that large quantities of Confederate gold might have induced the general to avert his eye while Davis fled North Carolina. After all, had not Sherman ordered Stoneman's cavalry to stop tearing up the western part of the state, thus permitting the Confederates to slip through the net?

These accusations were insulting and utterly without foundation, inspired solely by political malice. Sherman bristled with rage at the way his own side was now treating him. Indeed, for a time, he seemed to find more to admire in the foes he had recently vanquished than in the masters he had served so well. He would not hesitate, he wrote to one correspondent, to freely mingle with Southerners. In fact, if the occasion ever arose, he would be proud to lead them in battle, for he knew their mettle well after Bentonville and Averasboro.

Embroiled in controversy, William Tecumseh Sherman left North Carolina at the end of April. His arrival in the state had been trumpeted by every portent of doom save falling comets, and his march through the lower Piedmont had left a legacy of pillage and destruction that would not fade from regional emotions for more than a century. Yet he had acquired, on that same march, a hard-won respect for North Carolina and its people. He had met on the state's soil the only determined resistance he had encountered since Atlanta. He had also been impressed by the industry of the people, the beauty of the landscape, and the decent cleanliness of the villages he had taken. And he had proposed a set of peace terms which, if they had been accepted by an enlightened and compassionate government, would have spared the state most of the bitterness of Reconstruction.

Sherman had come to North Carolina as the incarnation of Satan. Yet now, the people of the state had ample reason to lament his departure, for during those few fragile days when he had held the fate of postwar North Carolina in his hands, he had proven to be a statesman as well as a conqueror.

"WE STACKED OUR GUNS IN A FIELD AND LEFT THEM THERE..."

Governor Zebulon Vance had left Hillsborough on April 15 and obeyed President Jefferson Davis's order to join him in Greensboro. Vance was traveling light: personal effects, a couple of aides, some pens and stationery in his saddlebags, and under his coat a big Navy-pattern revolver...just in case. But by the time Vance got to Greensboro, Davis and his band of political gypsies had trekked on. Somewhat at a loss about what to do next, Vance decided to tag along with Postmaster General John Reagan and War Secretary John Breckinridge when they returned to Hillsborough on the eve of the second peace conference at Bennett's farm.

When the three men arrived at General Wade Hampton's headquarters, Vance — still, after all, governor of North Carolina — went inside and joined the council of war that was underway. There was a great deal of coming and going during the evening, so it is impossible to say with complete certainty just who was present for what part of the evening. But, for certain, the Confederate generals included Hampton, Wheeler, Johnston, and M.C. Butler, along with sundry aides and staff members; Reagan; Breckinridge; and, for part of the time, Zebulon Vance.

The purpose of the meeting, obviously, was to analyze Sherman's terms of surrender. But at some point, one or several of the men present — mindful of Jefferson Davis's suspicions about the Vance-Graham-Swain peace delegation, and remembering the order to halt the delegates that had emanated from Davis's headquarters — turned on the misunderstood Vance and harshly accused him of selling out the cause, even of treachery. Vance replied to these unjust accusations with some fiery language of his own. For a few moments, it seemed as if a fistfight was in the offing. Exactly what words were said to him, and who spoke them, Vance never recounted — so deeply did the incident wound him.

Whatever transpired, Vance was so angered and humiliated that he stormed out of the meeting and spent the night outside under a blanket. He was joined by a staff officer named Saunders. When morning came, poor Saunders woke to a chill — Vance had rolled over in his sleep and taken all of the blanket. Saunders lit his pipe, tucked the governor in, fetched a basin of water for him, and watched over him until he woke.

Upon waking, Vance quickly washed up in the basin, drying himself with a handkerchief in lieu of a towel. He needed someone to talk to, and the solicitous Saunders was handy. As they strolled through the thin spring sunshine, watching the mist burn off the fields, Vance let his bitterness out. At the conference the night before, he said, he had not even been given a chance to explain his own dealings with Sherman — the governor of North Carolina had been told bluntly to sit down and shut up.

"I came here to explain that Sherman letter, and they wouldn't hear me!" he exclaimed, still incredulous. "Me, 'in communication with the enemy'! Me, 'making terms for my state unknown to the authorities'! Of all men, sir, I am the last man they can accuse of that infamy!"

To Saunders, the governor seemed in "an agony of shame"; tears filled his eyes as he recalled the humiliation of the night before.

Restless and smarting from his rebuff at Hillsborough, Vance rode south now to catch up with Davis's procession, joining the presidential party probably at Lexington, possibly in Charlotte (depending on which historian tells the tale). With Raleigh fallen to the enemy, and his own peace initiative stillborn and misinterpreted by his own side, Vance was offering, at this eleventh hour, consummate proof of his loyalty to the Confederate cause. When Davis learned that Vance had joined them, he convened the cabinet for a meeting with the governor. This final wartime meeting between the two men was charged with emotion. How long and often had they argued in their eloquent and often acrimonious correspondence! At this moment, however, most of those disagreements seemed irrelevant. Vance spoke first, and plainly: "Mr. President, I have come to see what you wish me to do…"

Davis then launched into a long, rambling discourse on future military options. They could rally an army in the trans-Mississippi area using Kirby-Smith's force as a nucleus, and Vance could raise a contingent of North Carolinian troops to join them. Vance listened in silent consternation, moved by the President's determination but unnerved by his casual manipulation of phantom armies. When Davis had finished, there was a somber silence. For one of the few times in his life, Zebulon Vance was at a loss for words.

Finally, Breckinridge gently broke the silence. "Mr. President, I don't think you have answered the governor's question…"

"Well," muttered Davis, "what would you tell him to do?"

Breckinridge looked at Vance with a level gaze. "I don't think we are dealing candidly with him. Our hopes of accomplishing what you set forth are so remote and uncertain that I, for my part, could not advise him to follow our fortunes further." Stepping closer to Vance, Breckinridge looked the governor in the eye and said, "My advice would be that you return to your responsibilities and do the best you can for your people, and share their fate, whatever it might be."

Davis exhaled a long, thin sigh, and nodded slightly toward Breckinridge. "Well, perhaps, General, you are right…" Then he rose with solemn dignity, clasped the governor's hand, and cried out with unfeigned sincerity: "God bless you, sir; God bless you and the noble old state of North Carolina."

Not knowing what else to do, Vance returned to Greensboro and set up a de facto state administration in the law offices of the Scott brothers on North Elm Street. He issued a few proclamations and wrote a few letters, including a very peevish one to General Joseph Johnston, asking why, as governor, he was not being included in the continuing peace negotiations. Johnston courteously wrote back and told Vance that no slight was intended, but this was soldiers' business and no one else's. Vance also got into an argument with Johnston about the way Old Joe's men were helping themselves to state supplies as they passed through the Greensboro area. Johnston by this time had virtually no control over most of those troops, and had more important things to worry about than the governor's precious supplies — which, in his opinion, Vance had hoarded too jealously anyway. Johnston couldn't be bothered with the problem and told Vance so in an unusually testy exchange of notes. If his men wanted the supplies, he felt they were entitled to take some.

All things considered, this was the low point of Vance's career, as well as of his spirits, and his last-minute tiff with Johnston did him no credit.

Vance's brief stay in Greensboro seems to have passed without much public attention. Perhaps, after the arrival of the entire Confederate government as well as a host of military heroes whom most people had only read about in the papers, the citizens were becoming jaded. In any case, it is now impossible even to determine where he slept at night.

Vance did make one attempt to return to Raleigh, but he was stopped by Federal authorities. He then tried to surrender to General Schofield on the Hillsborough road near Durham, but Schofield would not accept the gesture and told Vance to go home and stop fretting. Vance decided to do just that. He bought passage on a train for Statesville, where his family was waiting.

The train was crowded beyond endurance and the weather was unseasonably hot. Vance and his fellow travelers were crammed into their railroad car like sardines. Someone finally kicked a hole in the side of the car to permit a little air to circulate. During one of the numerous delays on the trip, with the train barely moving, a Confederate veteran with a hard-bitten face forced himself through the ventilation hole — dust, body odor, and all. Vance, who had withstood about all that one man could take in the past couple of weeks, lost his temper at this intrusion. He pulled his heavy pistol out of his belt and brandished it at the interloper.

The grizzled old soldier looked the governor squarely in the eye and took his measure: "You don't look like you'd shoot," he said calmly.

Nor could he. Laughing now, at himself and perhaps at the fickleness of destiny itself, Vance extended a hand to the man as he found a few inches of space for himself in the crowd. The train gathered speed and rolled on toward Statesville, carrying Zebulon Vance out of the war, out of the governorship, but ultimately into a career in national politics no less distinguished, if slightly less colorful, than his dramatic sojourn in Raleigh.

Meanwhile, moderate weather blessed the odyssey of Jefferson Davis and his motley band as they struggled southward out of Greensboro, but the roads were still in frightful shape from the prolonged spring rains and progress was slow. Davis, due to his rank, and Secretary of State Judah Benjamin, due to his girth, rode in wagons; everyone else was on horse or muleback. Davis rode with head downcast, shrouded in an aura of morose gloom. Only Benjamin, manifesting even now his customary waxen mask of geniality, continued to try and make lively conversation, in a voice whose cheerfulness seemed hollow. Benjamin also revealed a bizarre sense of occasion. For a long stretch of the trip, he insisted upon reading aloud the interminable verses of Tennyson's ode to the death of Wellington:

> Lead out the pageant: sad and slow, As befits an universal woe, Let the long, long procession go...and let the mournful, martial music blow; The last great Englishman is low....

Between the hub-deep mud, the weight of the wagons, and the pathetic condition of the animals, the caravan made, on that first day, a total of ten miles. They spent the night near Jamestown at the farm of a man named John Hiatt, who treated them well, fed them decently, and gave Davis a good horse the next morning.

The party did not enjoy such luck on the next afternoon. In High Point, they could find no one willing to shelter them. They pushed on until dark, getting almost as far as Lexington. Then, the weather being clement, they decided simply to camp out for the night. Around the campfire, Davis became another man. Relaxed, expansive, and mellow-voiced, he reclined with his head against a saddle, contentedly puffed on a cigar, and told nostalgic, colorful stories of his days at West Point, his adventures in Mexico, his fiery career in national politics. The other cabinet members listened, flabbergasted and altogether enthralled. In all their days in the Richmond administration, this was a side of their President they had never before seen, and it was sad to see it now, and to reflect on what a terrible price pride can exact from a man.

On Easter Sunday, April 16, the slow, sad caravan reached the Yadkin River. They crossed on the bridge that had been saved a short time before from General Stoneman's incendiaries by the spirited resistance of a few Salisbury Home Guardsmen and some "galvanized" Irish Yankees. Rumors continued to reach them of Federal cavalry in the area, but so far none had actually appeared.

In Salisbury itself, the infamous prison compound was still smoldering after Stoneman's raiders had put it to the torch. Davis and his entourage spent the night with the Reverend Thomas Haughton, pastor of St. Luke's Church. Once again, when the rigors and tension of the day's march were behind him, Davis became a changed man. Seemingly without a care in the world, he stayed up late, rocking back and forth on the good reverend's veranda, smoking cigars and telling stories.

After breakfast the next morning, Reverend Haughton's young daughter suddenly burst into tears. When asked what was wrong, the little girl wailed that surely now "Old Lincoln" would come and kill them all because they had sheltered the refugees. Davis knelt before the girl, took her tear-streaked face in his fine, long-fingered hands, and solemnly reassured her. "Oh no, little lady. Mr. Lincoln is not such a bad man, and he doesn't want to kill anybody, and certainly not a little girl like you."

Before the presidential gypsies departed Salisbury, a courier arrived with a telegram from General Johnston: Would Secretary of War John Breckinridge return to Greensboro and join him in his next round of negotiations with General Sherman? Breckinridge and Postmaster General John Reagan both mounted horses and rode back the way they had come. The others wearily turned south again on the next leg of their journey.

They spent one more night on the road, in Concord, before reaching their immediate destination, Charlotte. The cabinet members all found lodging with prominent local citizens, but for a time it appeared that no one was willing to come forward and offer the President shelter, out of fear of reprisal from Sherman. Finally, an ex-Northerner named Bates — a bachelor who was thought to be a Union sympathizer, and who may, in fact, have been a part-time

Union spy — offered Davis the hospitality of his home. It was an invitation Davis would regret having accepted.

What happened next, just as Davis was arriving at the Bates house, constitutes one of the war's best "UFO" stories — that is, dozens of people witnessed the event, but almost everybody who talked or wrote about it later gave a different account of what they saw and heard.

Davis was being cheered by some passing Kentucky cavalrymen when he was handed a telegram from Breckinridge informing him of the assassination of Abraham Lincoln. Davis read the message through twice, without changing his expression, and then passed it to the man closest to him, a wealthy Charlottean named William Johnston. Davis muttered that it was "an extraordinary communication," expressed doubts about its authenticity, and finally stated that, if true, it was indeed "sad news."

Several weeks later, Davis's putative host, Mr. Bates, would testify before Congress that Davis received the news with undisguised glee. According to Bates, Davis turned to General Breckinridge and quoted (or rather misquoted) Macbeth by saying, "If it were done, it were well that it was done well." Bates claimed that Davis then expressed the bloodthirsty desire that the same fate should befall Vice President Andrew Johnson and Secretary of War Edwin Stanton, so that "the job would be complete." All in all, Bate's account certainly made it sound as though Jefferson Davis approved of, if not actually conspired in, a well-oiled plot to exterminate the whole Lincoln administration in one night-of-the-long-knives swoop.

Bates's motives for spreading such slander is a matter of conjecture. Clearly, though, he was lying on an extravagant scale in at least one respect: How could Davis have turned and uttered his remarks to Breckinridge when it was Breckinridge himself who had sent the telegram from Greensboro? But the Northern press, already howling for Jefferson Davis's head on a pike, took Bates's canards for gospel and milked headlines from them for days.

Significantly, no other account of the incident reveals Davis expressing anything but regret over the news, although there is disagreement over the exact wording and timing of his remarks. What seems to have happened is this: Davis read the telegram, handed it to William Johnston, made his understated comment, and then passed the message around among the nearby cabinet members. When Navy Secretary Stephen R. Mallory read it, he remarked that the news might provoke violence. According to Mallory, Davis replied, "I certainly have no special regard for Mr. Lincoln; but there are a great many men of whose end I would much rather have heard than his. I fear it will be disastrous for our people, and I regret it deeply."

After this, Davis's attention was diverted by the Kentucky cavalrymen, who had heard the news by now and were cheering and demanding a speech from the President on this historic occasion. Davis did not feel like making a speech, but he mouthed a few homilies about continuing the struggle, thanked the men for their loyalty, and then, pleading exhaustion from his journey, turned to leave. Whatever his words, his obvious demeanor was that of a saddened and downcast man, not that of a man rejoicing over the fall of an enemy. Later that day, Davis confided to Burton Harrison, his executive secretary: "We have lost our best friend in the court of the enemy." Davis had, of course, no personal love for Lincoln, but he knew perfectly well that with Andrew Johnson and his clique at the helm instead of Honest Abe, the South would be made to groan and to feel the heel of retribution in ways, and to a degree, that Lincoln would never have countenanced.

More nails were driven into the Confederacy's coffin during Davis's stay in Charlotte. They received news of the fall of Mobile, the last important Confederate port, and General Robert E. Lee's written report of the final days of the Army of Northern Virginia. Amazingly, with everything crumbling around him, Davis still clung to his hope of eventual triumph. It had become a personal matter to him, now, inextricably tangled with his fierce, inflexible sense of pride. It was not so much that the South had not yet been beaten; rather, it was as he said to Harrison: "I *cannot* feel myself a beaten man!" This indicates once more the depths to which he had subsumed the larger cause into his own egotistic drives and needs.

Davis was momentarily cheered by the arrival of General Wade Hampton, who fed the President's fantasies with his own passionate avowals of resistance to the last horse and bullet. Neither man knew exactly what troops they could rally, or how they would find them, or how they would cross several hundred miles of impoverished and chaotic countryside to take command of them, but while they were in one another's company, the air rang once more with words of steel and brimstone.

Far more sobering were the words Davis heard when Reagan and Breckinridge returned to Charlotte. They carried with them a copy of the surrender instrument signed by generals Sherman and Joseph Johnston. Johnston had insisted that Davis approve and sign the documents. Davis was startled by the liberality of the terms, and predicted — correctly, as it turned out — that Lincoln's successor would never accept them.

The document was discussed at what appears to have been the next-to-last full-scale meeting of the Confederate Cabinet. Everyone, even the eupeptic Benjamin, agreed that these were the best terms they could hope for. So Davis signed the surrender, but still expressed doubt that Washington would let Sherman get away with such a generous arrangement. If the terms were rejected, Davis announced, he would not feel compelled to abide by them, but would continue his odyssey for an army.

After signing the document, Davis wrote a letter to his wife full of bitterness and uncertainty. He pleaded with her to embark for a foreign port, and intimated that he might make for Mexico, where he would try to enlist Emperor Ferdinand Maximilian's aid in finding a ship to take him to join his family. He closed with sentiments worthy of a Victorian gentleman: "Dear wife, this is not the fate to which I invited you when the future was rose-colored for us both; but I know you will bear it even better than myself...Farewell, my dear, there may be better things in store for us than are now in view, but my love is all I have to offer, and that has the value of a thing long possessed, and sure not to be lost...."

An hour after the signed surrender documents reached Johnston, so did news of their thundering rejection by Washington. Davis ordered the general to repudiate the agreement and march with all available cavalry to meet him. Thus reinforced, they could cut their way through to the West. In his reply, Johnston made little effort to hide his contempt for Davis, suggesting that such a plan would only bring further misery to his men and the country they marched through, and would benefit only the Confederate hierarchy. Johnston then disobeyed Davis's orders, got the best terms he could, and surrendered every Confederate soldier within his sphere of command.

Davis never forgave him, nor could he ever bring himself to admit the logic of Johnston's actions. To Davis, it was a final, Brutus-like wound from a man he had disliked since their cadet days at West Point.

The last formal meeting of the Confederate Cabinet was held in the Phifer house on North Tryon Street in Charlotte on April 24, 1865. The only matter of business under discussion was the plan of flight to be adopted, and the only dramatic thing that happened was the splintering of one of their host's antique chairs when Judah Benjamin sat down on it too emphatically.

For his last act in Charlotte, General Breckinridge — a man with a keen sense of history — turned over all the official records carried by the Presidential party to an officer who could be trusted to keep them safe until order was restored. Historians have been grateful to him ever since.

Jefferson Davis and his beleaguered caravan crossed the border into South Carolina on April 26. Ahead lay weeks of desperate flight and Davis's eventual capture, on May 10, near Irwinville, Georgia. On his way out of North Carolina, Davis was escorted by a gaggle of unruly cavalrymen, who came and went as they pleased and obeyed orders only when it suited them; many of them were so drunk they could barely stay in the saddle.

Meanwhile, news of Johnston's formal surrender occasioned a great outburst of celebration in Raleigh. Fireworks blazed in the sky, bands oom-pahed in the streets, people danced and cheered, and a mood of profound relief was manifested in the behavior of both Federal soldiers and civilians alike.

Around the campfires of Johnston's army, however, the mood was bitter and anguished. Doctor Alexander D. Betts, chaplain of the 17th North Carolina Regiment, recorded the following scenes on or about April 27:

> The night following the tidings of our contemplated surrender was a still, sad night in our camp...In little...groups [the men] softly talked of the past, the present, and the future. Old men were there, who would have cheerfully gone on, enduring the hardships of war and protracted absence from their families, for the freedom of their country. Middle aged men were there, who had been away from wives and children for years, had gone through many battles, had lost much on their farms or stores of factories or professional busi-

ness; but would that night have been glad to shoulder the gun and march forward for the defense of their "native land." Young men and boys were there, who loved their country and were unspeakably sad at the thought of failure to secure Southern Independence.

I walked out of the camp...and wept...As I started back to my tent...I passed three lads sitting together, talking softly...I paused and listened. One said, "It makes me very sad to think of our surrendering." Another said, "It hurts me more than the thought of battle ever did." The third raised his arm, clenched his fist, and seemed to grate his teeth as he said, "I would rather know we had to go into battle tomorrow morning." There was patriotism! There may have been in that camp that night generals, colonels and other officers who had been moved by a desire for worldly honor. Owners of slaves and of lands may have hoped for financial benefit from Confederate success. But these boys felt they had a country that ought to be free![1]

A more philosophical, long-range view would be expressed a year later on the first anniversary of the surrender by "Athos," the anonymous columnist in the *Greensboro Patriot*. In an article customarily cushioned in Victorian rodomontade, Athos wrote:

We have given up the contest, we have yielded the issue, we have surrendered our arms, we intend to obey the laws of the country, what more can or ought any one ask? We cannot say we are knaves — that we are sorry for doing that which we thought right and for which so many thousands of our best men bled and died. We fought a brave fight — we were conquered — we submit. Not since the first dawn of creation — not since the Almighty brought order out of chaos and "divided the light from the darkness" has there ever been a people more devoted, more determined, more terrible in their bravery...than the civilized, chivalrous, Christian people of the South...It surely cannot be considered treason to love and revere and honor the names and memories of our noble comrades, friends, and brothers who fought and died....[2]

Clearly, the Legend of the Confederacy — so much more potent and enduring than the rickety political system that spawned it — was already rising, phoenix-like, from the ashes of the real Confederacy.

And Old Joe Johnston, his weary frame all but cracked under the weight of all he had been called upon to do and feel, came back from signing the surrender papers, sat down at his headquarters on the outskirts of Greensboro, and wrote a starkly eloquent letter of explanation to the governors of all the states under his nominal command:

The disaster in Virginia, the capture by the enemy of all our work-shops for the preparation of ammunition and repairing arms, the impossibility of recruiting our little army, opposed by more than ten times its number, or of supplying it except by robbing our own citizens, destroyed all hope of successful war. I have, therefore, made a military convention with General Sherman to terminate hostilities in North and South Carolina, Georgia, and Florida. I have made this convention to spare the blood of the gallant little army committed to me, to prevent further sufferings of our people by the devastation and ruin inevitable from the marches of invading armies, and to avoid the crime of waging hopeless war.[3]

The task of paroling Johnston's army was given to General Schofield, who arrived at the end of April. Johnston's forces were camped all around Greensboro and to the southwest as far as High Point. Old Joe's own headquarters was nestled in a rural pine grove about a mile and a half west of town. A correspondent from the *New York Herald*, who had followed Schofield into town, interviewed Johnston there:

Yes, he could have given Sherman the slip, and dragged his whole army after him — he'd done it enough times in Georgia — but, eventually, they would have had to come to terms somewhere or other, if only when Johnston ran into the Mississippi River. But it was better, he insisted, to end it here and now, rather than scourge the countryside with two more foraging armies for as much as a single day more. Besides, Old Joe ruminated, "the fate of the Confederacy was decided in Virginia."

It took until May 1 to get the parole forms printed and the apparatus set up for handling the process. By that time, probably as many as 50,000 Confederate soldiers had already set out for home, usually without telling their officers, so the paperwork for the demobilization was almost hopelessly complicated.

The parole forms themselves, however, were simple and to the point:

[*Name of soldier*] has given his solemn obligation not to take up arms against the Government of the United States until properly released from this obligation; and is permitted to return to his home, not to be disturbed by the United States authorities so long as he observes this obligation and obeys the laws in force where he may reside.

Working together, Johnston and Beauregard devised a plan whereby only the officers would actually receive their signed

paroles on the spot where they signed them. The enlisted men's
documents were kept by their unit commanders and were not handed
out until the units were formally disbanded on the road home —
wherever that was. In this manner, some semblance of military discipline could be maintained among the long masses of trudging
men.

Those soldiers who had stayed with Johnston until the end could,
perhaps, take some pride from the fact that Johnston never actually
"surrendered" his men — he merely ended hostilities and "dispersed" them. They were never prisoners of war, but rather ended
the war as they had begun it: free men. As for General Joseph E.
Johnston himself, he was not asked to sign a parole — a handshake,
and his word, were all that Schofield deemed necessary.

For the Army of Tennessee, then, it was the end of an epic odyssey, a road that wound across the entire Southern heartland, measured off in milestones painted with blood: Shiloh, Chickamauga,
Chattanooga, Kenesaw Mountain, Atlanta, Nashville, Bentonville.

There remained but one task for Johnston, and that was to say
farewell to his "matchless troops." He did so by means of General
Order No. 22, issued on May 2, 1865. Given the scattered positions
of his units throughout Guilford County, it was not practical to hold
a final review, or for the commander to address his men in any great
numbers. Instead, General Order No. 22 was copied and distributed
to all units, where it was both posted and read aloud.

There was, however, one final council of war, held beneath the
vast and noble oak trees in front of the Gorrell house, near the now-
famous railroad siding in Greensboro. And it was to that small
audience, of officers whose divisions had shrunk to the size of companies, and privates from the ranks who had come by to get a last
look at their beloved "Old Joe," that Johnston spoke his farewell
words:

> Comrades: In terminating our official relations, I earnestly exhort
> you to observe faithfully the terms of pacifications agreed upon;
> and to discharge the obligations of good and peaceful citizens, as
> well as you have performed the duties of thorough soldiers in the
> field. By such a course, you will best secure the comfort of your
> families and kindred, and restore tranquility to our country.
>
> You will return to your homes with the admiration of our people,
> won by the courage and noble devotion you have displayed in this

long war. I shall always remember with pride the loyal support and generous confidence you have given me.

I now part with you with deep regret — and bid you farewell with feelings of cordial friendship; and with earnest wishes that you may have hereafter all the prosperity and happiness to be found in the world.

Slowly the men wandered off. Johnston himself walked a few blocks from the railroad siding to Blandwood, the handsome mansion of former governor John Morehead, intending to say a farewell now to his closest civilian friends in Greensboro. Lititia Morehead Walker, Morehead's daughter, saw Johnston coming up the wide, green, spring-flowered lawn, head down, shoulders bent, walking past the towering old oaks that surrounded Blandwood. She met him on the front steps. She tried to speak, but could not. Neither could Johnston; the iron will that had held him together for the past 90 days was broken at last. He stood there before the lady, unable to utter a word, tears pouring freely down his brown, leathery cheeks. It was as though one of the oak trees had started to cry.

Sergeant Daniel Dantzler, in the diary he had been keeping since he had left James Island, South Carolina, to march north and join Johnston's concentration before Bentonville, described his last day of Confederate service, May 3, 1865, very simply:

We were lined up and stacked our guns in a field and left them there....

Hustled into formation by their officers, Dantzler and his comrades marched away. When they were about a hundred miles south of Greensboro, their officers passed out their parole papers, wished them Godspeed, and left them to find their own ways home.

NOTES

CHAPTER 2: NORTH CAROLINA ON THE EVE OF WAR

1. Boykin, James, H., *North Carolina in 1861*, p. 136.

CHAPTER 3: 'YOU CAN GET NO TROOPS FROM NORTH CAROLINA!'

1. While it debated grave matters of state, the Assembly still conducted business as usual. Among the issues under discussion as 1861 opened were such burning questions as whether or not to allocate funds for the insertion of coal grates into the Capitol building's fireplaces, and Senate Bill No. 90, a piece of legislation intriguingly labeled "A Bill to Permit Persons to Remove the Remains of their Deceased Relatives When Buried Upon the Land of Another." The latter bill was tabled without action.

2. Robinson, Blackwell P., and Stoeson, Alexander R., *The History of Guilford County, North Carolina, to 1980 A.D.*, p. 89.

CHAPTER 4: GIRDING FOR A LONG WAR

1. Graham, Colonel H.C., "How North Carolina Went to War," p. 10.

2. Barrett, John G., *The Civil War in North Carolina*, p. 24.

3. A full account of the state's adventurous and remarkably successful blockade-running enterprises will be found in Volume III, *Silk Flags and Cold Steel: The Coast*.

CHAPTER 8: A WORD ABOUT THE RAILROADS

1. Price, Charles L., "North Carolina Railroads During the Civil War," p. 300.

2. Black, R.C., *Railroads of the Confederacy*, p. 228.

CHAPTER 9: ZEBULON VANCE — AN OVERVIEW

1. Lefler, Hugh T., and Newsome, Albert R. (editors), *North Carolina — The History of a Southern State*, 1963 edition, p. 448.

2. Kruman, Marc, *Politics and Parties in North Carolina, 1836-1865*, p. 243.

3. Ibid, p. 242, excerpted from the *Raleigh Standard*, September 4, 1861.

CHAPTER 13: CONSCRIPTION, DESERTION, AND RAMPAGING CAVALRYMEN

1. Tucker, Glenn, *Zeb Vance — Champion of Personal Freedom*; p. 258.

CHAPTER 15: HARD TIMES ON THE HOME FRONT

1. Mrs. A.J. Ellis, in the *Raleigh News and Observer*, January 1, 1928; copy in the archives of the Carolina Collection, Greensboro Public Library, Greensboro, North Carolina.

2. Massey, Mary Elizabeth, *Ersatz in the Confederacy*, pp. 88-89.

3. Weatherly, A. Carl, *The First Hundred Years of Historic Guilford*, p. 58. (Weatherly's unique philatelic history of Guilford County includes numerous well-preserved specimens of such envelopes, printed and mailed in the Piedmont region.)

4. Massey, Mary Elizabeth, "The Food and Drink Shortage on the Confederate Home Front," p. 322.

5. Boyd, W.K., "Fiscal and Economic Conditions in North Carolina During the Civil War," p. 215.

6. Anderson, Mrs. John H., *North Carolina Women of the Confederacy*, pp. 88-89.

7. Ellis, *Raleigh News and Observer*, January 1, 1928.

CHAPTER 16: ANARCHY IN THE PIEDMONT — A WAR WITHIN A WAR

1. Auman, William T., "Neighbor Against Neighbor — The Inner Civil War in the Randolph County Area of Confederate North Carolina," pp. 67-68.

2. Auman, William T., *North Carolina's Inner Civil War: Randolph County*, p. 48.

3. Cox, Waldo C., *Hoot Owls, Honeysuckle, and Hallelujah*, p. 70.

4. Auman, "Neighbor Against Neighbor," p. 71.

5. Ibid, pp. 71-72.

6. Ibid, p. 73.

7. Auman, *North Carolina's Inner Civil War*, p. 97.

8. Ibid.

9. Thomas W. Ritter to Zebulon Vance, January 25, 1864; cited in Auman, *North Carolina's Inner Civil War*, p. 153.

10. Cox, p. 72.

11. Ibid.

12. Auman, *North Carolina's Inner Civil War*, p. 286.

13. Ibid, p. 213.

14. Ibid, p. 220-221.

15. Ibid.

16. Auman, "Neighbor Against Neighbor," p. 86.

CHAPTER 17: NORTH CAROLINA'S 'ANDERSONVILLE' — THE PRISON AT SALISBURY

1. From "Pennsylvania at Salisbury," a booklet of addresses given at the unveiling of a monument to the Pennsylvania troops who died at Salisbury Prison, published by the State of Pennsylvania, 1912; copy in the Carolina Collection, Greensboro Public Library, Greensboro, North Carolina.

2. Small, Joseph, from a speech given in 1908 at the dedication of a monument to the Maine soldiers who died at Salisbury; see "Report of the Maine Commission on the Monument Erected at Salisbury, North Carolina," 1908; copy in the Greensboro Public Library's Carolina Collection.

CHAPTER 18: THE 'HEROES OF AMERICA'

1. Auman, William A., and Scarboro, David D., "The Heroes of America in Civil War North Carolina," p. 335.

CHAPTER 19: THE PEACE MOVEMENT AND THE ELECTION OF 1864

1. Yates, Richard E., "Governor Vance and the Peace Movement," p. 14.

CHAPTER 20: 'THEIR RUDE HANDS SPARED NOTHING BUT OUR LIVES...'

1. Bauer, K. Jack (editor), *Soldiering — The Civil War Diary of Rice*

C. Bull, pp. 228-229.

2. Barrett, John G., *The Civil War in North Carolina*, p. 315.

3. Johnson, Robert Underwood, and Buel, Clarence Clough (editors), *Battles and Leaders of the Civil War*, pp. 677-678.

CHAPTER 23: HARD FIGHTING AT AVERASBORO

1. Johnson, Robert Underwood, and Buel, Clarence Clough (editors), *Battles and Leaders of the Civil War*, pp. 689-691.

2. Barrett, John G., *The Civil War in North Carolina*, p. 315.

3. Nicols, George Ward, *The Story of the Great March*, p. 252.

4. Fowler, Malcolm, *They Passed This Way — A Narrative History of Harnett County*, p. 96.

5. Johnson and Buel, p. 679.

6. Fowler, pp. 97-98.

7. Glatthaar, Joseph T., *The March to the Sea and Beyond*, p. 167.

CHAPTER 24: BENTONVILLE — THE LAST REBEL YELL

1. Luvaas, Jay, "Johnston's Last Stand — Bentonville," p. 340 — from a letter by Lieutenant Charles S. Brown to his family, April 10, 1865.

2. Clark, Walter (editor), *Histories of the Several Regiments and Battalions from North Carolina in the Great War, 1861-65*, Volume IV, p. 21.

3. Upson, Theodore F., (edited by O.O. Winther), *With Sherman to the Sea*, pp. 158-160.

4. Barrett, John G., *The Civil War in North Carolina*; p. 343.

5. "The Last Important Battle," *Charlotte Observer*, March 18, 1934; same article includes interesting quotes from Bentonville citizens who actually remembered the battle; copy in the Carolina Collection, Greensboro Public Library, Greensboro, North Carolina.

CHAPTER 25: 'CALL FUR STONES FROM THE VASTY DEEP' — THE LAST MONTHS OF THE VANCE ADMINISTRATION

1. Yates, Richard E., "Governor Vance and the End of the War in North Carolina," p. 317.

2. Ibid, p. 319.

3. Tucker, Glenn, *Zeb Vance — Champion of Personal Freedom*, p. 378.

4. Ibid, p. 386.

CHAPTER 26: ENDGAME — THE FALL OF RALEIGH

1. Bauer, Jack, K. (editor), *Soldiering — the Civil War Diary of Rice C. Bull*, p. 233.

2. Tucker, Glenn, *Zeb Vance — Champion of Personal Freedom*, p. 396.

3. Barrett, John G., *Sherman's March Through the Carolinas*, p. 213.

4. Spencer, Cornelia Phillips, *The Last Ninety Days of the War in North Carolina*, p. 43.

CHAPTER 27: ALL THINGS CONVERGE AT GREENSBORO

1. Arnett, Ethel Stevens, *Confederate Guns Were Stacked at Greens-*

boro, p. 12.

CHAPTER 28: 'LIKE SNOW BEFORE THE SUN...'

1. Stock, Sallie W., *The History of Guilford County, N.C.*, p. 66.

2. Clement Eaton, *Life of Jefferson Davis*, New York, 1977 — quoted in Ballard, *A Long Shadow*, p. 77.

3. Arnett, Ethel Stephens, *Confederate Guns Were Stacked at Greensboro*, p. 39.

4. Ibid, p. 39.

5. Johnston, Joseph E., *Narrative of Military Operations*, p. 397.

CHAPTER 29: THE CONVERSATIONS AT BENNETT'S FARM

1. Spencer, Cornelia Phillips, *The Last Ninety Days of the War in North Carolina*, p. 169.

2. Ibid, pp. 170-171.

3. Arnett, Ethel Stephens, *Confederate Guns Were Stacked at Greensboro*, p. 56.

CHAPTER 30: 'WE STACKED OUR GUNS IN A FIELD AND LEFT THEM THERE...'

1. Arnett, Ethel Stephens, *Confederate Guns Were Stacked at Greensboro*; p. 66.

2. *Greensboro Patriot*, March 23, 1866.

3. Johnston, Joseph E., *Narrative of Military Operations*; p. 415.

BIBLIOGRAPHY

Sources relevant to the trilogy as a whole:

Ashe, Samuel A'Court, *History of North Carolina*, Vol. II, The Reprint Press, Spartinburg, 1971.

Barrett, John G., *The Civil War in North Carolina*, University of North Carolina Press, Chapel Hill, 1963.

Barrett, John G., and Yearns, W. Buck, *North Carolina Civil War Documentary*, University of North Carolina Press, Chapel Hill, 1980.

Butler, Lindley S., and Watson, Alan D., *The North Carolina Experience — An Interpretive and Documentary History*, University of North Carolina Press, Chapel Hill, 1984.

Clark, Walter (editor), *Histories of the Several Regiments and Battalions from North Carolina in the Great War, 1861-65*, Published by the State of North Carolina, Goldsboro, 1901 (four volumes).

Commager, Henry Steele (editor), *The Official Atlas of the Civil War*, Thomas Yoseloff Inc., New York, 1958.

Corbitt, D.L. (editor), *Pictures of the Civil War Period in North Carolina*, North Carolina Department of Archives and History, Raleigh, 1958.

Esposito, Vincent J. (editor), *The West Point Atlas of American Wars*, Frederick Praeger, New York, 1960 edition.

Gilham, William, *Manual of Instruction for the Volunteers and*

Militia, West and Johnson, Richmond, Virginia, 1861.

Johnson, Robert Underwood, and Buel, Clarence Clough (editors), *Battles and Leaders of the Civil War*, Commemorative Edition in four volumes, Thomas Yoseloff, Inc., New York, 1956.

Jordan, Weymouth T. (editor), *North Carolina Troops, 1861-65*, in ten volumes, North Carolina Department of Archives and History, Raleigh, 1981.

Lefler, Hugh, and Newsome, Albert R. (editors), *North Carolina — The History of a Southern State*, University of North Carolina Press, Chapel Hill, 1963 and 1975 editions.

McWhiney, Grady, and Jamieson, Perry, *Attack and Die — Civil War Tactics and the Southern Heritage*, University of Alabama Press, 1982.

Mitchell, Joseph R., *Military Leaders of the Civil War*, G. P. Putnam's Sons, New York, 1972.

Official Records, The War of the Rebellion, Vol. LXVII, "Operations in the Carolinas," Thomas Settle, 1865.

Tucker, Glenn, *Front Rank*, North Carolina Confederate Centennial Commission, Raleigh, 1962.

Sources mainly relevant to Volume I:

Alexander, Violet G., "The Confederate States Navy Yard at Charlotte, N.C., 1862-1865," *The North Carolina Booklet*, Volume XIV, April 1915.

Anderson, Mrs. John H., *North Carolina Women of the Confederacy*, privately published by Daughters of the Confederacy, Fayetteville, North Carolina, 1926.

A.O.W., *Eyewitness — Life Scenes from the Old North State, Depict-*

ing the Trials and Suffering of the Unionists During the Rebellion,
B.B. Russell and Co., Boston, 1866.

Arnett, Ethel Stephens, *Confederate Guns Were Stacked at Greensboro*, Piedmont Press, Greensboro, North Carolina, 1965.

Arnett, Ethel Stephens, *Greensboro, North Carolina*, University of North Carolina Press, Chapel Hill, 1955.

Auman, William T., "Neighbor Against Neighbor: The Inner Civil War in the Randolph County Area of Confederate North Carolina," *North Carolina Historical Review*, January 1984.

Auman, William T., *North Carolina's Inner Civil War: Randolph County*, unpublished thesis, University of North Carolina-Greensboro, 1978.

Ballard, Michael B., *A Long Shadow — Jefferson Davis and the Final Days of the Confederacy*, University of Mississippi Press, Jackson, 1986.

Barrett, John G., "Sherman's March Through the Carolinas," text of an address delivered to the North Carolina Literary and Historical Association, Raleigh, December 4, 1964.

Barret, John G., *Sherman's March Through the Carolinas*, University of North Carolina Press, Chapel Hill, 1956.

Bauer, Jack K. (editor), *Soldiering — The Civil War Diary of Rice C. Bull*, Presidio Press, San Rafael, California, 1977.

Beals, Carleton, *War Within a War — The Confederacy Against Itself*, Chilton Books, Philadelphia, Pennsylvania, 1965.

Black, John Logan, *Crumbling Defenses*, J. W. Burke Co., Macon, Georgia, 1960.

Black, R.C., *Railroads of the Confederacy*, University of North

Carolina Press, Chapel Hill, 1952.

Boyd, William K., "Fiscal and Economic Conditions in North Carolina During the Civil War," *The North Carolina Booklet*, Volume XIV, April 1915.

Boykin, James C., *North Carolina in 1861*, Bookman Associates, New York, 1961.

Brawley, James S., *Rowan County: A Brief History*, North Carolina Department of Archives and History, Raleigh, 1974.

Brown, Louis A., *The Salisbury Prison — A Case Study in Confederate Military Prisons*, Avera Press, Wendell, North Carolina, 1980.

Weatherly, A. Carl, *The First Hundred Years of Historic Guilford*, privately printed by the Greensboro Printing Company, Greensboro, North Carolina, 1972.

Carroll, Karen C., "Sterling, Campbell, and Albright: Textbook Publishers, 1861-1865," *North Carolina Historical Review*, April 1986.

Cartland, Fernando G., *Southern Heroes — The Friends in War Time*, Riverside Press, Cambridge, Massachusetts, 1895.

Channing, Steven A., *Confederate Ordeal — The Southern Home Front*, Time-Life Books, Alexandria, Virginia, 1984.

Connelly, Thomas Lawrence, *Autumn of Glory — The Army of Tennessee, 1862-1865*, Louisiana State University Press, Baton Rouge, Louisiana, 1971.

Cox, Jacob D., *The March to the Sea*, Blue and Grey Reprint Edition, New York, 1965.

Cox, Waldo C., *Hoot Owls, Honeysuckle, and Hallelujah*, Vantage

Press, New York, 1966.

Davis, Burke, *Sherman's March*, Random House, New York, 1980.

Davis, Burke, *The Long Surrender*, Random House, New York, 1985.

Fiore, Jannette C., *William C. Holden and The Standard — The Civil War Years*, thesis, University of North Carolina-Greensboro, 1966.

Fowler, Malcolm, *They Passed This Way — A Narrative History of Harnett County*, Harnett County (North Carolina) Centennial, Inc., 1976.

Fries, Adelaide, *Forsyth, History of a County on the March*, University of North Carolina Press, Chapel Hill, 1976.

Gibson, John M., *Those 163 Days — A Southern Account of Sherman's March from Atlanta to Raleigh*, Coward-McCann, Inc., New York, 1961.

Glatthaar, Joseph T., *The March to the Sea and Beyond*, New York University Press, New York, 1985.

Govan, Gilbert E., and Livingood, James W., *A Different Valor — The Story of Joseph E. Johnston, C.S.A.*, Bobbs-Merrill Co., Inc., New York, 1956.

Graham, H.C., "How North Carolina Went to War," reprinted in *The State Magazine*, March 1, 1968.

Hitchcock, Henry, *Marching With Sherman*, Yale University Press, New Haven, 1927.

Johnston, Frontis W., "Zebulon Baird Vance — A Personality Sketch," *North Carolina Historical Review*, April 1953.

Johnston, Joseph E., *Narrative of Military Operations*, D. Appleton & Co., New York, 1874.

Jones, Katharine M., *When Sherman Came — Southern Women and the "Great March"*, Bobbs-Merrill, Indianapolis, Indiana, 1964.

Korn, Jerry, *Pursuit to Appomattox — The Last Battles*, Time-Life Books, Alexandria, Virginia, 1987.

Kruman, Marc, "Dissent in the Confederacy — the North Carolina Experience," *Civil War History*, Vol. XXVII, No. 4, December 1981.

Kruman, Marc, *Politics and Parties in North Carolina, 1836-1865*, Louisiana State University Press, Baton Rouge, 1983.

Longacre, Edward G., "Judson Kilpatrick," *Civil War Times*, April 1971.

Luuvas, Jay, "Johnston's Last Stand — Bentonville," *North Carolina Historical Review*, July 1956.

Massey, Mary Elizabeth, *Ersatz in the Confederacy*, University of South Carolina Press, Columbia, 1952.

Massey, Mary Elizabeth, "The Food and Drink Shortage on the Confederate Home Front," *North Carolina Historical Review*, September 1961.

Mitchell, Memory F., *Legal Aspects of Conscription and Exemption in North Carolina, 1861-1865*, James Sprunt Studies in History, Vol. 47, University of North Carolina Press, Chapel Hill, 1965.

Moore, James, *Kilpatrick and Our Cavalry*, W. J. Widdleton, New York, 1865.

Nelson, B. H., "Some Aspects of Negro Life in North Carolina During the Civil War," *North Carolina Historical Review*, April

1948.

Nicols, George Ward, *The Story of the Great March*, Harper & Brothers, New York, 1865.

"Pennsylvania at Salisbury" — Dedication ceremonies and addresses for the memorial to Pennsylvania soldiers who died at the Salisbury Prison, published by the state of Pennsylvania, 1912.

Polk, Edgar E., and Shaw, Bynum, *W.W. Holden, A Political Biography*, John F. Blair, Winston-Salem, North Carolina, 1982.

Price, Charles L., "North Carolina Railroads During the Civil War," *Civil War History*, September 1961.

Raper, Horace W., *William Holden — North Carolina's Political Enigma*, University of North Carolina Press, Chapel Hill, 1985.

"Report of the Maine Commissioners on the Monument Erected at Salisbury, North Carolina," Sentinal Publishing Co., Waterville, Maine, 1908.

Rights, Douglas LeTell, "Salem in the War Between the States," *North Carolina Historical Review*, July 1950.

Robinson, Blackwell P., and Stoeson, Alexander R., *The History of Guilford County, North Carolina*, Guilford County Bicentennial Commission, 1981.

Scarboro, David D., "North Carolina and the Confederacy: The Weakness of States' Rights During the Civil War," *North Carolina Historical Review*, April 1972.

Scarboro, David D., "The Heroes of America in Civil War North Carolina," *North Carolina Historical Review*, October 1981.

Shirley, Franklin Ray, *Zebulon Vance, Tar Heel Spokesman*, McNally and Loftin, Charlotte, 1962.

Sloan, John A., *Reminiscences of the Guilford Grays*, R. O. Polkin-horn, Washington, North Carolina, 1883.

Spencer, Cornelia Phillips, *The Last Ninety Days of the War in North Carolina*, Watchman Publishing Co., New York, 1866.

Spraggins, Tinsley Lee, "Mobilization of Negro Labor in the Department of Virginia and North Carolina, 1861-1865," *North Carolina Historical Review*, April 1947.

Stock, Sallie W., *History of Guilford County, N.C.*, Knoxville, 1902.

Tatum, Georgia Lee, *Disloyalty in the Confederacy*, University of North Carolina Press, Chapel Hill, 1934.

Tucker, Glenn, *Zeb Vance — Champion of Personal Freedom*, Bobbs-Merrill Co., New York, 1965.

Upson, Theodore F., *With Sherman to the Sea*, Louisiana State University Press, Baton Rouge, 1943.

Weatherly, A. Carl, *The First Hundred Years of Historic Guilford*, privately printed by the Greensboro Printing Company, Greensboro, North Carolina, 1972.

Wellman, Manly Wade, "Bentonville — The Last Might-Have-Been," *The State Magazine*, August 9, 1958.

Wesley, Charles H., *The Collapse of the Confederacy*, The Associated Publishers, Inc., Washington, 1937.

Wharton, Don, *Smithfield As Seen By Sherman's Soldiers*, Smith-field Herald Publishing Co., Smithfield, North Carolina, 1977.

Yates, Richard E., *The Confederacy and Zeb Vance*, Confederate Publishing Co., Inc., Tuscaloosa, Alabama, 1958.

Yates, Richard E., "Governor Vance and the End of the War," *North*

Carolina Historical Review, October 1941.

Yates, Richard E., "Governor Vance and the Peace Movement,"
North Carolina Historical Review, April and June 1940.

Yearns, W. Buck (editor), *The Confederate Governors*, University of
Georgia Press, Athens, 1985.

INDEX

Guilford County, 5-9, 14, 32, 47, 49, 145-146, 148, 182-183, 313-314, 316, 321, 324, 361

Guilford Grays, 6-10, 20, 25, 28, 313

H

Halifax County, 28, 83

Hampton, General Wade, 203, 217, 225-226, 232-233, 235-236, 239, 241-242, 253, 255-256, 258-259, 279, 282, 284, 304-305, 322, 337-338, 341-342, 347, 349, 356

Hardee, General, 226-227, 232, 239, 248-251, 253-259, 262-263, 266-267, 281-282, 284, 304-305

Heroes of America, 181-188; founding of, 181-184; gubernatorial campaign of 1864, 181, 187-188; sabotage, 185-188

High Point, 28, 32, 183, 353, 360

Hoke, General Robert, 37, 59, 96, 155, 157, 190, 257-258, 262-267, 271, 274, 279-281, 284-285, 289, 307-309

Holden, William, 74-77, 87, 102-103, 109, 158, 291; gubernatorial campaign of 1864, 158, 187-188, 193-205; Heroes of America, 181, 187-188; relations with Governor Zebulon Vance, 75-77, 103, 109-110, 187, 192-205, 291

House of Commons, 25

Hood, General John B., 212, 224-225, 257, 274-275, 287

Howard, General O.O., 241, 243, 248, 254, 256-257, 279, 282, 284, 299

J

Johnston, General Joseph E., 10, 60; appointment by General Lee, 225;

Atlanta, 223-225; Battle of Bentonville, 255-285; Battle of Seven Pines (Fair Oaks), 221-222; Bennett's farm, 339-347; Greensboro, 315, 319-320, 328-333, 338, 354, 359-362; military career (background), 219-225; surrender of the Army of Tennessee, 339-347, 357-362; Vicksburg, 222-223

K

Kansas-Nebraska Act, 18

L

Leventhorpe, General Collett, 158

Lincolnites, 150

Lincolnton, 32, 204

M

Manumission Society, 40, 47

McDowell County, 87

Mecklenberg Declaration of Independence, 25

Merrimac (U.S. warship), 34

Monroe's Cross-Roads, 232, 235, 239, 337

Moore County, 145-146, 153, 158

Morehead City, 99

Morehead, John, 6, 17, 20, 326-328, 362

Morehead, Mary Harper, 6-8

N

North Carolina, Richmond, and Danville Line (see also "Piedmont Line"), 56

O

Onslow County, 43

Owens, William, 146, 152, 157

Jefferson Davis, 63-67, 86, 95-96, 103, 105-110, 117-120, 122-124, 191, 197-198, 201-202, 349-351; relations with William Holden, 75-77, 103, 109-110, 187, 192-205, 291; U.S. Congressman, 23, 72-73

W

Wadesboro, 132, 217
Warren County, 29, 83
Washington Peace Conference, 20-21
Waterhouse, James, 34-35
Wilmington and Weldon Line, 56, 59, 94, 128

Y

Yadkin County, 145, 155

1st North Carolina Regiment, 29, 36
4th North Carolina Regiment, 112
5th North Carolina Regiment, 108
6th North Carolina Regiment, 190, 301
11th North Carolina Regiment, 159
14th North Carolina Regiment, 73, 91, 112
17th North Carolina Regiment, 358
26th North Carolina Regiment, 73, 77
45th North Carolina Regiment, 323
48th North Carolina Regiment, 184
67th North Carolina Regiment, 300